"*Reconfiguration of Business Models and Ecosystems: Decoupling and Resilience* is a distinguished scholarly work that provides a very convincing analysis of how business plans can be adapted in a highly competitive and evolving context."

     – **Eric Milliot**, *University of Nantes*

Reconfiguration of Business Models and Ecosystems

Decoupling of business models and ecosystems is the disconnection of certain characteristic activities originally planned and completed in coincidence. It could bring in an immense adverse shock in the functioning of established business models and ecosystems possibly bringing them to resilience. Core causes for decoupling and resilience of business models and ecosystems are jolts, known as global crisis, universal pandemics, etc. The undesirable outcomes of critical events can reveal unique circumstances for business model and ecosystem resilience. Business model and ecosystem resilience represents a mandatory prerequisite for firms challenging their functioning and even very existence. Research has been conducted thus far, nevertheless this theme requires significantly more consideration.

The key objective of this book is to bring further insights in the field delivering a thorough examination of the ways in which business models and ecosystems can develop resilience under extraordinary conditions. In the book, the resilience of business models and ecosystems is analysed aiming to investigate further the specifics of the relevant processes securing resilience and its outcomes. The resilience of business models and ecosystems is scrutinised as a credible way for enhancing the predispositions of a firm's survivability.

Svetla T. Marinova is Professor of International Business and International Marketing and Head of the International Business Research Group at Aalborg University Business School, Aalborg University, Denmark.

Marin A. Marinov is Professor of International Business at Aalborg University Business School, Aalborg University, Denmark.

Routledge Frontiers in the Development of International Business, Management and Marketing
Series Editors: Marin A. Marinov and Svetla T. Marinova

Economic Transition and International Business
Managing through Change and Crises in the Global Economy
Edited by Eric Milliot and Sophie Nivoix

Value in Marketing
Retrospective and Perspective Stance
Edited by Marin A. Marinov

Cross-Cultural Challenges in International Management
Edited by Bruno Amann and Jacques Jaussaud

COVID-19 and International Business
Change of Era
Edited by Marin A. Marinov and Svetla T. Marinova

Open Internationalization Strategy
Edited by Nadine Tournois and Philippe Very

Philosophy of Marketing
The New Realist Approach
Matteo Giannasi and Francesco Casarin

Business Models and Firm Internationalisation
Edited by Christian Nielsen, Svetla T. Marinova and Marin A. Marinov

Consumer Culture Theory in Asia
History and Contemporary Issues
Edited by Yuko Minowa and Russell W. Belk

Reconfiguration of Business Models and Ecosystems
Decoupling and Resilience
Svetla T. Marinova and Marin A. Marinov

For more information about this series, please visit: https://www.routledge.com/ Routledge-Frontiers-in-the-Development-of-International-Business-Management/book-series/RFDIBMM

Reconfiguration of Business Models and Ecosystems

Decoupling and Resilience

Edited by Svetla T. Marinova
and Marin A. Marinov

NEW YORK AND LONDON

First published 2023
by Routledge
605 Third Avenue, New York, NY 10158

and by Routledge
4 Park Square, Milton Park, Abingdon, Oxon, OX14 4RN

Routledge is an imprint of the Taylor & Francis Group, an informa business

© 2023 selection and editorial matter, Svetla T. Marinova and Marin A.
Marinov; individual chapters, the contributors

The right of Svetla T. Marinova and Marin A. Marinov to be identified
as the authors of the editorial material, and of the authors for their
individual chapters, has been asserted in accordance with sections 77 and
78 of the Copyright, Designs and Patents Act 1988.

All rights reserved. No part of this book may be reprinted or reproduced
or utilised in any form or by any electronic, mechanical, or other means,
now known or hereafter invented, including photocopying and
recording, or in any information storage or retrieval system, without
permission in writing from the publishers.

Trademark notice: Product or corporate names may be trademarks or
registered trademarks, and are used only for identification and
explanation without intent to infringe.

Library of Congress Cataloging-in-Publication Data
Names: Marinova, Svetla Trifonova, editor. | Marinov, Marin,
1948- editor.
Title: Reconfiguration of business models and ecosystems : decoupling
and resilience / edited by Svetla T. Marinova and Marin A. Marinov.
Description: New York, NY : Routledge, 2023. |
Series: Routledge frontiers in the development of international business,
management and marketing | Includes bibliographical references and index.
Identifiers: LCCN 2022039275 | ISBN 9781032354026 (hardback) |
ISBN 9781032354064 (paperback) | ISBN 9781003326731 (ebook)
Subjects: LCSH: Management. | Strategic planning. | Organizational
change. | Organizational resilience.
Classification: LCC HD31.2 .R43 2023 | DDC 658--dc23/eng/
20220930
LC record available at https://lccn.loc.gov/2022039275

ISBN: 978-1-032-35402-6 (hbk)
ISBN: 978-1-032-35406-4 (pbk)
ISBN: 978-1-003-32673-1 (ebk)

DOI: 10.4324/9781003326731

Typeset in Bembo
by MPS Limited, Dehradun

Contents

List of Figures	x
List of Tables	xii
Acknowledgement	xiv
Notes on the Editors	xv
List of Contributors	xvii

1 Decoupling and Resilience of Business Models and
   Ecosystems   1
   SVETLA T. MARINOVA AND MARIN A. MARINOV

2 What Is Ahead? Impact of The Current Economic
   Volatility on Business Models and Ecosystems   18
   WINFRIED MUELLER

3 Overcoming Barriers in Creating Ecosystem Business
   Models: Achieving Resilience in an Uncertain and
   Competitive Setting   26
   SEBASTIAN EVALD STÜCK, PETER THOMSEN, AND
   CHRISTIAN NIELSEN

4 Offshoring vs Further Offshoring: A Multi-level Analysis
   on the Firm-, Country- and Industry-Specific Drivers of
   Business Model Reconfiguration   47
   STEFANO ELIA AND GIORGIO RENNA

5 Reconfiguring Digital Business Models to Enter the
   Japanese Market   66
   ARTO OJALA AND WILLIAM W. BABER

viii *Contents*

6 Data-Driven Business Model Innovation – When Is Decoupling Necessary? 82

TAINA ERIKSSON, NIINA NUMMELA, AND MARIKKA HEIKKILÄ

7 Value-creating and Value-eroding Decoupling in B2B Platforms – A Multiple Case Study 98

MIKA YRJÖLÄ, MALLA MATTILA, AND MARJUKKA MIKKONEN

8 Critical Junctures and Their Role in Reconfiguration of Business Models and Ecosystems 118

SVETLA T. MARINOVA, MARIN A. MARINOV, AND WINFRIED MUELLER

9 Tensions of Coopetition and Integration into the Multiplatform Ecosystems in Digital Care 131

MAHMOUD MOHAMED, PETRI AHOKANGAS, AND MINNA PIKKARAINEN

10 Customer Orientation: The Case of Creating Value in Ecosystems 163

MIKA YRJÖLÄ, ALEKSI NIITTYMIES, AND ABDOLLAH MOHAMMADPARAST TABAS

11 How Global Virtual Teams Are Innovating the Business Models of MNEs and Higher Education Institutions 185

ERNESTO TAVOLETTI

12 Healthcare Ecosystems and Business Models Reconfiguration: Decoupling and Resilience in the Context of Data-Driven Technologies: A Systematic Literature Review 204

ANNA ŻUKOWICKA-SURMA, MAGNUS HOLMÉN, JEANETH JOHANSSON, AND SVANTE ANDERSSON

13 IT Entrepreneur Resilience in Geopolitical Turbulence 236

LIUBOV ERMOLAEVA AND DARIA KLISHEVICH

14 Old-School Gender Values in a New Labour Model: A Case Study of Women's Entrepreneurship in Israel 258

GUY ABUTBUL-SELINGER, ANAT GUY, AND AVARAHAM SHNIDER

Contents ix

15 The Emergence of Open Banking and its Implications 281
SASCHA STRUWE

16 Trans-fur-able Resources? Strategic Responses to a
Crisis in the Danish Mink-Related Ecosystem 294
MICHAEL S. DAHL, LOUISE BRØNS KRINGELUM,
AGNIESZKA NOWINSKA, AND THOMAS ROSLYNG OLESEN

Index 315

Figures

3.1	The current transaction flows around service solutions in Esbjerg	39
3.2	The dream scenario platform ecosystem	40
3.3	A potential tier 1/tier 2 innovation ecosystem	41
4.1	Multi-level framework and hypotheses development	52
4.2	Graph of the interaction market-seeking location advantage – firm's size	58
5.1	First business model in Japan	73
5.2	Second business model in Japan	74
5.3	Third business model in Japan	75
7.1	Preliminary framework for decoupling in B2B platform ecosystems	103
7.2	Decoupling in B2B platforms	113
9.1	The planned integrations into the digital care pathway	140
9.2	Data structure	142
9.3	Coopetition-related tensions in MPEs	151
10.1	Preliminary framework for customer orientation in ecosystems	168
10.2	How managers understand customer value creation in the ecosystem context and activities through which managers advance customer orientation in their organisational contexts	171
12.1	Distribution of the published articles	210
12.2	Citations distribution in the three domains	212
13.1	Resilience model of start-ups	243
13.2	Model for resilience of Russian start-ups	252
14.1	Study subject by gender	262
14.2	Entrepreneurs' education level	271
14.3	The participants' previous occupations	272
14.4	Business sector distribution	273
14.5	Sector division in salaried jobs compared to self-employed businesses	273

14.6	Income gaps between women and their spouses	274
15.1	Closed vs open banking value chain	283
15.2	Business model configurations for open banking	286
15.3	Transformation of the value chain – traditional vs open banking	289
16.1	Overview of actors in the Danish mink production industry	296
16.2	Immediate strategic responses of the actors in the Danish mink production industry	303
16.3	Ecosystem dependency and resource fungibility in the Danish mink-related industry	308

Tables

1.1	Dimensions and levels of value embedded in business models	3
3.1	Descriptive data about the case companies	32
3.2	Business models used in the service hub	34
3.3	Primary business model configurations in the service hub	35
3.4	Value propositions of the companies to the service hub	36
4.1	Correlation matrix, descriptive statistics and VIF of all the variables considered	56
4.2	Results of the main Probit regression model and of the interaction model	57
5.1	People interviewed	70
6.1	Overview of the case companies	85
6.2	List of codes	87
7.1	Summary of the cases and conducted interviews	104
7.2	Research agenda	114
9.1	Summary of the case companies and interview rounds	137
10.1	Participants in the study	169
12.1	Operational definitions for the key concepts	206
12.2	Interdisciplinary keywords and key concepts used to construct search queries	207
12.3	Distribution of interdisciplinary articles published between 2001 and 2022	209
12.4	The top 10 cited articles	211
12.5	Citation distribution analysis in the three periods	212
12.6	Citations distribution between domains in the three periods	212
12.7	Citations and (citations per article) distribution (in each domain and period)	213
12.8	Top 25 journals' citation impact and productivity	214
12.9	The top 10 cited articles from the healthcare domain	218
12.10	The top 10 cited articles from the engineering domain	221
12.11	The top 10 cited articles from the management domain	223
12.12	Digitalisation in healthcare	225

		Tables	xiii
13.1	Data analysis results		247
16.1	Data sources		298
16.2	Summary of main findings regarding firm characteristics and strategic response		311

Acknowledgement

This book is based on the activities of the project "Enhancing Value Creation and Value Capture through Business Model Configuration: An Ecosystem Perspective (ENHANCE)", number 327110, funded by NOS-HS Nordic Council of Ministers, project lead Svetla T. Marinova.

Notes on the Editors

Dr Marin A. Marinov has accomplished his PhD degree in Production/Operations Management from the Bulgarian Academy of Sciences. He is Professor in International Business at Aalborg Business School of Aalborg University, Denmark. He has taught and done extensive research on both sides of the Atlantic as well as in Asia and Africa in numerous countries including Austria, Bulgaria, China, Finland, France, Germany, Portugal, Spain, Sweden, the United Kingdom and the United States, among others. His research interests are in internationalisation, multinational firms, and business development with a focus on emerging economies, as well as business policy and strategy. He has delivered keynote addresses at academic events world-wide. His publications include numerous books with world-leading publishers, many book chapters, as well as numerous scholarly articles in renowned academic journals, for instance, *European Journal of Marketing*, *International Marketing Review* and *Journal of Marketing Management*, among many others. He has obtained numerous research grants for international projects and is on the editorial boards of renowned scholarly journals and world-famous publishers and has consulted for various multinational firms and national governments world-wide on international business and educational matters. He is joint Series Editor of book series with Taylor and Francis and Palgrave Macmillan Springer.

Dr Svetla T. Marinova has gained her MBA degree from the University of Warwick, the United Kingdom, and her PhD degree in International Business from Copenhagen Business School, Denmark. She is Professor of International Business and International Marketing at Aalborg Business School of Aalborg University, Denmark, where she is the Head of the International Business Research Group. She has a prolific teaching experience from major universities world-wide and has conducted extensive research. Her research interests are in firm internationalisation and the role of institutions, strategy of multinational firms, as well as value creation and value capture from business activities, as well as business models, ecosystems and firm internationalisation. Professor Marinova has received funding from various granting bodies and is regularly invited to

xvi *Notes on the Editors*

deliver keynote speeches at world forums of academic and banking significance. She has published many books with world-famous publishers, numerous book chapters as well as many scholarly papers in leading academic journals, such as *Journal of World Business, International Business Review, Management and Organization Review, International Marketing Review, European Journal of Marketing,* among many others. She is on the editorial boards of numerous renowned scholarly journals and is joint Series Editor of book series with Taylor and Francis and Palgrave Macmillan Springer.

Contributors

Dr Guy Abutbul-Selinger is a senior lecturer and Dean of the Bnei–Brak Campus at the College of Management in Israel. He developed his PhD degree at the Sociology Department at Brandeis University, the United States and he developed his PhD degree at the Sociology Department of Brandeis University in the United States and his post-doctoral studies at the Department of Sociology of Tel Aviv University in Israel. His research interests are in the ethnicity of the Israeli middle class, multi-ethnic families' issues in Israel, Israeli periphery and current characteristics of the Israeli-Palestinian conflict.

Dr Petri Ahokangas is a professor of Future Digital Business at Martti Ahtisaari Institute, Oulu Business School, University of Oulu, Finland and an adjunct professor at Aalborg University (Denmark), University of Vaasa (Finland) and University of Oulu (Finland). He got his MSc degree in 1992 and DSc degree in 1998, both from the University of Vaasa, Finland. During 1990–1999 Ahokangas worked in various positions of the University of Oulu. During 2000–2007 he worked in the telecom industry. In 2008, he became a professor of International Business and a head of department at Oulu Business School. His multidisciplinary research is in the intersection of entrepreneurship, strategic management, international business, futures research and technology management. The focus of his research topics encompasses internationalisation, strategies, business models, ecosystems and data in various fields of technology, e.g., next-generation mobile communication, smart energy systems, software, platforms and artificial intelligence in different industries and sectors ranging from ICT to telecommunication, healthcare, mining and raw materials, public services and smart city.

Dr Svante Andersson is a professor in Business Administration at Halmstad University, Sweden. His research areas include innovation, marketing, entrepreneurship and international business. He has published in scholarly journals, including *Journal of Business Venturing*, *Journal of International Marketing*, *International Marketing Review*, *International Business* xviii Contributors

Review, European Journal of Marketing and *International Studies in Management and Organization*. He has extensive international experience as export manager and guest professor/researcher.

Dr William W. Baber has combined education with business throughout his career. His professional experience includes economic development in the State of Maryland, the United States, language services in the Washington, DC area, the United States, supporting business starters in Japan, and teaching business students in Japan, Europe and Canada. He taught English in the Economics and Business Administration Departments of Ritsumeikan University, Japan before joining the Graduate School of Management at Kyoto University, Japan, where he is an associate professor in addition to holding courses at the University of Vienna, Austria, and the University of Jyväskylä, Finland. He teaches courses including Business Negotiation, Cross Cultural Management and Management Communication. He is the lead author of the 2020 textbook *Practical Business Negotiation* and conducts research in the areas of negotiation, acculturation and business models, especially in related to Japan. In 2016, he got his PhD degree on intercultural adjustment of expatriate workers in Japan from the University of Jyväskylä, Finland. In 2004, he earned a Master of Education degree from the University of Maryland, the United States, in Instructional Systems Design.

Dr Michael S. Dahl is a professor at Aalborg University Business School, Aalborg University, Denmark. His research focuses on organisations, entrepreneurship and economic geography with a special interest in career trajectories, gender inequality and mental health. His extensive research has been published in numerous scholarly journals, including *Administrative Science Quarterly, Management Science, Organization Science, American Sociological Review, Research Policy, Industrial and Corporate Change* and *Social Forces*. Professor Dahl's research was awarded the 2020 Responsible Research in Management Award, the Jorck's Foundation Research Award in 2016, the Tietgen Gold Medal Research Award in 2006, the Spar Nord Foundation Research Award in 2005, the Tuborg Foundation Business Research Award in 2001, and the European Management Review Best Paper Award in 2009.

Dr Stefano Elia is an associate professor of International Business at Politecnico di Milano, Italy. He was "Dunning Visiting Fellow" at University of Reading, "Visiting Research Fellow" at University of Leeds, both in the United Kingdom, and "Marie Curie Fellow" at Shanghai Jiao Tong University, China. He is part of the Dunning Centre Europe for International Business, of the "Digital Export" Observatory of Politecnico di Milano, and of the Reshoring Group RE4IT. He took part to part the "Offshoring Research Network" of the

Duke University, the United States, the European project "POREEN on Partnering Opportunities between Europe and China" and the European COST Action "The Emergence of Southern Multinationals and their impact on Europe". His research interests are in multinational firms from emerging economies, offshoring of business services, reshoring of manufacturing activities, micro-foundation of international business, new technologies and internationalisation. He has published in reputable scholarly journals, namely, *Journal of International Business Studies, Journal of Economic Geography, Economic Geography, Journal of World Business, Global Strategy Journal, Journal of Business Research, Long Range Planning, Journal of International Management, Management International Review, International Business Review, International Journal of Production Economics, Journal of Purchasing and Supply Management* and *European Journal of International Management*.

Dr Taina Eriksson is a research director at Turku School of Economics, University of Turku, Finland. She leads Laboratory of Business Disruption Research examining the drivers and characteristics of market disruptions. Her research interests are in the dynamic capabilities of business organisations. She studies capabilities in relation to innovations, digital transformation and internationalisation of small- and medium-sized enterprises. Her over ten-year experience in collaborative research links universities and companies. Her research has been published in journals as *International Business Review, International Marketing Management, Journal of Small Business and Enterprise Development, Journal of International Management* and *Thunderbird International Business Review*.

Dr Liubov Ermolaeva is an assistant professor at the Graduate School of Management (GSOM) of the St. Petersburg State University, Russia. She got her PhD degree at GSOM. Her research interests include cross-border M&As, emerging economy multinationals, as well as migrant and international entrepreneurship. Her research has been published in *Regional Studies, European Business Review*, and *Eurasian Geography and Economics*.

Dr Anat Guy has a PhD degree in Social Work from the Hebrew University of Jerusalem, Israel. She is a senior lecturer at the School of Behavioural Science, College of Management in Israel. She has published numerous book chapters and journal articles on gender, parenting and shifts of personal values. Her current research projects deal with gender entrepreneurship, intersectionality and lives of Ultra-Orthodox women in Israel.

Dr Marikka Heikkilä is a research director specialised in Industrial Innovation studies at the School of Economics, University of Turku, Finland. She is leading a research group studying innovation and renewal in organisations. She has more than years of experience on joint research xx *Contributors*

projects including companies, organisations and universities. She has authored numerous scientific articles, the most recent ones appearing in *Journal of Small Business and Enterprise Development, European Management Review, Electronic Markets, International Journal of Information Management,* and *Business Horizons.*

Dr Magnus Holmén is a professor of Innovation Science with a focus on Industrial Management at Halmstad University, Sweden. Previously, he worked at Chalmers University of Technology, Sweden, and the Australian National University. He is a visiting professor at Gothenburg University and Linköping University, both in Sweden and has been a visiting fellow at the Scandinavian Consortium for Organizational Research (SCANCOR) at Stanford University, the United States. His research interests relate to innovation, industrial transformation and evolutionary processes. His current research includes business model innovation processes and ecosystem formation, relating to areas such as artificial intelligence, additive manufacturing, healthcare, transportation and energy. He has published in various scholarly outlets such as *Research Policy, Industrial and Corporate Change, R&D Management* and *Industrial Marketing Management.* He has also edited numerous books and has been involved in developing educational programmes for practitioners, e.g., Education in AI and Managing Additive Manufacturing for Professional Engineers.

Dr Jeaneth Johansson is a professor of Business Administration, Accounting and Financial Decision Making at Halmstad University, Sweden. She also works as a professor of Entrepreneurship and Innovation at Luleå University of Technology, Sweden. Her research interests include innovation and entrepreneurship, digital transformation and sustainability mainly in relation to financial decision-making and assessment of business potentials, development of collaboration models and business models as well as organisational change. Professor Johansson's current research is on commercialisation and implementation of MedTech and innovation management. She has published in scholarly outlets such as *Journal of Management Studies, Entrepreneurship Theory and Practice, Small Business Economics* and *Harvard Business Review.* She has been involved in developing educational programmes for practitioners and has been a board member in the New Entrepreneur's Business Centre Nord.

Daria Klishevich is a research fellow at the Centre for Russian Multinationals and Global Business at the Graduate School of Management (GSOM), Russia. She has finished the PhD programme at GSOM, awaiting defence, and holds a master's degree in Sociology and European Studies from St Petersburg State University and Universität Bielefeld, Germany. Her research interests focus on international business, emerging economy multinationals and international entrepreneurship. She has published articles in *Journal of International Business Policy*, *Multinational Business Review* and *Asian Business & Management*.

Dr Louise B. Kringelum is an associate professor at Aalborg University Business School, Aalborg University, Denmark. Her research is focused on business models, strategy development and inter-organisational collaboration. She has been published articles in journals such as *Research in Transportation Business and Management, Journal of Industrial Ecology, The Learning Organization* and *Journal of Critical Realism*.

Dr Malla Mattila works as a university lecturer and academic director of the master's degree programme in Leadership for Change at the Faculty of Management and Business, Tampere University, Finland. She has been the leader of the ROBINS TAU research project, which focuses on developing models for digital B2B customer journeys, platform business, and appropriate use of intelligent sales tools (2019–2022). Her research interests include networks in innovative technology business, business models and organising of food waste. She has published her research in such scholarly periodicals as *Industrial Marketing Management, Public Policy & Marketing, Journal of Personal Selling and Sales Management, Time & Society, Journal of Cleaner Production*, and *International Journal of Entrepreneurship and Innovation Management*. She has also co-edited a book titled *Food Waste Management: Solving the Wicked Problem* published by Palgrave Macmillan.

Marjukka Mikkonen holds an MSc degree in Administrative Sciences from the University of Agder, Norway, and works as a doctoral researcher at the Faculty of Management and Business, Tampere University, Finland. Her research interests include business models, platforms & digitalisation and gender, as well as sport leadership and management. Her work has been published in scholarly journals such as *Administrative Sciences* and chapters in edited books.

Mahmoud Mohamed is a doctoral researcher at Martti Ahtisaari Institute, Oulu Business School, University of Oulu, Finland. In 2019, he was awarded an MSc degree in Marketing from the University of Oulu, Finland. His research interests focus on platforms, ecosystem emergence, co-opetition, multi-platform ecosystems, business models, platform governance and inter-platform collaborative and competitive relationships. Before starting his doctoral research, he has two years of experience as a data-driven marketer in Finnish high-tech firms.

Dr Winfried Mueller is a CFO and a member of the board of a large international bank located in Munich, Germany. Prior to his current position he held several key international posts in different areas of banking, finance, and risk management. He has worked and lived in Hong Kong, Mainland China, and Italy. His PhD degree is from the

University of Gloucestershire, the United Kingdom and MA degree from ESB European School of Business, Reutlingen, Germany.

Dr Christian Nielsen is an adjunct professor at Bologna University, Italy and a professor at Aalborg University, Denmark. He is head of Aalborg University Business School. He is a global thought leader in the design of disruptive and scalable business models. His work combines business model design with corporate performance and benchmarking. He is also the founding Editor of the *Journal of Business Models* as well as on the Editorial Board of the *Accounting, Auditing and Accountability Journal* and *Journal of Behavioural Economics and Social Systems*. Since initiating the establishment of the Business Design Lab in 2011, over 300 companies ranging from local start-ups and SMEs to large multinationals with a global presence have seen the value of collaborating with Professor Nielsen and his research team. The contributions of the research have led to published works in leading international scholarly journals. This reflects his broad international research network spanning Europe, the United States, Australia and Asia.

Dr Aleksi Niittymies is a postdoctoral researcher at the Faculty of Management and Business at Tampere University, Finland. His research interests relate to managerial decision-making and international business, especially to how cognition shapes firms' internationalisation processes. He has published his research in scholarly journals including *International Business Review*.

Dr Agnieszka Nowinska is an assistant professor at Aalborg Business School, Aalborg University, Denmark. In 2018, she received her PhD degree in Management and Economics from Copenhagen Business School, Denmark Her research focuses on formation and persistence of collaborations, career evolution and individual decision-making. She published in *Journal of Business Research* and in edited book with Taylor & Francis publishing.

Dr Niina Nummela is a professor of International Business and a vice dean at the Turku School of Economics at the University of Turku, Finland. Her areas of expertise include international entrepreneurship, cross-border acquisitions and research methods. She has published widely in academic journals including, e.g., *Journal of International Business Studies, Journal of World Business, International Business Review, Management International Review*, among others, and has contributed to several internationally published books, also as an editor. She has also co-edited special issues for journals. She has several years of editorial experience (for example with the *International Small Business Journal, Journal of International Business Studies*). In a recent bibliometric analysis, she was ranked among the 30 most impactful scholars in the international entrepreneurship field.

Contributors xxiii

Dr Arto Ojala is a professor of International Business at the University of Vaasa, Finland. He is also an adjunct professor in Knowledge Management from the University of Tampere, Finland, and in entrepreneurship from the Jyväskylä University School of Business and Economics, Finland. His research is at the cross-section of international business, information systems and entrepreneurship. His articles have been published in *Journal of World Business, International Business Review, Journal of International Marketing, International Marketing Review, Journal of Small Business Management, Information Systems Journal, IEEE Software*, among numerous others. In 2008, he received his doctorate degree in Economics from the University of Jyväskylä, majoring in information systems science.

Dr Thomas Roslyng Olesen is a special consultant and a project manager at the Department of Strategy and Innovation at Copenhagen Business School, Denmark. He holds a master's degree in history & political science from University of Copenhagen, Denmark, and a PhD degree in Business History from University of Southern Denmark. His research has focused on entrepreneurship and innovation processes during industrial transformations. He has furthermore conducted studies of supply chain dynamics with a specific focus on value creation and business strategies in the shipping and energy sector. His research has been published in books, reports and scholarly journals including *Journal of Regional Science, Økonomi og Politik*, and *Erhvervshistorisk Årbog.*

Dr Minna Pikkarainen works in Oslo Metropolitan University in the Faculty of Health Sciences and the Faculty of Technology, Art and Design (TKD) as a professor in Digitalisation of Healthcare Services. She conducts research on the effects of digitalisation in healthcare services and healthcare professionals as well as the innovations related to and consequences of digitalisation on healthcare services. She works also as a connected health professor at University of Oulu of the Oulu Business School, Martti Ahtisaari Institute. Professor Pikkarainen has extensive record of external funding. Her research has been published in more than 110 journal and conference papers, e.g., in the field of nursing science, innovation management, software engineering and information systems. Prior to entering academia, she has had very significant and extensive experiences as an applied researcher in a variety of industries. Her employment locations span the globe including Norway, Sweden, Finland, Ireland, Belgium, incorporating business experiences developed in France, Italy, Germany, Finland and Sweden.

Giorgio Renna is an associate at PwC Italy, working in the M&A advisory, PwC Deals, and in the specifics in the Deals Strategy & Operations. He is part of the PwC Edge EMEA graduate programme, a xxiv *Contributors*

three-year programme which supports the most promising graduates at the start of their career by making them experience different lines of business of the M&A advisory with a variety of local and international clients and teams. He obtained his BSc degree in Management Engineering and the MSc degree in Management Engineering with a major in International Business, both at Politecnico di Milano, Italy.

Dr Avaraham Shnider received his PhD degree in Sociology from Ben Gurion University of the Negev, Israel. He is Dean of Students and a lecturer in the School of Behavioural Sciences and Psychology at the College of Management in Israel. His research focuses on future labour organisational shifts and analysis of rural areas, such as Kibbutzim, as well as settlements in Israel.

Dr Sascha Struwe is a research assistant at the Aalborg University Business School. After receiving his MSc in Innovation Management from the Aalborg University and the University of Chinese Academy of Sciences, he obtained a PhD in Business and Management focusing on B2B Service Innovation from the Aalborg University. He has been a visiting scholar at the Nordic Center at Fudan University. His research interests include service innovation, service design, servitisation and value creation, and his work has been published in the *Journal of Business Research*.

Sebastian Stück is a research assistant at Aalborg University Business School, Aalborg University, Denmark. He holds a double master's degree in Innovation Management. His work revolves around business model mapping and reporting of business model patterns for start-ups, SMEs and ecosystems, carried out at the Business Design Lab at Aalborg University Business School. Within this, his attention is focused on the development of a rigid tool for the business model mapping process of how to facilitate a consensus on the understanding of approaches to the mapping of the business model patterns and value drivers, across company-specific contexts.

Abdollah Mohammadparast Tabas is a doctoral researcher at the Oulu Business School, the University of Oulu, Finland. His research interests are internationalisation, entrepreneurial ecosystem, high-growth ventures, and healthcare. He has published in the *International Journal of Export Marketing*, *Journal of Business and Industrial Marketing* and *Small Enterprise Research,* among others.

Dr Ernesto Tavoletti is an associate professor of Management, International Marketing and International Business Strategy at the University of Macerata, Italy. He received his PhD degree in Economics and Management of Enterprises and Local Systems from the University of Firenze, Italy, in 2004. He was a board member of the

PhD in Management at the University of Rome Tor Vergata from 2011 to 2013, and of the PhD in Governance and Management for Business Innovation at the University Niccolò Cusano from 2015 to 2021. He is a member of the Academy of International Business and the European Academy of Management. He has served in the Council of Directors of the Master in Relations with Eastern Countries from 2004 to 2011, as co-director from 2009 and as director in 2011. Since 2019 he has been the chair of the master's degree programme in International Relations. His research interests focus on international business and innovation management. He has published books, book chapters and articles in scholarly journals, including *International Business Review, Harvard Business Review, European Journal of Innovation Management, Energy Policy, International Journal of Operations & Production, European Journal of International Management, International Journal of Emerging Markets, Management Research Review, Journal of the Knowledge Economy,* among others.

Dr Peter Thomsen is a post-doc at the Business Design Lab of Aalborg University Business School, Aalborg University, Denmark. Previously, he has worked as a business consultant. His main research interests include strategy and business development – hereunder business models. He has worked extensively with business model innovation as well as the prospects for generating quantitative datasets of business models to expand the theoretical field of knowledge and build best practice theories on business models. His research has involved and engaged more than 200 companies and opened an international collaboration network with research institutions in Italy, Switzerland and Scotland.

Dr Mika Yrjölä is a university lecturer of Marketing at the Faculty of Management and Business, Tampere University, Finland, where he teaches marketing management. His research background is in the field of strategic marketing, including themes such as executive decision-making and mental models, business models and value propositions, digital services, and omni-channel retailing. He actively participates in international conferences in the fields of marketing, services, and retailing, and he has published his research in scholarly journals such as *Journal of Retailing and Consumer Services, European Business Review, Journal of Cleaner Production, Journal of Marketing Management* and *Journal of Business and Industrial Marketing.*

Dr Anna Żukowicka-Surma is a post-doc at the School of Business, Innovation and Sustainability (FIH), Halmstad University, Sweden. She obtained her PhD degree in Management and Quality Sciences in 2020 from Kozminski University in Poland, and her master's degree in pharmacy in 2003 from the Medical University in Białystok, Poland.

xxvi *Contributors*

Prior to her academic career, she accumulated extensive professional experience in the healthcare sector. She is a member of the EURAM (The European Academy of Management) and EAHP (European Association of Hospital Pharmacists). She has reviewed for academic journals and conference submissions. Her research is on business development, and healthcare innovation.

1 Decoupling and Resilience of Business Models and Ecosystems

Svetla T. Marinova and Marin A. Marinov

Business Model and Value

The concept of business model has attracted booming scholarly interest, yet it has been often interpreted as a structure, e.g., the widely cited Business Model Canvas (Osterwalder & Pigneur, 2010) upon which strategies emerge and develop, activities are performed and relationships are built. Such a schematic approach to business model is somehow related to the fact that there is a tension between the established strategy literature and the growing business model perspective in academic publications. Business models have been questioned to be a substitute to firm strategy and strategy formulation (Sánchez & Ricart, 2010), but the conceptual hierarchy has not been clarified as to whether strategy is a prerequisite to developing a business model, or the other way round (Sánchez & Ricart, 2010; DaSilva & Trkman, 2014). Nevertheless, there is a generally accepted agreement of the integrative nature of business models as enablers of the operations of firms and thus a re-cognition of the complexity of the business model concept at the core of which stands the construct of value, with value proposition, value segment, value configuration, value network and value capture as suggested by the 5V framework (see Taran et al., 2016). Hence, the business model of a firm is a "blueprint" for its strategic and operational logic, governance, architecture and arrangement of internal resources to exploit business opportunities (Casadesus-Masanell & Ricart, 2010; Lee, Shin & Park, 2012; Rask, 2014; Saebi, Lien & Foss, 2017). This blueprint is founded on managers' assumptions of how the specific environment functions (including for example customer behaviour and institutional aspects) and how the firm should be functioning within the set conditions (Dunford, Palmer & Benveniste, 2010; Saebi et al., 2017). Additionally, such a functional interpretation of business model assumes that context has somewhat limited effect on the working business logic of the firm. Ostewalder's Business Model Canvas (BMC) is likely to be the most prominent example of this approach, where a snapshot-like workflow of the firm is developed within a singular context to describe aspects such as the core product and the target audience of the firm, the means of value delivery to said audience, the critical internal and external assets, and

DOI: 10.4324/9781003326731-1

processes of the business, as well as cost and revenue models (Chesbrough & Rosenbloom, 2002). By comparison, integral business model understanding is about the integrative logic of the firm across multiple contextual settings focusing on how the business can be maintained as an integral unit in the most efficient way across various contexts of operation. These concepts feature elements such as the divisional logic of the firm, its systems of governance in view of integral and specific units, the flow of knowledge and its channels among the individual units, etc. Such a perspective is the response to the call from Onetti et al. (2012) to include a geographical dimension in the business model view not only for external transactions and exchange, but for internal ones as well. Sánchez and Ricart (2010) also argue for highlighting the interdependency between a firm's business model and its ecosystem. Understanding the nature and depth of these transactions within a firm's business model bears the utmost importance in conceptualising how it creates and captures value (Kesting & Günzel-Jensen, 2015).

Business model is constructed on the pillar of individuals inside the firm who drive and execute company activities and others who are served by the firm's value proposition and its worthiness. Such an understanding goes well beyond the only product, customer and distribution argument (Hennart, 2014), although structurally, these building blocks are at the foundation of each business model. In line with this, Teece (2010, pp. 173–174) defines a business model as yielding "… value propositions that are compelling to customers, achieves advantageous cost and risk structures, and enables significant value capture by the business that generates and delivers products and services" (Dunford et al., 2010). Further, Ghemawat (2010) suggests that business model elements should not be isolated and looked at individually, but in the context of the whole with increased complexity and synergy (Rask, 2014). Moreover, Voelpel, Leibold and Tekie (2004) argue that the combination of business model elements ought to generate additional system level value, distinguishable from the value of the same elements individually. Thus, value has centrality in the business model research as it has progressed from a more structural element orientation towards a more business-reasoning orientation, addressing the questions of how and why in the existence and purpose of a firm. In addition, the understanding of value is not only individual firm focused, but it is rather integrative, indicating that a firm exists in its environment, in its ecosystem and is thus also dependent on the value created by others in that ecosystem. In this regard, the value concept integrates the meaning and purposefulness of business models. They should create value for, should have worthiness to, individuals, organisations, communities and society. Moreover, value is not only unidimensional, instead, it is a complex multidimensional construct (Holbrook, 1999) in which economic value in terms of economic gains is only one dimension. Instead, value is also psychological, sociological and ecological and every economic value at all four levels should also be associated with creating and delivering the other three types of worthiness (or the lack of such) to individuals, organisation, ecosystem and society (Table 1.1).

Table 1.1 Dimensions and levels of value embedded in business models

Value dimensions *Value levels*	*Economic value* *Monetary utility*	*Psychological value* *Emotional level*	*Sociological value* *Social significance*	*Ecological value* *Environmental level*
User	Value for money	Happiness	Belonging	Footprint
Organisation	Profit, new market and product expansion, new utility creation	Core and aspirational values	Social fit (e.g., legitimacy), contribution and responsibility (e.g., CSR)	Eco-effectiveness
Ecosystem	Mutual economic gains	Shared drivers	Mutuality and reciprocity	Sustainability
Society	Wealth and income security	Well-being and safety	Meaningful life in a social context	Environment and living conditions

Source: Based on Marinova (2021); Boztepe (2007); and den Ouden (2011).

Business Model Reconfiguration

Companies and their respective business models are not static as the latter just depicts a snapshot at a certain point in time. McGrath called for a better understanding of business model erosion, whereby existing business models are challenged by the changing external environment, thus requiring experimentation of refinement or even major changes (Dunford et al., 2010).

Exploring business model change Ritter and Lettl (2018) adopted the business model concept in conjunction with dynamic capability literature as they refer to a firm's dynamic capabilities as the conceptual connection between the focal firm's current business model, and its future business model development, which is the consequence of the reconfiguration or renewal of business model elements and the employment of managerial capability.

In the context of how dynamic capabilities influence business model change, Saebi et al. (2017) highlight that business literature lacks a well-justified empirical understanding. Established views on business model evolution perceive that business models change through innovation and adaptation, and their difference lies in the nature, purpose and direction of what initiated the change (Lee et al., 2012). Bucherer, Eisert and Gassmann (2012) suggest that business model adaptation is an organisational response to external causes, while innovation can be driven by the process of aligning organisational elements to changes in the environment. The changes involve aspects such as "changes in the preferences of customers, supplier bargaining power, technological changes, competition, etc." (Saebi et al., 2017, p. 569), whereas business model innovation has more to do with inducing said changes with a market disruptive organisational strategy. Saebi et al. (2017) analysed the relationship between business model adaptability, innovativeness and managerial risk-taking behaviour when identifying business opportunities and threats, as well as with elements from institutional theory and cultural idiosyncrasy, explaining why organisations may act differently when faced with threats and opportunities in their marketplace. Yahagi and Kar (2009) as well as Rask (2014) describe firm internationalisation with business model innovation, regardless of whether the exploitation of market opportunity has a disruptive strategy behind it or not. Furthermore, not only the geographical dimension has a role to play, but the temporal one as well. In this regard, a more dynamic process view has been developed by Dunfort et al. (2010) who argues that a global business model development process involves (1) clarification, (2) localisation, (3) experimentation and (4) co-option. Clarification is the managerial act of defining the core elements and logic of the firm and formulating a set of assumptions that underpin, support and validate the coherence of the firm's building blocks. Localisation is about establishing a global governance structure, while adapting the business model to the emerging contextual differences of a host market. Experimentation is an optional step in the development of a global business model, where, if applicable, the individual subsidiaries innovate their respective local business models beyond their derived, adapted or initially established one. Lastly, co-option technically entails the knowledge transfer internally within the global subsidiary network for the growth and development of the whole organisation. This four-step process describes how a firm's functional business model(s) in individual contexts and its global, integral business model evolves simultaneously. Similarly, Yahagi and Kar (2009) also emphasise the significance of business model localisation. A business model could be standardised across various host markets, but some degree of adaptation may also be required due to contextual specificity. Localisation also implicitly assumes the isolation of core business model blocks, that need to remain intact, and identifying the ones which need to be adapted to the new context (Rask, 2014). It also explains that the most successful international business strategies also combine the standardisation of some core elements with the localisation of ones that need adapting (Rask, 2014) and a greater institutional distance between home and host countries requires greater adaptation.

Ritter and Lettl (2018) explore the theoretical merit of business model and suggest that its versatility allows to integrate a great number of business-related concepts and act as a theoretical "membrane". It is not only a concept which mediates "between technological inputs and economic value creation" (Chesbrough & Rosenbloom, 2002, p. 532), but also connects theories (Ritter & Lettl, 2018) and models (Boztepe, 2007). The reason the "membrane" is a fitting metaphor is due to the business models' conceptual complexity integrating and offering a system where lower-level concepts cannot only co-exist but be inter-related.

Global Decoupling, Resilience and Change

While there is a consensus that the static nature of business models could be relevant and reflected as a snapshot at a specific point of a business' existence, and dynamism leads to business model reconfiguration through reproduction by adaptation or gradual transformation, knowledge on how business models change at a time of disruptive critical jolts is still emerging. Do they survive such a jolt and return to their previous state of configuration as a result of an abrupt change and business continuity as a result of the change, or they suffer breakdown and replacement of the business model because of an abrupt change and business model discontinuous process of change (Streeck & Thelen, 2005)? For example, the COVID-19 pandemic created a severe juxtaposition between attempts to drive business models to survival and return and pressures pushing many business models towards breakdown and replacement. At a chaotic disruptive situation, such as COVID-19 (for a discussion see Marinov & Marinova, 2021) and the sudden military confrontation in the Ukraine, not only the cause cannot be forecast, but the relationship between cause and effect is impossible to define. Hence, businesses are forced to immediately adopt novel practices, apply an approach of act-sense-respond, use stability-oriented interventions to buy time and employ crisis management. When such swift, deep and simultaneous critical events act as massive accelerators of change processes, economic effects are disruptive and almost instantaneous.

The process of change is associated with unprecedented volatility leading to larger fluctuations than in the past. The time of hyper-globalisation driven by efficiency gains and almost indiscriminate access to host country resources and market skimming strategies is left behind. Expectations of consistency, which is deeply ingrained in the predictive stability-oriented European mindset, is replaced by insecurity – with huge uncertainty in supply and value chain relationships, in value capture, and even in the ability of firms to create value within the near future. Decoupling of production and markets, of supply and value chains is not by managers' choice; current business model reconfiguration is not data driven, but rather decision- or even situation driven. Under such complexity, suggested solutions using past data-based correlational thinking to assess cause-effect relationship may turn out to be more of a fiction than future reality. Hence, under the disruptive conditions of unprecedented ambiguity and conflict, the business model reconfiguration knowledge held by researchers is still at a nascent stage of comprehension and, not to say, hardly usable for predictive purposes.

Research interest in business model resilience has also grown exponentially in the last couple of years in relation to critical jolts. For example, Slepniov (2021) has found out that in handling the effects of the COVID-19 pandemic Danish firms in China have made structural, relational and geographical dispersion changes in their value networks – supply chains and institutional players, reconfigured the channels through which they capture value, as well as provided greater value to users through payment incentives, product co-creation and customer involvement, and to employees through workforce protection. Jaklič and Burger (2020) explore Slovenian firms and their analysis shows that small- and medium-sized firms have changed their business models through mostly localising their value segment, reducing product diversification and export markets and using export channel digitalisation and automation. In the case of small US exporters, Tesar (2021) argues that small manufacturing enterprises can be resilient if that are well connected to the Internet, maintain relationships with their value segment and value networks to secure longer-term value capture and survive a systemic shutdown, but the "reluctant passive exporters" that hesitate and cannot act quickly in the rapidly changing environment have a questionable ability to survive. In a similar vein, some scholars study resilience beyond individual company business models, i.e., in global value chains (GVCs) that have increased risks and vulnerabilities to shocks and argue that more localised production might ensure greater resilience at a time of global decoupling of supply and value chains (Jaklič, Stare & Knez, 2020; OECD, 2020). Eduardsen (2021) suggests that firms should very carefully re-think the balance between efficiency gains, based mostly on maximising the economic value to the firm, and resilience as companies in GVCs are vulnerable to systemic disruptions and face the dilemma of achievement of efficiency in activities, while managing the risks assumed in carrying out those activities. However, the understanding of business model's reconfiguration and firm resilience under the conditions of global decoupling is still in an infant stage.

One might place this issue of decoupling, business model reconfiguration and resilience in a more philosophical perspective introduced by Aaron Antonovsky (1979) who writes that the sense of coherence is "a global orientation that expresses the extent to which one has a pervasive, enduring though dynamic feeling of confidence that (1) the stimuli deriving from one's internal and external environments in the course of living are structured, predictable and explicable; (2) the resources are available to one to meet the demands posed by these stimuli; and (3) these demands are challenges, worthy of investment and engagement" (1979, p. 123). In reference to business models reconfiguration that can ensure resilience this may mean that managers have to respond (to act) without any delay to the stress caused by global decoupling critical jolts without allowing this stress to affect negatively the sense of coherence. Whereas any changes may not be related to knowing what comes next, focusing on those elements of the business model that can be within the firm's control and management can take care of them, the firm may be resilient to survive the critical jolt. If management understand what is happening, but cannot deal with the changes, they can continue with some necessary business model adaptations and hold on while the challenge is believed to be "worthy of investment and engagement". If the latter is not present, then resilience can only harm the people who are trying to safe the firm. Such a case is further explicated in the case of the mink farms in Denmark shown in this book.

The Chapters in the Book

Chapter 2 by Winfried Mueller evaluates how the present economic conditions impact on business models and ecosystems. The foresight abilities of firms relating to the most unfavourable risks threatening the existing business models and ecosystems have at best brought hybrid results that can be either labelled as success or otherwise taking into consideration what has happened during the past few years. Considering that the present economic situation consisting of five specific features disrupting the *status quo* when dishevelled they reinforce: rise of inflation, return of high interest rates, revitalisation of risk-based crediting, incessant intermissions of supply chains as pioneering processes of further de-globalisation, as well as augmenting risk of stagflation. These characteristics destabilise existing business models and ecosystems augmenting risks in a variety of ways calling for firm actions regarding necessary consequential changes. Accordingly, there is a need for all factors relating to production, strategic and operational planning as well as treasury and cash management to be revisited, refocused and consequently changed. The challenges to the increased complexity, disruptions, velocity of reconfigurations in firm business models and whole ecosystems necessitate renewed knowledge by firms about all relevant areas including behavioural psychology and complexity theory. The chapter deals with the above stated issues offering relevant insights in these aspects.

In Chapter 3, Sebastian Evald Stück, Peter Thomsen and Christian Nielsen relate to the preparatory work of creating a network-based business model in the maritime sector in connection with a particular port. The network comprises of loosely coupled maritime firms and other organisations has been uncovered to have a potential to construct the existing ecosystem, which would foster partnerships and collaboration among firms rather than competition. The authors deliver a non-interventionist case study the analysis of which extends the current knowledge base concerning how partnerships and value propositions are formed in supposedly highly competitive environments in times of augmenting global uncertainty, where decoupling from global value chains is a part of enhancing the resilience of firms. The case study provides a clear illustration in view that numerous factors must be considered when shaping innovation and platform ecosystems despite strong common value propositions and distinct business models. It has been found out that the case firms needed inspiration on how to structure the process of designing and implementing the desired ecosystem. Furthermore, the chapter illustrates the application of service innovation and business modelling tools in the implementation of analytical and structured approaches.

Chapter 4 by Stefano Elia and Giorgio Renna deals with the issues of offshoring and further offshoring via conducting a multi-level analysis on the firm-, country- and industry-specific drivers of business model reconfiguration. Over the years, certain firms have adopted offshoring as a core strategy of expanding their business in order to improve and develop their competitive advantage, for instance, by gaining access to new markets and/or to cost-saving or value-enhancing resources. Nevertheless, over the past decade, some firms have begun to re-evaluate their preceding offshoring initiatives by revising their location choice. This phenomenon is known as further offshoring and has been implemented by firms to protect, pursue and further develop their competitive advantage in response to the ongoing changes that are taking place in the global business arena. The specific motives underlying the further offshoring phenomenon has not been explored by the international business literature thus far. Consequently, the purpose of this chapter is to identify the drivers of further offshoring against the traditional drivers of offshoring, by adopting a multi-level framework that considers the role of country-specific, industry-specific and firm-specific dimensions of the ecosystem. Using a sample of 114 further offshoring and offshoring initiatives, the authors have found out that the former are mainly driven by the resources availability of the firm, while the latter is particularly

Decoupling and Resilience of Business Models and Ecosystems   9

driven by the capital intensity of the sector, in which firms operate and by the efficiency-seeking and strategic asset-seeking location advantages. The results of the study provide theoretical and practical foundations concerning the use of further offshoring as a way of revising the decoupling strategy associated to the first offshoring initiative and as a form of reconfiguration of business models that allows firms to be resilient, by offering also useful insights on the post COVID-19 economic scenarios.

The purpose of Arto Ojala and William W. Baber authoring Chapter 5 is to analyse the reconfiguration of digital business models when entering the Japanese market. Digitalisation of products and services has led to a situation where firms have to constantly reconfigure, adjust and innovate their business models for new market conditions predominately foreign. In addition, when a firm enters a new foreign market, the environment, culture, local customer preferences and numerous other considerations may lead to the reconfiguration of the existing business model. However, recent business model studies provide very limited insight as to how business models might change and evolve over time when a firm enters an unknown foreign market. To improve our understanding of this phenomenon, the authors present a longitudinal study encompassing 10 years of a Finnish digital service provider's market entry experiences with the Japanese market. The empirical data, presented in the chapter, are built on 13 in-depth face-to-face interviews conducted in a ten-year period between 2011 and 2021. Based on the empirical data, the authors determine how and why the case firm's digital business model changed over time and how the studied firm found a lucrative business model for the firm's operations in Japan. The findings indicate that the case firm continuously reconfigured its business model three times to find an effective and relevant model. The re-configurations were related to the service, value network and revenue model elements of the business model. The findings have clearly highlighted that particularly in Japan, networking based on personal re-lationships, ability to innovate new digital services based on customer re-quirements and the capability to change the business model constantly have played key roles for surviving in the Japanese market. From a more general point of view, this indicates that firms cannot always apply the same business model in all markets. In numerous cases, there is clearly a need to adopt new business models for the specifics of certain foreign markets.

In Chapter 6, Taina Eriksson, Niina Nummela and Marikka Heikkilä investigate the issues relating to data-driven business model innovation relating them to the need of decoupling. More specifically, their study investigates how small- and medium-sized enterprises (SMEs) innovating new business by utilising data analytics techniques improve their future competitiveness and resilience. The authors set their goal to understand how SMEs innovate their existing business models to support new business ideas and whether such an approach leads to the decoupling of business models. The chapter adopts a "matched-pair" case study of two Finnish

10   *Svetla T. Marinova and Marin A. Marinov*

SMEs applying an inductive approach and data triangulation. The authors uncovered the emergence of business model innovation in real time. They have identified the focal factors that led the SMEs to decouple the novel business from the established one and develop a parallel business model for the new offering of the studied SMEs. The findings have proved that in the case SMEs, decoupling has been necessary for resilience building purposes. The key contribution of the study is in uncovering that forward firms' strategies help managing multiple business models in SMEs when decoupling takes place.

Chapter 7 by Mika Yrjölä, Malla Mattila and Marjukka Mikkonen represents a multiple case study on value-creating and value-eroding decoupling in business-to-business (B2B) platforms. B2B platforms have been progressively transforming customer behaviour with major implications for existing value chains and business ecosystems. For instance, platform players typically act as both complementors and competitors to incumbents through the business model innovation of decoupling (i.e., the breaking of links in customer relation processes). The purpose of the chapter is to identify, explain and analyse how B2B platforms utilise decoupling to disrupt value creation in business ecosystems. From a theoretical point of view, this chapter builds upon the existing literature on business model decoupling, value creation and B2B platforms. From an empirical point of view the study has been conducted via the utilisation of 14 case studies of Finnish SMEs offering knowledge-intensive business services through their own or partnering platforms. The broad selection of cases illustrates the different types of decoupling, including value-creating and value-eroding activities, that target different stages of the customer processes. The case firms represent different industrial sectors, such as construction, education, software, artificial intelligence (AI) and industrial Internet of Things (IoT). The study contributes to the existing literature on business model decoupling by furthering the focus of the study to B2B contexts of various industries. Thus, the study demonstrates how decoupling is a more complex phenomenon in the B2B context compared to business-to-consumer (B2C) market context. The findings show that B2B platforms have targeted multiple stages of customer processes to effectively create value for customers, stakeholders and the business ecosystems. It has become evident that B2B platforms can also decouple value-eroding activities by removing time, place and resource constraints. In conclusion, the chapter suggests an agenda for future research and provides clear implications for managers.

Chapter 8 by Svetla T. Marinova, Marin A. Marinov and Winfried Mueller explores how critical junctures impact the reconfiguration of business models and ecosystems. The authors suggest that while the dynamic changes in business model configuration apply the firm as an unit of analysis, the business ecosystem represents a higher level of analysis of a complex system where diverse firm business models are interlocked to secure access to limited resources and market power. On this background

Decoupling and Resilience of Business Models and Ecosystems 11

reconfiguration of business models allow companies to adapt to changing environmental conditions caused by critical jolts through various coping mechanisms that use structural, relational, financial and logistics mechanisms, as well as ecosystem-related changes to achieve a better balance between efficiency and security. By exploring major impacts of the recent pandemic on firms, the authors demonstrate that the ecosystem changes have forced companies to reconfigure value networks, value segments, value configuration, but less so value propositions experiencing reduced value capture. The authors also explore the pressure on business models and ecosystems by the magnified uncertainty leading to heightened risk created by the ongoing critical jolts caused by the decoupling of economic and socio-political systems, of production, supply and value chains, previously interlocked ecosystems, relationships, markets and knowledge flows. This impact of the current critical jolt on companies is very significant in its scope, scale and depth due to the unprecedented non-transitory inflation, complexities in supply, energy price and interest rate rise, huge government debt and increased cost of borrowing combined with debt servicing in conditions of stagflation. All these necessitate significant changes in the business models and ecosystem alignment for companies across the world.

Chapter 9 by Mahmoud Mohamed, Petri Ahokangas and Minna Pikkarainen studies the coopetition and integration in multiplatform ecosystems in digital care. Platforms integrate into multiplatform ecosystems (MPEs) to expand their business scope and achieve global reach. Via integrating into MPEs, each platform may share part of or the whole infrastructure with other platforms due to complementarity and knowledge sharing between platforms. The authors apply qualitative research to explore the coopetition-related tensions when complementing entrant and incumbent platforms integrate into MPEs. The study finds out that MPEs provide a mediating ecosystem enabling the multi-layered coopetition between new entrants and incumbent platforms to create more collective value than individual platforms could create independently. Tensions in integration arise from the unbalanced leadership power that may hinder the establishing of collective governance agreements between platforms in MPEs. Incumbent platforms struggle for market dominance intensifying the governance tensions as a precaution for the appearance of a sudden competition or dropouts from MPEs. The authors argue that platforms integrating into MPEs need to be opportunistically aligned; otherwise, sudden competition or dropouts from MPEs will inevitably occur if the unbalanced leadership roles pressurise the new entrant platform's ability of autonomy allowing to grant access to new stakeholders.

Studying customer orientation in the process of creating value in ecosystems is the topic address by Mika Yrjölä, Aleksi Niittymies and Abdollah Mohammadparast Tabas in Chapter 10. Innovations in technology, business models and value propositions create changes in value chains and ecosystems. Firms operating in ecosystems and networks can create value for

12 *Svetla T. Marinova and Marin A. Marinov*

customers in novel ways. Moreover, value creation in ecosystems is theoretically interesting because of the multiple interrelated and overlapping roles that actors perform. For instance, two firms can at the one and the same time be considered competitors and complementors while also being in a customer–supplier relationship. In such a context, the terms "customer" and "customer orientation" become very complex and particularly nuanced because it is not always easy to identify who eventually is the customer and how value is being created. Therefore, the purpose of this chapter is to identify and analyse how managers understand customer value creation in the ecosystem context and to elucidate activities through which managers advance customer orientation in their organisational contexts. From a theoretical perspective, the authors have built upon the extant literature on business models, customer orientation and customer value. They have interviewed 34 managers from firms growing by using networks and ecosystems. The findings of the study illustrate that there are various ways in which managers create value for their customers. They vary depending on the role of context and the dimensions of value promised to customers. This chapter contributes by providing useful insights into how customer orientation is understood and managed within ecosystems. The authors discuss the findings and provide recommendations for future research into the reconfiguration of business models and ecosystems, concluding with implications for managers navigating value creation within ecosystems.

Chapter 11, authored by Ernesto Tavoletti, deals with global virtual teams and how they innovate the business models of multinational enterprises (MNEs) and higher education institutions (HEIs). More specifically, the chapter explores how global virtual teams (GVTs) have innovated the business models of MNEs and HEIs in the pre- and post-pandemic world. A GVT is a workgroup whose members are dispersed around the planet and rely on online tools for communication. It is an evolutionary form of team organisation made widespread by the globalisation and enabled by the advances in information and communication technology. The term "virtual team" appeared in the literature in the mid-1980s and became increasingly popular in the early 1990s as the advent of the Internet making electronic communication tools ubiquitous. The term GVT first appeared in literature in 1999 to define a team whose members transcend time, space and culture. By that time, GVTs were already popular and recognised organisational settings in international business, especially in the neo-global corporation idea of fragmentation of country subsidiaries and virtuality of corporate headquarters. The COVID-19 pandemic gave a booster to adopting GVTs in all areas of international business practice and education at every level of organisations, overcoming status quo inertia through health emergence. The widespread adoption of GVTs in multinational corporations, management consulting and international business education makes their business models increasingly virtual based, sustainable and resilient to external factors.

Decoupling and Resilience of Business Models and Ecosystems 13

Chapter 12 by Anna Żukowicka-Surma, Magnus Holmén, Jeaneth Johansson and Svante Andersson researches the reconfiguration of ecosystems and business models in relation to decoupling and resilience in the context of data driven technologies via conducting a systematic literature review. New data-driven technologies such as AI and IoT have been largely introduced to different sectors. Digitalisation may lead to disruptive changes in any industry, including creating or entering new business models, lowering or changing entry barriers into markets and enabling the breakup of sectorial silos. A significant aspect of digitalisation is the increased abundance of data, increased role of automatic or semi-manual data analysis approaches and the associated value potential. For healthcare, digital transformation brings enormous opportunities for quality improvement and efficiency. Although the COVID-19 pandemic accelerated significantly the digitalisation of the healthcare sector, innovation adoption in the sector proceeds slower than in most other industries. Furthermore, there is a scarcity of research on data-driven management in healthcare, implying a lack of consensus on how to handle the challenges of data-driven technologies in healthcare practice. Although researchers, practitioners and policymakers have paid significant attention to digitalisation issues in healthcare, a systematic overview of the implications of data-driven use in healthcare is still lacking. Thus, this chapter reviews systematically the existing literature on this area and develops a research agenda aiming at answering the pre-set research question: Whether and how do healthcare actors explore new business opportunities in the context of digitalisation? To address the research question, a systematic literature review (SLR) methodology has been applied to provide insights, critical reflections, managerial implications and a research road maps for future research. The qualitative analysis of studies from innovation management, healthcare implementation and medical informatics fields, using NVivo 10 Software, addresses the healthcare reconfiguration in innovative data-driven technology by investigating and describing the current state of the interdisciplinary research and tendencies. The chapter identifies the potential benefits of the use of data-driven technology in healthcare at organisational, institutional, ethical and macro-level dimensions. It discusses the adoption of digitalisation and healthcare management practices to enhance data-driven outcomes. Based on the conducted literature review and the bibliometric analysis of articles included in the chapter, the authors propose the development of an integrative conceptual framework for digital healthcare (for the data-driven value creation and co-creation through co-ordinating building capacity in the ecosystem of people, projects and systems) in the future research agenda.

In Chapter 13, written by Liubov Ermolaeva and Daria Klishevich, the issue of IT entrepreneur resilience in geopolitical turbulence is investigated. Resilience has progressively become one of the essential capabilities of any business in today's uncertain and unpredictable environment. Business start-ups possess specific characteristics determining the way they respond to global disruptions. Scholars acknowledge that start-ups often lack resources and experience, but at the same time they are innovative and agile, and the latter characteristics help them survive at a time of crisis. In this study, the authors investigate four case studies of Russian start-ups that have recently experienced critical external shocks caused by a geopolitical crisis and subsequent transformation. Radical change in the business ecosystem enforced the studied start-ups to react immediately, which led to a significant business model transformation. The authors analyse in depth the four cases and explain how Russian start-ups responded to a disruptive change and how they became resilient in conditions of unprecedented external turmoil.

Guy Abutbul-Selinger, Anat Guy and Avaraham Shnider authoring Chapter 14 analyse the issues of old-school gender values in a new labour model focusing on a case study of female entrepreneurship in Israel. The modern labour market is characterised by the transition from traditional employment to novel employment models. One of the interesting expressions of this change is found in the growing rate of freelance workers and entrepreneurs. The trend of women venturing into entrepreneurship, for various reasons, has been documented in scholarly literature. The literature points at some similarities between male and female entrepreneurs and their motives; yet it is often argued that women, unlike men, are more influenced by intransient motives, such as the search for work-life balance or financial independence. Other significant differences between the two genders include the lack of role models for women, scarce experience in opportunity hunting and utilisation, smaller social networks, a smaller financial security network and a greater reluctance to take risks. Entrepreneurship in Israel is synonymous with the high-tech sector, which is seen as prestigious, lucrative and essentially masculine. The current study aims to reveal another aspect: women's entrepreneurship in Israel. The study focuses on those women who have chosen to establish small businesses – an afterschool day-care, a clothing store, a styling business, consultancy on issues related to children or babies, etc. The study aims to shed light on the common characteristics of these women, their socio-demographic characteristics, their reasons for establishing small businesses and their unique voice. All of this allows us to portray how these women use entrepreneurship to shape their work-life balance and how this discourse is anchored in the socio-cultural Israeli context. The findings of the study suggest that the structure of the traditional labour market is replicated in the new one, i.e., while women do become entrepreneurs, they do so by returning to traditionally "feminine" fields, using this employment as part of their mothering (placing work as secondary to the home and allowing home demands to bleed into work hours, etc.).

Chapter 15 by Sascha Struwe deals with the emergence of open banking and its implications. Open banking as a business model fundamentally challenges how value is created and captured within financial service

Decoupling and Resilience of Business Models and Ecosystems 15

ecosystems. Traditional bank–customer relationships are broken up by the introduction of additional actors into the value chain under the promise of enhanced value creation opportunities. These developments are driven by diverse forces such as regulative pressure, changing customer demands, or technological developments. This chapter introduces the concept of open banking, highlights implications on actor value creation and provides an account of the current developments, including an outlook for the future.

In Chapter 16, Michael S. Dahl, Louise Brøns Kringelum, Agnieszka Nowinska and Thomas Roslyng Olesen deal with the strategic responses to a crisis in the Danish mink concerned ecosystem caused by the COVID-19 related decisions. The chapter investigates the interchange among organisational and inter-organisational resilience of an ecosystem exemplified by the Danish mink-related industry. The interdependent activities are interlinked in order to establish a value proposition throughout organisational boundaries. While each organisation in an ecosystem has its business model, in the ecosystem itself the organisational business models are interrelated in creating a joint value proposition. Adopting the ecosystem standpoint, the authors focus on the multilateral set of actors that maintain value creation processes central to the creation of the joint value proposition of high-quality mink fur. By presenting the process of ecosystem breakdown as an effect of the total shutdown of Danish mink production during COVID-19 pandemic, the authors explore the resilience of every individual mink-related firm when they become decoupled from the joint ecosystem value proposition, that they previously were part of. In this case, mink-related industries cover feed kitchens and affiliated sub-suppliers, equipment producers, wholesalers, veterinarians, transportation providers, pelters and auction houses that are directly dependent on the breeding of mink. Firms stated in media outlets reporting on the collapse of the mink industry and its consequences industry-wide have been approached and interviewed. Interviewee selection has had multiple goals. A semi-structured protocol has been adopted with four interview parts using the first part of the interviews to analyse firms' value propositions and activities using the BMC. The authors have investigated the immediate strategic responses by different types of actors along with factors driving the strategic responses. Specifically, the research has studied the crisis that hit the Danish mink-related industry ecosystem when the government decided to close all activities in November 2020. Exploring the response of the individual actors in the ecosystem, the authors have found that firms engaged in midstream and downstream activities pursued an exit strategy. In contrast, firms involved in upstream activities pursued retrenchment or innovation strategies. The research has uncovered that firms highly dependent on the ecosystem have chosen an exit strategy. Low dependency on the ecosystem has allowed firms to retrench and continue their activities outside the initial ecosystem. Exit is usually not a preferred strategy for firms with low dependence on the ecosystem, as the business will generally be able to continue its activities. At all times the role of the owner of the firm needs always to be taken into consideration.

16   *Svetla T. Marinova and Marin A. Marinov*

References

Antonovsky, A. (1979). *Health, Stress and Coping*. San Francisco, CA: Jossey-Bass Publishers.

Boztepe, S. (2007). "User value: Competing theories and models", *International Journal of Design*, vol. 1(2), pp. 55–63.

Bucherer, E., Eisert, U. & Gassmann, O. (2012). "Towards systematic business model innovation: Lessons from product innovation management", *Creativity and Innovation Management*, vol. 21(2), pp. 183–198.

Casadesus-Masanell, R. & Ricart, J.E. (2010). "From strategy to business models and onto tactics", *Long Range Planning*, vol. 43, pp. 195–215.

Chesbrough, H. & Rosenbloom, R.S. (2002). "The role of the business model in capturing value from innovation: Evidence from Xerox Corporation's technology spin-off companies", *Industrial and Corporate Change*, vol. 11, pp. 529–555.

DaSilva, C. & Trkman, P. (2014). "Business model: What it is and what it is not?" *Long Range Planning*, vol. 47(6), pp. 379–389.

den Ouden, E. (2011). *Innovation Design: Creating Value for People, Organizations and Society*, London: Springer Science & Business Media.

Dunford, R., Palmer, I. & Benveniste, J. (2010). "Business model replication for early and rapid internationalisation: The ING direct experience", *Long Range Planning*, vol. 43(5–6), pp. 655–674.

Eduardsen, J. (2021). "Covid-19, global value chains, risk, and resilience", In M.A. Marinov & S.T. Marinova (Eds.), *Covid-19 and International Business: Change of Era*, London and New York, NY: Taylor and Francis, 180–191.

Ghemawat, P. (2010). *Strategy and the Business Landscape*, 3rd ed. Upper Saddle River, NJ: Pearson.

Hennart, J.-F. (2014). "The accidental internationalist: A theory of born globals", *Entrepreneurship Theory and Practice*, vol. 38(1), pp. 117–135.

Holbrook, M.B. (1999). *Consumer Value: A Framework for Analysis and Research*, New York: Routledge.

Jaklič, A. & Burger, A. (2020). "Complex internationalisation strategies during crises: The case of Slovenian exporters during the great recession and Covid-19 pandemic", *Teorija in Praksa*, vol. 57(4), pp. 1018–1041.

Jaklič, A., Stare, M. & Knez, K. (2020). "Changes in global value chains and the Covid-19 pandemic", *Teorija in Praksa*, vol. 57(4), pp. 1042–1064.

Kesting, P. & Günzel-Jensen, F. (2015). "SMEs and new ventures need business model sophistication", *Business Horizons*, vol. 58(3), pp. 285–293.

Lee, Y., Shin, J. & Park, Y. (2012). "The changing pattern of SME's innovativeness through business model globalization", *Technological Forecasting and Social Change*, vol. 79(5), pp. 832–842.

Marinov, M.A. & Marinova, S.T. (Eds.) (2021). *Covid-19 and International Business: Change of Era*. London and New York, NY: Taylor and Francis.

Marinova, S. (2021). "Disrupting globalization: Prospects for states and firms in international business", in M.A. Marinov & S.T. Marinova (Eds.), *Covid-19 and International Business: Change of Era*, London and New York, NY: Taylor and Francis, 365–377.

OECD (2020). "Shocks, risks and global value chains: Insights from the OECD METRO model", OECD Publishing, Paris. Accessible at http://www.oecd.org/trade/documents/shocks-risks-gvc-insights-oecd-metro-model.pdf, June 2022.

Onetti, A., Zucchella, A., Jones, M. & McDougall-Covin, P. (2012). "Internationalization, innovation and entrepreneurship: Business models for new technology-based firms", *Journal of Management and Governance*, vol. 16(3), pp. 337–368.

Osterwalder, A. & Pigneur, Y. (2010). *Business Model Generation: A Handbook for Visionaries, Game Changers, and Challengers*. New Jersey: Wiley.

Rask, M. (2014). "Internationalisation through business model innovation: In search of relevant design dimensions and elements", *Journal of International Entrepreneurship*, vol. 12(2), pp. 146–161.

Ritter, T. & Lettl, C. (2018). "The wider implications of business-model research", *Long Range Planning*, vol. 51(1), pp. 1–8.

Saebi, T., Lien, L. & Foss, N.J. (2017). "What drives business model adaptation? The impact of opportunities, threats, and strategic orientation", *Long Range Planning*, vol. 50(5), pp. 567–581.

Sánchez, P. & Ricart, J. (2010). "Business model innovation and sources of value creation in low-income markets", *European Management Review*, vol. 7(3), pp. 138–154.

Slepniov, D. (2021). "Danish companies in China during COVID-19: Staying afloat and post-pandemic trends", in M.A. Marinov & S.T. Marinova (Eds.), *Covid-19 and International Business: Change of Era*, London and New York, NY: Taylor and Francis, 330–338.

Streeck, W. & Thelen, K. (2005). "Introduction: Institutional change in advanced political economies", in W. Streeck & K. Thelen (Eds.), *Beyond Continuity: Institutional Change in Advanced Political Economies*. Oxford: Oxford University Press, 1–39.

Taran, Y., Nielsen, C., Montemari, M., Thomsen, P. & Paolone, F. (2016). "Business model configurations: A five-V framework to map out potential innovation routes", *European Journal of Innovation Management*, vol. 19(4), pp. 492–527.

Teece, D. (2010). "Business models, business strategy and innovation", *Long Range Planning*, vol. 43(2–3), pp. 172–194.

Tesar, G. (2021). "Effects of COVID-19 on the export operations of smaller manufacturing enterprises", in M.A. Marinov & S.T. Marinova (Eds.), *Covid-19 and International Business: Change of Era*. London and New York, NY: Taylor and Francis, 268–277.

Voelpel, S.C., Leibold, M. & Tekie, E.B. (2004). "The wheel of business model re-invention: How to reshape your business model to leapfrog competitors", *Journal of Change Management*, vol. 4(3), pp. 259–276.

Yahagi, T. & Kar, M. (2009). "The process of international business model transfer in the Seven-Eleven Group: US – Japan – China", *Asia Pacific Business Review*, vol. 15(1), pp. 41–58.

2 What Is Ahead? Impact of The Current Economic Volatility on Business Models and Ecosystems

Winfried Mueller

Introduction

Are we currently witnessing one of the rare economic turning points in history? Answering the question will be probably still difficult right now as generally the answer will be only visible in hindsight.

It is fair to say that we are living through times of truly exponential changes. Goldman Sachs' Chief Operating Officer John Waldron described this in early June 2022 when speaking about the global economy and financial markets: "This is among, if not the most complex, dynamic environment I've ever seen in my career. We've obviously been through lots of cycles, but the confluence of the number of shocks to the system to me is unprecedented" (Mandl & Marshal, 2022). In 2019, the year before COVID-19 appeared, the motto of the Venice Biennale that is attributed to a Chinese curse "May you live in interesting times" (Biennale, 2019) sounded like a Casandra call.

Since then, despite massive governmental support (Müeller, 2021), traditional business models have been destroyed by pandemic protective measures within weeks and well-established sound ecosystems got interrupted – while new ones have been created and respectively pushed beyond expectations. Yet, some of the new ones still must prove their economic viability.

Now, two and a half years after the outbreak of the corona pandemic, the speed of changes has further increased, inflation is back and the costs of funds are on the rise. Apart from the health crisis, interruptions have subsequently shaken the global clockwork-like flow of people, raw materials and goods lasting almost for two years so far.

As if that wasn't enough, the outbreak of the military confrontation between Russia and the Ukraine has further deepened the perception of a fragmented world by shortening supply and putting stress on markets, especially in the area of agricultural products, energy prices and selected prefabricated goods, e.g., cable harness in the automotive industry. In an unprecedented manner, financial sanctions have been put on Russia and, under pressure of public opinion and considerations of sustainable corporate governance, most international firms have abandoned or at least frozen their

DOI: 10.4324/9781003326731-2

Russian business. What sounds like a concerted punitive measure of the Western countries is at the same time probably the most severe interference in business models of virtually all industries that occurred within days (Kolhatkar, 2022).

Limited Foresight Quality

Substantial research has been done on the lessons learned from the recent financial crisis, but not many firms have made themselves "weatherproof" (see, for instance, Gennaro & Nietlispach, 2021). Especially, the foresight quality on developments that threaten the resilience and continuity of business models and ecosystems has not been outstanding, rather it has lagged behind environmental dynamics (Aschoff & Heitmann, 2020). For example, who could draw out conclusions in 2014 from the draft papers leading to the Paris Agreement on climate change just one year later? In 2016, the year Donald Trump became US president, tariff and trade restrictions were not even on the bottom of the list of the expected economic perils. Neither was a pandemic incident included in the priority of corporate risk management in 2019 (Aschoff & Heitmann, 2020). Finally, in 2021 a European war seemed to be out of imaginal reach until it became reality (Allianz, 2021). So, what do we possibly have to expect today about for the future?

The aim of the following lines is to draw a rough situational analysis as of summer 2022 paired with an attempt to imagine and identify areas of potential significance and economic relevance for business models and ecosystems.

The development of the economic situation, as visible today, consists of five specific disrupters that are intertwined and partially reinforcing. The disrupters affect financial business drivers and via transmission mechanisms accelerate existing sociological, demographic and ecological developments.

The Current Economic Situation

Already before the outbreak of the Ukrainian war, energy prices ended a long bear market that had found its bottom in the famous negative oil prices during the first corona wave (Saefong, 2021). Since then, the hope for rebound of the post-COVID industrial production paired with increasing CO_2 prices have fuelled rising prices. Secondly, supply chain interruptions resulted in various material and spare part shortages thus putting additionally pressure of prices.

Both effects impelled inflation that woke up from a decade-long absence. In an act of fundamental misjudgement, both central banks, which have flooded the markets for years with enormous stimulus packages and full of fear of deflation, and governments, sitting on a rising level of public debts, resisted long to reality in a cognitive-dissonance-style, calling the price rise only "transitory" (Koranyi & Canepaand, 2022; N.A., 2022) and thus, postponing counter measures. In the meantime, both institutions had to learn the permanence of an environment of rising prices.

While the rise of inflation was pushing real interest rates deep into negative territory, with a time lag of about six months, capital markets since early 2022 woke up emancipating interest rate from negative yields and ultra-low interest rates of the years of central bank unparalleled bond purchase programmes.

Besides the financial indicators, at the same time, one should not forget the effect of measures against COVID. For an untransparent mix of health and political reasons, China has been sticking to its zero-tolerance policy adamantly slowing down the exchange of people and goods and pushing its trade partners even deeper in disruptions that are not yet even reflected in actual inflation rates. At the same time, with China as economic engine slowing down, rising cost of living and depressing geopolitical incidents, the threat of further cooling down that enables stagflation could become the worst-case scenario for central banks and governments. This development will be reinforced by the painful boomerang-effects of all economic sanctions against Russia.

What are the adverse impacts of the "cocktail" of these external effects influencing the future path of economic development and business models?

Risks for Business Models Ahead

The strength and viability of any business model lies in its ability in uncertain times to either predict and pre-eliminate negative effects or to become resilient and able to absorb shocks to the business model and to recover up and above the pre-shock levels (Brunnermeier, 2021).

So far, public attention is widely on consumer price inflation, while spill over effects from **producer prices** may harm all businesses with limited pricing power towards customers. In fact, per mid-2022, most of the substantially higher producer price inflation (Statistisches Bundesamt, 2022) has not yet found its way through the entrepreneurial performance, an effect still to come. Furthermore, second-round effects may occur on the labour cost side, if wage requests close or above the inflation level are realising in the corporate profits/losses in labour intensive industries.

On the customer demand side, *psychological behaviour* will influence future inflation. Besides the already reduced purchasing power of customers, in fear of rising future prices anticipating investments and consumptions create in times of limited supply a self-fulfilling inflation prophesy: higher velocity of circulation of money stimulates inflation by its own. At the same time, an opposite development is possible: if rising fear hampers willingness to invest and consume, inflation may slow down, but at the price of overall lower economic activities. What is for sure is the fact that already today's inflation paired with rising interest expense cut into available household income and will likely continue to do so.

Deepening *social inequality* is the ugly face of inflation due to its nature as general "tax" (Kupiec, 2021). Nothing new here, debtors (government!) and real asset holders are favoured while owners of financial assets and salary earners suffer real losses. Governments are likely to address the polarising development with non-market conforming transfer payments, taxation and reallocation of income and wealth to prevent from social unrest. What is true for industrialised countries is even more relevant for frontier and developing economies. In addition to inflation, the interest rate rise in the United States makes foreign debts of those countries more expensive, both from an interest cost point but also from a currency aspect.

Already before the first interest rate rise by the European Central Bank took place, a crack between the risk-spreads of the northern members of the Eurozone and the slow-growing and highly indebted southern peripheral "Club-Med" countries got visible again. A normal differentiation due to the issuer's different credit quality, one could argue – but not the European Central Bank (2022). Economically questionable, monetary instruments are announced to be applied preventing from *fragmentation* and unjustified expansion of spreads.

Fragmentation is not only a risky development the ECB fears, but it is also a geopolitical concern: concepts of *on- and nearshoring*, opposite to off shoring, refer to more geographical closeness between producer and purchaser. Winding back from global (fair) trade concepts, supply may be more secure and potential ecological effects due to shorter delivery routes may be improved, but probably at the expense of higher prices driven by higher costs, pushing inflation further in the next round. A similar effect might be driven by fostering ecological standards towards producer and consumer. The fear of *greenflation* has, however, been seen in connection with new business models around the environmental, social and corporate governance (ESG) framework.

In the light of the Ukrainian war and rising tensions with China, one may criticise the European and especially the German economic policy concept of "change-through-trade" (Fulda, 2022), whereas opposite ideas are by far less dangerous. The concept of *friend-shoring* proposed by Janet Yellen (Atlantic Council, 2022) aims for slicing the world in dichotomist good-bad dimensions by limiting trade relationships to politically friendly countries only, which is a short-sighted and costly undertake (Subramaniam, 2022). Continuous political tensions, economic decoupling, de-globalisation are buzzwords indicating a risk of segregation and permanently welding apart ecosystems to an extent that would be unparalleled in recent history. Putting all business models, which are relying on manufacturing upside down, the mental model of economic worldview of this generations' decision maker, would equally collapse.

Corporate Actions to Address Economic Challenges

Business models are likely to be affected by the accelerating mix of presumably manageable risk and complete uncertainty. Handling changes within all parts of the business model and all aspects of the corporate value chain as well as the surrounding ecosystem seems to be relevant.

Strategic, as well as operational, planning will have to be based much more on *scenario thinking* taking into consideration crisis types, contagion effects and second round courses. Instead of trust in past solutions, creative – even counter-factual – thinking opens for imagination and related scenarios to operational business context. For this, risk identification will play a pivotal role in addressing corporate vulnerabilities, especially in times where even some mid-sized companies still do not have a risk management function in place. Challenging the status quo of the individual business model and developing scenarios for "what-if?" questions will become essential. Especially, emergency planning based on the effects of low probability but high-impact cases, the famous black swan effects (Taleb, 2008) is recommended.

Being a synonym for global economy (Rickards, 2022), the conditions of *supply chains* are likely to be of highest importance for the viability and success of most business models. Weakened and unsecure channels will lead to subsequent fluctuating prices more than in the past as the deflationary and market-broadening effect of globalisation came, at best, to a halt. Low-cost single sourcing strategies to optimise volume and gain better conditions have to be questioned as overlooking the inherent risks of one-sided dependency. Counting on alternative sources in geopolitically secure regions or countries seems necessary. Own experiences show that personal relationships to key-provider staff matters in times of shortage. Fair treatment during "good" past times far outweighs gag contracts and the one-sided focus on legally binding contracts.

Even if costly, geopolitical tensions are likely to foster *redundancies* in organisations. Threats of tariffs and trade restrictions, import barriers and transport difficulties force managers to think about partial or full duplications of dedicated supply chains, flexible production ability in formerly specialised locations without stepping into the trap described above as the concept of friend shoring.

Similarly, important is the economic effect that political actions during the pandemic have now on the labour base. While unemployment at a much bigger scale could be avoided during the crisis, buzzwords as *great resignation and great retention* indicate a behavioural change in self-esteem and loyalty of qualified staff (Riley, 2021). Paired with demographic development, keeping knowledgeable and diverse staff as the true assets of any company is of growing importance as any otherwise thinking leads to undermining the success of companies' business models.

As a practical example, apart from risk management, the importance of *treasury and cash management* abilities will celebrate a renaissance. With the end of virtually priceless liquidity and availability of funds not as "natural" as in the past decade, committed credit lines and cash truly will become king – to ensure solvency but also to make use of opportunities in the market.

The higher interest rates in combination with widening risk-oriented credit spreads will put pressure on the financial returns of business models. With the end of the time of negative risk-free interest rates, the expectations towards a minimum profitability and returns of any investors, stakeholders and venture capitalists will rise as well. As Warren Buffet has stated in the Letter to Shareholders 2001 (Berkshire Hathaway, 2002), "you only find out who is swimming naked when the tide goes out", especially some of those business models that contain higher risk profiles, will probably have problems with delivering the demanded higher returns. A first sign of this selection process can be found in the stock underperformance of highly leveraged and loss-making technology firms during the first half of 2022 (N.A., 2022).

Last, but not least, companies will need to change their managerial mindset to stay *resilient in a complex environment* by being more comprehensive, focused and sophisticated than in the past. In contrast to complicated situations, where individual knowledge helps to solve problems, resilience in complex situations involves many uncertain but interrelated elements. The nature of complex systems is that they are in many indirect relations, often without a specific and predictable cause-effect relations and inability of being solved by subject-matter experience alone (Sterman, 2000). Instead, (life-) experiences from various fields are exceeding the standard call for (gender-)diversity, bringing the topic to a new level.

Protecting the business while at the same time opening up for changes in the model of doing business, requires internal structures, where the before mentioned challenges are brought into decision and execution. Speed will be of pivotal importance. Preparing the organisation by defining decision paths, meeting formats and the development of specific measure toolboxes need to be in place and has to be regularly the subject to resilience drills in companies.

Outlook

The challenges from today's dull, uncertain and risky economic outlook should neither depress not paralyse companies. Both inflation and interest rate rise are results of over-exaggeration of the past and can be seen as a normalisation process. Since ever, the development of businesses and business models occurs along the famous "wall of worry," a notion of the famous US investor Ken Fisher who claims that there is permanently a wall of unexpected, immovable bad forces (Fisher, 2014) that must, however, not prevent from identifying and realising the splendid new business opportunities non-existing in "normal" times.

In fact, building up and focusing on corporate qualities as understanding behavioural psychology, managing by usage of complexity theories (Rickards, 2016) and strengthening risk management will strengthen foresight and improve business models and surrounding ecosystems continuously in the future.

24 *Winfried Mueller*

References

Allianz (2021). "Allianz risk barometer 2022: The most important business risks for the next 12 months and beyond based on the insight of 2,650 risk management experts from 89 countries and territories", https://www.agcs.allianz.com/content/dam/onemarketing/agcs/agcs/reports/Allianz-Risk-Barometer-2022.pdf. Accessed on 10 April 2022.

Aschoff, D. & Heitmann, J. (2020). "Klassische Risiken im Überblick", in A. Mahnke & T. Rohlfs (Eds.), *Betriebliches Risikomanagement und Industrieversicherung: Erfolgreiche Unternehmenssteuerung durch ein effektives Risiko- und Versicherungsmanagement*, Wiesbaden: Springer Fachmedien, 89–114.

Berkshire Hathaway (2002). Letter of Warren Buffett, https://www.berkshirehathaway.com/letters/2002pdf.pdf.

Biennale (2019). https://www.labiennale.org/en/art/2019/58th-exhibition. Accessed on 10 April 2022.

Brunnermeier, M. (2021). *The Resilient Society*. London: Endeavor Literary Press.

European Central Bank (2022). "Press release: Statement after the ad hoc meeting of the ECB Governing Council 15 June 2022", https://www.ecb.europa.eu/press/pr/date/2022/html/ecb.pr220615~2aa3900e0a.en.html. Accessed on 25 May 2022.

Fisher, K. (2014). "Only two things can stop the bull market", https://www.forbes.com/sites/kenfisher/2014/03/26/only-two-things-can-stop-the-bull-market/?sh=7a186fe66a7b. Accessed on 10 April 2022.

Fulda, A. (2022). "Germany's China policy of 'Change Through Trade' has failed", https://www.rusi.org/explore-our-research/publications/commentary/germanys-china-policy-change-through-trade-has-failed. Accessed on 20 May 2022.

Gennaro, A. & Nietlispach, M. (2021). "Corporate governance and risk management: Lessons (not) learnt from the financial crisis", *Journal of Risk and Financial Management*, vol. 14(9), p. 419. 10.3390/jrfm14090419.

Kolhatkar, S. (2022). "The consequences of the unprecedented rush of companies leaving Russia", https://www.newyorker.com/business/currency/the-consequences-of-the-unprecedented-rush-of-companies-leaving-russia. Accessed on 20 May 2022.

Koranyi, B. & Canepa, F. (2022). "Euro zone inflation not as transitory: ECB's de Guindos", https://www.reuters.com/world/europe/euro-zone-inflation-not-transitory-thought-ecbs-de-guindos-2022-01-13/. Accessed on 5 May 2022.

Kupiec, P.H. (2021). "The inflation tax is not only real, it's massive", https://www.aei.org/op-eds/the-inflation-tax-is-not-only-real-its-massive/. Accessed on 2 April 2022.

Mandl, C. & Marshall, E.D. (2022). "Goldman Sachs COO Waldron sees unprecedented shocks in economy", https://www.reuters.com/markets/wealth/goldman-sachs-coo-waldron-says-lower-valuations-wealth-management-open-ma-2022-06-02/. Accessed on 10 June 2022.

Müeller, W. (2021). "Market conforming and non-market conforming financial support measures during COVID-19", in M.A. Marinov & S.T. Marinova (Eds.), *COVID-19 and International Business: Change of Area*. London and New York, NY: Routledge, 140–147.

N.A. (2022). "Gorillas und Co.: Startups stecken in der Todesspirale", https://www.boerse-am-sonntag.de/aktien/markt-im-fokus/artikel/gorillas-und-co-startups-stecken-in-der-todesspirale-12491.html. Accessed on 10 May 2022.

New Atlanticist (April 13, 2022). Transcript: US Treasury Secretary Janet Yellen on the next steps for Russia sanctions and 'friend-shoring' supply chains, https://www.atlanticcouncil.org/news/transcripts/transcript-us-treasury-secretary-janet-yellen-on-the-next-steps-for-russia-sanctions-and-friend-shoring-supply-chains/

Rickards, J. (2016). *The Road to Ruin*. London: Penguin.

Rickards, J. (2022). "The supply chain is the economy", https://dailyreckoning.com/the-supply-chain-is-the-economy/. Accessed on 20 May 2022.

Riley, R. (2021). "The great resignation, the great reset, the great reshuffle and the great retention", https://blog.bham.ac.uk/cityredi/the-great-resignation-the-great-reset-the-great-reshuffle-and-the-great-retention/. Accessed on 10 April 2022.

Saefong, M.P. (2021). "Commodities corner: Oil prices went negative a year ago: Here's what traders have learned since", https://www.marketwatch.com/story/oil-prices-went-negative-a-year-ago-heres-what-traders-have-learned-since-11618863839#:~:text=On%20April%2020%2C%202020%2C%20the,the%20New%20York%20Mercantile%20Exchange. Accessed on 10 April 2022.

Statistisches Bundesamt (2022). "Producer prices on May 2022: + 33.6%", in May 2021. Pressrelease #252 from 20 June 2022. https://www.destatis.de/EN/Press/2022/06/PE22_252_61241.html. Accessed on 22 June 2022.

Sterman, J.D. (2000). *Business Dynamics: System Thinking and Modeling for a Complex World*. Boston, MA: Irwin McGraw Hill.

Subramaniam, S. (2022). "Friend shoring is bad for politics but even worse for business", https://qz.com/2173562/what-is-friendshoring/. Accessed on 22 June 2022.

Taleb, N.N. (2008). *The Black Swan: The Impact of the Highly Improbable*. London: Penguin.

3 Overcoming Barriers in Creating Ecosystem Business Models: Achieving Resilience in an Uncertain and Competitive Setting

Sebastian Evald Stück, Peter Thomsen, and Christian Nielsen

Introduction

Corporations worldwide are experiencing immense pressure to innovate and create new products, services and technologies, as well as to be able to market these globally. For many companies, achieving a competitive speed to market and global reach and innovating one's finance, business model and product development (among other goals) is a difficult, if not impossible, task. While a handful of large global companies may be able to do this alone, most companies require collaboration with others. However, this opens a whole new avenue of risk scenarios and problems. In addition, companies are experiencing mounting pressure to compete in global markets that have become increasingly unstable due to recent geopolitical issues, such as financial crises, pandemics and armed conflicts.

Regardless of the geopolitical situation, the fact that many companies cannot by themselves compete in innovation due to their small size is problematic. In most European countries, the main thrust of economic growth is through small- and medium-sized enterprises (SMEs), characterised as having fewer than 250 employees. Typically, SMEs have less capital for investment purposes and likely have less strategic ability than larger corporations and multinational companies. Therefore, if economies characterised by a large proportion of SMEs must continue or improve their growth trajectories, they need to ensure that SMEs – and even smaller companies and start-ups – become experts at creating value in collaborative ecosystems. Research into value creation mechanisms has indicated that forming strategic partnerships is key to building scalable business models (Nielsen & Lund, 2018).

Therefore, this study contributes to the field by providing insights into how partnerships and value propositions are formed in highly competitive environments in times of global uncertainty, where decoupling from global value chains forms part of enhancing resilience. Moreover, the chapter aims to shed light onto how companies can begin the process of creating

DOI: 10.4324/9781003326731-3

innovation and platform-based ecosystems. Both contributions are essential elements of increasing competitiveness and corporate resilience. The research context is the creation of two network-based business models, one being an innovation ecosystem and the other a platform ecosystem, both situated in the maritime sector of a port. Ports are an exciting context in which to study collaboration between companies because they are often hubs for different services and, therefore, natural places for companies to locate.

The study is grounded in a *structured systems of action* approach (Crozier & Friedberg, 1980). This methodological and analytical approach lends itself naturally to the analysis of collective systems of action, such as business ecosystems and network-based business models. The remainder of the chapter is structured as follows: The next section covers the link between business models and value creation in ecosystems. The third section presents the applied methodology, including an introduction to the data, data collection methods and the analytical and interpretive perspective. The fourth section provides empirical evidence of the two collaborative ecosystems, and the conclusions are presented in the fifth section.

Business Models and Ecosystems

Nielsen and Roslender (2015) defined business models as describing a given company's concept for earning "money", which would entail identifying the platform that connects value creation and delivery between the enterprise, its stakeholders and its customers in order to capture value. In this sense, Nielsen and Roslender (2015) argued that business models are not confined to the so-called focal firm. This perspective has otherwise been proposed in several alternative ways for defining a business model.

Business models can assume different roles within a company. They can guide strategy and reporting processes, serve as management representations of value creation mechanisms and act as cognitive models. What is most important is that the depiction of a business model assists the company in understanding how to succeed and perform well. However, the dimensions by which we determine good performance are open for interpretation.

According to Magretta (2002), a successful business model entails two aspects that must be present simultaneously. The first is the narrative test, which is to say that a successful business model is coherent. The second aspect is the numbers test. Positive financial outcomes illustrate the success of a business model. Similarly, Osterwalder and Pigneur (2010) described a business model as the rationale of how an organisation creates, delivers and captures value. They offered the Business Model Canvas (BMC) for describing a business model through nine basic building blocks, which allows the logic of how a company intends to make money to become evident. The nine building blocks (customer segments, value proposition, channels, customer relationships, key resources, key activities, strategic partnerships, revenue streams and cost structure) cover four main areas that constitute a business: customers, product/service offerings, value chain infrastructure and financial viability.

Much like a strategy blueprint, a business model is implemented through organisational structures, processes and systems (Montemari & Nielsen, 2013). In this regard, a BMC (Osterwalder & Pigneur, 2010) connects the different building blocks for a shared understanding of the business model within the company and, notably, to the external stakeholders who interact with it.

Baden-Fuller perceived business models from a typology perspective (Baden-Fuller & Morgan, 2010). His Business Model Zoo framework identifies four elemental business model pathways for business development. Each describes an ideal model of how a company can engage with its customers, deliver value, and monetise the result. Recent research has evaluated more specific business model configurations from an ontological level. Two contemporary examples are Gassmann et al.'s (2014) Business Model Navigator, comprising over 55 business model patterns, and Taran et al.'s (2016) 5-V framework, which identified 71 business model configurations. Such configurations are specific modes of conducting business, and each entails particular strengths and weaknesses; for instance, the latter example was built around 251 specifically identified value drivers.

The existing literature tells us that business models seldom work in isolation; instead, they almost always interact with other companies' business models, either upstream or downstream in the value chain or in the ecosystem in which they function. Jacobides, Cennamo and Gawer (2018) suggested that ecosystem emergence allows a set of interdependent organisations to coordinate without full hierarchical fiat. Thinking in terms of functional modularity is essential in allowing this to happen. Ecosystems include dependences based on different complementarities: unique, unidirectional or bidirectional. Jacobides et al. (2018) further argued that non-generic complementarities and the creation of sets of roles that face similar rules lie at the core of ecosystems. However, Jacobides et al.'s (2018) definition of an ecosystem – namely as a network where there is a focal firm in the hub – could be argued to be problematically narrow.

Lingens (2021) provided a helpful typology of ecosystems according to four archetypes: industry, knowledge, innovation and platform ecosystems. It is worth bearing in mind that ecosystems come in many forms and that there is not necessarily a firm at the centre of such a network. Nielsen and Montemari (2012) described an ecosystem wherein two companies act out an equal relationship and draw upon other companies in the total ecosystem. Lingens (2021) argued that the ultimate purpose of an innovation ecosystem is the creation of an innovation that a company could not create in isolation and is thus the most fruitful avenue from which to further collaborative business models. The innovation ecosystem fosters a distinct worldview on acquiring collaborative advantage (Boemenburg & Gassmann, 2022), which requires a collaborative leadership approach.

Overcoming Barriers in Creating Ecosystem Business Models 29

Working with a collaborative advantage requires companies to shift from a transactional or transformational perspective into a collective mindset. Companies are motivated by being socially responsible, inclusive, and focused on creating community. A collaborative approach is crucial for many companies to develop scale and reach SMEs. Both collaborative advantage and business models have been studied for some years now, and despite the scholarly attention these have received, core knowledge gaps remain. These are addressed in the current chapter. A notable longitudinal study by Lund and Nielsen (2014) on business models and their roles in creating ecosystem-based value illustrated how an ecosystem-based business model transforms through stages.

Jacobides et al. (2018) described how ecosystems – as a form of interactive, collaborative organisation – differ from such other business constellations as markets, alliances, or hierarchically managed supply chains. They also argued that modularity enables them not to be hierarchically managed and bound together by their collective investment. The ability to create a collaborative organisation, and thus a partnership mindset (Lund & Nielsen, 2018), is a foundational element of creating growth and scalability (Nielsen & Lund, 2018). However, the current literature seems to lack models and insights into how to initiate and implement ecosystems in practice.

Methodology

Analytical and interpretive perspectives use concrete systems of action, which are structured ensembles of human and organisational agents linked by relatively stable mechanisms that coordinate and regulate their participants' activities. March (1994) noted that the factors influencing action and relationships on a multiple-actor level include inconsistencies in preferences and identities within the group. Crozier and Friedberg's (1980) methodology can be applied in instances where understanding the systems of contingent power relationships are inherent in any form of organisation, whether single-firm or ecosystem-based. The methodology constitutes an experimental and inductive approach to studying organisations, ecosystems and decision-making. At the same time, it is a method of analysis of social reality. It analyses the organisation as a system of action and reflects its constituent groups or individuals. It comprises a "sociology of organised action" (Crozier & Friedberg 1980, p. 54). Crozier and Friedberg's (1980) framework critiques traditional research into organisational action, inapplicable as it does not transcend a static description of reality. The basic concepts of their paradigm of collective action are games, power and uncertainty. However, we focused primarily on the theoretical elements concerning decisions in a multi-stakeholder setting due to the current research purpose.

30 *Sebastian Evald Stück et al.*

Crozier and Friedberg (1980) defined concrete systems of action as:

> A structured human ensemble, which employs relatively stable game mechanisms to coordinate the actions of its participants. Furthermore, it maintains its structure, i.e., the stability of its games and the relationships among them, through regulation mechanisms. These, in turn, form the content of still other games. (p. 153)

The backbone of Crozier and Friedberg's (1980) theory is the proposition that strategy precedes structure (i.e., becoming the determinant of the organisational system). Chandler (1962) illustrated that a firm's strategy over a period determines its structure. The former should be analysed by assessing the firm's willingness to make the best use of its resources as a function of market possibilities. Chandler (1962) emphasised the importance of changes in the environment for making new strategic choices and considered such changes to be critical factors in selecting new modes of conducting business. Chandler (1962) may be viewed as a seminal contribution to our current understanding of business models as a way of thinking that creates links and synergies among the various constituents of a company's value creation.

The above discussion allows us to analyse organisations from two perspectives: strategy and a systematic point of departure. As with Chandler's (1962, p. 121) ideas, the strategic argument starts with the strategy before discovering the system, and vice versa. However, the strategic analysis remains confined within phenomenological interpretation without an articulated system argument. Without confirmation in terms of strategy, systems analysis remains speculative, needing the stimulus of the strategic argument to prevent it from being deterministic. As these two underlying logics of strategic and systemic arguments are contrasting – i.e., one inductive and the other deductive – the integration calls for a new logic. From this basis, Crozier and Friedberg (1980) proposed "concrete systems of action" as the missing logic, in which analysis takes precedence over theory.

Power is an essential aspect of concrete systems of action because of the relations between actors. In Crozier & Friedberg's (1980) terminology, power is a relation, rather than an attribute, of the actors and can only develop through exchanges among them (i.e., negotiation). They defined power as a reciprocal but unbalanced relation of force from which one party can obtain more than the other. However, neither party is defenceless nor therefore lies in the margin of liberty available to each in a relation to power (Crozier & Friedberg 1980, pp. 30–32). Crozier and Friedberg (1980, p. 40) identified four broad sources of power: (1) power deriving from special skills and functional specialisation; (2) power connected with the relations between an organisation and its environment; (3) power engendered by control of communication and information; and (4) power through the existence of general organisational rules.

Crozier and Friedberg's (1980) work naturally lent itself to the qualitative study of ecosystems due to its focus on understanding relationships and how they form the total value creation of the system. Hence, it offers a framework for analysis that can rest upon the case study-based data collections.

This study focuses on creating a service hub at the Port of Esbjerg, one of the larger Danish ports with a long-standing export history. Currently, Esbjerg concentrates on the energy sector and maritime activities around the renewable energy sector. We sought to investigate how to create a network-based business model around a service hub with the potential of becoming an innovation or platform ecosystem. It presents the non-interventionist part of an action research project combining interventionist and non-interventionist methods. Nine companies were involved in this study, presented in Table 3.1.

We collected data on the nine companies through primary and secondary sources. As part of the primary data collection methods, each company was mapped using a mapping tool that could identify business model configurations. Simoni, Schaper and Nielsen (2022) proposed this more granular and accurate content analysis methodology for investigating business models by inserting an additional "layer" of analysis based on Taran et al.'s (2016) business model taxonomy. By classifying the sample of companies according to this taxonomy, it is possible to identify the main value drivers of each company. Taran et al.'s (2016) taxonomy boil the companies' business models down to 71 potential business model configurations, each with a predefined set of value drivers.

In addition, we conducted semi-structured interviews to uncover qualitative aspects of these business model configurations and their value drivers. This enabled us to identify the value propositions of each organisation in the ecosystem and thus analyse how each could create value in collaboration in the ecosystem using the motivation matrix methodology. The semi-structured interviews comprised the following questions:

- In your value chain, do you feel rising risk scenarios on quality, price, or timeliness?
- Is this pressure smaller or greater than that of your competitors?
- How do these pressures emerge in terms of the decisions made by the company?
- And is this different for other companies in your sector? Please explain.
- Do these pressures influence your business model and how you collaborate? Please explain.
- Do they influence risk management and how risk is treated financially?
- Have the latest market developments affected the coupling and the relationships in the network/value chain?

The interviews focused on the potential of the service hub solution by identifying standard value creation potentials. We collected secondary data

Table 3.1 Descriptive data about the case companies

	Name	Nation	Industry affiliation	Revenue (DKK)	Total number of employees	No. of employees in the operations related to the PoE
A	Blue Water Shipping A/S	Denmark	Freight forwarding	5,490,427,000 kr. (2021)	~1,800	804
B(A)	Granly Diesel A/S	Denmark	Wholesale and repair of diesel engines, generators and other propulsion systems and equipment	Have not disclosed their revenue	41	41
B(B)	Granly Gruppen	Denmark	Non-financial holding company	27,220,000 kr. (2021)	10	10
C	Maersk Drilling A/S	Denmark	Oil and gas drilling services	1,741,182,000 kr. (2020)	~2,481	675
D	NorSea Denmark A/S	Denmark	Oil and gas drilling services	200,629,000 kr. (2017)	250	217
E	Port of Esbjerg	Denmark	Commercial port	208,650,687 kr. (2020)	50–99	50–99
F	Semco Maritime A/S	Denmark	Engineering, design, manufacturing, installation, project management, repairs and services in offshore	997,643,000 kr. (2020)	~1,700	821
G	Rig Quip Drilling Services Ltd.	Scotland, United Kingdom	Drilling equipment and service	**N/A**	~51–200	27
H	Jacking Solutions International	United Arab Emirates	Oil and gas, and jacking systems equipment, repairs and services	N/A	~1–10	No presence in Port Esbjerg
I	West Diesel Engineering A/S	Denmark	Wholesale and repair of diesel engines, generators and other propulsion systems and equipment	Have not disclosed their revenue	23	23

Source: The authors.

on the companies through annual reports and materials describing the solutions the nine case companies were offering to the market.

Empirical Evidence of Collaborative Ecosystems

Let us begin by providing an overview of each company individually. The QUANT business model analyses of the nine companies showed that each company uses two to three distinct business model configurations. Table 3.2 illustrates the 14 different business models in the service hub that we identified.

The dispersion becomes evident when focusing on each company's most prominent business model configurations (see Table 3.3).

We identified the companies' potential value propositions to the service hub by analysing these business model configurations in-depth (see Table 3.4).

Value Creation in Collaboration

We illustrated an AS-IS ecosystem by analysing the interviews and data collected on the current state of the network (see Figure 3.1). Both Semco and Granly saw their current business as already being that of the intended service hub solution. Therefore, they had conflicting roles and were naturally reluctant to participate. They feared missing out on business that "should have been theirs" from the beginning and fought hard for every penny when forced to take in partners and subcontractors. These two companies needed to be convinced that the ecosystem would be able to draw in additional business opportunities and that the port as a whole was missing out on because the companies themselves were not attractive to or visible in the market. Other participating companies were of the same belief that the shift towards an ecosystem business model would hurt their business in the short term but could have positive effect on the long-term advantages.

Through our interaction with the participating companies, we observed a general uncertainty about the scope and volume of the overall potential market in the North Sea region. While detailed insights were provided about current customers and their reason for choosing Port of Esbjerg, it remained unclear to what extent traffic and general offshore activity was dispersed among "neighbouring" ports, i.e., those in Holland, Britain and Norway. Ports individually possess different characteristics such as distance, water depth, on-site facilities and supply chains, which are decisive factors for the choice of port some customers make. Rotterdam is, for example, strong on its cargo logistics network, while Norway on its low electricity price and deep basins to service to oil rigs. However, according to several of the interviewed companies, some customer patterns seem to be rather indiscriminate and/or inexplicable as to why they would choose a certain port.

Table 3.2 Business models used in the service hub

	3 (Value chain service provider	1 (Customer focused)	7 (8) (Full-service provider)	2 (Value chain coordinator)	1 (Integrator)	1 (Leasing)	1 (Procurement)	1 (Breakthrough markets)	1 (Trusted advisor)	2 (Pay-as-you-go)	1 (Trusted operation)	1 (Incomparable product/service)	1 (Upfront payment)	1 (Collaboration platforms)
A	X	X	X											
B	–	–	(X)	–	–	–	–	–						
C	X		X	X										
D	X		X	X										
E					X	X	X							
F			X					X	X					
G			X							X	X			
H			X							X		X		
I			X										X	X

Source: The authors.

Table 3.3 Primary business model configurations in the service hub

	Main BM Configuration
A	Value chain service provider
B	Full-service provider
C	Value chain service provider
D	Value chain service provider
E	Integrator
F	Breakthrough markets
G	Full-service provider
H	Full-service provider
I	Upfront payment

Source: The authors.

General knowledge about the market appeared to be fragmented and somewhat limited, leading us to conclude that further investigation of the market is paramount in order to ensure the right configuration and position on the market from a differentiation perspective.

Furthermore, the role of the port itself was found to be unclear. The port acted as a landlord, information gatherer and infrastructure provider, but its exact involvement in specific jobs was not always apparent. Some stakeholders viewed the port as an added expense with marginal value creation due to labour union control dictating the presence of port employees when new vessels landed. This critique could be answered by the port's introduction of a model with a low-service/low-cost arm or even a freemium solution (see Anderson, 2013).

Figure 3.1 illustrates that customers currently have many options when landing in the port due to the well-updated status of its information and website regarding potential services. Figure 3.1 further shows the network of companies included in the current data collection, as well as the high level of interaction between them. This network diagram is by no means complete. It would most likely differ if other potential partners were introduced or if the focus were shifted to another service category at the port. In visualising the current network, we hoped that the companies would begin to realise how they could increase their business through collaboration simply because new and more complex opportunities could be seized in conjunction.

Dream Scenario – a Platform Ecosystem

In a dream scenario, the potential customer experiences a single point of contact with the service hub that would be able to coordinate the service needs of the drilling contractors with equipment suppliers, service companies, logistics suppliers and other support functions, such as consultancies, data and software companies, and legal, financial and insurance firms (Olesen, 2015).

Table 3.4 Value propositions of the companies to the service hub

	Company name			
A	Blue Water Shipping A/S	Specialise in a specific link in the value chain. Use special expertise and handle the function for customers in a more efficient manner than they themselves could. This also forms the basis for large-scale operating benefits.	Focus on customer needs and decentralise infrastructure management and product innovation activities so that they take place at, and in, close collaboration with, local customers.	Offer a complete range of products and services within a specific subject area. Create convenience, reliability and savings for the customer by offering such a wide selection that the customer only needs one provider.
B	Granly Diesel A/S	Offer a complete range of products and services within a specific subject area. Create convenience, reliability, and savings for the customer by offering such a wide selection that the customer only needs one provider.	N/A	N/A
C	Maersk Drilling A/S	Specialise in a specific link in the value chain. Use special expertise and handle the function for customers in a more efficient manner than they themselves could. This also forms the basis for large-scale operating benefits.	Offer a complete range of products and services within a specific subject area. Create convenience, reliability and savings for the customer by offering such a wide selection that the customer only needs one provider.	Offer coordination services related for communication and organisational work processes for parties in the same value chain

D	NorSea Denmark A/S	Specialise in a specific link in the value chain. Use special expertise and handle the function for customers in a more efficient manner than they themselves could. This also forms the basis for large-scale operating benefits.	Offer a complete range of products and services within a specific subject area. Create convenience, reliability and savings for the customer by offering such a wide selection that the customer only needs one provider.	Offer coordination services related for communication and organisational work processes for parties in the same value chain
E	Port of Esbjerg	The majority of the links from the company's value chain are handled in-house. Accordingly, the company remains in control of its resources and value creation opportunities. The low degree of dependence on key partners or suppliers creates the foundation for stability in value creation and economies of scale.	Offer the customer to lease, rather than buy, a product. The customer obtains many of the benefits of full ownership for a limited period, but at a fraction of the purchase price. The lower capital requirement means that the product becomes relevant for a larger customer segment.	Continuously put goods and services out to tender for a bidding war between suppliers. The outcome of the bidding war is typically lower purchase prices.
F	Semco Maritime A/S	Keep yourself updated on the latest knowledge and specialise in a given subject area so you can advise customers on complex challenges.	Offer a complete range of products and services within a specific subject area. Create convenience, reliability, and savings for the customer by offering such a wide selection that the customer only needs one provider.	Invest regularly in creating or exploring new markets to gain temporary monopolies to begin with. Subsequently consolidate one's market position through continuous price adjustment and streamlining of operations.

(*Continued*)

Table 3.4 (Continued)

	Company name			
G	Rig Quip Drilling Services Ltd.	Offer a complete range of products and services within a specific subject area. Create convenience, reliability and savings for the customer by offering such a wide selection that the customer only needs one provider.	Offer a service up charge only payment for the customer's actual consumption of it.	Offer safe handling of activities where they can have major consequences for the customer if mistakes are made.
H	Jacking Solutions International	Offer a service up charge only payment for the customer's actual consumption of it.	Take advantage of proprietary technologies to create and offer unique products or services that can be sold with a high coverage rate.	Offer a complete range of products and services within a specific subject area. Create convenience, reliability and savings for the customer by offering such a wide selection that the customer only needs one provider.
I	West Diesel Engineering A/S	Get the customer to pay in advance and generate high profits by maintaining a low inventory.	Offer a complete range of products and services within a specific subject area. Create convenience, reliability and savings for the customer by offering such a wide selection that the customer only needs one provider.	Offer a platform with relevant, reliable and user-friendly tools that can facilitate collaboration between companies. Base earnings on sales of access to the platform through, for example, membership or usage fees, and minimise costs through economies of scale.

Source: The authors.

Overcoming Barriers in Creating Ecosystem Business Models 39

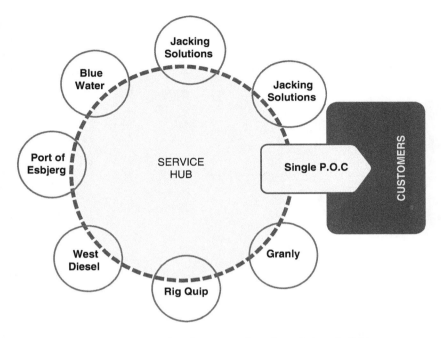

Figure 3.1 The current transaction flows around service solutions in Esbjerg.

Figure 3.2 illustrates this dream scenario that was formed from interviews with the port, the participating companies, and the business developers in the region's maritime sector. Having a single point of contact was frequently mentioned in the interviews and preparations for business model mappings, albeit with a reluctant tone. It had been tried, and it had failed. A company attempted to create such a network called the One-network. Among explanations for its failure was a lack of commitment from partners, who saw it as conflicting with their business scope. While having clear advantages, the idea of having an independent company to undertake customer contact seemed to be too drastic a power shift for the service hub's central players. They worried about not receiving their fair share of profits.

Our business model analysis further clarified this issue by identifying the extent to which some companies were already operating as full-service providers, and consequently, worried about or were reluctant to relinquish customer jobs to others and promote yet another full-service provider (i.e., a service hub) in the Port of Esbjerg. Individually, the full-service companies already identified and promoted themselves as one point of contact, thus they did not perceive this as a value proposition for the service hub.

This led to questioning whether a platform ecosystem with one controlling company at the core could be transformed into an innovation

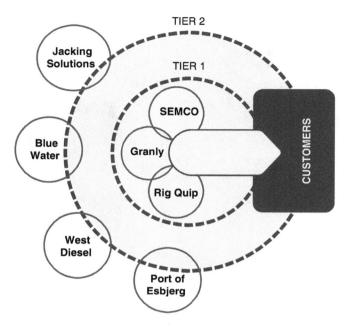

Figure 3.2 The dream scenario platform ecosystem.

ecosystem with a more nuanced governance structure. To evaluate this proposition, we analysed the companies' interactions and their own understanding of the business models of each company. The solution hub needed a more robust platform for creating a co-understanding that could eventually lead to forming an active ecosystem. The potential partners would need to work on how they could be more strategic in bringing in larger inflows of business to the port, not interfering with or cannibalising their existing activities. In this way, the service hub would constitute a bonus solution and not a potential disruptor. Consequently, the service hub would need to take ownership of customers recruited through this channel and establish a fair basis of distribution among the partner companies. To do so, they would need to collaborate with information-consulting, financing, investment and insurance partners for information flows.

One way to initiate this ecosystem development process that could enable the inclusion of additional value-creating partners to an already-established ecosystem in an efficient manner would be to create a tier 1/tier 2 solution to the service hub. This could involve constructing a tier 1 organisation of two to three service providers with a clear governance structure and a one-year rolling contract to evaluate marketing, pricing and collaboration mechanisms. Around this tier 1 group, a tier 2 network of organisations with a semi-annual appraisal dialogue could be established.

Therefore, the second tier might constitute a flexible access platform to the network where existing and potential partnerships could be explored, enhanced or eliminated. The governance structure developed must be able to handle applications to leave and join and should ideally include both tier 1 and 2 members (see Figure 3.3).

There are several problems and threats that must first be overcome for such an ecosystem to become potentially successful. As is evident from the above discussion, there are apparent difficulties in forming and implementing the ecosystem and problems in its governance. The data identifies apparent links between the value drivers of the individual companies' business models and the transactional links between them through the structured systems perspective. The structured systems of action approach focus on both the characteristics of the relationships and the underlying motivation in the collaborations. A potential method to improve this understanding for further development would be to apply the motivation matrix methodology (Jegou, Manzini & Meroni, 2004). This would require a workshop process wherein the companies are all summoned to identify strong, weak and potential relations.

There is an interesting paradox in that innovation ecosystems do not necessarily have a central stakeholder but instead rely on dispersed power in the organisation of the value creation and must therefore factor in the network's relative strength in forming a governance structure that can contain contradictions of interest. Our data illustrates that this carries with it both opportunities and challenges. We found that the network's power

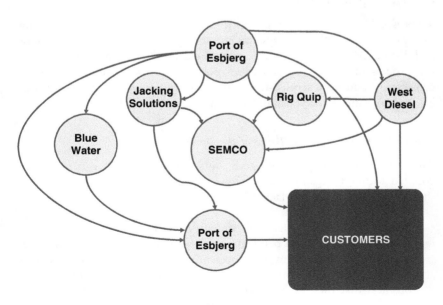

Figure 3.3 A potential tier 1/tier 2 innovation ecosystem.

42 *Sebastian Evald Stück et al.*

structure and the transactions serve to bind the various actors involved, which fully aligns with Crozier and Friedberg's findings (1980, p. 80). A challenge is to create a gatekeeping function between the organisations and the environment of external organisations. In Crozier and Friedberg's (1980) approach, collective action is a construct of human relations and their organisation. They argued that individual, relational capacities are inseparable from the structures within which social action must unfold. In this sense, they perceive the organisation (or system) as comprising two mutually conditioning elements: relations and structures. It seems evident that, in the case of the solution hub, it is necessary to work on improving personal ties and creating a collaborative culture within the port environment. Major obstacles include a lack of trust, an absence of collaboration and a reluctance to pay it forward.

External challenges include trends in decoupling local supply chains from a global world and global forces to increase resilience. Creating an ecosystem approach around a product/technology is thought to enhance the probability of resilience through loose coupling between businesses and business models in geographic proximity. According to Lingens (2021), actors in ecosystems tend to be loosely connected only in situations of stronger substantive uncertainty. Adner (2017) argued that discussing business model compatibility – and identifying "missing links" or potential value orchestrators – could motivate partners to collaborate, rather than compete, in creating resilience.

Concluding Remarks

The cases illustrate that other factors must also be considered when forming innovation and platform ecosystems and strong common value propositions and distinct business models. The cases also shed light on how to structure the process of identifying ecosystem potentials, how to implement such ecosystems, and how service-innovation and business modelling tools can be used in a more analytical and structured manners.

What Can Increase the Resilience of the Service Hub?

The empirical probing of this study indicates that resilience in a loosely coupled form of organisation, such as that of an innovation ecosystem, should be built on certain factors:

- First, while having a clear overview of how the governance structures support the interaction between each organisation is essential, the level of trust between them is a prerequisite for collaboration-induced business growth. It is only when the stakeholders begin to bring in new business that they do not necessarily profit from themselves that the ecosystem can build strength, thereby resilience.

Overcoming Barriers in Creating Ecosystem Business Models   43

- Second, and leaning on the notion of "paying it forward", resilience is built when interactions can also occur in the ecosystem's subgroups without the entire ecosystem wanting a slice of the pie, as it were. Again, unselfish behaviour, trust and a commitment to enhancing the overall value creation of the system play a vital role in building resilience.

Identifying (Potential) Ecosystems

An understudied theme is the identification of possible ecosystems and the potentials of an ecosystem-based organisation in a given context. From Jacobides et al.'s (2018) perspective, identifying the ecosystem's central node is a crucial first step. However, not all ecosystems have a central organising stakeholder. Some have two (Nielsen & Montemari, 2012), while others have none (Lund & Nielsen, 2014). So, what is to be done when this is the case? The current study offers some preliminary insights into this. However, further research specifically focused on this issue should be conducted. We found evidence of the following:

First, some form of initiative must occur, and there needs to be prior knowledge of the existence of potential stakeholders. These previous relations need not be strong and could even be in the form of a personal relationship outside of business. The initiative can come from potential or external stakeholders, either customers who have identified a gap in the market or private or public consultants.

Second, the initiative must come from the business side – not the venture side. Elaborate understanding of the potential market with its gaps and opportunities, must be established. This knowledge should constitute a guiding factor to the configuration and activities of the service hub. Forcing collaboration without a clear business opportunity, is unlikely to produce positive results.

In terms of engaging stakeholders, two situations presented themselves in the service hub, namely positive or reluctant stakeholders. When a stakeholder is immediately interested and engaged in the process, the data indicates that the focus should be on ensuring that they focus on pitfalls and constraints in capacity. For reluctant stakeholders, however, we found that focusing on the potential motivations of other collaborating stakeholders helped overcome reluctance, negativity and insecurity. Typically, insufficient trust in other stakeholders and a lack of persuasion of the business case were reasons for either reluctance or even outright refusal to participate in the ecosystem.

Implementing Ecosystems

Once a potential ecosystem is identified, the next step is to implement it. Here we lean upon discussions of priorities and roles. Depending on these indications, we suggest that the companies wanting to launch an innovation ecosystem should do the following:

44 *Sebastian Evald Stück et al.*

- Create brief narratives for each company about what motivates their value creation, what the company aims to assist its customers in achieving (their jobs to be done), and which pains they seek to avoid. These narratives do not need a full-blown BMC process but could instead use the right-hand side of the Value Proposition Canvas as inspiration (Osterwalder et al., 2014).
- Create a clear storyline about what each company's product/service/ technology offers the ecosystem's customers and the comparative strengths of said product/service/technology.
- Map this among all the potential participants and communicate it actively among the stakeholders.
- Investigate and evaluate the market. Utilise and merge the knowledge of participating companies to fully understand the market context of the potential service hub.
- Perform a comparative analysis between market opportunities and stakeholder offerings and competences to identify opportunities and gaps.
- Invite two to three pilot customers for the ecosystem solution, ensuring that serving them includes as many of the partners in the innovation ecosystem as possible.
- Evaluate the pilot cases and use the motivation matrix line of thought to refine the interactions and collaborations among the ecosystem stakeholders.
- Each company should evaluate the business model they are using in the solution hub ecosystem against the business model of the ecosystem. When the innovation ecosystem is in full operation, are there potential conflicts, such as resource allocation, mindset, and bottlenecks?

Further research should focus on successes and failures in different types of innovation ecosystems, thus, creating a checklist of dos and don'ts at various stages of the implementation, and when and how it is an advantage to include external consultants in the process.

The Role of Technology

The role of technology was an aspect that was somewhat important in the individual company mappings and interviews – and especially its role in business model innovation – but disappeared in the latter ecosystem phases. While technology could potentially play a role in collaboration and communication among the stakeholders, our findings were not evident.

Implications for Society 5.0

Finally, the work of Boemenburg and Gassmann (2022) provided an exciting connection to the current trends in societal development – typically denoted by the Society 5.0 movement. The underlying mechanisms in a Society 5.0

perspective rest on a Penta-Helix mindset where human and artificial intelligence enrich one another, and stakeholders collaborate across traditional boundaries. Currently, cities and regions worldwide, such as Tokyo and the Eindhoven region, are actively working towards this. Here, they are not afraid to take action, and communities, local governments, organisations and companies are more than willing to invest in this movement with time, resources and money. The outcomes of a Society 5.0 are, among others:

- Innovation often occurs across sectors and disciplines and can usually be transferred from one area to another.
- Initiatives are open and collaborative, and constantly include a wide range of actors.
- Ideas and implementation are often bottom-up processes, although usually with support from the public system or companies and characterised by co-production.
- Innovation often results in the creation of formal communities of interest, such as associations and organisations.
- Innovation focuses on discovering, using, and coordinating the mobilisation of both physical and human resources.
- Innovation often results in new partnerships (among public actors, companies, associations, individual citizens, etc.) or new distribution roles in existing partnerships.

As such, the mindset here is akin to collaborative thinking regarding ecosystems. Therefore, one could expect that the idea of doing business and competing based on collaborative ecosystems will be increasingly applied in future. Hence, as Hamel (2000) argues in his book, *Leading the Revolution* (2000), "Competition now increasingly stands between competing business concepts, and not only between constellations of firms linked together in linear value chains". However, this may well eventually be rewritten as: "In the future, competition will not stand primarily between individual companies in solitude, but rather competition will be between rivalling business ecosystems".

References

Adner, R. (2017). "Ecosystem as structure: An actionable construct for strategy", *Journal of Management*, vol. 43(1), pp. 39–58.

Anderson, C. (2013). *Free: How Today's Smartest Businesses Profit by Giving Something for Nothing*. New York, NY: Random House.

Baden-Fuller, C. & Morgan, M.S. (2010). "Business models as models", *Long Range Planning*, vol. 43(2-3), pp. 156–171.

Boemenburg, R. & Gassmann, O. (2022). *Collaborative Advantage: A Modern Approach to Innovating, Scaling and Transforming Your Organization*. Working paper: St. Gallen University, Switzerland.

46 *Sebastian Evald Stück et al.*

Chandler Jr., A.D. (1962). *Strategy and Structure: Chapters in the History of the American Industrial Enterprise.* Boston, MA: MIT Press.

Crozier, M. & Friedberg, E. (1980). *Actors and Systems: The Politics of Collective Action.* Chicago, IL: University of Chicago Press.

Gassmann, H., Frankenberger, K. & Csik, M. (2014). *The Business Model Navigator.* New York, NY: Pearson Education.

Hamel, G. (2000). *Leading the Revolution.* Brighton, MA: Harvard Business School Press.

Jacobides, M.G., Cennamo, C. & Gawer, A. (2018). "Towards a theory of ecosystems", *Strategic Management Journal,* vol. 39(8), pp. 2255–2276.

Jegou, F., Manzini, E. & Meroni, A. (2004). "Design plan. A design toolbox to facilitate solution-oriented partnerships", in E. Manzini, L. Collina & S. Evans (Eds.), *Solution Oriented Partnership: How to Design Industrialised Sustainable Solutions.* Cranfield: Cranfield University, 107–118.

Lingens, B. (2021). "Ecosystems: Unlocking the potentials of innovation beyond borders", in O. Gassmann & F. Ferrandina (Eds.), *Connected Business.* New York, NY: Springer Publishing Company Inc., 55–69.

Lund, M. & Nielsen, C. (2014). "The evolution of network-based business models illustrated through the case study of an entrepreneurship project", *Journal of Business Models,* vol. 2(1), pp. 105–121.

Lund, M. & Nielsen, C. (2018). "The concept of business model scalability", *Journal of Business Models,* vol. 6(1), pp. 1–18.

Magretta, J. (2002). "Why business models matter", *Harvard Business Review,* vol. 80(5), pp. 86–92, 133.

March, J.G. (1994). *A Primer on Decision Making: How Decisions Happen.* New York, NY: Free Press.

Montemari, M. & Nielsen, C. (2013). "The role of causal maps in intellectual capital measurement and management", *Journal of Intellectual Capital,* vol. 14(4), pp. 522–546.

Nielsen, C. & Lund, M. (2018). "Building scalable business models", *MIT Sloan Management Review,* vol. 59(2), pp. 65–69.

Nielsen, C. & Montemari, M. (2012). "The role of human resources in business model performance: The case of network-based companies", *Journal of Human Resource Costing & Accounting,* vol. 16(2), pp. 142–164.

Nielsen, C. & Roslender, R. (2015). "Enhancing financial reporting: the contribution of business models", *British Accounting Review,* vol. 47(3), pp. 262–274.

Olesen, T.R. (2015). *Offshore Supply Industry Dynamics: The Main Drivers in the Energy Sector and the Value Chain Characteristics for Offshore Oil and Gas and Offshore Wind.* Frederiksberg, Denmark: CBS Maritime.

Osterwalder, A. & Pigneur, Y. (2010). *Business Model Generation: A Handbook for Visionaries, Game Changers and Challengers.* Hoboken, NJ: John Wiley & Sons.

Osterwalder, A., Pigneur, Y., Bernarda, G., Smith, A. & Papadakos, T. (2014). *Value Proposition Design: How to Create Products and Services Customers Want.* Hoboken, NJ: John Wiley & Sons.

Simoni, L., Schaper, S. & Nielsen, C. (2022). "Business model disclosures, market values, and earnings persistence: Evidence from the UK", *Abacus,* vol. 58(1), pp. 142–173.

Taran, Y., Nielsen, C., Thomsen, P., Montemari, M. & Paolone, F. (2016). "Business model configurations: A five-V framework to map out potential innovation routes", *European Journal of Innovation Management,* vol. 19(4), pp. 92–527.

4 Offshoring vs Further Offshoring: A Multi-level Analysis on the Firm-, Country- and Industry-Specific Drivers of Business Model Reconfiguration

Stefano Elia and Giorgio Renna

Introduction

During the 1970s, companies in manufacturing industries identified the opportunity to internationalise and expand their business at the global level. The diffusion and development of offshoring initiatives involving production and service activities gained the attention of scholars, who started to study the motivations and effects of this phenomenon (e.g., Lewin, Massini & Peeters, 2009). Offshoring reached a huge global dimension in 2008, when it was worth around 80 billion dollars (Daub, Maitra & Mesøy, 2009). However, during the last 15 years, while offshoring was still spreading, some companies started to re-evaluate their location and internationalisation decisions due to some changes in both internal and external factors, thus leading to the rise of the so-called Relocation of Second Degree (RSD) phenomenon (Barbieri et al., 2019). This is a second location decision that modifies the prior offshoring, and that can take the form of either the decision to go back to the home country, i.e., *backshoring*, or to go elsewhere, i.e., *further offshoring*. However, while the international business and supply chain literature has largely explored the driver of the former type of RSD (see, for instance, Fratocchi et al., 2016), little is known about the phenomenon of further offshoring.

This is a gap that we aim to fill in with this chapter, considering that the COVID-19 pandemic (and more recently the war in Ukraine) are changing the geopolitical scenarios and affecting the business model of the firms by forcing governments to adopt exceptional recovery policies and companies to re-evaluate their priorities and goals, including their relocation strategy. In addition, the acceleration of some macro-trends, such as the digitalisation of production processes and the central role given to sustainability within the political agendas of several countries (UNCTAD, 2020), have opened new possibilities that may accelerate firms' decision to revise the initial offshoring location choice.

DOI: 10.4324/9781003326731-4

48 *Stefano Elia and Giorgio Renna*

While offshoring and further offshoring show some common character-istics, they also exhibit interesting differences that have led some researchers to study them as two independent location decisions. Nevertheless, nowa-days, many scholars highlight the importance to study the reshoring phe-nomenon in connection with the previous offshoring decision (Barbieri et al., 2019), recognising that offshoring and further offshoring are considered as two steps of the same manufacturing location strategy that share a strong path dependency (Wan et al., 2019; Boffelli & Johansson, 2020).

The purpose of this chapter is to identify the main drivers underlying companies' decision to undertake offshoring and further offshoring deci-sions, by looking at the latter as a form of reconfiguration of the business model (implemented through a relocation choice) that is triggered by changes involving factors that are internal and external to the firm, thus affecting the entire ecosystem. In doing so, we build on the literature that emphasises the importance of considering the drivers of offshoring and reshoring at different levels of analysis (e.g., Di Mauro et al., 2018) and we adopt a holistic framework based on a multi-level perspective that captures three different dimensions of the ecosystem, i.e., the country, the industry and the firm itself.

Our empirical analysis, based on a unique database of 141 observations of relocation initiatives of manufacturing activities obtained from the European Restructuring Monitor, shows that country and industry factors motivate companies in carrying out offshoring initiatives, while the fur-ther offshoring is driven more by firm's characteristics. Our results can provide some suggestions for managers on when and how to use further offshoring as a strategy to reconfigure firm's business models and to in-crease their resilience, and for policymakers on the implementation of policies supporting reshoring.

Theoretical Framework and Hypotheses

Building on the location decision-making model developed by Joubioux and Vanpoucke (2016), we employ a multi-level framework with the aim to capture the factors underlying the offshoring and further-offshoring decisions.

The framework, which represents the ground for our hypothesis's de-velopment, shows the relocation of the main drivers (in terms of offshoring and further-offshoring), defined as a set of specific factors that are categorised into three levels:

- The macro-level factors refer to the features of the external environ-ment that influence the firm's relocation decision, namely the country characteristics.
- The meso-level factors examine the industry in which companies operate, i.e., the sector characteristics affecting the decision of relocating an activity.

- The micro-level factors explore the relationship between the firm's characteristics and the decision of carrying out a relocation.

Our aim is to define which factors are more related to offshoring and which elements influence more the further offshoring decision. For both initiatives, we evaluate the reasons and barriers associated to each factor considered, as well as the evolution of these elements in the period prior to the decision.

The Macro-Level Factors: Country-Specific Location Advantages

The macro-level factors refer to the location advantages of a country that allow firms to achieve the target profitability. Based on Dunning (1977), we identify three main location advantages that firms search for when investing in foreign countries: *Market-seeking location advantage*, which refers to those economic and financial characteristics reflecting the robustness of the national economy and the attractiveness of the country that allow companies to grow in terms of profitability and sales opportunities (Callen, 2020); *Efficiency-seeking location advantage,* which is related to the cost of the main production factors and to the average productivity that allows companies to increase their profitability through cost reduction and productivity enhancement (Dunning, 2000); *Strategic asset-seeking location advantage,* which refers to the access and exploitation of knowledge-based resources and skills in other locations that are usually superior or not available in the home environment, due to the localised nature of technology and knowledge (Jaffe, Trajtenberg & Henderson, 1993; Almeida, 1996).

Moving the activities from the home to a foreign country entails several costs for a company, such as information, implementation, transportation and inventory costs (Joubioux & Vanpoucke, 2016). For this reason, in the first offshoring initiative, the foreign investment must be sufficiently profitable to cope with these costs, granting the company a positive net gain. Besides this, companies have a lower level of internationalisation experience when doing offshoring than when doing further-offshoring, simply because the latter takes place after the former; therefore, they are likely to be more risk adverse due to lack of confidence. Hence, we expect that during the decision process of the first offshoring initiative, the firm will pay more attention to the macro-level factors by targeting locations that entails less risk and that also grants high returns in terms of market performances, efficiency gains and/or acquisition of strategic assets, in order to offset the costs of the initial investment and the lack of experience.

Conversely, firms undertaking further offshoring can rely on higher internationalisation experience that can be leveraged to increase the efficiency and reduce the costs of the next internationalisation process, and to decrease the risk-aversion towards international investments, thus reducing the importance of location advantages. In addition, the accumulated experience increases the capacity of managers in evaluating a foreign direct investment through a broader perspective (Johanson & Vahlne, 1977), thus leading decision-makers to better adapt the business model to the external context. Therefore, managers are likely to give less importance to the location advantages *per se* given their higher ability to revise and adapt the business model to the macro-level factors. Hence, we expect the following hypotheses to hold:

- *HP 1a:* The market-seeking location advantage of a country is a more relevant driver for the first offshoring than for the further offshoring decision.
- *HP 1b:* The efficiency-seeking location advantage of a country is a more relevant driver for the first offshoring than for the further offshoring decision.
- *HP 1c:* The strategic asset-seeking location advantage of a country is a more relevant driver for the first offshoring than for the further offshoring decision.

The Meso-Level Factors: Capital and Technology Intensity of the Industries

We assess the meso-level factors by looking at the capital and technology intensity of a sector. Capital intensive industries are composed of firms investing huge amounts of financial resources in fixed assets and equipment to generate profits. Furthermore, these sectors have many barriers to entry, meaning that additional resources are required to overcome such barriers and compete with incumbents. Therefore, firms operating in capital-intensive industries face much higher sunk costs when offshoring for the first time (Contractor et al., 2010). In addition, capital-intensive sectors are usually characterised by a stringent regulation in the area where they operate (Hasan, Mitra & Sundaram, 2013), which leads managers to carefully assess the place where to locate the first offshoring investment. The higher sunk costs, market barriers and restrictive regulations that firm operating in capital-intensive industries face when undertaking the first offshoring makes the option of further offshoring less convenient and, hence, less likely.

Conversely, when an industry is technology intensive, firms face higher volatility and uncertainty due to the continuous evolution of information and communication technologies (ICTs). The rise of digital transformation and Industry 4.0 technologies continue to open new possibilities, by supporting remote coordination, extending the span of control and reducing coordination costs (UNCTAD, 2020). Moreover, such technologies allow companies to "fine-slice" and decouple their value-adding activities and to locate them in the best possible locations, as in the "global factory" scenario (Fratocchi & Di Stefano, 2020). The technological development allows to exploit new innovative processes, as in the case of production automation and additive manufacturing, leading to a more flexible and resilient supply chain development. In addition, a recent paper by Barbieri et al. (2022) has shown that companies developing Industry 4.0 technologies are more likely to pursue their internationalisation strategy when deciding to revise their first offshoring decision, by relocating to a new host country rather than going back to their home country (unless the latter offer a policy supporting the adoption of Industry 4.0 technologies). As a consequence, we expect technology intensity to be a more relevant driver for further offshoring than for the first offshoring.

Hence, we formulate the following two hypotheses:

- *HP 2a:* The high capital intensity of an industry is a more relevant driver for the first offshoring than for the further offshoring decision.
- *HP 2b:* The high technology intensity of an industry is a more relevant driver for the further offshoring than for the first offshoring decision.

The Micro-Level Factors: Firm's Size and Productivity

The company size is defined as the amount of resources available to a company. Large firms can profit more from transferring business across countries. Unlike small firms, large companies own more resources to finance and absorb the costs of the relocation investment. Furthermore, large firms can typically rely on wider and more structured organisations, since on average they can count on higher managerial capabilities and more analytical organisational processes, which provide them with a better support in detecting the need to revise the business model of a firm and, hence, in the adoption and implementation of relocation decisions. Therefore, we expect large firms to be more involved in further offshoring decisions than small firms, due to the high resource availability and higher organisational and managerial ability in co-ordinating and (re)organising their foreign activities.

We also consider firm's productivity, which represents one of the possible competitive advantages that can be leveraged to undertake the first offshoring decision. Companies with a firm-specific advantage are likely to be not sa-tisfied with a single offshoring process. A continuous internationalisation process allows to increase and evolve firms' ownership advantage. The dy-namic development and accumulation of specific advantages allows the firms to integrate, renew and upgrade their tangible and intangible resources in order to sustain their competitive advantages in a changing environment (Ho, Lin & Lin, 2010). In this sense, productivity can be interpreted as a firm-specific advantage, which is developed and improved with a continuous process of relocations, as shown also by Barbieri et al. (2019). Hence, we expect that a high productivity level motivates companies to undertake a continuous internationalisation process, favouring more the further off-shoring decision than the stable offshoring.

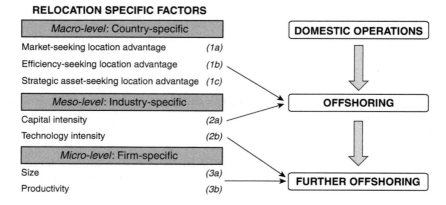

Figure 4.1 Multi-level framework and hypotheses development.
Source: The authors.

To summarise, we formulate the following two hypotheses:

- *HP 3a:* The size of the firm is a more relevant driver for the further offshoring than for the first offshoring decision.
- *HP 3b:* The high productivity of a firm is a more relevant driver for the further offshoring than for the first offshoring decision.

Figure 4.1 sums up the links between the theoretical framework and the hypotheses presented.

Empirical Analysis

Database Structure

The main database employed in our research is the European Restructuring Monitor (ERM) developed by Eurofound, which monitors the employment impact of large-scale restructuring events in Europe (27 EU members plus Norway). This database is built on secondary external information reporting announcements of international relocations activities. We collected information about 141 relocation cases, from 2002 to 2018, concerning the first offshoring and the further offshoring decisions.[1]

Variables

Dependent Variables

The dependent variable, *Location Decision,* is a binary variable that assumes the value 1 in case the firm undertakes a further offshoring and 0 in case the firms undertake an offshoring decision. In our sample, 43 observations refer to offshoring initiatives, while 98 observations refer to further offshoring.

Country Variables

Country variables are computed as the difference between the host and the home country as regards the average value of each indicator in the three years before the announcement of the relocation (Barbieri et al., 2019). The proxies are all continuous variables and have been standardised in order to smooth the heterogeneity of the different measures and scales of each indicator. The country variables are the following:

- *Market-seeking location advantage:* It is measured as the difference in the GDP annual growth rate between the host country, which is the first host in case of offshoring or the second host in case of further offshoring, and the home country. Gross Domestic Product (GDP) is globally recognised as a reference measure for understanding the size and the health of a country's economy and evaluating its attractiveness in terms of market opportunity for companies, investors and policymakers. Using the annual growth rate of the GDP it is possible to assess the economic growth of the country and how it is performing. GDP annual growth rate data have been retrieved from the World Bank, World Development Indicators.
- *Strategic asset-seeking location advantage:* We used the Research and Development (R&D) expenditure as a percentage of the GDP as proxy. R&D expenditure evaluates the attractiveness of a country in terms of innovation (Barbieri et al., 2022) and high-quality resource acquisition and it is related to increase of a country technological capabilities and knowledge (Celikay & Gumus, 2015). R&D expenditure for each (first and second) host country refers to capital and current expenditures by all entities in private and public sector, including government. Data for this variable have been gathered from World Bank, Sustainable Development Goals.
- *Efficiency-seeking location advantage:* We used the Unit Labour Cost (ULC) as a proxy, which represents the average cost of labour per unit of output produced and which allows understanding the competitiveness in terms of costs and, hence, the potential gain in terms of productivity.[2] Data for ULC have been extracted from OECD Data, Compendium of Productivity Indicators, where the indicator is measured as unit labour cost by person employed with respect to 2015.

54 Stefano Elia and Giorgio Renna

Industry Variables

Industry factors are captured through dummy variables, as reported below:

- *Industry's capital intensity:* This is a binary variable, which takes value 1 for a high capital-intensive sector and 0 for a low capital-intensive sector. We divided the sectors into two groups based on the median value of the capital intensity, calculated as the ratio of gross investments in tangible goods over the number of employees. Data have been gathered from the Eurostat database, which collects aggregated values for the EU28 firms by sectors between 2010 and 2017.
- *Industry's technology intensity:* This is a binary variable, which takes the value 1 for companies operating in high-tech sectors and 0 for low-tech sectors. This distinction was based on the Eurostat (2007)[3] classification of manufacturing sectors according to the technological intensity.

Firm Variables

Firm variables are continuous values and have been computed using the same average approach employed for country variables. Also in this case, variables have been standardised to smooth the differences regarding the measures and scales. The firm variables are the following:

- *Firm's size:* It is measured as the total assets of the firm. Data have been gathered from Orbis – Bureau Van Dijk.
- *Firm's productivity:* It is measured as the ratio of total sales over the number of employees. Data have been obtained from the Orbis – Bureau Van Dijk database.

Control Variables

In addition, we included several control variables:

- *Economic freedom*: It is the Index of Economic Freedom (EFW Index) provided by the Fraser Institute (2019), which represents the degree of economic freedom of a country in five areas: size of government, legal system and security of property rights, sound money, freedom to trade internationally and regulation.
- *Tax revenue's location advantage:* It is measured as tax revenues as share of the GDP. Data have been gathered from the World Bank.
- *Firm's EU headquarters location:* This is a binary variable, which takes value 1 if home country is in the European Union and 0 if it is located outside the EU.
- *Eastern first host country*: This is a binary variable, which takes value 1 if the first host country belongs to Eastern Europe and 0 if it does not.

This variable has been introduced to capture whether Eastern countries are more likely to be an attractive destination for offshoring initiatives (especially after the enlargement of European Union in 2004) or, rather, a trigger for further offshoring (particularly after the increase of economic wealth – and, hence, of production costs – occurred during the last 15 years following the financial support provided by European Union).

- *Financial crisis:* This is a binary variable, assuming value 1 if the year of the announcement belongs to the period in which financial crisis displaced most of its effects (i.e., 2008–2015) and 0 otherwise.
- *Age of the initiative:* It counts the number of years since the beginning of the initiative, i.e., the difference between 2018 and the year of announcement of the relocation.

Table 4.1 reports the descriptive statistics and the correlations among the variables. The Variance Inflator Factors (VIFs) exhibit values lower than 5, while the mean VIF is 1.60, thus ruling out multicollinearity problems (Akinwande, Dikko & Samson, 2015; Kim, 2019).

Results

Main Model

We employed a Probit regression model for our econometric analysis, given the binomial nature of the dependent variable *Location Decision,* which assumes dichotomous values (0 for offshoring cases, 1 for further offshoring cases). The first column of Table 4.2 displays the regression results.

The market-seeking location advantage exhibits a negative but not significant coefficient, thus rejecting the hypothesis 1a. The other two country variables, strategic asset-seeking and efficiency-seeking location advantage, show a negative and significant correlation with the dependent variable ($p < 0.01$ and $p < 0.05$, respectively), meaning that they are more likely to be drivers of the first offshoring decision, thus confirming hypotheses 1b and 1c. Moreover, marginal effects (available upon requests) suggest that an increase of 10% of strategic asset-seeking and efficiency-seeking factors decreases the probability of undertaking a further offshoring initiative by 0.97% and 0.56%, respectively.

As regards the meso-level variables, the industry's technology intensity is not significant ($p = 0.263$), so the model rejects hypothesis 2a. Conversely, industry's capital intensity exhibits a negative significant correlation with the dependent variable ($p = 0.054$), suggesting that a high capital-intensive industry is associated with offshoring initiatives, thus confirming hypothesis 2b. Furthermore, the associated marginal effects suggest that switching from a low to a high capital-intensive industry decreases the probability of undertaking a further offshoring initiative by 12.4 percentage points.

Table 4.1 Correlation matrix, descriptive statistics and VIF of all the variables considered

Variables	(1)	(2)	(3)	(4)	(5)	(6)	(7)	(8)	(9)	(10)	(11)	(12)	(13)	(14)
1. Further offshoring	1.000													
2. Market-seeking location advantage	−.348	1.000												
3. Strategic asset-seeking location advantage	−0.079	−0.154	1.000											
4. Efficiency-seeking location advantage	0.063	−0.238	−0.135	1.000										
5. Industry's capital intensity	0.004	0.061	0.201	0.066	1.000									
6. Industry's technology intensity	−0.200	0.244	−0.032	0.144	0.106	1.000								
7. Firm's size	0.234	−0.154	−0.003	0.077	0.117	−0.113	1.000							
8. Firm's productivity	0.062	−0.066	−0.037	−0.047	−0.056	0.075	−0.056	1.000						
9. Economic freedom	−0.022	−0.048	0.328	−0.013	0.098	−0.041	−0.104	0.107	1.000					
10. Tax revenues location advantage	−0.328	0.314	−0.037	−0.079	0.024	0.040	−0.281	−0.055	0.027	1.000				
11. Firm's EU headquarters location	−0.414	0.272	−0.089	−0.086	−0.115	0.168	−0.337	−0.096	0.323	0.431	1.000			
12. Eastern first host country	−0.658	0.285	−0.117	−0.154	−0.168	0.186	−0.198	−0.053	−0.054	0.320	0.468	1.000		
13. Financial crisis	0.132	−0.085	−0.292	−0.015	0.017	0.121	−0.056	0.048	−0.010	−0.185	0.063	0.022	1.000	
14. Age of the initiative	−0.114	0.127	−0.099	0.053	−0.042	0.085	0.033	−0.041	−0.013	0.086	0.050	0.097	0.506	1.000
Obs.	141	141	141	141	141	141	141	141	141	141	141	141	141	141
Mean	0.695	0.000	0.000	0.000	0.000	0.000	0.000	0.000	0.305	0.596	0.574	0.277	0.780	0.000
Std. dev.	0.462	1.0000	1.000	1.000	1.000	1.000	1.000	1.000	0.462	0.492	0.496	0.449	0.416	1.000
Min	0.000	−1.969	−1.666	−5.007	−2.060	−2.341	−0.293	−0.634	0.000	0.000	0.000	0.000	0.000	−1.784
Max	1.000	4.599	2.698	3.554	2.912	2.209	11.782	4.706	1.000	1.000	1.000	1.000	1.000	2.588
VIF	2.19	1.54	1.59	1.28	1.23	1.25	1.09	1.25	1.49	1.55	2.06	2.19	1.99	1.64

Source: The authors.

Offshoring vs Further Offshoring 57

Table 4.2 Results of the main Probit regression model and of the interaction model

Variables	Main model		Interaction model	
	Coefficient	Std. Error	Coefficient	Std. Error
Market-seeking location advantage	−0.275	0.275	−0.458	0.240[*]
Strategic asset-seeking location advantage	−0.713	0.181[***]	−0.814	0.266[***]
Efficiency-seeking location advantage	−0.412	0.178[**]	−0.542	0.234[**]
Industry's capital intensity	−0.911	0.423[*]	−1.036	0.461[**]
Industry's technology intensity	−0.568	0.466	−0.514	0.423
Firm's size	0.675	0.262[***]	0.588	0.313[*]
Firm's productivity	20.602	15.407	27.788	15.756[*]
Economic freedom	0.416	0.182[**]	0.504	0.231[**]
Tax revenue location adv.	−0.001	0.227	0.477	0.203
Firm's EU headquarters location	−1.434	0.443[***]	−1.562	0.585[***]
Eastern first host country	−2.673	0.483[***]	−3.119	0.660[***]
Financial crisis	1.794	0.647[***]	1.970	0.661[***]
Age of the initiative	−0.408	0.189[*]	−0.448	0.242[*]
Constant	3.723	1.504[**]	4.373	1.587[***]
Market-seeking location advantage * Firm's size			−0.448[*]	0.314
Observations	141		141	
Wald Chi2 (9)	88.65		107.9	
Prob > Chi2	0.000		0.000	
Pseudo R^2	0.599		0.622	

Source: The authors.

Notes
* $p < 0.1$
** $p < 0.05$
*** $p < 0.01$

Regarding variables at the firm-level, the model confirms hypothesis 3a, as firm's size displays a positive significant relationship with further off-shoring ($p < 0.01$), while, although firm's productivity exhibits a positive coefficient, hypothesis 3b is rejected as the variable is not significant ($p = 0.285$). The marginal effect for firm's size is also significant ($p < 0.01$) and it shows that an increase of 10% this variable increases the probability of carrying out a further offshoring by 0.92%

As regards control variables, economic freedom proves to be positively and significantly related with the dependent variable ($p = 0.049$), meaning that a higher economic freedom in the host country can trigger more further offshoring initiatives. The two dummies describing the geographical location of home and first host country are both significant ($p = 0.006$ and $p < 0.001$, respectively) and negatively correlated with the dependent variable. This means that, on the one hand, European firms are less likely to undertake further offshoring initiatives than non-European firms; on the other hand, Eastern countries are more likely to be a trigger of offshoring than of further offshoring initiatives. The variable identifying the financial crisis is also significant ($p = 0.003$), but it is positively correlated with the dependent variable, meaning that financial crisis was one important trigger of further offshoring initiatives. Lastly, the age of the initiative is significant ($p = 0.051$) and negatively correlated with further offshoring, meaning that further offshoring is a more recent phenomenon.

Additional Evidence: Interaction Effects

We also tested some interactions effects between country-level and firm-level variables, since these two groups exhibit opposite correlation with the dependent variable. The only significant interaction is between market-seeking location advantage and firm's size ($p = 0.066$). The fifth column of Table 4.2 shows the Probit regression model with this interaction.

The interaction displays a negative correlation with further offshoring, meaning that a higher market-seeking location advantage and a higher firm's size increase the probability of undertaking an offshoring initiative. To get a clear view of this relationship, the interaction term was plotted as shown in Figure 4.2. The graph shows that market-seeking location advantage seems to mitigate the probability that large firms undertake a further offshoring

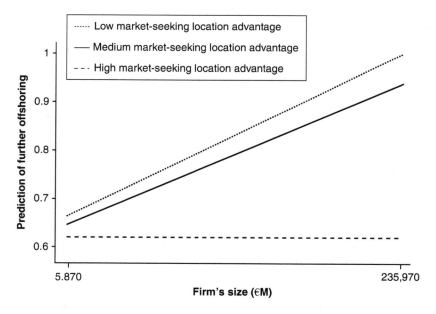

Figure 4.2 Graph of the interaction market-seeking location advantage – firm's size.
Source: The authors.

initiative. Indeed, when the market-seeking location advantage is high (dashed line) the relationship between firm's size and the dependent variable is flat and the prediction of further offshoring is lower with respect to a low market-seeking location advantage (dotted line).

Discussions and Conclusions

Using a multi-level analysis, we identified the main drivers underlying the decision to undertake a first offshoring vs. a further offshoring initiative. First interesting evidence is that firms undertaking their first offshoring initiative pay more attention to external macro- and meso-level factors of the ecosystem rather than to internal firm-level aspects. Indeed, on the one hand, companies that carry out their first offshoring investment are attracted by the competitive advantage of the host country they invest to; on the other hand, their offshoring decision depends on the industry firms belong to. More specifically, our results show that the efficiency-seeking and strategic-asset seeking location advantages are the main drivers of the offshoring decision, meaning that companies undertaking offshoring usually target countries where the cost of labour is favourable or where more strategic resources are available with respect to the home country. As regards the industry, firms belonging to capital-intensive sectors face higher barriers to internationalisation and higher fixed costs, meaning that they are more involved in stable offshoring initiatives and that their first location decision is aimed at finding long-term competitive advantage.

Conversely, firms undertaking further offshoring seem to be more motivated by firm-specific factors. More specifically, results show that large firms seem to be more likely to undertake further offshoring with respect to small firms, thus confirming our expectations. A possible explanation is that only large companies can afford to re-organise their international business model and to implement a relocation choice towards a new host country, since they can rely on more resources and capabilities to recover the sunk costs and the loss in performances related to the previous offshoring and to persist with their decoupling and internationalisation strategy.

Our analysis also shows that the financial crisis and post-crisis period influence the tendency to relocate, given that during periods of economic recession, companies carried out more further offshoring initiatives. The explanation of this result may be twofold. On the one hand, the crisis caused a general reduction in performances of offshored companies, leading them to relocate towards more profitable locations. On the other hand, it discouraged companies to carry out offshoring, due to significant productivity losses in domestic markets, draining the firm's excess resources needed to internationalise. We also find that high country's economic freedom attracts companies at the second step of relocation. This represents a greater incentive for governments to implement policies aimed at increasing the openness to trade and sustain the business development to attract foreign companies.

60 *Stefano Elia and Giorgio Renna*

Finally, the interaction between the market-seeking location advantage and the firm's size suggests that a higher market-seeking advantage decreases the propensity of large firms to carry out further offshoring initiatives. This finding suggests that a long-lasting market opportunity can motivate the large companies to continue investing in that country rather than relocate elsewhere.

Contribution to Previous Literature

We believe that our chapter can provides some contributions to the international business literature on location and relocation choice. The large majority of previous studies, indeed, focused mainly on offshoring and backshoring, while further offshoring has been neglected. Also previous studies adopting a comparative approach have mainly considered the comparison between offshoring and backshoring, leading to the result that reshoring decisions can be based on the previous unsuccessful offshoring outcomes (Kinkel & Maloca, 2009). Authors rarely discussed the differences between the initial decision of offshoring from the home country to a first host country, and the following relocations, from the first host to a second host location (Barbieri et al., 2019). Our work fills this gap, as we study the differences between the drivers of offshoring and further offshoring initiatives.

Furthermore, we provide a wider perspective on the relocation decision motivations. Indeed, previous relocation studies usually evaluated implications at one level, namely the firm (Di Mauro et al., 2018) or the country (Johansson & Olhager, 2018), or at two levels, identifying company and location specific factors (Fratocchi et al., 2016). Nevertheless, the industry perspective can also play a relevant role to understand the reshoring dynamics (Fratocchi et al., 2014). In addition, researchers have recently addressed the need for a more comprehensive view to capture the dynamics of the relocation decision (Barbieri et al., 2019). Following this suggestion, we provide a multi-level analysis, including firm, industry and country-level factors affecting offshoring and further-offshoring choices.

Finally, we offer insights regarding the motivations of the further offshoring initiatives, which are relatively understudied in the international business literature. Our results show that firm's size and industry's low capital intensity are drivers of the further offshoring.

More in general, our results allow us to offer also some further insights on the factors of the ecosystem that affect the possibility to re-organise the business model of a company and to decouple the manufacturing production. Indeed, while country-factors dominates when undertaking the first step of reconfiguration through the first offshoring initiatives, industry- and firm-level factors prevail in the second step in which firms exhibit resilience through further offshoring initiatives.

Implications for Managers and Policymakers

The outcomes of our research can give useful suggestions to both managers and policymakers. For what concerns managers, one of the main findings of our work is that companies undertake offshoring mainly as consequence of country-level factors and further offshoring mainly as consequence of internal factors. This seems to suggest that firm's and country's performance are not directly correlated. In other words, it is not sufficient to relocate a subsidiary in a country with lower costs or higher skills to obtain gains and knowledge. The relationship must consider the firm's capability to exploit a specific location advantage. Hence, managers should consider performing some investments in tangible and intangible resources before starting an offshoring initiative, in order to be able to capture the benefits arising from country-specific advantages. Managers should also be aware that a further-offshoring initiative requires large resources to offset the sunk costs associated to the first offshoring initiative.

As regards the policymakers, our results confirm the importance of creating a favourable institutional and economic environment in which firms can operate in order to attract foreign investments, by offering a high level of skills, a low cost of labour (in terms of taxes rather than in terms of wages), a high level of regulatory quality and economic freedom. Our results seem to suggest also that the creation of a favourable market environment can inhibit large firms from disinvesting and undertaking further offshoring initiatives.

COVID-19 Implications

Since COVID-19 drastically changed the global socio-economic scenario, we believe it is important to discuss its effect on the relocation phenomenon in the short and long term. Indeed, due to the strong effect of the pandemics, some offshoring companies had to review their location choice.

The manufacturing sectors that were most negatively affected by the pandemics are machinery and equipment, information and technologies, telecommunications and energy, and utilities (Aoi, 2021), although pandemics favoured some other industries, such as medical and digital technologies (Lloyd & Borgese, 2020). The short-term reactions of companies were various. On the one side, some firms have engaged in the accumulation of stocks and started searching for alternative supplies. On the other side, other companies have engaged in better monitoring, understanding and reorganisation of the supply chains (Aoi, 2021). This secular shift in the international order highlights the fragility and vulnerability of global value chains (GVCs) to the effects of exogenous shocks (Raza et al., 2021). Thus, the necessity of managers to increase the supply chain resilience is a main

62 *Stefano Elia and Giorgio Renna*

issue, with initiatives related to diversification, digitalisation, increase of stockpiling and improvement of the due diligence.

The World Investment Report 2020 (UNCTAD, 2020) outlined four possible trajectories for the post-pandemic future of GVCs as consequences of some mega-trends such as political tensions, digitalisation and sustainability. The four scenarios are replication, backshoring, diversification and regionalisation. While the first two are considered less likely, as they do not allow firms to leverage the heterogeneity of country's comparative advantage, diversification and regionalisation, which entails a geographic reconfiguration of the value chains, are considered the most likely scenarios. Given that offshoring and further offshoring are two important contributors of geographic reconfiguration, our results provide some insights on the macro-, meso- and micro-level factors of the ecosystem that might affect the post-pandemic (and maybe the post-war) evolution of GVCs in the nearby future.

Limitations and Avenues for Future Research

The main limitations related to our study can act as a starting point for future research. The first limitation is related to the source of our data, the European Restructuring Monitor. This database gathers announcements of relocation initiatives and the actual implementation is uncertain. Furthermore, the expansion of the research to other geographical areas outside Europe, such as east Asia or America, are not available in the database, while they could bring additional relevant findings. We also recognise that companies have been classified as either capital-intensive or technological intensive based on their industry, but this does not guarantee that, for example, a company in a technological intensive sector will actually operate with a high level of technological intensity. The third limitation is related to the sample composition. A sample composed of the same companies doing offshoring and further offshoring allows a more realistic observation of the phenomena. In addition, a suggestion for future research is to consider the effect of policies on the decision of whether to carry out relocation, in order to suggest to policymakers what government initiatives are more able to increase the country's attractiveness. Finally, future researches could measure the effect of the location decision on firm's performance.

Conclusion

In this study, we investigate the motivations and the main drivers behind the decision of carrying out offshoring and further offshoring initiatives. We performed a multi-level econometric analysis to test our hypotheses, and we find that companies rely more on country and industry factors during the offshoring decision-making process, while they are more

Offshoring vs Further Offshoring 63

affected by firm factors when choosing further offshoring. We conclude by providing some theoretical insights and some suggestions to managers and policymakers. We believe that this work can be a starting point for future researches investigating the dynamics underlying the offshoring and further offshoring decisions.

Notes

1 In our sample, the firms undertaking offshoring and further offshoring decisions are not the same companies. Indeed, the majority of firms undertaking further offshoring made their first offshoring decision before the time span considered; hence, it was not possible to retrieve all data that are needed to account for the multi-level factors underlying these choices. However, we believe that comparing firms undertaking offshoring with firms undertaking further-offshoring decisions can still offer the possibility to identify the most relevant drivers for these choices similarly to what happens in counterfactual analyses. Therefore, in line with this empirical sampling strategy, regarding offshoring observations we kept only those initiatives in which the companies have not subsequently relocated, in order to capture more stable and long-lasting offshoring initiatives and to better identify the long-term underlying drivers in comparison with further-offshoring.

2 In this case, we measured the difference between home and host countries, since higher values of such difference reflect a cost advantage for the host country.

3 High technological intensive manufacturing sectors according to Eurostat (2007) classification are: chemicals and chemical products; basic pharmaceuticals and pharmaceutical preparations; computer, electronic and optical products; electrical equipment; machinery and equipment n.e.c.; motor vehicles, trailers and semi-trailers; other transport equipment. Low technological intensive manufacturing sector according to Eurostat (2007) are: food products; beverages; tobacco products; textile; wearing apparel; leather and related products; wood and wood products; paper and paper products; printing and reproduction of recorded media; coke and refined petroleum products; rubber and plastic products; other non-metallic mineral product; basic metals; fabricated metals excepts machinery and equipment; furniture; other manufacturing; repair and installation of machinery and equipment.

References

Akinwande, M., Dikko, H. & Samson, A. (2015). "Variance inflation factor: As a condition for the inclusion of suppressor variable(s) in regression analysis", *Open Journal of Statistics*, vol. 5, pp. 754–767. 10.4236/ojs.2015.57075

Almeida, P. (1996). "Knowledge sourcing by foreign multinationals: Patent citation analysis in the U.S. semiconductor industry", *Strategic Management Journal*, vol. 17, pp. 155–165. 10.1002/smj.4250171113

Aoi, S. (2021). "Covid-19 riporta le aziende vicino a casa", *La Repubblica*, 7 January, available at: https://www.repubblica.it/dossier/economia/i-gioielli-del-made-in-italy/2021/01/07/news/covid-19_riporta_le_aziende_vicino_a_casa-281514894/ (Accessed: 25 January 2021).

Barbieri, P., Elia S., Fratocchi, L. & Golini, R. (2019). "Relocation of second degree: Moving towards a new place or returning home?", *Journal of Purchasing and Supply Management*, vol. 25, pp. 1–14. 10.1016/j.pursup.2018.12.003

64 *Stefano Elia and Giorgio Renna*

Barbieri, P., Boffelli, A., Elia, S., Fratocchi, L. & Kalchschmidt, M. (2022). "How does Industry 4.0 affect international exposure? The interplay between firm innovation and home-country policies in post-offshoring relocation decisions", *International Business Review*, vol. 31, no. 4, p. 101992. 101992. 10.1016/j.ibusrev.2022.101992

Boffelli, A. & Johansson, M. (2020). "What do we want to know about reshoring? Towards a comprehensive framework based on a meta-synthesis", *Operations Management Research*, vol. 13, pp. 53–69. 10.1007/s12063-020-00155-y

Callen, T. (2020). "Gross domestic product: An economy's all", International Monetary Fund, 24 February, available at: https://www.imf.org/external/pubs/ft/fandd/basics/gdp.htm (Accessed: 15 January 2021).

Celikay, F. & Gumus, E. (2015). "R&D expenditure and economic growth: New empirical evidence", *The Journal of Applied Economic Research*, vol. 9(3), pp. 205–217. 10.1177/0973801015579753

Contractor, F., Kumar, V., Kundu, S. & Pedersen, T. (2010). "Reconceptualising the firm in a world of outsourcing and offshoring: The organizational and geographical relocation of high-value company functions", *Journal of Management Studies*, vol. 47(8), pp. 1417–1433. 10.1111/j.1467-6486.2010.00945.x

Daub, M., Maitra, B. & Mesøy, T. (2009). "Rethinking the model for offshoring services", *McKinsey & Company*, 1 September, available at: http://www.mckinsey.com/business-functions/strategy-and-corporate-finance/our-insights/raising-your-digital-quotient (Accessed: 14 March 2022).

Di Mauro, C., Fratocchi, L., Orzes, G. & Sartor, M. (2018). "Offshoring and backshoring: A multiple case study analysis", *Journal of Purchasing and Supply Management*, vol. 24(2), pp. 108–134. 10.1016/j.pursup.2017.07.003

Dunning, J.H. (1977). "Trade, location of economic activity and the MNE: A search for an eclectic approach", *The International Allocation of Economic Activity*. London: MacMillan, pp. 395–418.

Dunning, J.H. (2000). "The eclectic paradigm as an envelope for economic and business theories of MNE activity", *International Business Review*, vol. 9(2), pp. 163–190. 10.1016/S0969-5931(99)00035-9

Eurostat (2007). "Eurostat indicators on high-tech industry and knowledge – intensive services", Annex 3 – High-tech aggregation by NACE Rev. 2, available at: https://ec.europa.eu/eurostat/cache/metadata/Annexes/htec_esms_an3.pdf (Accessed: 20 January 2021).

Fraser Institute (2019). "Economic freedom of the world – methodology – approach", available at: https://www.fraserinstitute.org/economic-freedom/approach (Accessed: 10 November 2020)

Fratocchi, L., Ancarani, A., Barbieri, P., Di Mauro, C., Nassimbeni, G., Sartor, M., Vignoli, M. & Zanoni, A. (2016). "Motivations of manufacturing reshoring: An interpretative framework", *International Journal of Physical Distribution and Logistics Management*, vol. 46(2), pp. 98–127. 10.1108/IJPDLM-06-2014-0131

Fratocchi, L., Di Mauro, C., Barbieri, P., Nassimbeni, G. & Zanoni, A. (2014). "When manufacturing moves back: Concepts and questions", *Journal of Purchasing and Supply Management*, vol. 20, pp. 54–59. 10.1016/j.pursup.2014.01.004

Fratocchi, L. & Di Stefano, C. (2020). "Industry 4.0 technologies and manufacturing back-shoring: A European perspective", *Acta IMEKO*, vol. 9(4), art. 3. 10.21014/acta_imeko.v9i4.721

Hasan, R., Mitra, D. & Sundaram, A. (2013). "The determinants of capital intensity in manufacturing: The role of factor market imperfections". *World Development*, vol. 51, pp. 91–103. 10.1016/j.worlddev.2013.05.012

Ho, S., Lin, E. & Lin, Y. (2010). "Model for the internationalization process of construction firms: A dynamic OLI view", EPOC 2010 Conference. 10.13140/2.1.2764.3681

Jaffe, A.B., Trajtenberg, M. & Henderson, R. (1993). "Geographic localization of knowledge spillovers as evidenced by patent citations", *The Quarterly Journal of Economics*, vol. 108(3), pp. 577–598. 10.2307/2118401

Johanson, J. & Vahlne, J.E. (1977). "The internationalization process of the firm — a model of knowledge development and increasing foreign market commitments", *Journal of International Business Studies*, vol. 8, pp. 23–32. 10.1057/palgrave.jibs.84 90676

Johansson, M. & Olhager, J. (2018). "Comparing offshoring and backshoring: The role of manufacturing site location factors and their impact on post-relocation performance", *International Journal of Production Economics*, vol. 205, pp. 37–46. 10.1016/j.ijpe.2018.08.027

Joubioux, C. & Vanpoucke, E. (2016). "Towards right-shoring: A framework for off- and re-shoring decision making", *Operations Management Research*, vol. 9(3-4), pp. 117–132. 10.1007/s12063-016-0115-y

Kim, J.H. (2019). "Multicollinearity and misleading statistical results", *Korean Journal of Anesthesiology*, vol. 72(6), pp. 558–569. 10.4097/kja.19087

Kinkel, S. & Maloca, S. (2009). "Drivers and antecedents of manufacturing offshoring and backshoring – a German perspective", *Journal of Purchasing and Supply Management*, vol. 15, pp. 154–165. 10.1016/j.pursup.2009.05.007

Lewin, A.Y., Massini, S. & Peeters, C. (2009). "Why are companies offshoring innovation? The emerging global race for talent", *Journal of International Business Studies*, vol. 40(8), pp. 1406–11406. 10.1057/jibs.2008.92

Lloyd, K. & Borgese, A. (2020). "Is offshoring a victim of COVID-19?", *MinterEllison*, 5 August, available at: https://www.minterellison.com/articles/is-offshoring-a-victim-of-covid-19 (Accessed: 25 January 2021)

Raza, W., Grumiller, J., Grohs, H., Essletzbichler, J. & Pintar, N. (2021). "Post Covid-19 value chains: Options for reshoring production back to Europe in a globalised economy", *European Parliament's Committee on International Trade*. 10.2861/118324

UNCTAD (2020). *World Investment Report 2020: International production beyond the pandemic*. New York and Geneva: United Nations.

Wan, L., Orzes, G., Sartor, M., Di Mauro, C. & Nassimbeni, G. (2019). "Entry modes in reshoring strategies: An empirical analysis", *Journal of Purchasing and Supply Management*, vol. 25(3), p. 100522. 10.1016/j.pursup.2018.11.002

5 Reconfiguring Digital Business Models to Enter the Japanese Market

Arto Ojala and William W. Baber

Introduction

In the fields like software and other purely digital services, firms are commonly expanding their businesses to countries that provide huge market potential for their services (Bell et al., 2003; Ojala & Tyrväinen, 2007; Ojala, 2015). In general, firms apply a certain business model in their home country. When they internationalise, firms have to estimate how the same business model can be applied in a host country or the market area (e.g., in EU). In the most favourable situation, there is no need for changes in the business model, and in these cases, firms can save cost and resources that are needed to reconfigure the business model to a target country. However, in some cases changes to the business model are required and might become necessity for the foreign market entry (see e.g., Baber et al., 2022). This can be the case especially if a firm is entering to a market that is very attractive by offering a huge business potential, but operations in the country requires reconfiguration of the recent business model. This might be the case especially in the countries where the culture and the way of doing business differs greatly from the home country. However, current studies on internationalisation of technology based new ventures provides only little guidance (see, e.g., Casadesus-Masanell & Ricart, 2010; Sosna, Trevinyo-Rodriguez & Velamuri, 2010; Rissanen et al., 2020; Baber et al., 2022) how firms should reconfigure their business model when entering to a new location (Onetti et al., 2012). Based on this, the aim is to contribute to business model literature in the context where a firm internationalises and reconfigures its business model for the new geographical location.

Based on the above discussion, we investigate a Finnish digital service provider's market entry into the Japanese market and especially how the business model evolved during this process. As it is commonly viewed, Japan is one of the most attractive markets for digital services, and Finland, despite being a small country, has numerous innovative digital service providers. That being so, Japan is a very attractive country for Finnish digital service providers, yet also very distant, culturally and geographically (Ojala & Tyrväinen, 2007). This research setting helps us to make a detailed

DOI: 10.4324/9781003326731-5

study of how and why the business model and related business model elements change, over time, when a firm reconfigures its business model during foreign market entry. This also answers the call for more studies on how new location impacts business models and their evolution (Onetti et al., 2012).

In this chapter, we first define the business model and identify the elements of the business model that are most relevant to this study. Thereafter, we review literature to better understand how and why business models might change over time. This is followed by a short discussion on how business models might impact a firm's foreign market entry (Nielsen, Marinova & Marinov, 2022). Next, we present the longitudinal case-study method used in this study. The method section is followed by description of the changes in the case firm's business model. Finally, we discuss research findings and present the conclusions of the study.

Business Models

The term "business model" is defined in several manners in the academic literature. One common characteristic of all these definitions is that they describe how firms create, capture, and deliver value to partners, customers, and other actors in their network. A very common definition used in the academic literature on business models is given by Osterwalder, Pigneur and Tucci (2005, p. 17–18) who define business models as follows: "A business model is a conceptual tool that contains a set of elements and their relationships and allows expressing the business logic of a specific firm. It is a description of the value a company offers to one or several segments of customers and of the architecture of the firm and its network of partners for creating marketing, and delivering this value and relationship capital, to generate profitable and sustainable revenue streams." Business model "thinking" can include planned decisions or merely application of a certain model without detailed planning and thinking. As explained by Chesbrough (2007, p. 12), "every company has a business model, whether they articulate it or not" and "at its heart, a business model performs two important functions: value creation and value capture".

Although a description of the business model delivers a rather static image, business models change and evolve over time as firms reconfigure business models while they react to changes in the market, costumer needs, or when they innovate new services or products. This has been covered also in business model innovation (BMI) literature that focuses on how entrepreneurs innovate new business models (see, e.g., Chesbrough, 2007; Cavalcante, Kesting & Ulhoi, 2011; Bohnsack, Pinkse & Kolk, 2014; Saebi, Lien & Foss 2017; Baber, Ojala & Martinez, 2019a, 2019b, 2020). Recent studies have also found that business models might change when firms enter to new foreign markets (Baber et al., 2022). Internationalisation and new foreign customers might require new value networks, customisation and localisation of the services, consideration of local standards, regulations, polices, etc. These all will impact how the current business model can be implemented in a new foreign market (Ojala & Tyrväinen, 2006; Child et al., 2017).

Elements of Business Model

A business model is commonly described to include various elements which form the business model and the way how a firm works (Ojala, 2016). Academic literature has recognised several different elements (Luoma, 2013; Baber et al., 2022). However, in this chapter, we focus on only the most relevant business model elements for this study. These elements are (1) Service (or product), (2) Value Network and (3) Value Delivery. Changes in these elements are interactive, so that a change in one element might lead to chance in one or several elements (Kindström & Kowalkowski, 2014; Baber & Ojala, 2021). For example, new customer requirements (locally or globally) might impact how a service is implemented. New characteristics of the service might lead to new ways to deliver it and consequently lead to changes in the Value Network (Baber et al., 2020). Further, by studying business models based on elements, we can form a better understanding of the interactions between the environment where the firm operates and the firm's internal development. Below we describe three business model elements that we apply in this study.

Firstly, the Service element (also called the product element in some studies) refers to a firm's innovations that it develops, markets and sell (Baber et al., 2020). Further, the Service element may indicate how a firm's service is related to other services or products in the market and how it impacts their evolution (Adomavicius et al., 2008; Arthur, 2009). When a firm expands its business to other industries or foreign markets, the service commonly requires customisation and/or localisation based on the needs and requirements of customers, authorities, regulations and so on (Ojala & Tyrväinen, 2006). The Service element maintains a very important role in the business model as it largely defines how other elements will be formed. It also specifies largely who are the customers, partners, stakeholders and other actors within the firm's network (Osterwalder et al., 2005; Ojala & Tyrväinen, 2006; Osterwalder & Pigneur, 2013).

Secondly, the Value Network element shows all the key actors that the focal firm interacts with when creating value. That is, the Value Network forms a broader ecosystem around the firm (Chesbrough, 2007) including customers, regulators, partners and others that are involved in the creation of value. To build the Value Network, firms have to understand the value of their service, meaning how it benefits other members within the Value Network who contribute to value creation (Walter, Ritter & Gemünden, 2001; Zain & Ng, 2006). This element also provides an understanding of how and why firms act within the same Value Network (Osterwalder & Pigneur, 2010;

Teece, 2010; Ojala & Helander, 2014). Depending on the service, the Value Network might vary greatly. If a firm develops and markets services directly to the end users without outsourcing any activities, the Value Network remains very simple. However, nowadays firms are very specialised and might represent only a smaller (but important) part of a larger service within an ecosystem. For instance, digital platforms form a service that are commonly enabled by large group of firms acting in the same Value Network (Autio et al., 2017; Ojala & Lyytinen, 2022).

Thirdly, the Value Delivery element explains how the actual value is delivered between different actors in the Value Network (Osterwalder et al., 2005). It demonstrates how and by which routes the focal firm delivers the service and how and what kind of value different partners exchange (Al-Debei & Avison, 2010; Osterwalder & Pigneur, 2010; Teece, 2010). This value can be related to the focal firm's service in the form of financial benefits or knowledge and know-how (Ojala & Helander, 2014). At a macro level, the Value Delivery element can be a subset of the Value Network, however, examined in greater detail, it can specify the actions and partners needed to reach customers and end users.

Methodology

To better understand the evolution of business models in the international location, Japan, we applied a longitudinal single-case study method (Yin, 2009). The longitudinal approach was selected as it enables following, in real-time, how business operations and related business models evolve. The case method also makes it possible to understand and track cause-and-effect relationships (Eisenhardt, 1989; Pettigrew, 1990). We also studied a rather unexplored phenomenon, evolution of a business model within a foreign market entry (Onetti et al., 2012). In this context, a single-case study offers detailed understanding of the processes involved (Doz, 2011) as a firm's business models develop.

Data Collection and Analysis

The empirical data for this study were collected between 2011 and 2021. That is, the data collection started the same year that the case firm started their operations in Japan. The interviewed persons include all the key players involved with the market entry to Japan and business model development there. We interviewed the top management team (Chief Executive Officer [CEO], Chief Operating Officer [COO], Chief Technology Officer [CTO], Art Director, and Vice President of Sales) to build an overall understanding of the firm's business, business model development in general, international operations, and interest toward the Japanese market. To acquire more detailed understanding of the business activities in Japan, we interviewed the case firm's representatives in Japan as well as their Sales Manager operating in

70 Arto Ojala and William W. Baber

Table 5.1 People interviewed

Person interviewed	Time of the interview(s) (month/year)	Duration of the interview(s) (hour/minute)
CEO (co-founder)	4/2011	1:10
	4/2017	1:15
	2/2018	1:20
	1/2019	1:00
	5/2021	2:15
	11/2021	0:50
COO (co-founder)	4/2011	1:00
CTO (co-founder)	3/2013	1:10
Art director (co-founder)	6/2011	0:55
Vice president, sales	8/2011	1:00
Sales manager, South-East Asia (in Singapore)	12/2014	0:45
Representative in Japan (Sales)	5/2012	1:00
Representative in Japan (technical director)	5/2012	1:10

Source: The authors.

South-East Asia. The number, date and length of the interviews between 2011 and 2021 is displayed in Table 5.1.

We conducted 13 interviews for this study lasting from 45 to 135 minutes. We had 11 face-to-face interviews (eight in Finland, two in Japan and one in Singapore) and held two Zoom interviews in 2021 because of COVID-19 pandemic restrictions. In the first interviews, we focused on the firm's history and early development of the business model. Thereafter, our research questions focused more on internationalisation and business model evolution in general and especially in Japan. Two last interviews (in 2021) with the CEO were conducted to summarise the business operations in Japan and clarify inconsistences in the previously collected data.

We took notes and recorded all the interviews. All the interviews were transcribed verbatim and reviewed. Over the years, we also developed good relationships with the case firm representatives. This enabled us to delve into confidential data that would be otherwise difficult to collect. In addition to these face-to-face interviews, we went through a large amount of secondary data to confirm dates, events and other facts while validating the collected primary data. Secondary data was also used to find new insights from various point of views. This secondary data was based on the firm's websites, social media pages (LinkedIn, Facebook, Instagram), news, magazines and advertisement material. Inconsistences that emerged from secondary data and new insights were clarified and discussed either in interviews or by using email as a mode of communication. This also helped us to minimise the retrospective bias (see, e.g., Huber & Power, 1985).

During analysis of the data, we followed mainly advice by Miles, Huberman and Saldana (2013) regarding data reduction. That is, we reduced data so that we had only row data related to the topic of this study. This was conducted by first identifying all important events related to the market entry to Japan and business model development there. Second, we organised the data into chronological order to identify potential causal links and develop more comprehensive understanding among various actions in the Japanese market and business model development. These steps helped us to organise and comprehend the data so that we were able to write a case narrative illustrating the case firm's operations in Japan.

The Case Firm

The case firm, Vivo (pseudonym), was established in 2006 in Finland. It offers digital services based on their own cloud service and which can be used to visualise customers' physical products (e.g., bookshelves, sofas and other home furnishings) as three-dimensional (3D) digital models. Their main target groups for the service are furniture manufacturers, furniture retailers, home improvement and design firms, and firms offering renovation products and services. Basically, the service can be used as a sales tool by customer firms that interact with retail users. The firm's size has varied over the years between 10 and 50 employees. Currently they employ around 40 staff members. Vivo maintains offices or representatives on four continents and has a global clientele.

Foreign Market Entry and Business Models in Japan

Generally, firms in all sizes and all industries tend to enter those markets that provide good business potential for their products and/or services (Dunning, 2001; Bell et al., 2003; Ojala & Tyrväinen, 2007). However, factors like geographical distance and cultural distance might reduce the attractiveness of large markets, or at least, make business operations more challenging in distant markets (Blum & Goldfarb, 2006; Dow & Karunaratna, 2006; Ojala & Tyrväinen, 2007; Gooris & Peeters, 2014; Ojala, 2015). According to Ojala (2015, p. 826), geographic distance in this context refers to "... physical separation between one location and another, typically involving the space between the home of a firm and the foreign location in which it is selling, or exploring possible sales", whereas cultural distance is related to "... differences between groups of people regarding values, communication styles, and stereotypes" (Ojala, 2015, p. 827).

Although Japan is a very distant country (geographically and culturally) from Finland, Vivo saw it as a very interesting market for several reasons. The market size was seen as offering a huge growth potential for their digital services. Further, it is widely thought that Japanese consumers are very accepting of new technological solutions, tools, and services and this attitude makes the market very interesting. Accordingly, Japan entered their focus, in addition to Scandinavian markets, soon after the establishment of the firm. However, this foreign market entry was not easy, and success required several changes over the years to the original business model as elaborated below.

First Business Model 2011–2013

Vivo started their operations in the Japanese market in 2011. The first market entry was more a coincidence than a planned or intentional establishment of foreign operations in Japan. In 2010, one of Vivo's employees moved to Japan and started to do remote work from Japan for Vivo. One year later, in 2011, he established his own firm for the purpose of bringing foreign technological innovations to Japan. He started to represent Vivo's digital service in Japan among other imported products and services.

At that time, Vivo's business in Japan was based on the same concept used in Finland. They provided a digital sales tool for furniture manufacturers and furniture retailers so that they could demonstrate their offering in 3D form and show how a furniture item looked from different angles, how different modules could be combined, and so on. However, the main problem at that time was that even though the Service element existed, the Value Network and delivery elements of the business model were lacking. That is, the representatives of Vivo in Japan were not able to develop reliable relationships with potential partners, delivery channels or end-customers to establish the value network. The CEO explained this as follows:

> Even if these guys [representatives in Japan] were really good and knew the service, they had a lack of networks within the target industry. They were also very young, so it caused difficulties to establish reliable networks.

Based on this first "trial" to enter the Japanese market, only one direct customer was found. As Figure 5.1 demonstrates, there was a lack of local distributors who knew the market. Further, only one customer was reached even though there was a vast number of potential customers in the market. Further, because the digital service in Japan was exactly the same as what they had available in other countries, there was a clear need for more customised services that targeted especially the Japanese market. However, at that time, Vivo was not capable of customising content provision for the market needs of Japan, for instance by using a value-added reseller. Based on the first business model, Vivo learned that in Japan (1) there are very high-quality requirements that require customisation of the service, (2) there is a need for Japanese language skills in sales and marketing processes and (3) it is important to develop personal relationships with customers.

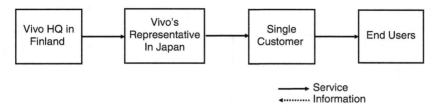

Figure 5.1 First business model in Japan.
Source: The authors.

Second Business Model 2014–2015

Because of the unsuccessful first business model, Vivo recruited an expatriate in Singapore (with some personal contacts in Japan) that replaced the first representative operating in Japan. The idea was that the expatriate in Singapore would take care of business activities in Australia and Japan. The aim was to use the expatriate to find and establish a Value Network including delivery channels, value-added resellers, furniture retailers, content developers and end users in Japan. However, the expatriate was not able to handle this task and expansion of the operations in Japan without being inside the market proved impossible. For this reason, the contract with the expatriate was terminated in 2015. However, during the expatriate's work for Vivo, he identified a Japanese consultancy firm. The consultancy firm was run by a senior Japanese manager with in-depth knowledge of Japanese IT-markets and with very good personal networks among different actors in the market. The firm itself was not a reseller but started to look for suitable resellers for Vivo's digital service. This was explained this as follows:

> I'll have to emphasise that you have to have a contact that you can use to get into the market, otherwise the successful market entry is impossible. The fact that we found this person [with aconsultancy firm] and the fact that he believed us, was the way how we finally get into the market.

The development of the Service element of the business model also helped attract the interest of the consultancy firm to the market entry. Vivo had just launched an iPad version of their digital platform with augmented reality (AR) functionality. These new features helped end users to see for instance how the furniture looked and fit into their rooms before taking the decision to pay. Because of these new features, the Japanese consultancy firm saw the potential of digital service in the Japanese market. The second business model is demonstrated in Figure 5.2. As it can be seen from the

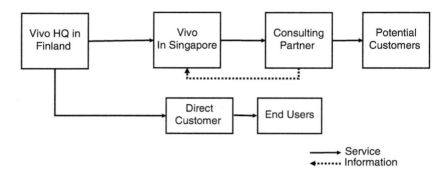

Figure 5.2 Second business model in Japan.
Source: The authors.

figure, the customer found by Vivo's representative in the first business model became their direct customer who was dealt with from the headquarters (HQ). In this model, Vivo also started to receive better market information from the consulting partner. While this second model aided Vivo in exploring potential customers, none were converted into actual customers. Thus, this model was of necessity converted into the third model described next.

Third Business Model 2016 Onwards

Changes to the Service element and the capability to expand the Value Network and Value Delivery enabled growth in Japan. The consultancy firm is currently working as the country manager and they are further developing the distributor and reselling networks. From 2016, Vivo gained a partner who worked as a value-added reseller (VAR) and was able to integrate new content into Vivo's platform. This activity had been performed previously only in Finland. Content development in Japan allowed conservation of resources and made it possible to tailor the content better for the Japanese market. This tailoring boosted content development significantly as most of the customers had their own content, such as furniture or renovation materials, that they modelled for the platform. As a result, since 2016 Vivo has had a functioning Value Network in Japan where the service creates value for different partners, including additional B2B partners and end users. The third business model (see Figure 5.3) also included updates to the Service element as Vivo launched new services that were targeted first to the Japanese market and which then expanded into other markets. They developed High-Quality Rendering (HQR) and virtual show rooms first for the Japanese market as there was an enquiry from the customer side for these kinds of services. These changes enabled Vivo to

Reconfiguring Digital Business Models 75

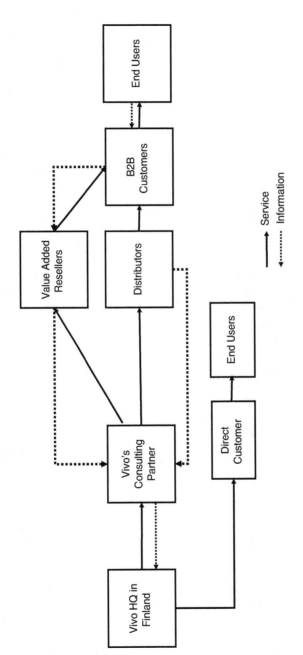

Figure 5.3 Third business model in Japan.
Source: The authors.

expand their business from 3D modelling of furniture to modelling of different renovation solutions as well as interiors. Vivo has also expanded their service portfolio. Also, other new technologies, like Virtual Reality (VR) solutions, have opened markets in Japan, even though these innovations have not been as successful in other markets, such as Europe. As it can be seen from Figure 5.3, there are also several routes that help Vivo to receive feedback also from end users. Vivo top manager commented on this as follows:

> In Japan, people have much more willingness to take new technologies into the use compared for example to Finland or Europe. In Europe, constructors are wondering how to use VR in different projects, and we have not sold much VR based services there. However, in Japan, all customers are eager to use VR and other new technologies. Even old ladiesthere use VR helmets to see how their new house will look like.

Discussion

In this section, we discuss the empirical findings and especially how and why different business model elements changed during the foreign market entry in Japan. Related to the Service element, the basic platform service for furniture retailers developed further when Vivo added new functionalities like connectivity with iPad and AR integration. Even though the platform service was designed so that there were not many country-specific elements that required localisation and/or customisation (cf., Ojala & Tyrväinen, 2006), they developed extensions for their platform based on the needs of Japanese customers (like HQR). These extensions helped to gain access to the market and evoke customers' interest towards Vivo's digital platform. These changes to the platform showed that Vivo's partner cared about and was equipped to understand the local market. Through the partner, Vivo received new ideas from their Japanese customers and end users. Vivo was able to utilise these ideas in their service development for Japanese market and also globally.

For Vivo, the Value Network element and its development further created the biggest challenge to growth business in Japan. Development of the Value Network required, in addition to the excellent digital service, networking with the right persons. It became evident that this was exceptionally hard when relying on non-Japanese persons. This networking challenge was also the main reason why the two first business models failed. Only the third business model, where Vivo was able to use the experience of the Japanese partner (consultancy firm), with in-depth knowledge of the industry, opened up the market. This contact helped to find key customers and expand the network of various partners where VAR was the most significant enabler for success. This finding contributes to previous business model literature that highlights the evolution of Value Network based on the attractiveness of the product and the value it brings to different actors within the network (e.g., Osterwalder & Pigneur, 2010; Teece, 2010; Ojala & Helander, 2014). However, our findings demonstrate that building a Value Network requires also the right personal relationships in addition to the value that the service brings. This is especially valid in the markets where personal relationships are highly valued such as in Japan (Nishiyama, 2000).

The Value Delivery element played a very minor role in Vivo's first and second business models as the Value Network was not fully developed. However, in the third business model, Value Delivery included, in addition to monetary value, many kinds of know-how and knowledge. Especially the value provided by the Japanese consultancy firm, the VAR, and distributors proved important providers of different kinds of knowledge about the market. Additionally, the VAR provided knowledge necessary to innovate in the overseas market and that innovation disseminated back to the headquarters in Finland and the established markets of Vivo in Europe. The flow of information was from users and B2B customers, to the VAR, to Vivo and Vivo headquarters. This kind of knowledge movement about user preferences and behaviors and process related to innovations in the foreign and home markets is less common than the usual dissemination from headquarters to target countries. More specifically, this knowledge was related to new business ideas, improving the existing service and using different functionalities of the platform.

Conclusion

Based on our empirical findings, the successful market entry into the Japanese market was a long process for Vivo. It required reconfiguration of the business model over the years. Even though they had workable digital platform services that they were selling to several countries, all the business model elements required changes to operate successfully in Japan. However, the most critical element was creation of a Value Network that required personal relationship with a trustful actor in Japan. Thereafter, the characteristics of the service became critical. These characteristics required innovating with customers to customise the digital service for the market. After reconfiguring these two business model elements, it become possible to establish the Value Delivery element and successful business operations.

From a theoretical point of view, our findings indicate the importance of personal network relationships (Chetty & Blankenburg Holm, 2000; Coviello, 2006) especially in the case where a firm is entering a culturally distant country. This finding indicates that closer investigation to the development of personal relationships is needed when studying evolution of a Value Network. Here the network theory of internationalisation (Johanson & Mattsson, 1988, 1992) would bring valuable insights and better understanding how these relationships can be built with foreign actors. It might also provide insights how different types of network relationships (formal, informal and mediated) bring value (Birley, 1985; Chetty & Blankenburg Holm, 2000; Ellis & Pecotich, 2001; Rialp, Rialp & Knight, 2005; Ojala, 2009) when reconfiguring business models when entering and operating in a foreign market.

Overall, this chapter contributes to business model literature especially in the context of digital service providers entering foreign markets. It moves forward our understanding of requirements that firms might encounter when they enter new locations and reconfigure their business model for new markets. By doing so, this study answers to the call made by Onetti et al. (2012) by forming better understanding how locations impact business model reconfiguration.

References

Adomavicius, G., Bockstedt, J.C., Gupta, A. & Kauffman, R.J. (2008). "Making sense of technology trends in the information technology landscape: A design science approach", *MIS Quarterly*, vol. 32(4), pp. 779–809.

Al-Debei, M.M. & Avison, D. (2010). "Developing a unified framework of the business model concept", *European Journal of Information Systems*, vol. 19(3), pp. 359–376.

Arthur, W.B. (2009). *The Nature of Technology: What It Is and How It Evolves*. London, UK: Penguin.

Autio, E., Nambisan, S., Thomas, L.D.W. & Wright, M. (2017). "Digital affordances, spatial affordances, and the genesis of entrepreneurial ecosystems", *Strategic Entrepreneurship Journal*, vol. 12(1), pp. 72–95.

Baber, W., Ojala, A. & Martinez, R. (2019a). "Effectuation logic in digital business model transformation: Insights from Japanese high-tech innovators", *Journal of Small Business and Enterprise Development*, vol. 26 (6/7), pp. 811–830.

Baber, W., Ojala, A. & Martinez, R. (2019b). "Transition to digital distribution platforms and business model evolution", *Proceedings of 52nd Hawaii International Conference on System Science (HICSS 2019)*, Maui, Hawaii, 8–11 January 2019.

Baber, W., Ojala, A. & Martinez, R. (2020). "Digitalization and evolution of business model pathways among Japanese software SMEs", in A. Khare, H. Ishikura & W.W. Baber (Eds.), *Transforming of Japanese Business: Rising to the Digital Challenge*. Singapore: Springer, 154–165.

Baber, W.W. & Ojala, A. (2021). "Change of international business models during Covid-19", in M.A. Maronov & S.T. Marinova (Eds.), *Covid-19 and International Business: Change of Era*. London and New York, NY: Taylor and Francis, 103–112.

Baber, W.W., Ojala, A., Sarata, M. & Tsukamoto, M. (2022). "Business model transformation during internationalization: Stretching from Japan to the US market", in C. Nielsen, S.T. Marinova & M.A. Marinov (Eds.), *Business Models and Firm Internationalisation*. London and New York, NY: Routledge, 91–105.

Bell, J., McNaughton, R., Young, S. & Crick, D. (2003). "Towards an integrative model of small firm internationalization", *Journal of International Entrepreneurship*, vol. 1(4), pp. 339–362.

Birley, S. (1985). "The role of networks in the entrepreneurial process", *Journal of Business Venturing*, vol. 1/1, pp. 107–117.

Blum, B.S. & Goldfarb, A. (2006). "Does the Internet defy the law of gravity?" *Journal of International Economics*, vol. 70(2), pp. 384–405.

Bohnsack, R., Pinkse, J. & Kolk, A. (2014). "Business models for sustainable technologies: Exploring business model evolution in the case of electric vehicles", *Research Policy*, vol. 43(2), pp. 284–300.

Casadesus-Masanell, R., & Ricart, J.E. (2010). From Strategy to Business Models and onto Tactics. *Long Range Planning*, 43, 195–215.

Cavalcante, S., Kesting, P. & Ulhoi, J. (2011). "Business model dynamics and innovation: (Re)establishing the missing linkages", *Management Decisions*, vol. 49(8), pp. 1327–1342.

Chesbrough, H. (2007). "Business model innovation: It's not just about technology anymore", *Strategy and Leadership*, vol. 35(6), pp. 12–17.

Chetty, S. & Blankenburg Holm, D. (2000). "Internationalisation of small- to medium-sized manufacturing firms: A network approach", *International Business Review*, vol. 9/1, pp. 77–93.

Child, J., Hsieh, L., Elbanna, S., Karmowska, J., Marinova, S., Puthusserry, P., Tsai, T., Narooz, R. & Zhang, Y. (2017). "SME international business models: The role of context and experience", *Journal of World Business*, vol. 52(5), pp. 664–679.

Coviello, N. (2006). "The network dynamics of international new ventures", *Journal of International Business Studies*, vol. 37/5, pp. 713–731.

Dow, D. & Karunaratna, A. (2006). "Developing a multidimensional instrument to measure psychic distance stimuli", *Journal of International Business Studies*, vol. 37(5), pp. 578–602.

Doz, Y. (2011). "Qualitative research for international business", *Journal of International Business Studies*, vol. 42(5), pp. 582–590.

Dunning, J.H. (2001). "The eclectic (OLI) paradigm of international production: Past, present, and future", *International Journal of the Economics of Business*, vol. 8(2), pp. 173–190.

Eisenhardt, K.M. (1989). "Building theories from case study research", *Academy of Management Review*, vol. 14(4), pp. 532–550.

Ellis, P. & Pecotich, A. (2001). "Social factors influencing export initiation in small- and medium-sized enterprises", *Journal of Marketing Research*, vol. 38/1, pp. 119–130.

Gooris, J. & Peeters, C. (2014). "Home–host country distance in offshore governance choices", *Journal of International Management*, vol. 20(1), pp. 73–86.

Huber, G.P. & Power, D.J. (1985). "Retrospective reports of strategic-level managers: Guidelines for increasing their accuracy", *Strategic Management Journal*, vol. 6, pp. 171–180.

Johanson, J. & Mattsson, L.-G. (1988). "Internationalisation in industrial systems – a network approach", in N. Hood & J.-E. Vahlne (Eds.), *Strategies in Global Competition*. London: Croom Helm, 287–314.

Johanson, J. & Mattsson, L.-G. (1992). "Network positions and strategic action: An analytical framework", in B. Axelsson & G. Easton (Eds.), *Industrial Networks: A New View of Reality*. New York: Routledge, 205–217.

Kindström, D. & Kowalkowski, C. (2014). "Service innovation in product-centric firms: A multidimensional business model perspective", *Journal of Business and Industrial Marketing*, vol. 29(2), pp. 96–111.

Luoma, E. (2013). "Examining business models of software-as-a-service companies", University of Jyväskylä, Finland.

80 *Arto Ojala and William W. Baber*

Miles, M.B., Huberman, A.M. & Saldana, J. (2013). *Qualitative Data Analysis: A Methods Sourcebook*. Thousand Oaks, CA: SAGE Publications.

Nielsen, C., Marinova, S.T. & Marinov, M.A. (Eds.) (2022). *Business Models and Firm Internationalisation*. London and New York, NY: Routledge, 97–113.

Nishiyama, K. (2000). *Doing Business with Japan: Successful Strategies for Intercultural Communication*. Honolulu: University of Hawaii Press.

Ojala, A. (2016). Business models and opportunity creation: How IT entrepreneurs create and develop business models under uncertainty. *Information Systems Journal*, vol. 26(5), pp. 451–476.

Ojala, A. (2009). "Internationalization of knowledge-intensive SMEs: The role of network relationships in the entry to a psychically distant market", *International Business Review*, vol. 18(1), pp. 50–59.

Ojala, A. (2015). "Geographic, cultural, and psychic distance to foreign markets in the context of small and new ventures", *International Business Review*, vol. 24(5), pp. 825–835.

Ojala, A. & Helander, N. (2014). "Value creation and evolution of a value network: A longitudinal case study on a platform-as-a-service provider", in Proceedings of 47th Hawaii International Conference on System Sciences, pp. 975–984.

Ojala, A. & Lyytinen, K. (2022). "How do entrepreneurs create indirect network effects on digital platforms? A study on a multi-sided gaming platform", *Technology Analysis & Strategic Management*. https://www.tandfonline.com/doi/pdf/10.1080/09537325.2022.2065977?needAccess=true

Ojala, A. & Tyrväinen, P. (2006). "Business models and market entry mode choice of small software firms", *Journal of International Entrepreneurship*, vol. 4(2–3), pp. 69–81.

Ojala, A. & Tyrväinen, P. (2007). "Market entry and priority of small- and medium-sized enterprises in the software industry: An empirical analysis of cultural distance, geographical distance, and market size", *Journal of International Marketing*, vol. 15(3), pp. 123–149.

Onetti, A., Zucchella, A., Jones, M.V. & Mcdougall-covin, P.P. (2012). "Internationalization, innovation and entrepreneurship: Business models for new technology-based firms", *Journal of Management & Governance*, vol. 16(3), pp. 337–368.

Osterwalder, A. & Pigneur, Y. (2010). *Business Model Generation: A Handbook for Visionaries, Game Changers, and Challengers*. New York, NY: John Wiley & Sons.

Osterwalder, A. & Pigneur, Y. (2013). "Designing business models and similar strategic objects: The contribution of IS", *Journal of the Association for Information Systems*, vol. 14, pp. 237–244.

Osterwalder, A., Pigneur, Y. & Tucci, C.L. (2005). "Clarifying business models: Origins, present, and future of the concept", *Communications of the Association for Information Systems*, vol. 15(1), pp. 1–43.

Pettigrew, A.M. (1990). "Longitudinal field research on change: Theory and practice", *Organization Science*, vol. 1(3), pp. 267–292.

Rialp, A., Rialp, J. & Knight, G.A. (2005). "The phenomenon of early internationalizing firms: What do we know after a decide (1993–2003) of scientific inquiry?" *International Business Review*, vol. 14/2, pp. 147–166.

Rissanen, T., Ermolaeva, L., Torkkeli, L., Ahi, A. & Saarenketo, S. (2020). "The role of home market context in business model change in internationalizing SMEs", *European Business Review*, vol. 23(2), 257–275.

Saebi, T., Lien, L. & Foss, N.J. (2017). "What drives business model adaptation? The impact of opportunities, threats and strategic orientation", Long *Range Planning*, vol. 50(5), pp. 567–581.

Sosna, M., Trevinyo-Rodríguez, R. & Velamuri, S.R. (2010). "Business model innovation through trial-and-error learning: The Naturhouse case", *Long Range Planning*, vol. 43(2-3), pp. 383–407.

Teece, D.J. (2010). "Business models, business strategy and innovation", *Long Range Planning*, vol. 43(2–3), pp. 172–194.

Walter, A., Ritter, T. & Gemünden, H.G. (2001). "Value creation in buyer-seller relationships", *Industrial Marketing Management*, vol. 30(4), pp. 365–377.

Yin, R.K. (2009). *Case Study Research: Design and Methods*. Los Angeles, CA: Sage Publications.

Zain, M. & Ng, S.I. (2006). "The impacts of network relationships on SMEs' internationalization process", *Thunderbird International Business Review*, vol. 48(2), pp. 183–205.

6 Data-driven Business Model Innovation – When is Decoupling Necessary?

Taina Eriksson, Niina Nummela, and Marikka Heikkilä

Introduction

Whether we like it or not, the world in which companies operate today is volatile, uncertain, complex and ambiguous (VUCA), and this forces them to continuously adapt and renew their activities in order to succeed (Schoemaker, Heaton & Teece, 2018). This is reflected in companies' business models, which need to be flexible in order to survive strategic discontinuities and disruptions (Doz & Kosonen, 2010).

The impact of a turbulent environment is both direct and indirect, as international business is heavily interconnected via global value networks. The success of a global value network is dependent on its resilience to external shocks and particularly on small- and medium-sized enterprises' (SMEs) need to assure their position in global value networks by convincing the leading companies of their continuous resilience in the future (Kano & Hoon Oh, 2020). Unfortunately, our knowledge of SME resilience building and the capabilities needed for business model innovation is limited (Randhawa, Wilden & Gudergan, 2021).

One strategy that SMEs have applied to improve their resilience is digitalisation: The increased use and integration of digital technologies in products and services by including more functionalities and making better use of the data that the product or service already collects (Björkdahl, 2020). Adding a digital element to company activities is a major business model innovation and requires that the company reconfigure its resource base and develop novel dynamic capabilities, which are needed to co-ordinate and manage the renewed business model (cf. Wollersheim & Heimeriks, 2016).

This study investigates how SMEs that innovate new business by embedding data analytics into their products or services improve their future competitiveness and resilience. In particular, we want to understand how these SMEs innovate their existing business models to support new business ideas and whether this leads to the decoupling of business models. We conducted a "matched-pair" case study of two Finnish SMEs that have introduced new data-driven services to their customers. Based on

DOI: 10.4324/9781003326731-6

various data sources, including semi-structured, in-depth interviews with key informants, we learned how the implementation of digital elements affected their business models and ecosystem constellations. We identified, for example, the focal factors that led the SMEs to decouple the novel business from the established one and to develop a parallel business model for the new offering. The key contribution of this study lies in bringing forward the interrelatedness of business model innovation and strategic changes in the ecosystem.

Literature Review

A business model is a widely accepted concept to describe the logic of how a company creates, captures and delivers value to its customers (Wirtz et al., 2016). Its core elements are value proposition, customer segments, revenue logic and organisation of activities and resources. The business model of a company is not static, but in response to the changing environment or to expand its business, the company needs to innovate the element(s) of its business model to ensure its viability. This topic of business model innovation has been investigated widely during the past decade (Foss & Saebi, 2017; DaSilva & Trkman, 2014; Schneider & Spieth, 2013), also with a focus on SMEs (Albats, Podmetina & Vanhaverbeke, 2021; Rissanen et al., 2020; Asemokha et al., 2019; Heikkilä, Bouwman & Heikkilä, 2017; Sainio et al., 2011) and/or on data-driven business models (Eriksson, Heikkilä & Nummela, 2022; Bouwman, Nikou & de Reuver, 2019; Müller, 2019). However, existing research often seems to ignore the role of digitalisation in business model innovation (Ritter & Lund Petersen, 2020).

When a company is seizing a novel opportunity that involves digitalisation and leveraging data for services or solutions, the need for business model innovation is evident. Recently, there has been a growing interest among SMEs to search for new business opportunities based on data generated in their or their customers' operations (Ulander, Ahomäki & Laukkanen, 2019). Data-driven innovations use data as a core ingredient (Jetzek, Avital & Bjorn-Andersen, 2014) to produce value added for a company's internal use or for its customers. From the viewpoint of this study, it is significant that data-driven innovations can potentially change the underlying value-creation mechanisms and, in turn, have a significant impact on business models (Huberty, 2015).

Exploitation of the identified digital business opportunities requires flexibility of the business model; the company may need to switch between business models, modularise business processes, switch between parallel models or decouple activities (Doz & Kosonen, 2010). Digitalisation of business promotes decoupling and often results in changes in the company's value chains (Autio et al., 2018). However, it also requires novel capabilities to handle the challenges related to the decoupling and reorganisation of existing value chains (Warner & Wäger, 2019).

84 *Taina Eriksson et al.*

To our knowledge, the concept of "decoupling" was first introduced by Meyer and Rowan (1977), then referred to organisational buffering to protect the core of the company. Later, in organisational studies, it has been applied to describe the gap between company goals, institutional needs and organisational practices (Stål & Corvellec, 2018; Bromley & Powell, 2012). Inherently, the concept also includes the idea of separation or disengagement, in line with the colloquial use of the term. However, over the years, the concept has received more detailed definitions, and its interpretation varies considerably across disciplines (besides management, the concept has been used, for example, in environmental sciences, finance and information technology).

In this study, we examine decoupling as an element of business model innovation in which organisational resources and value chains are re-organised. In this process, activities are coupled with other activities to contribute to a firm's value creation and capture (Stål & Corvellec, 2018). However, tight coupling may result in rigidity; therefore, the degree of coupling is "a trade-off between efficiency and resilience" (Roberts, 2004, 68). Business model innovation requires flexibility of the organisation and therefore too tight coupling may decelerate or even prevent business model innovation. Instead, it may be that decoupling is needed to secure the future resilience of the business.

In this study, we are interested in organisational resilience – that is, a company's ability to return to a stable state after disruptive events and its tolerance for turbulence and discontinuities (Bhamra, 2015). Business model innovation is considered one way to build organisational resilience (Niemimaa et al., 2019). However, given our focus on SMEs, we do not ignore entrepreneurial resilience but acknowledge that it is conceptually distinct from the organisational resilience of the venture (Hartmann et al., 2022; Ayala & Manzano, 2014). For us, organisational resilience incorporates two characteristics: Adaptability and robustness. They combine endurance, preparedness and recovery with identification of opportunities, innovation and continuous learning (Buliga, Scheiner & Voigt, 2016). Business model innovation can boost all these characteristics.

Methodology

Research Strategy

Our exploratory study was set up to understand how innovative SMEs adapt their existing business models when exploiting novel business opportunities related to the adoption of data-driven business ideas. Our focus lies in particular in the potentially resulting decoupling of the business model. We adopted an inductive approach and conducted a qualitative case study. We focused on two firms to combine a deep understanding of the cases with the possibility of pattern matching between

Data-driven Business Model Innovation   85

Table 6.1 Overview of the case companies

Company	Established	Employees (2021)	Industry/Sector	Product/Service
HygieFix	2007 (has a history of 70+ years)	44	Metal and engineering	Furniture and fixtures made of steel
ITguru	2004	19	Information technology	Information technology services

Source: The authors.

them (Eisenhardt, 1989). In this respect, our study can be labelled a "matched-pair" case study (cf. Piekkari, Welch & Paavilainen, 2009). The selection of appropriate cases was based on the study's purpose – what the researcher wants to be able to say about the unit of the analysis – and access to information (cf. Fletcher et al., 2018). In this exploratory study, we searched for companies that aimed to increase resilience through business renewal with the help of digital technology.

Two suitable case companies were found through a business development programme that facilitated the development of data-driven innovations. Both are Finnish-based SMEs, but they also operate in international markets (for detailed information, see Table 6.1). One of them offers ICT services, and the other manufactures steel products. Both companies search for growth through diversification from international markets. The following quote illustrates their aims well:

We search for new business with an open mind as well as value added to our current business to secure survival and resilience.

Case Companies

HygieFix has over 70 years of history in industrial manufacturing. Its products include specialised metal furniture and fixtures, which can be used in spaces that require high hygiene and ease of maintenance, such as hospitals, marine catering and professional kitchens. At the start of the business development programme, the standard product line consisted of physical products, but for quite some time, the top management of the company had played with ideas on how to increase the value added to their products as a response to fierce competition. Then, COVID-19 started to severely affect one of its product lines.

COVID-19 has affected some of our business areas very severely, including the marine side, which has lost about 40% of its turnover this financial year. This

86 *Taina Eriksson et al.*

has pushed us to find a new direction. While COVID was a strong driver, I guess that without the slowdown of the market we would not have had time even to think about new business model innovations.

They decided to put an effort into developing a digital solution that adds data-driven service elements to physical products.

ITguru specialises in Apple-based technology maintenance services for business customers. Over the years, it has developed technology tools to be used internally for running its own operations based on this technology; the company gets information on customers' computers, for example, on the usage patterns, configurations and status of updates. The owner of the company set the aim to grow internationally; thus, they were looking for ways to expand.

We have the goal to grow quite aggressively and internationalise our business, but it is not possible with our current services and products. Therefore, we started to create our new internationally scalable business by building on our organisation's expertise and capabilities, instead.

The company decided to develop its internal tools further into a product that could be offered to the customers because they saw the need on the market accompanied by a lack of solutions.

Data Collection and Analysis

The operations of the case companies were monitored for two years. The selected SMEs applied to the business development programme shortly after the pandemic hit the world. They started business model innovation in the autumn of 2020. This innovation has continued till present. We followed this development process in real time from the start of the programme in 2020, and different data sources were available to us throughout this period. Furthermore, we had access to the companies' applications to the programme, where they described their initial ideas and motivations. In addition, we had access to the business plan materials that they worked on during the programme. In addition, secondary materials from companies' web pages have been utilised to better understand the context in which they operate.

When applying to the programme, the companies had to describe their business model with a "business model canvas" (Osterwalder & Pigneur, 2010). During the programme, the business model canvases were updated, and in the interviews, we asked them to evaluate how their business models changed. For the interviews, key informants (i.e., the most knowledgeable persons related to the expected business model innovation and its aims) from each company were chosen. Typically, these persons were also actively involved in the business development programme as participants;

Table 6.2 List of codes

Code	Description
Trigger for data-driven business model innovation	The reasons why the company has decided to embark on innovating on the use of data
Data-driven innovation	Description of the data-driven innovation the company has been working on
Value proposition	Customer value proposition
Customers, relationship and channels	Customer segments, what kind of relationship is formed with the customers and how the potential customers are reached
Earnings and revenue flows	Earnings logic of the data-driven innovation
Resources, processes, capabilities and costs	What new resources and processes the company needs to develop to deliver the new solution, what kinds of capabilities it needs and what kinds of costs are related to the production
Networks	What kind of new partners the company needs to first develop the data-driven innovation and later on to deliver the expected customer value
The relationship between old and new business models	What is the role of the new business model in relation to the existing business model when the data-driven innovation is launched and what is the plan for the future

Source: The authors.

additionally, they were responsible for business development and data-driven innovation initiatives in their respective organisations.

The analysis started with systematic thematic coding of the data using NVivo software. The thematic codes were derived from the literature, particularly from the business model canvas (Osterwalder & Pigneur, 2010). Additionally, we used codes to analyse the motivation for business model innovation, the description of the data-driven innovation, the research context and the informants' perceptions of the relationship between the existing and the new business models. A list of the codes is compiled in Table 6.2.

Findings

Business Model Innovation in the Case Companies

Although the integration of a physical product and data-driven service is considered necessary for the international growth of *HygieFix*, top management does not expect any major changes in the value proposition to the customer. High-level hygiene, safety and easiness of the fixtures and cabinets will remain at the core of the value proposition as the new services will be offered, for example, to hospitals, to provide better data on the

88   *Taina Eriksson et al.*

material flows that are stored or passed through the cabinets. The data are utilised in monitoring the consumption of materials in the customers' processes. This information will help the customer to design their materials logistics better and to, for instance, make better estimates of future needs.

> *The data is collected on the flow of materials which are passed through our products e.g., to the operating theatre. We gather data on the inflow and usage and are able to tell when there is a need for replenishment.*

This means that instead of "dumb" steel products, customer value is delivered through a clever cabinetry that plays an essential role in the customer's materials management process.

> *In the new business model we are no longer the supplier of a single piece of steel or a wall element, but deliver something else to the customer's value chain, thereby bringing them cost savings and also increasing patient safety.*

The new business model differs significantly from the existing model in terms of how customers are reached and the relationships formed with them. In addition, the purchasing decision-maker is likely to be different, even though the end users remain the same. Although, in the current business, the new deals are won by participating independently in the tendering processes of big building projects (such as hospitals), in the new model, the company needs to become part of an alliance that offers a more complete solution to the building. In addition, the new business model requires the company to become involved in the daily operations of the buildings, which means significant changes in the partner network. Earlier, it was enough to collaborate with specialised construction and engineering companies; now, it needs partners that are involved in material flow processes in hospitals. In principle, the company can either collaborate independently with multiple international partners or decide to make an exclusive agreement with a selected international solution provider.

> *Now we can provide that data to either the hospital directly or its logistics companies who are taking care of daily material supply. If the information is utilized to the fullest extent they can save unnecessary work effort and improve their supply processes.*

The new data-driven solution requires additional resources and capabilities, as some completely new activities in the domain of software development are crucial parts of customer value creation. On the one hand, the company needs to perform some new activities when its solution is integrated into the daily material flows of the user organisation. In addition, the company needs to coordinate and manage the activities acquired from its partners. This requires a sufficient level of technological understanding that the company does not yet have, but it is developing. In addition, the new kind of collaboration with sales or delivery partners challenges the company in developing new capabilities in the area of partnership management.

> *If we start with the key partners, key activities and resources, so in the same way as [name of the managing director] mentioned that we're moving from welders to coders, so the domain of software and apps becomes even more important. And the question of how we integrate with the customers' logistics systems. So in that sense our whole approach towards accessing the hospital changes.*

Furthermore, although the end users of the new solution may at least partly be the same as the users of existing physical products, customers may acquire the new solution in multiple alternative ways, as hospitals are being built with different contract models. In addition to the variety of new construction productions, there is the potential to retrofit existing buildings. As a result, the company will have several parallel sales channels to reach potential customers. In the future, independent of the sales channel, customer relationships are expected to become more stable and long lasting, thus gradually replacing existing transaction/project-based customer relationships. This will hopefully result in more continuous and predictable revenue streams, which will improve the resilience of the company.

ITguru is developing a new business model to first diversify and eventually replace the current business model built around the use of its technology. In essence, the novel data-driven service will build on the same core technology that has been the key resource in the earlier business model, but its user base has expanded beyond the internal users within the company, and the service has become more holistic; instead of offering a specific IT service, the company will provide an outsourced IT management function.

> *We have been developing tools to support our own work processes and have noticed that there are no similar tools available anywhere in the world.*

The data-driven service solution will be applied in multiple ways, in what will eventually be a platform solution around the core technology and tools that are offered to customers. The company is seeing multiple different use cases for the technology, and in the first phase, it is focusing on a data-driven service in which the customer gets access to specific tools and data that partially replace what services the company has been offering.

In the earlier business model, they used the technology to produce outsourced technology management services for one customer group: Companies using Apple computers. By developing a new user interface, the company is able to broaden the potential user base since the user does not have to have deep technological expertise.

90   *Taina Eriksson et al.*

> *Opening the use of the technology to customers necessitates a different kind of user interface ... But the fact that it [technology] could be exploited by someone else means that tool needs to be rebuilt and similarly also the business model around it.*

Further development into a platform solution opens doors to a larger customer base, and it can be expected that this will broaden the customer base of the case company in the end. The customers can be individual Apple users or information technology staff at the company level. *ITguru* also recognised some user groups outside customer organisations that would find the data valuable. However, to enable this, the company needs to combine, analyse, enrich, aggregate and anonymise the data to meet the needs of each customer group. There are multiple potential revenue streams to be realised in the future, but the value creation logics differ.

> *This is a platform business, i.e., a technology platform where end-users can access services either free of charge or for a small fee. And a company customer pays a monthly fee for having data covering the entire organisation. Moreover, differing service providers also pay for the use of the platform. The platform also provides an easy way to order for example maintenance, i.e., a button to order maintenance. It tells you where the nearest Apple service is and provides cost estimates. These service providers pay us when we pass on to them customers.*

The addition of data-driven services and platform operating logic increases the complexity of the business. The company is expecting to operate through multiple distribution channels – alongside the existing one – and there will also be parallel revenue streams from various customer groups, some of which are very different from existing customers. Besides current organisational customers, the company is also preparing to serve individuals and, at the same time, to serve very different kinds of organisational customers with quite a different use for the data. Overall, the complexity of the business model will increase considerably.

This also implies the need for additional resources and capabilities, as well as refined or even completely new processes. Customer service processes are a focal process to be developed when the company grows internationally with data-driven services.

> *We are changing our processes so that as we begin to attract international users, so that we are capable of offering support and to do selling and marketing internationally. We have been building that platform for a while now. When we launch the product, it needs to be done so that the users get support, we have means to support our internal operations, we invoice and so on.*

The company needs to broaden and further develop its existing capabilities. To serve a multitude of different customer or user groups, there is a need for diversity in the use of key resources.

Cross-Case Analysis

When comparing the companies, there are many similarities but also significant differences. Starting with the technology that is the basis for the data-driven solution, and hence a focal resource, there is a considerable difference in the newness of technology. *ITguru* is leveraging an existing technology with which it is very familiar. On the contrary, *HygieFix* is adopting many new technologies; therefore, there is a considerable need for new capabilities and partners, which would enable a new kind of customer relationship. However, neither company has sufficient data to build the data-driven innovation at the moment, so both are facing a new situation in that sense. Nevertheless, compared to *HygieFix*, *ITguru* is not expecting to develop many new processes and capabilities, but it needs to put more emphasis on developing already existing ones further. For example, the availability of customer support for *ITguru* customers necessitates that the support language selection be broadened, whereas *HygieFix* has not even provided customer support for the ongoing customer relationship.

Due to the introduction of a data-driven service, *HygieFix* needs to restructure its business network significantly, as it needs to integrate into a more comprehensive solution. In other words, to reach customers and become part of new building projects, the company needs to collaborate with new partners. On the other hand, *ITguru* does not need to expand its partner network; instead, it needs to broaden its customer base.

Both companies will need to renew their earnings logic. *ITguru* already has monthly subscription-based invoicing, but *HygieFix* is now preparing for it. Then again, *ITguru* expects multiple revenue streams from different kinds of customer groups, which is a more complex setup than the present arrangement. In parallel with the changing earnings logic, customer relationships are also changing. *HygieFix* strives to build partnerships with its customers, and these partnerships will be enabled by the ongoing value delivery of the data-driven service. *ITguru* is preparing for a gradual increase in the different types of customers but acknowledging that not all possible customer groups are realised.

Management of Parallel Business Models

While the innovative new data-driven business model provides potential for international growth in both companies, they also pointed out that as the new business model radically differs from the original business model, the complexity within the organisations' operations has increased. At the same time, markets are also changing. All this creates challenges in managing the business and maintaining the resilience of the company.

HygieFix, which originally served two industry segments, began offering a new business model in only one of the segments: Hospitals. One of the reasons for the selection of this specific segment was that new building projects are increasingly adopting the alliance model. In the alliance model, the parties – contractors, architects, structural designers, civil engineering designers, building consultants and clients – work much more closely together than in the contract model projects. Consequently, smaller parties, such as HygieFix, can have more voice, get a better understanding of customer's challenges and have a better possibility of introducing innovations into hospitals.

> *Surely the changes [in our business model] will take place in stages, and the development will continue all the time ... But there will certainly be a gradual transition, the old operating models will disappear and be forgotten, but some small hospitals will certainly still want certain old-fashioned cabinets for smaller units.*

However, in autumn 2021, after one year of business model development, the company announced that its business had been divided into two parallel companies. The new company focuses on demanding health care fixtures, and the original company continues its operations with marine catering and professional kitchen furniture. By decoupling the two business segments, the company is securing its resilience, particularly the adaptability of operations and the ability to develop business models in the future.

> *The division will strengthen the identity of both companies and create better opportunities for both companies to focus on developing their own business areas.*

Moreover, there are some differences in the resources and capabilities needed to run the operations of the new business compared to the old business, which may also be an important driver in separating the two units. The company is preparing to operate the new business model in domestic and international markets. The market niche in the domestic market does not offer the growth potential that the company is looking for, so international growth appears necessary to reach its goals.

ITguru continues to operate as one company. Based on the similarity of customer needs, the solution can be offered in the home market and for international customers; the needs seem to be similar across the world. The company does not have experience in operating with international customers, although some of its domestic customers do have overseas operations. Despite similar customer needs across markets, the company has decided to provide the platform-based service only outside its home markets to avoid competing against the company's current offering.

> *In fact, we have made a decision that we will probably not launch the service in Finland, due to the fact that we would be cannibalizing our own current business.*

Thus, in the home market, the company will continue operating the existing business model for now. It is actually treating the domestic market as a testbed for the functioning and development of technology.

Discussion and Conclusions

This study responds to the call for a better understanding of digitalisation in business model innovation (Ritter & Lund Petersen, 2020). In particular, we want to understand how SMEs innovate their existing business models to support new business ideas and whether this leads to the decoupling of business models. We followed the emergence of business model innovation in two SMEs for two years and identified the focal factors that led the SMEs to innovate new data-driven business models and how the adoption of the new business model resulted in the decoupling of organisational activities, even affecting the organisational structure of the companies.

The companies examined in this study have embarked on a journey towards new kinds of business models for data-driven innovations. The development of data-driven innovation and the parallel development of the business model were motivated by the companies' need to grow internationally and develop their resilience. Similar needs for increased resilience, international growth and resilience building have also been noted in other studies during the COVID-19 pandemic (Fath et al., 2021).

Our analysis of the case companies suggests that the motivations behind the decision to seek international growth via data-driven services may be different for each company. On the one hand, *HygieFix* was facing multiple challenges: Declining market in one business area, fierce competition from low-cost international providers in another business area and the changing purchasing models related to how hospitals are being built. On the other hand, *ITguru* was seeing opportunities in globally similar customer needs that could be solved with its technology and with the potential of creating a platform solution around it.

Both companies bring forward interesting insights from the viewpoint of decoupling. Although the same physical product is the core of both business models of *HygieFix*, the business model innovation calls for substantial renewal in resources, processes, capabilities, customer channels and relations, as well as partners. The new business model is therefore developed as an independent organisation, and the other business areas continue operating the old model. Thus, *HygieFix* is decoupling the novel business model from the existing business model, mainly because adding data-based services to its offering adds too much complexity to its current organisational structure. For *HygieFix*, the aim of decoupling the business models – separating the new

94 Taina Eriksson et al.

business model into an independent company – is to find a way to manage complexity. Top management believes that the management of two different businesses parallel to each other is simpler than the management of one very complex business. In other words, with decoupling, it is increasing the fluidity of its resources and decreasing inertia due to existing structures (cf. Doz & Kosonen, 2010).

However, the starting point for decoupling in the case of *ITguru* is quite different. Its aim in decoupling was to better meet the needs of the markets and customers. It has decided to decouple the home market business model from the one it applies to international markets. Interestingly, top management plans to serve all international markets with one business model without any adaptations. However, when the plans materialise, it is possible that although the business models in different markets may appear similar at first glance, a closer look may reveal minor differences (cf. Sainio et al., 2011). In the case of *ITguru*, decoupling seems market- or customer driven, as both models serve similar customer needs, but the role of the company is different in the models; therefore, it is possible that one cannibalises the other.

In addition to organisational or customer-related factors, it is possible that the core technology leveraged in data-driven innovation may play a role in explaining the need for decoupling business models. Building on the use of technologies with which the company is familiar allows the company to utilise its existing capabilities. On the contrary, the novelty of the core technologies for the company entails that the company needs to develop new capabilities to be able to at least collaborate with technology providers (cf. Cohen & Levinthal, 1990, on absorptive capacity).

In our opinion, this study provides an interesting new perspective for scientific discussion on the role of business model innovation as a means to increase the resilience of internationally growing companies. Earlier literature on resilience and continuity management has studied and even provided tools to analyse how resilient existing business models are with respect to market uncertainties. For example, Haaker et al. (2017) introduce a method to test the resilience of different elements of the business model against various risk scenarios (Haaker et al., 2017). However, this study deviates from prior research, as it makes it explicit that companies can increase resilience by radically innovating their business models and this may result in a decision in which the existing and new business models are decoupled.

Our exploratory study offers interesting insights into a topic that has received relatively little attention thus far. We were able to shed some light on data-driven business model innovation and decoupling from the viewpoint of resilience building in international markets. However, we must admit that we have only scratched the surface and that the phenomenon would definitely deserve more attention. We hope that in the future, scholars will conduct further studies on the topic, addressing, for example, the question of when a new business model is needed. An interesting approach could be to link organisational resilience and business model innovation with serial entrepreneurship and to study what kind of reasoning serial entrepreneurs use when making decisions on the (de) coupling of organisational activities. For example, how much resilience or changes in the business model drive their decisions to establish a new company. We think that introducing insights from the entrepreneurship literature to this discussion would offer fruitful avenues for further discussion on the emergence of serial entrepreneurship, for example.

References

Albats, E., Podmetina, D., & Vanhaverbeke, W. (2021). "Open innovation in SMEs: A process view towards business model innovation", *Journal of Small Business Management*, pp. 1–42. doi:10.1080/00472778.2021.1913595

Asemokha, A., Musona, J., Torkkeli, L., & Saarenketo, S. (2019). "Business model innovation and entrepreneurial orientation relationships in SMEs: Implications for international performance", *Journal of International Entrepreneurship*, vol. 17(3), pp. 425–453.

Autio, E., Nambisan, S., Thomas, L.D., & Wright, M. (2018). "Digital affordances, spatial affordances, and the genesis of entrepreneurial ecosystems", *Strategic Entrepreneurship Journal*, vol. 12(1), pp. 72–95.

Ayala, J.C. & Manzano, G. (2014). "The resilience of the entrepreneur. Influence on the success of the business. A longitudinal analysis", *Journal of Economic Psychology*, vol. 42, pp. 126–135.

Bhamra, R. (Ed.). (2015). *Organisational Resilience: Concepts, Integration, and Practice.* CRC Press/Taylor & Francis Group: Boca Raton.

Björkdahl, J. (2020). "Strategies for digitalization in manufacturing firms", *California Management Review*, vol. 62(4), pp. 17–36.

Bouwman, H., Nikou, S., & de Reuver, M. (2019). "Digitalization, business models, and SMEs: How do business model innovation practices improve performance of digitalizing SMEs?" *Telecommunications Policy*, vol. 43(9), pp. 11–18.

Bromley, P. & Powell, W.W. (2012). "From smoke and mirrors to walking the talk: Decoupling in the contemporary world", *Academy of Management Annals*, vol. 6(1), pp. 483–530.

Buliga, O., Scheiner, C.W., & Voigt, K.I. (2016). "Business model innovation and organizational resilience: Towards an integrated conceptual framework", *Journal of Business Economics*, vol. 86(6), pp. 647–670.

Cohen, W.M. & Levinthal, D.A. (1990). "Absorptive capacity: A new perspective on learning and innovation", *Administrative Science Quarterly*, vol. 35(1), pp. 128–152.

DaSilva, C.M. & Trkman, P. (2014). "Business model: What it is and what it is not", *Long Range Planning*, vol. 47(6), pp. 379–389.

Doz, Y.L. & Kosonen, M. (2010). "Embedding strategic agility: A leadership agenda for accelerating business model renewal", *Long Range Planning*, vol. 43(2–3), pp. 370–382.

Eisenhardt, K.M. (1989). "Building theories from case study research", *Academy of Management Review*, vol. 14(4), pp. 532–550.

Eriksson, T., Heikkilä, M., & Nummela, N. (2022). "Crafting SME business model for international expansion with data-driven services", in C. Nielsen, S.T. Marinova & M.A. Marinov (Eds.), *Business Models and Firm Internationalization*. London and New York, NY: Routledge, 137–151.

Fath, B., Fiedler, A., Sinkovics, N., Sinkovics, R.R., & Sullivan-Taylor, B. (2021). "International relationships and resilience of New Zealand SME exporters during COVID-19", *Critical Perspectives on International Business*, vol. 17(2), pp. 359–379.

Fletcher, M., Zhao, Y., Plakoyiannaki, E., & Buck, T. (2018). "Three pathways to case selection in international business: A twenty-year review, analysis and synthesis", *International Business Review*, vol. 27(4), pp. 755–766.

Foss, N.J. & Saebi, T. (2017). "Fifteen years of research on business model innovation: How far have we come and where should we go?" *Journal of Management*, vol. 43(1), pp. 200–227.

Haaker, T., Bouwman, H., Janssen, W., & de Reuver, M. (2017). "Business model stress testing: A practical approach to test the robustness of a business model", *Futures*, vol. 89, pp. 14–25.

Hartmann, S., Backmann, J., Newman, A., Brykman, K.M., & Pidduck, R.J. (2022). "Psychological resilience of entrepreneurs: A review and agenda for future research", *Journal of Small Business Management*. doi:10.1080/00472778.2021.2024216

Heikkilä, M., Bouwman, H., & Heikkilä, J. (2017). "From strategic goals to business model innovation paths: An exploratory study", *Journal of Small Business and Enterprise Development*, vol. 25(1), pp. 107–128.

Huberty, M. (2015). "Awaiting the second big data revolution: From digital noise to value creation", *Journal of Industry, Competition and Trade*, vol. 15(1), pp. 35–47.

Jetzek, T., Avital, M., & Bjorn-Andersen, N. (2014). "Data-driven innovation through open government data", *Journal of Theoretical and Applied Electronic Commerce Research*, vol. 9(2), pp. 15–16.

Kano, L. & Hoon Oh, C. (2020). "Global value chains in the post-COVID world: Governance for reliability", *Journal of Management Studies*, vol. 57(8), pp. 1773–1777.

Meyer, J.W. & Rowan, B. (1977). "Institutionalized organizations: Formal structure as myth and ceremony", *American Journal of Sociology*, vol. 83(2), pp. 340–363.

Müller, J.M. (2019). "Business model innovation in small-and medium-sized enterprises: Strategies for industry 4.0 providers and users", *Journal of Manufacturing Technology Management*, vol. 30(8), pp. 1127–1142.

Niemimaa, M., Järveläinen, J., Heikkilä, M., & Heikkilä, J. (2019). "Business continuity of business models: Evaluating the resilience of business models for contingencies", *International Journal of Information Management*, vol. 49, pp. 208–216.

Osterwalder, A. & Pigneur, Y. (2010). *Business Model Generation: A Handbook for Visionaries, Game Changers, and Challengers*, vol. 1. Hoboken, NJ: John Wiley & Sons.

Piekkari, R., Welch, C., & Paavilainen, E. (2009). "The case study as disciplinary convention: Evidence from international business journals", *Organizational Research Methods*, vol. 12(3), pp. 567–589.

Randhawa, K., Wilden, R., & Gudergan, S. (2021). "How to innovate toward an ambidextrous business model? The role of dynamic capabilities and market orientation", *Journal of Business Research*, vol. 130, pp. 618–634.

Rissanen, T., Ermolaeva, L., Torkkeli, L., Ahi, A., & Saarenketo, S. (2020). "The role of home market context in business model change in internationalizing SMEs", *European Business Review*, vol. 32(2), pp. 257–275.

Ritter, T. & Lund Pedersen, C. (2020). "Digitization capability and the digitalization of business models in business-to-business firms: Past, present, and future", *Industrial Marketing Management*, vol. 86, pp. 180–190.

Roberts, J. (2004). *The Modern Firm: Organizational Design for Performance and Growth*. Oxford, UK: Oxford University Press.

Sainio, L.M., Saarenketo, S., Nummela, N., & Eriksson, T. (2011). "Value creation of an internationalizing entrepreneurial firm: The business model perspective", *Journal of Small Business and Enterprise Development*, vol. 18(3), pp. 556–570.

Schneider, S. & Spieth, P. (2013). "Business model innovation: Towards an integrated future research agenda", *International Journal of Innovation Management*, vol. 17(1), pp. 1–34.

Schoemaker, P.J., Heaton, S., & Teece, D. (2018). "Innovation, dynamic capabilities, and leadership", *California Management Review*, vol. 61(1), pp. 15–42.

Stål, H.I. & Corvellec, H. (2018). "A decoupling perspective on circular business model implementation: Illustrations from Swedish apparel", *Journal of Cleaner Production*, vol. 171, pp. 630–643.

Ulander, M., Ahomäki, M., & Laukkanen, J. (2019). *The Future of European Companies in Data Economy*. Helsinki: Sitra.

Warner, K.S. & Wäger, M. (2019). "Building dynamic capabilities for digital transformation: An ongoing process of strategic renewal", *Long Range Planning*, vol. 52(3), pp. 326–349.

Wirtz, B.W., Pistoia, A., Ullrich, S., & Göttel, V. (2016). "Business models: Origin, development and future research perspectives", *Long Range Planning*, vol. 49(1), pp. 36–54.

Wollersheim, J. & Heimeriks, K.H. (2016). "Dynamic capabilities and their characteristic qualities: Insights from a lab experiment", *Organization Science*, vol. 27(2), pp. 233–248.

7 Value-creating and Value-eroding Decoupling in B2B Platforms – A Multiple Case Study

Mika Yrjölä, Malla Mattila, and Marjukka Mikkonen

Introduction

Digitalisation has brought about the rise of platform business models in many industries (Mody et al., 2020; Van Alstyne, Parker & Choudary, 2016). A platform is a type of digital intermediary which enables interactions and/or transactions between two or more distinct groups of users (McIntyre & Srinivasan, 2017). Platform business models can exhibit innovations that have implications for multiple industries (Cusumano, Gawer & Yoffie, 2019). They transform industries such as retailing (Hokkanen et al., 2021) by innovating the mechanisms and channels of distribution and value delivery (Crittenden et al., 2017). Examples of successful business-to-consumer (B2C) platform business models include social media (e.g., Meta, Twitter and YouTube), collaborative consumption (e.g., Airbnb and Uber) and marketplaces (e.g., eBay and Alibaba).

Platforms disrupt competition in new ways by typically acting as both complementors and competitors to incumbents. Against this backdrop, platform business models provide an interesting context to study decoupling – the separation of two or more previously linked customer value-creating activities (Leavy, 2020; Teixeira & Jamieson, 2014). While platformisation has been previously studied from the business model perspective, no research has yet analysed it through the conceptual lens of decoupling. Decoupling would represent a more customer-oriented approach to platform business models, as it highlights the role of customer value and customer processes (Leavy, 2020). This chapter aims to fill this gap and bring a balanced perspective to the literature on platform business models. Thus, joining the researchers who analyse platforms from the business model perspective (Hagiu & Wright, 2013; Yrjölä, Hokkanen & Saarijärvi, 2021) enables us to look at the processes of value creation and value capture from both a firm-centric viewpoint and a broader viewpoint that considers platform actors and interconnected activities (Gawer & Cusumano, 2014; Ondrus, Gannamaneni & Lyytinen, 2015).

The objective of this chapter is to identify, describe and analyse how business-to-business (B2B) platforms utilise decoupling to disrupt value

DOI: 10.4324/9781003326731-7

creation in business ecosystems. This objective is met by utilising 14 case studies of Finnish small and medium-sized enterprises (SMEs) that offer knowledge-intensive services through their own or partnering platforms. We contribute to the current literature on platform business models and business model decoupling by extending the focus to a B2B context. This is important because value creation is inherently different and more complex in business markets, meaning that decoupling can take on new forms not yet seen in research focusing on consumer markets.

The rest of the chapter is organised as follows: First, this chapter discusses the literature on business model decoupling, value creation and B2B platforms, building a tentative framework on the phenomenon. Next, the methodological choices and procedures are outlined. A presentation of the analysis and findings follows. This chapter concludes with a discussion together with implications for managers and a research agenda.

Theoretical Framework

Business Model as a Lens to Value Creation

Businesses exist to create value for customers and other stakeholders while seeking to capture some of this value in terms of cost savings, added revenue and valuable information. This value creation and value capture can be understood through a firm's business model (Arend, 2013; Osterwalder & Pigneur, 2010; Richardson, 2008).

For the purposes of this chapter, a business model is defined as "a representation of a firm's underlying core logic and strategic choices for creating and capturing value" (Shafer, Smith & Linder, 2005, p. 202). Business models are therefore strategic tools that represent a firm's business logic and enable its managers to explore market opportunities (Doganova & Eyquem-Renault, 2009; Magretta, 2002). Business model innovations enable competitive differentiation by matching external opportunities with internal strengths (Amit & Zott, 2012; Teece, 2010).

The Internet and other advances in technology have allowed companies to find novel ways of creating and capturing value (Haucap & Heimeshoff, 2014; Mattila, Mesiranta & Heikkinen, 2020; Mattila, Yrjölä & Lehtimäki, 2019; Yrjölä, Hokkanen & Saarijärvi, 2021). Already the earliest business models allowed a wide range of innovations that encouraged value creation by supporting parts of the value chain (e.g., payment handling) or integrating multiple parts of the value chain (Amit & Zott, 2001; Timmers, 1998). One example would be unbundling, where content that has been previously sold together is now made available for purchase in smaller packages (e.g., instead of buying an entire album, a consumer can now simply buy individual songs). Industries such as music, video and print media have been hit hard by business models that unbundle products for customers (Papies & van Heerde, 2017). Another example is the business model innovation of disintermediation: Eliminating "middlemen" in industries such as air travel, financial services and vacation packages (Clemons & Lang, 2003; Haucap & Heimeshoff, 2014; Leavy, 2020). Many of these business model innovations specifically target customers and end users, inspiring Dawar (2013) to note that competitive advantage seems to be moving downstream in value chains.

Platform business models represent an opposing force to disintermediation – as they are digital intermediaries or meta-organisations – that allow organisations and other actors to pool together and coordinate resources for value creation and capture (Cusumano, Gawer & Yoffie, 2019; Gawer, 2014; Haucap & Heimeshoff, 2014; Mathmann et al., 2017). Platforms can therefore be seen as a new type of intermediary (Hagiu & Wright, 2015), competing with or complementing existing value chains and networks (Yrjölä, Hokkanen & Saarijärvi, 2021). Due to this ability to transform how customers, suppliers and other participants interact and transact, platforms have received considerable scholarly attention (Mathmann et al., 2017; Yrjölä, Hokkanen & Saarijärvi, 2021).

Parker, Van Alstyne and Jiang (2017) characterise the value creation of platform business models as involving *resource orchestration* instead of resource control, *interactions* instead of transactions and *network effects* instead of sales volume as key value-creating and value-capturing mechanisms. First, in terms of resource orchestration, it is important to note that many platforms do not own valuable resources, and, therefore, their business models can be characterised as "asset-lite" (Parente, Geleilate & Rong, 2018). Instead, platforms orchestrate the combination and use of external resources. They create value by enabling interactions between different types of users that otherwise might not be able to interact with each other due to barriers such as transaction costs (Gawer, 2014; Hagiu & Wright, 2015). This value creation can be based on various mechanisms, such as aggregating supply and demand, offering complementary products or services, and providing protection against parties with asymmetric information or negotiation power (Hagiu & Wright, 2013; Van Alstyne, Parker & Choudary, 2016).

Second, while many business models focus on selling products and services (transactions), platforms can create and capture value through multiple methods. Platforms can, for example, facilitate innovation, social interaction and knowledge sharing (McIntyre & Srinivasan, 2017). Platform businesses can also focus on production (Thomas, Autio & Gann, 2014). Therefore, while market intermediary platforms, such as eBay and Alibaba, are perhaps the most well-known platforms, it is important to note that platforms need not necessarily take a transaction focus, especially in B2B contexts (McIntyre & Srinivasan, 2017; Yrjölä, Hokkanen & Saarijärvi, 2021).

Third, the ability of platforms to succeed is typically related to their ability to drive and take advantage of network effects. The network effect refers to the phenomenon where the value for all platform participants increases as the number of participants increases (Van Alstyne, Parker & Choudary, 2016;

Yrjölä, Hokkanen & Saarijärvi, 2021). Therefore, the survival and success of platforms is dependent on their ability to attract a large enough number of high-quality users (Gawer & Cusumano, 2014; Haucap & Heimeshoff, 2014). The value propositions of their business models therefore play a significant role as a key motivational mechanism to attract users to platforms (Ondrus, Gannamaneni & Lyytinen, 2015). However, a rapid increase in the number of platform participants can sometimes lead to misbehaviour or low-quality platform content, which is why the governance of platform access, rules and incentives is a key issue for platform business models (Van Alstyne, Parker & Choudary, 2016).

Platforms and other business model innovations and strategies can be characterised based on whether they aim to leverage current resources and capabilities or create new ones (Lahtinen, Kuusela & Yrjölä, 2018; March, 1991; Medlin & Törnroos, 2015). The former category, labelled exploitation, involves placing emphasis on established and more certain resources, capabilities and revenue streams, while the latter category, exploration, targets future value creation, which is more uncertain and risk-seeking in nature (March, 1991; Medlin & Törnroos, 2015). Business model innovations founded on exploitation involve elements such as efficiency, refinement and execution, while those founded on exploration include aspects such as discovery, innovation and experimentation (Lahtinen, Kuusela & Yrjölä, 2018; March, 1991).

Decoupling Value Creation

This chapter focuses on the business model innovation of decoupling (Teixeira & Jamieson, 2014). Decoupling is a customer-oriented business model innovation that targets customers' purchase and/or consumption processes. It involves the breaking of links in customers' purchase processes and creating value in one or more customer activities, while leaving the rest of the customer processes untouched (Leavy, 2020; Teixeira & Jamieson, 2014). Decoupling can therefore be seen as a new type of competition: The company that decouples one or more customer activities will only compete in terms of those activities (e.g., customer search) while leaving the rest of the activities to the incumbent market leaders (Leavy, 2020).

Decoupling, driven by digitalisation, is affecting multiple industries, such as retail, video game and transportation (Leavy, 2020). For instance, in the dawn of multichannel and omnichannel retailing, the practice of "showrooming" effectively decoupled the activity of touching and testing of products in physical stores from the activity of purchasing the products (Gensler, Neslin & Verhoef, 2017; Yrjölä, Spence & Saarijärvi, 2018) – meaning that many brick-and-mortar retailers were left with offering customer service offline while the customers made orders online from competitors (Yrjölä, 2014). Moreover, digital content has enabled disruptions related to music, entertainment and gaming, as mobile and online services have decoupled customer activities in these industries (Cusumano, Gawer & Yoffie, 2019; Leavy, 2020). Given decoupling has previously been studied exclusively in B2C contexts, such as music and news (Clemons & Lang, 2003) or video games (Leavy, 2020), the current chapter contributes by analysing companies in B2B markets.

When designing business models, managers make assumptions and have expectations regarding the behaviour of customers and competitors (Teece, 2010). Often at the early stage of business model change, it might be difficult to assess the economic potential of a decoupling innovation (Pieroni et al., 2021). Regarding decoupling especially, the focus is on customer processes (Teixeira & Jamieson, 2014). These processes can be purchase processes (as in the showrooming example) or consumption/production processes (as in the case of streaming services). To drive innovation efforts, managers must carefully evaluate the decoupling potential of different resources and activities (Pieroni et al., 2021). Decoupling can thus be divided into value-creating decoupling, value-eroding decoupling and value-charging decoupling (Leavy, 2020).

Value-creating decoupling involves breaking the links between two value-creating activities and performing one of them. Leavy (2020) gives the streaming service Twitch.tv as an example here: The company leaves the activity of "playing games" to incumbents, while it decouples the activity of "watching games" to itself. In cases where value creation is relatively expensive (e.g., in cases where incumbents have previously controlled costly physical production and distribution channels), new entrants are likely to find opportunities to decouple and offer some value-creating activities at a lower cost (Clemons & Lang, 2003).

Value-eroding decoupling refers to breaking the links between value-creating and value-eroding activities that have typically been coupled in the industry (Teixeira & Jamieson, 2014). For example, Steam, a video game digital distribution platform, has decoupled the value-creating activity of playing the game from the value-eroding activity of having to purchase it from a physical store (Leavy, 2020). Many circular economy business models act as examples of value-eroding decoupling as they decouple resource consumption from the value created by the resources (Pieroni et al., 2021).

Finally, value-charging decoupling involves breaking the links between value-creating and value-charging activities, in essence, letting customers enjoy certain activities free of charge. This type of decoupling is typical for B2C digital content that offers disruptive pricing models, for example, Supercell giving mobile games for free, while charging for in-app purchases of add-on content (Leavy, 2020). Another example would be companies offering consumers free content that they previously had to pay for, such as news and music, while building their business models on alternative revenue streams (Clemons & Lang, 2003).

Building on the earlier theoretical discussion, a preliminary framework is constructed. This framework is presented in Figure 7.1.

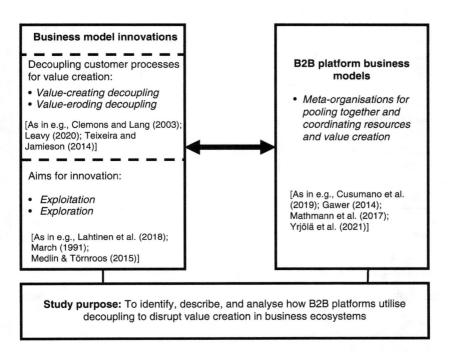

Figure 7.1 Preliminary framework for decoupling in B2B platform ecosystems.
Source: The authors.

Research Methodology

To empirically explore the value-creating and value-eroding decoupling in the context of B2B platforms, we adopted a multiple case study strategy due to its potential to achieve a holistic – yet reasonably detailed – real-life understanding of the fragmented research phenomenon under study (Eisenhardt, 1989; Stake, 2005). We utilised qualitative interview data generated from several Finnish knowledge-intensive enterprises as part of a research project focusing on B2B sales in the digital and ecosystem era between 2019 and 2021. The interviews were conducted with enterprise representatives all of whom either held executive positions or otherwise had decision-making authority on activities related to the firm's platform business at the time the interviews were held. All interviews were conducted online, recorded and then transcribed.

For this study, the enterprise cases were selected based on the following criteria. First, because of the previous research emphasis on large B2C companies, we decided to use the definition of SMEs followed by the European Union (European Commission, 2003) and chose only those knowledge-intensive enterprises that are SMEs and operating in the B2B

104   *Mika Yrjölä et al.*

market. We also focused solely on firms that have their own digital platform or provide products/services to their business customers' digital platforms. Finally, we only selected those firms that were perceived by the authors of this chapter to strongly exhibit instances of the business model innovation of decoupling. Therefore, those firms that were identified as only providing comprehensive solutions for customers were omitted from further investigation. The resulting 14 enterprise cases, anonymised for reasons of confidentiality, are summarised in Table 7.1.

The analysis and interpretation process of the transcribed interviews was highly iterative, including both separate and joint activities of data coding, sorting and writing. The process started with a meeting where all authors of

Table 7.1 Summary of the cases and conducted interviews

Case enterprise (year founded)	Industry (turnover in million Euros, no. of employees in 2020)	Interviewee's position	Date of the interview (duration of interview)
Alpha (2015)	Software/AI (0.7 M€, 7)	Head of Business Development	25 May 2020 (01:07:31)
Beta (2019)	Business Consultancy (0.1 M€, 1)	Chief Executive Officer	17 December 2021 (01:01:34)
Gamma (2016)	Software/Industrial IoT (2.3 M€, 25)	Chief Executive Officer	26 May 2020 (01:00:59)
Delta (1998)	Software/Industrial IoT (0.4 M€, 13)	Chief Executive Officer	27 May 2020 (01:02:43)
Epsilon (2017)	IT Consultancy (1.9 M€, 18)	Chief Executive Officer	12 November 2021 (01:07:57)
Zeta (2013)	Business Consultancy (0.3 M€, 6)	Chief Executive Officer & Partner	10 February 2021 (00:49:50)
Eta (1990)	Construction/ Consultancy (2.3 M€, 29)	Chief Executive Officer	11 December 2019 (01:10:38)
Theta (2001)	Software/Industrial IoT (1.8 M€, 24)	Chief Executive Officer	26 June 2020 (00:55:37)
Iota (2013)	Software/IT Consultancy (25.1 M€, n/d)	Chief Executive Officer	11 November 2021 (00:59:54)
Kappa (2020)	IT Consultancy (n/d)	Chief Executive Officer	12 February 2021 (00:52:28)
Lambda (2017)	IT Consultancy (4.5 M€, 19)	Chief Executive Officer	10 March 2021 (00:58:25)
Mu (2013)	Cleantech/Consultancy (0.2 M€, 6)	Chief Executive Officer	21 February 2020 (01:08:01)
Nu (2011)	Software (n/d)	Chief Executive Officer	27 February 2020 (00:52:46)
Xi (2015)	Software/IT Consultancy (0.6 M€, 12)	Chief Executive Officer	21 February 2020 (00:56:54)

Source: The authors.

Note: n/d = no data; IoT = Internet of Things.

this chapter discussed the relevancy of the enterprise cases in terms of assessing the suitability of the generated interview data for exploring value-creating and value-eroding activities taking place in B2B platforms. This discussion was facilitated by the authors' preunderstanding of the data, as some of them have been utilised in joint scientific publications (Mattila, Yrjölä & Hautamäki, 2021; Yrjölä, Hokkanen & Saarijärvi, 2021). In this meeting, the authors made a preliminary identification of the different customer processes that the digital platforms were changing or replacing.

After the first joint meeting, the second and third authors read the transcriptions separately and marked interesting aspects related to value-creating and value-eroding decoupling in digital B2B platforms. These markings and related data excerpts were then jointly discussed with the purpose of identifying and detailing the key themes. Thematic analysis was adopted because of its flexible orientation to coding and the development of themes (Braun & Clarke, 2006). The subsequent detailed analysis included several joint meetings during which conflicting or otherwise deviating viewpoints were openly deliberated to achieve commonly agreed understanding of the key themes. This phase can be seen as a convergence mode of triangulation (Farquhar, Michels & Robson, 2020) wherein subjective views and interpretations were contrasted to clarify the findings. Finally, the analysis resulted in the identification of several key themes related to value-creating and value-eroding decoupling in B2B platforms that are discussed in the next section.

Findings

Focusing on the adoption and the use of digital platforms by the case enterprises and their customer companies, our data analysis identifies four key themes for value-creating decoupling in B2B platforms: Supporting operational decision-making, searching information and assessing alternatives, predicting maintenance needs and enabling supplier network relationships and three key themes for value-eroding decoupling: Offering pre-made digital B2B platforms, digitalising previously physical activities and enabling efficient competence and expertise sourcing. These seven identified key themes are elaborated in the following section.

Value-Creating Decoupling

The analysis demonstrates that digital B2B platforms are currently replacing several activities in customer processes and, consequently, disrupting existing value creation logics. The analysis highlights such value-creating decoupling activities where digital platforms are adopted and used with the aim of achieving improved performance (i.e., operational and cost) efficiencies. Thus, decoupling in a B2B market involves more than focusing on one or more of customers' purchasing and consumption activities

106   *Mika Yrjölä et al.*

(cf. Leavy, 2020; Teixeira & Jamieson, 2014). In particular, the data analysis identifies supporting operational decision-making; searching information and assessing alternatives; predicting maintenance needs; and enabling supplier network relationships as the key themes for value-creating decoupling in digital B2B platforms. These four key themes are discussed next.

Supporting Operational Decision-Making

The first identified theme of value-creating decoupling is the ability of the digital platforms to *support operational decision-making*. According to our data analysis, this support occurs through two main mechanisms: By providing data to customers that they cannot themselves produce, or improving customers' data usage.

Regarding the first mechanism, the majority of interviewees reported how they are targeting customers who are now either running or planning different digitalisation projects and, consequently, are willing to invest in advancing data-driven decision-making in their organisations. The following excerpt exemplifies customers' needs for improved data usage in operational decision-making:

> *In one production site, we managed to improve the production lead time by over 3% by verifying from data where they had a bottleneck in production. They thought that it would be somewhere else. Well, we collected data from the entire line of industrial robots, and then we managed to see from data and factually show that 'this is your bottleneck. Fixing this would increase your lead time 3% on an annualised rate'. (Beta)*

Several interviewees also emphasised that their platforms are facilitating the production of (visual and/or textual) data for their customers. Depending on the customers' needs, data are generated from the customers' internal systems or derived using their own, partners' and/or public sources. The interviewees perceived these data to be valuable for their customers when making production-related decisions as in the case of manufacturing where different platform solutions enable customers to, for example, *"see an average reliability percentage of deliveries ... you can utilise aggregated data [formed from all firms using the case enterprise's platform] in setting up new factories"* (Kappa), *"monitor a pump, compressor, railroad track, or other device"* (Delta), *"collect automatically and continually data from big machines and devices"* (Theta) or *"bring several parameters to production decisions that are currently limited to product price"* (Kappa). Also, data were considered valuable for marketing communication-related decisions and decisions concerning end customers' consumption experiences, as illustrated in the following quote:

> *For example, shopping malls are fiercely competing [in a certain area of Finland]. They want to track what is said about them in social media. This*

Value-creating and Value-eroding Decoupling in B2B Platforms 107

kind of data are valuable for them. They can use that to change activities in some ways, be that marketing or other communication, or even update how they guide people in shopping malls. (Epsilon)

With respect to the second mechanism of improving customers' data usage, some case enterprises especially highlighted customers who are willing to *"move away from these kinds of purely technical discussions and focus more on how these [platforms] can be utilised"* (Beta). These customers were perceived as being able to not only generate such data but also utilise them to improve their operational performance. The excerpt below by Beta exemplifies the perceived importance of data usage in operational decision-making processes:

The value of AI is not that you know what happened last time – historical knowledge – but that you can tell how much you are going to sell next month with existing selling activities or how much you will lose sales because you have X number of internal meetings that take away time from serving your clients. I mean, if you only use data for verifying that things are going well or what has happened in the past ... competitiveness comes from understanding that if 20% of our internal meetings would be removed from our management model, it would leave this number of more hours to our sales efforts and serving clients. Or, based on data, we can estimate that minimizing 25% of our internal meetings we can increase our turnover by 25% because of this and that within this time frame. (Beta)

Also, enterprises are providing advanced technological solutions such as AI to B2B platforms that allow customer companies to improve their data usage. The following interview excerpt exemplifies this notion:

We make the customer's data more valuable. They have data on experts; we improve its usage. To speed up and improve recruitment processes, I mean, we enable higher quality searches so that it would not be subjective and based on human labour. You know, less searches based on human eyes and more machine-based, objective results, and then the human can still look at it. Their business will be more effective, remarkably faster, and the search results are much better. We improve the quality of data through machine-based operations. (Alpha)

Searching Information and Assessing Alternatives

The second identified theme, *searching information and assessing alternatives*, focuses on how digital platforms enable more effective information search and related assessments. From our data, we could see that the digital platform solutions offered by Alpha, Iota, Lambda and Xi were facilitating customers' information search and related assessments in the areas of innovation and business development, expertise recruitment and competence development, and customer/firm contacts and improved customer experiences. Using the

108   *Mika Yrjölä et al.*

case firms' B2B platforms, customers were able to access various private and public data sources, pool information based on their current or envisioned needs, and assess the alternatives. Hence, the digital platforms provide effective means for customers, for example, to "*intelligently connect actors and data that flow between them*" (Beta), "*enable them to become more agile in their operations*" (Lambda) and acquire "*strategic market insights*" (Xi).

Further, with the digital platforms, customers are able to not only pool information based on their current situation or needs but also generate an outlook for their near future. This future-oriented information search and its ability to provide feasible alternatives is illustrated in the following excerpt:

> *It [case enterprise's platform] has a machine learning algorithm, which starts searching companies with similar information ... This features different models, so by experimenting and finding the right way to search and find actors that fit the firms' current situation ... we can now provide a little outlook around the corner, to future, I mean, what companies may need within half a year from now. ... It is valuable that we can see what they need in the next year or half a year to come ... Data processing is evolving in a direction where we dive deeper into customer relationships. We go to customer's own data, and we will enrich it further ... if we see, for example, that [a large multinational company] wants to build a research centre in [place], we can search information about existing [schools] whether they can provide the needed training. (Lambda)*

Predicting Maintenance Needs

In the third identified theme, *predicting maintenance needs*, value-creating decoupling takes place when an anticipation phase included in the maintenance processes of production is replaced by real-time data analytics that digital platforms provide to customer companies via, for example, technologies that are integrated into customers' production systems. Overall, several of the case enterprises are currently providing cutting-edge data expertise to their customer companies facilitating the digitalisation of existing business processes. This concerns, for example, scalable industrial Internet of Things (IoT) platform solutions for manufacturing companies to "*move from an old-fashioned automation to this kind of futuristic architecture*" (Gamma). While facilitating customer efforts for "*digitalising the whole knowledge surface*" (Eta), our analysis shows that data produced by platform solutions enable the generation of more detailed and accurate estimates of customers' maintenance needs and, consequently, improve customers' asset management. The following excerpts from the interviews exemplify this observation:

> *Our platform aims to maximise machine health. Instead of speaking about maintenance control, we speak about lifecycle governance ... what needs to be done, who needs to do it, and when? The idea is to simplify the task so that the device gets appropriate maintenance, care, and attention when it is needed and*

then we can ensure that it does not break down. ... *The resulting measured value is that the device produces more, runs optimally, lasts longer and doesn't break down too early. Basically 90% of all breakdowns can be traced to operator or human error. We can remove these. ... We speak about a change of logic in the [maintenance] process, you don't need to go to that machine but, instead, we produce remote consultation and automation. ... digital platforms take ready-made digital data and start mining them.* (Delta)

One [use case] is based on this kind of IoT data. If an abnormal situation emerges ... an alert will follow. ... So, we send a message that now this kind of abnormality has occurred. This message is for an administrator that 'Hey, now you should go and see it, your machines may break in a moment'. A threshold value has been exceeded. (Epsilon)

Enabling Supplier Network Relationships

The fourth identified theme, *enabling supplier network relationships*, focuses on the ability of digital platforms to support long-term network relationships of business actors operating on the platforms. Hence, and besides replacing certain processes included in supply chain management such as supplier scouting, digital platforms can support leveraging collective strength in the form of long-term supplier network maintenance. As the data expert given below illustrates, this can occur when companies not only enrol their supplier partners to digital platforms and interact with them on the platforms but also receive more refined information (produced by the digital platforms) that further assist their efforts in developing and maintaining fruitful supply network relationships:

We embarked with the thought that marketplace and platform functionality are not the primary drivers in a manufacturing context. Instead, they need to smoothly work as built-in and integrated with supply chain functionalities and tools. Therefore, we started with giving tools that these professionals need so they can effectively handle their own purchasing and production chains and collaborate with their partners. This collaboration is, in a way, the marketplace function, I mean, if you collaborate with existing partners, well that's not a marketplace, it's a closed system. On [the platform] you can collaborate both with your existing partners and all other companies that can be found on it ... you bring your existing suppliers to it, you are not replacing or changing your suppliers, you just get a better tool to manage existing suppliers and compare them. At the same time, it forms data from them – key performance indicators from every firm. (Kappa)

Value-Eroding Decoupling

Four case firms (Iota, Mu, Nu and Zeta) utilised value-eroding decoupling in their operations. In the analysis, three different themes for value-eroding

110   *Mika Yrjölä et al.*

decoupling were identified: (1) Offering pre-made digital B2B platforms, (2) digitalising previously physical activities and (3) enabling efficient competence and expertise sourcing. These three themes are elaborated next.

Offering Pre-made Digital B2B Platforms

In the first identified theme, *offering pre-made digital B2B platforms*, value-eroding decoupling is utilised to reduce customers' sacrifice of time and their need for specific resources, such as IT capabilities and coding. Traditionally, firms that have wanted to set up their own digital B2B platform have had to do it ab initio. This requires specific capabilities and resource-heavy activities such as planning and testing the architecture and coding the platform. Two case enterprises (Zeta and Mu) cater to this need with white label offerings (i.e., offerings that can be rebranded by other companies). They thus decouple the link between sacrifices needed to set up a digital B2B platform and the value involved in running a platform business model:

> *We have built this ... platform, which can meet the different situations and needs of our customers. Our customers want to build a digital education business through a ready-made platform. Currently, the business situation is that we are selling our own educational programmes through this platform, and we are also selling the platform itself. For example, we are building an entire training program with a customer service consulting company for their needs on the platform. (Zeta)*

Digitalising Previously Physical Activities

In the second identified theme, *digitalising previously physical activities*, value-eroding decoupling occurs in a rather analogous form compared to the example of Steam discussed in the theoretical part of this chapter (Leavy, 2020). Two of the firms base their business on digital learning, meaning they are decoupling the link of time and place constraints of traditional teaching by offering impactful teaching through a digital platform. Naturally, digital learning as such is not a novel idea. However, what makes these cases interesting is that both these organisations have also been able to include the pedagogical and social aspects of learning, essential in traditional face-to-face learning, into the digital platform environment, thus providing the benefits of traditional face-to-face teaching but at the same time removing the time and place demands. Furthermore, the firms have been able to enrich the learning experience with digital tools such as tracking individual learning.

> *If you think about digital learning, it is done extremely poorly globally. And usually, it means taking classroom material and storing it on some digital platform, whatever it is. And then it doesn't matter if it [the teaching material]*

Value-creating and Value-eroding Decoupling in B2B Platforms 111

is lying somewhere in Moodle or Dropbox or something because if it doesn't have any pedagogical service design, you only have the same material in a new channel. And that will not deliver any results. The biggest problems with digital learning are that there is no support, no guidance, and no social interaction. If it's done from an administrative perspective, then it doesn't focus on the learning itself. And in a way, this kind of online pedagogical perspective is very often missing. (Nu)

Enabling Efficient Competence and Expertise Sourcing

In the third identified theme, *enabling efficient competence and expertise sourcing*, value-eroding decoupling occurs in the field of recruitment. Two of the case enterprises (Iota and Mu) base their business logic on detaching the link between traditional sacrifices related to sourcing experts and specific competencies (e.g., time, money and uncertainty) and successful recruitments by offering a B2B platform that enables finding a suitable expert with one click:

Our business idea was born. There is a need for a digital platform that can effectively bring together the know-how of experts and different solutions that meet various customer needs. ... we started as a networked expert organisation to solve those challenges. Previously, we worked as a consultancy firm that has a network of experts and links them with problems. In this linking, we utilised our platform as it was at the time to find the right experts. The platform also has the possibility to bring the customers, their problems, and their stakeholders together. ... But this has probably been the main idea all along, that we've been thinking how much more efficient and faster you can be, how can we scale and solve these global challenges. ... ow for 6 years we have been developing our own solution and technology platform for this problem, so that customers' problems can be solved more effectively by bringing the right experts from different organisations and companies around the problem, and we act as an intermediary in it. (Mu)

In addition to making sourcing for expertise easier and faster, the platform solutions utilise algorithms and AI to provide even more efficient "matchmaking" services for customer companies and experts. For instance, one firm offers two sets of intelligent search engines for differing needs. On the digital platform, the customer may search for experts using the basic "Tinder-like" search or the more advanced "engineering-like" search, which allows for more precise search terms.

There will be two versions of the [search engine]. One very easy to use, light, 'Tinder-like' and one 'engineering' version ... [In the Tinder-like version] you can search using, for example, one keyword. The keyword can be a role, a skill, an industry – whatever. So, you can with one keyword just click and search and that's it. And then in the engineering version, there are fields that can be filled from location to starting date. Then if you take Java coding experience as an example, there will be two more footnotes, one for years of experience, meaning what is sought and wanted, and another one for weight, meaning if this [Java experience] is necessary, nice to have, or something in between. So, it is very easy to use, more refined, and based largely on the parameters that we have seen during the 10 years of dealing with these assignments [finding experts]. In some cases, weighting is very important, and you need to be able to express them [weights], and of course, the more accurate the search specs are, the better matches you can get. (Iota)

In sum, the aforementioned analysis and accompanying data quotations illustrate how B2B platforms utilise decoupling to disrupt value creation in business ecosystems.

Discussion and Conclusions

This chapter set out to analyse how B2B platforms utilise value-creating and value-eroding decoupling to disrupt value creation in business ecosystems. Theoretically, the chapter is founded on the literature on business model decoupling, value creation and B2B platforms. Empirically, we utilised 14 case studies of Finnish SMEs that offer knowledge-intensive business services through their own or partnering platforms. Based on the qualitative interview data generated, we identified and analysed seven types of decoupling used by the analysed enterprises. Four of these themes related to value-creating decoupling in B2B platforms: Supporting operational decision-making, searching information and assessing alternatives, predicting maintenance needs, and enabling supplier network relationships. The remaining three themes involved value-eroding decoupling: Offering pre-made digital B2B platforms, digitalising previously physical activities and enabling efficient competence and expertise sourcing. The analyses of these themes spark interesting contributions and implications.

First, this chapter contributes to the studies of decoupling by extending them into the B2B context. Our findings demonstrate how decoupling is a more complex phenomenon in the B2B context compared to B2C markets. In consumer markets, decoupling takes on simpler forms because consumers' value-creating processes themselves are relatively simple when compared to how businesses create value for themselves. The value-eroding and value-creating decoupling innovations identified in this study therefore target relatively broad areas of customer processes, involving multiple interconnected activities (e.g., predicting maintenance needs by monitoring production machinery).

Second, our study highlights how decoupling is a useful lens for analysing digital platforms. It moves beyond the notions of intermediation and disintermediation and suggests a more nuanced understanding of the ways in

Value-creating and Value-eroding Decoupling in B2B Platforms 113

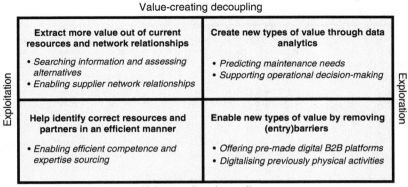

Figure 7.2 Decoupling in B2B platforms.
Source: The authors.

which digital platforms can disrupt competition and value creation. For instance, while some of the findings of this chapter highlight the role of platforms in matchmaking (e.g., enabling efficient competence and expertise sourcing), others involve maintaining long-term relationships, improving decision-making and operations using data, and using platforms to digitalise physical activities.

Third, the seven types of decoupling identified in the analysis provide a useful starting point for future research into value creation in business ecosystems. Based on our analysis and reflection of the findings, we put forth a framework for decoupling in B2B platforms, which is shown in Figure 7.2.

As shown in the framework, some types of decoupling clearly fall under exploitation strategies, while others rely more on exploration (March, 1991). Decoupling that relies on exploitation involve efficiently using existing resources and network relationships (Medlin & Törnroos, 2015).

Moreover, based on a reflection of our findings, we put forth the research agenda in Table 7.2.

Managerial Implications

The findings of this chapter, together with the framework in Figure 7.2, provide implications for managers operating in B2B ecosystems. Managers already operating in the digital platform business or contemplating entry can use the framework as a starting point for strategic discussions. Further, incumbents suspecting that parts of their value creation might be decoupled by start-ups can use the framework to anticipate possible moves by the competition. As the framework illustrates, value-creating and value-eroding decoupling can be used to drive an exploitation or an exploration strategy.

114   *Mika Yrjölä et al.*

Table 7.2 Research agenda

Research area	Description	Research questions
Underlying mechanisms of decoupling	While decoupling is a useful lens and a tool for business model innovation, its usefulness is clearly dependent on context (some customer activities and processes are easier to decouple than others). Many of the findings of this chapter involve the use of data and analytics as a driving mechanism for decoupling. It would be valuable to understand these contextual factors more systematically.	• Which contextual factors act as drivers for or barriers to decoupling? Are these factors different for B2B and B2C markets? • What moderating variables can be identified? • Through which mechanisms do companies successfully decouple customer activities and processes?
Decoupling in digital platforms	It should be noted that there are different types of digital platforms (e.g., transaction platforms and innovation platforms). Digital platforms bring together multiple types of actors, which can have different implications for the mechanisms of decoupling.	• How does the type of platform used affect decoupling? Do different types of decoupling (i.e., value-creating or value-eroding) work better with certain types of platforms? • How can decoupling be used as a way to understand value creation for different platform actors and stakeholders?
Temporal lens to decoupling	Decoupling represents one way in which digital transformation is changing competition, but there are no long-term studies on decoupling. Further, the SMEs and start-ups studied in this research have limited resources and it is uncertain whether their decoupling innovations will prove to be successful or not.	• For businesses utilising decoupling, do their value creation broaden or focus over time? • Is decoupling a successful innovation for B2B platforms in the long term or does it represent just one phase in the evolution of these enterprises?

Source: The authors.

Four approaches are suggested in the framework. First, in terms of exploitation, companies can use digital platforms to *extract more value out of current resources and network relationships*, thus improving the efficiency of value creation. Second, value-eroding decoupling can be used to drive an exploitation strategy by *helping to identify correct resources and partners in an efficient manner*, thus automating the labour-intensive parts of value creation. Third, value-creating decoupling can be used in an exploratory manner to *create new types of value through data analytics*. In our analysis, we noted how the data generated on digital platforms represent an untapped source of potential growth and innovation. Fourth, companies can leverage value-eroding decoupling to *enable new types of value by removing (entry) barriers*. Many businesses can potentially be digitalised through the use of modular/white label digital platforms.

Limitations

While the SME context provides a novel environment for studying the decoupling phenomenon, it can also act as a limitation. Most of the case enterprises are tech start-ups, which means they are experimenting with multiple forms of value creation to find a sustainable profit model. Therefore, the business model innovations identified in this chapter are not proven and tested, but instead their viability will be shown over time.

Acknowledgement

The work in this chapter is also part of the ROBINS research project, funded by Business Finland 2019–2022 (document number 7885/31/2018).

References

Amit, R. & Zott, C. (2001). "Value creation in E-business", *Strategic Management Journal*, vol. 22(6–7), pp. 493–520.

Amit, R. & Zott, C. (2012). "Creating value through business model innovation", *MIT Sloan Management Review*, vol. 53(3), pp. 41–49.

Arend, R.J. (2013). "The business model: Present and future—beyond a skeumorph", *Strategic Organization*, vol. 11(4), pp. 390–402.

Braun, V. & Clarke, V. (2006). "Using thematic analysis in psychology", *Qualitative Research in Psychology*, vol. 3(2), pp. 77–101.

Clemons, E.K. & Lang, K.R. (2003). "The decoupling of value creation from revenue: A strategic analysis of the markets for pure information goods", *Information Technology and Management*, vol. 4(2), pp. 259–287.

Crittenden, A.B., Crittenden, V.L., & Crittenden, W.F. (2017). "Industry transformation via channel disruption", *Journal of Marketing Channels*, vol. 24(1–2), pp. 13–26.

Cusumano, M.A., Gawer, A., & Yoffie, D.B. (2019). *The Business of Platforms: Strategy in the Age of Digital Competition, Innovation, and Power.* New York: Harper Business.

Dawar, N. (2013). "When marketing is strategy", *Harvard Business Review*, vol. 91(12), pp. 100–108.

Doganova, L. & Eyquem-Renault, M. (2009). "What do business models do?" *Research Policy*, vol. 38(10), pp. 1559–1570.

Eisenhardt, K.M. (1989). "Building theories from case study research", *Academy of Management Review*, vol. 14(4), pp. 532–550.

European Commission (2003). "European Commission recommendation 2003/361/EC of 6 May 2003 concerning the definition of micro, small and medium-sized enterprises", *Official Journal of the European Union*, vol. 124, pp. 36–41.

116 *Mika Yrjölä et al.*

Farquhar, J., Michels, N., & Robson, J. (2020). "Triangulation in industrial qualitative case study research: Widening the scope", *Industrial Marketing Management*, vol. 87, pp. 160–170.

Gawer, A. (2014). "Bridging differing perspectives on technological platforms: Toward an integrative framework", *Research Policy*, vol. 43(7), pp. 1239–1249.

Gawer, A. & Cusumano, M. (2014). "Industry platforms and ecosystem innovation", *Journal of Product Innovation Management*, vol. 31(3), pp. 417–433.

Gensler, S., Neslin, S.A., & Verhoef, P.C. (2017). "The showrooming phenomenon: It's more than just about price", *Journal of Interactive Marketing*, vol. 38, pp. 29–43.

Hagiu, A. & Wright, J. (2013). "Do you really want to be an eBay?" *Harvard Business Review*, vol. 91(3), pp. 102–108.

Hagiu, A. & Wright, J. (2015). "Multi-sided platforms", *International Journal of Industrial Organization*, vol. 43, pp. 162–174.

Haucap, J. & Heimeshoff, U. (2014). "Google, Facebook, Amazon, eBay: Is the internet driving competition or market monopolization?" *International Economics and Economic Policy*, vol. 11(1–2), pp. 49–61.

Hokkanen, H., Hänninen, M., Yrjölä, M., & Saarijärvi, H. (2021). "From customer to actor value propositions: An analysis of digital platforms", *The International Review of Retail, Distribution, and Consumer Research*, vol. 31(3), pp. 257–280.

Lahtinen, S., Kuusela, H., & Yrjölä, M. (2018). "The company in society: When corporate responsibility transforms strategy", *Journal of Business Strategy*, vol. 39(4), pp. 11–18.

Leavy, B. (2020). "Decoupling: Customer-centric perspectives on disruption and competitive advantage", *Strategy and Leadership*, vol. 48(1), pp. 3–11.

Magretta, J. (2002). "Why business models matter", *Harvard Business Review*, vol. 80(5), pp. 86–92.

March, J.G. (1991). "Exploration and exploitation in organizational learning", *Organization Science*, vol. 2(1), pp. 71–87.

Mathmann, F., Chylinski, M., de Ruyter, K., & Higgins, E. (2017). "When plentiful platforms pay off: Assessment orientation moderates the effect of assortment size on choice engagement and product valuation", *Journal of Retailing*, vol. 93(2), pp. 212–227.

Mattila, M., Mesiranta, N., & Heikkinen, A. (2020). "Platform-based sustainable business models: Reducing food waste in food services", *International Journal of Entrepreneurship and Innovation Management*, vol. 24(4/5), pp. 249–265.

Mattila, M., Yrjölä, M., & Hautamäki, P. (2021). "Digital transformation of business-to-business sales: What needs to be unlearned?" *Journal of Personal Selling & Sales Management*, vol. 41(2), pp. 113–129.

Mattila, M., Yrjölä, M., & Lehtimäki, H. (2019). "Drivers and barriers to networked commercialization: Business model perspective", *International Journal of Entrepreneurship and Innovation Management*, vol. 23(5), pp. 479–495.

McIntyre, D.P. & Srinivasan, A. (2017). "Networks, platforms, and strategy: Emerging views and next steps", *Strategic Management Journal*, vol. 38(1), pp. 141–160.

Medlin, C.J. & Törnroos, J.Å. (2015). "Exploring and exploiting network relationships to commercialize technology: A biofuel case", *Industrial Marketing Management*, vol. 49, pp. 42–52.

Mody, M., Wirtz, J., So, K.K.F., Chun, H.H., & Liu, S.Q. (2020). "Two-directional convergence of platform and pipeline business models", *Journal of Service Management*, vol. 31(4), pp. 693–721.

Ondrus, J., Gannamaneni, A., & Lyytinen, K. (2015). "The Impact of openness on the market potential of multi-sided platforms: A case study of mobile payment platforms", *Journal of Information Technology*, vol. 30(3), pp. 260–275.

Osterwalder, A. & Pigneur, Y. (2010). *Business Model Generation: A Handbook for Visionaries, Game Changers, and Challengers*. Hoboken, NJ: John Wiley.

Papies, D. & van Heerde, H.J. (2017). "The dynamic interplay between recorded music and live concerts: The role of piracy, unbundling, and artist characteristics", *Journal of Marketing*, vol. 81(4), pp. 67–87.

Parente, R.C., Geleilate, J.M.G., & Rong, K. (2018). "The sharing economy globalization phenomenon: A research agenda", *Journal of International Management*, vol. 24(1), pp. 52–64.

Parker, G., Van Alstyne, M., & Jiang, X. (2017). "Platform ecosystems: How developers invert the firm", *MIS Quarterly*, vol. 41(1), pp. 570–583.

Pieroni, M.P., McAloone, T.C., Borgianni, Y., Maccioni, L., & Pigosso, D.C. (2021). "An expert system for circular economy business modelling: Advising manufacturing companies in decoupling value creation from resource consumption", *Sustainable Production and Consumption*, vol. 27, pp. 534–550.

Richardson, J. (2008). "The business model: An integrative framework for strategy execution", *Strategic Change*, vol. 17(5–6), pp. 133–144.

Shafer, S., Smith, H., & Linder, J. (2005). "The power of business models", *Business Horizons*, vol. 48(3), pp. 199–207.

Stake, R.E. (2005). "Qualitative case studies", in N.K. Denzin & Y.S. Lincoln (Eds.), *The Sage Handbook of Qualitative Research*, 3rd ed. Thousand Oaks, CA: Sage Publications, 443–466.

Teece, D. (2010). "Business models, business strategy and innovation", *Long Range Planning*, vol. 43(2–3), pp. 172–194.

Teixeira, T.S. & Jamieson, P. (2014). *The Decoupling Effect of Digital Disruptors*, Working Paper No. 15-031. Boston, MA: Harvard Business School Press.

Thomas, L., Autio, E., & Gann, D. (2014). "Architectural leverage: Putting platforms in context", *Academy of Management Perspectives*, vol. 28(2), pp. 198–219.

Timmers, P. (1998). "Business models for electronic markets", *Electronic Markets*, vol. 8(2), pp. 3–8.

Van Alstyne, M.W., Parker, G.G., & Choudary, S.P. (2016). "Pipelines, platforms, and the new rules of strategy", *Harvard Business Review*, vol. 94(4), pp. 54–62.

Yrjölä, M. (2014). "Value creation challenges in multichannel retail business models", *Journal of Business Models*, vol. 2(1), pp. 89–104.

Yrjölä, M., Hokkanen, H., & Saarijärvi, H. (2021). "A typology of second-hand business models", *Journal of Marketing Management*, vol. 37(7–8), pp. 761–791.

Yrjölä, M., Mattila, M., Hautamäki, P., & Mikkonen, M. (2022). "Digital platforms as disrupting business models for internationalisation", in C. Nielsen, S.T. Marinova & M.A. Marinov (Eds.), *Business Models and Firm Internationalisation*. London and New York: Routledge, 114–133.

Yrjölä, M., Spence, M.T., & Saarijärvi, H. (2018). "Omni-channel retailing: Propositions, examples and solutions", *The International Review of Retail, Distribution and Consumer Research*, vol. 28(3), pp. 259–276.

8 Critical Junctures and Their Role in Reconfiguration of Business Models and Ecosystems

Svetla T. Marinova, Marin A. Marinov, and Winfried Mueller

The Ecosystem Perspective and Business Models

The concept of ecosystem comes from biology and was first used by Arthur Tansley in 1935, who was influenced by the Danish botanist Johannes Eugenius Bülow Warming and the German scholar Alexander von Humboldt who studied the relationship between organisms and their environment (Tansley, 1947). The ecosystem understanding in biology was developed by Odum (1953) to describe an ecosystem (originating from the Greek word *oikos*, meaning house) as an ecology, as a system of interlocked communities of living and non-living organisms interacting with each other in their environment, where they compete and collaborate for obtainable resources, they change and co-evolve to grow, adapt, merge or die in adapting to external disruptions. This concept has been adopted in business research to argue that companies are interlocked in communities and do not exist as individual firms in an industry, rather they are members of a business ecosystem with actors that can span several industries (Moore, 1993). Subsequently, this idea was extended to address the stages in the development of business ecosystems, i.e., pioneering, expansion, authority and renewal, and the key leadership challenges faced respectively in each stage, including value definition, achieving maximum market coverage, lead vision that can inspire the co-evolution with customers and suppliers, and performance improvement through innovation (for details, see Moore, 1996, p. 83). What makes such an ecosystem thinking interesting is that the ecosystem organisms collaborate and compete to allow the ecosystem to achieve continuous development, simultaneously protecting itself from other ecosystems with similar offers, defeat the implementation of similar ideas, define the market standard through own offers and create high entry barriers for new ecosystem entry in a market, and high customer switching costs. This thinking is aligned with the idea of Bionomics, i.e., the economy as an ecosystem, transcending ideas from biology to business organisation and underlying company dynamic interlocking systems, promoted by Rothschild (1992).

DOI: 10.4324/9781003326731-8

Thus, ecosystemic business thinking represents a higher level of analysis, the level of complex systems of interconnected and interlocked organisations in their environment with lead firms competing and collaborating with suppliers and customers, offering a vision of value proposition and innovation, aiming to achieve market dominance, and adopt protective measures against those that might have similar offers. In effect, this is a higher order complex organisation in a specific environment that strives to access limited resources. As such, business ecosystems are supposed to have their own unique business models that allow them to face critical events, to accelerate learning and make use of ideas and innovation in developing a sustained competitive advantage vis-à-vis other ecosystems. Thus, the business models of ecosystems can develop internal resilience and renewal, external resource access and market restraints, which business scholars are still to explore. Within this argument, we recognise that the understanding of business models on firm level is much better conceptually developed compared to the comprehension of ecosystem business models.

Business models have so far been mostly used with reference to individual firms that create, deliver and capture value (Davenport, Leibold & Voelpel, 2006; Gassmann, Frankenberger & Csik, 2014; Taran et al., 2016, Nielsen et al., 2018; Nielsen, Marinova & Marinov, 2022). The unit of business model analysis is the firm and there is a general agreement that firm business models may be various, but they are configured by core dimensions (Taran et al., 2016; Zott, Amit & Massa, 2011). For example, Osterwalder, Pigneur and Tucci (2005) suggest a business model ontology that includes several business model blocs. Taran et al. (2016) have developed the understanding of the five value dimensions configuring a business model. Johnson, Christensen and Kagermann (2008) focus on value proposition, profit formula, key resources and key processes, whereas Wirtz et al. (2015) identify common blocs in business model configuration studies, which are strategic, customer, market and value creation. The business model of a firm is therefore a configuration of elements that allows a firm to develop and implement its strategy and create a unique competitive position. However, Demil and Lecocq (2010) argue that business model configurations are dynamic, as business model reconfiguration reflects the changing interplay between the building blocks, enabling companies to adapt to changing environmental conditions caused by critical junctures.

The Nature of Critical Junctures

Critical junctures have been explored by scholars with a different disciplinary research interest. For example, critical junctures have been used in comparative historical analysis to explore the origins and development of institutions, the activities inherent to implementing institutional change, and its effects on the socio-political environment in a particular context (Capoccia, 2015; Capoccia & Kelemen, 2007; Shapiro & Bedi, 2006). Development of society throughout history is thus analysed by recognising the duality of development that is founded on the alterations of change and stability periods, whereby critical junctures act as triggers of change. Such an argument, that applies to institutions and societies in research of political scientists and sociologists, assumes that critical events are relevant when there is path dependency as the outcomes of critical junctures (Soifer, 2012) lead to provisions shaping a behaviour that becomes entrenched over a time period and provides stability or space for some adaptations. This also means that critical events are inherently associated with agency, choice and action by principal actors.

In a broader sense, institutions are forms of organisation and it means that the organisation studies literature delves into understanding critical junctures. However, apart from applying critical juncture analysis only in cases of path dependency, scholars also explore the emergence of new organisational fields whereby the very process of emergence is triggered by institutional actors and emergence is considered a process with its specific critical junctures, engaged institutional and other social actors, and entrepreneurial activities they perform (Child, Lu & Tsai, 2007). In this case, critical junctures not only trigger but also accelerate and enable the appearance of new organisational fields required by socio-economic development. The key ingredients here are also agency, choice and action that can create a new space enabling stability.

Business research has also drawn upon existing paradigms on critical events with the 2007 subprime mortgage collapse in the US real estate that led to the subsequent financial crisis. The notion of a Black Swan event is of an event that is unexpected, rare, with extreme impact, and usually rationalised in hindsight (Taleb, 2007). The term was pinned down emphasising the precariousness of any economic system and the recognition that impossible events might occur to disrupt an established system. In this sense, unpredictable events as Black Swans may be unexpected by many thinkers, but this may be a misconception as process developments and data leading to the critical event may well be existent, and at least foreseen to an extent by people with broader historical, economic and social system knowledge, although the temporal dimension of such events may not be easy to predict. In the first few days of January 2007, one of the co-authors of this chapter attended a conference on risk management in firms that took place in London and was approached by a US financial expert who told him that a global financial crisis was eminent, and it would start with the collapse of the housing market in the United States. None were mentioning the threat of such a critical juncture, yet. In May that year, at a management training workshop with the participation of managers and owners of real estate and production companies they were in utter disbelief that such a critical juncture would ever occur as their businesses were running strong. They laughed off the warning that was given to them. Consequently, many of the participating companies collapsed a year later or so under the effects of the subsequent global financial crisis. Therefore, we align our thinking on Black Swan events with that of Taleb who warns that the ability to mitigate the effects of such critical junctures depends on the observer (Webb, 2008) and their capacity to listen to and process unconventional views. Overall, such big events are indeed largely unexpected and with an overwhelming impact, with the so-called effect of the unknown that goes against anything known before, at least within the specificity of the dominant mental models in a socio-economic and business system, and more specifically, with reference to its temporal dimensions.

Therefore, we see critical junctures that may have a different degree of unpredictability for those who evaluate their likelihood of happening. For instance, some may argue that the collapse of the USSR was expected, others may say that the COVID-19 pandemic could be seen coming, but for the majority they were a complete surprise, something entirely unexpected and unpredictable. What is common among all these critical junctures is their scope, complexity, velocity, severity and interdependability (Schwab & Malleret, 2020; Marinov, 2021). Whereas the financial crisis disrupted and led to the decoupling of financial systems and flows, by 2017 decoupling of global trade and production flows was exacerbated, the COVID-19 global pandemic triggered decoupling of GVCs and augmented uncertainties, and the war in Ukraine has decoupled states, energy markets and overall, economic interconnectedness. As a result, such critical junctures have underlined the dual nature of business systems and have required agency, choice, and action to create new conditions for the functioning of the system players in the environment. Here, we suggest that critical events affect whole business ecosystems – their structure, processes, choices, relationships and scope and, consequently, the business models of their constituent entities.

Reconfiguration of Business Models under the Impact of the COVID-19 Critical Jolt

The size of the domestic market and the size of the foreign markets a company operates in have affected the business model and ecosystem reconfiguration under the impact of the COVID-19 jolt. Companies coming from big domestic markets and operating in big foreign markets that substantially contribute to value capture have localised production, supply and distribution, brought back to the home market their explorative innovations and expanded exploitative innovations in the host market. Generally, their key orientation has changed to their domestic market that could absorb the losses from the external jolt. Knowledge exploration has become concentrated in key markets that are within the comfort zone of the firm and aligned with the national innovation priorities of key home country institutional players. Thus, global innovation has become more decoupled and fragmented, and within the reach of ecosystems actors with market power. Firms from small open economies have also reconfigured the geographical exposure of their business models by localising production, concentrating on ensuring supply from and distribution to key big markets using them as second home market or creating an export platform for various actors in specific ecosystems with competitive innovation driven value proposition. Exploratory innovation has become more focused in the home country or in host countries with high innovation capability that can enhance the value proposition and value capture for the firm in the long term. When operating in small foreign host markets, these companies have become to rely greatly on digitalisation of exporting and importing of only key factor inputs they lack.

The consequences of the critical jolt were also somewhat varying for companies positioned differently along the global value chain (Marinova, Freeman & Marinov, 2019). For example, companies in orchestrator position that have closeness to end customers as they deliver high value through their brand/product have experienced challenges in terms of supply since their suppliers have been impacted by lockdowns and/or other companies were competing for the same supplies of raw materials and components. This has led to delays in supply, which was so much needed to create value for the end customer, as suppliers were located overseas. Furthermore, orchestrators have experienced difficulties in maintaining their supplier value network relationships due to restrictions on travel. This situation has negatively affected their product development and required some reconfiguration of product innovation actors, physical space, organisation structure and flow of communication between product development teams. The value delivery network has also been impacted negatively and forced a reconfiguration from physical stores to online sales and home deliveries, but one key consideration was not to cannibalise the already existing value segment, but to maintain it through better personalised communication for maintaining its value capture potential.

Market exploiters who rely on relationships in local value networks to target their value segment by selling imported products supplied by companies overseas suffered big impediments due to reduced connectivity with suppliers, lockdowns and social distance from customers. By comparison, companies focusing on product excellence had been dependent on suppliers to provide factor inputs of raw materials and components to produce their specialised knowledge-intensive products. Consequently, supplier selection has been adopted, where special attention is paid to supplier reliability and ease of communication, as well as geographical reconfiguration of value networks to reduce logistics distance and ensure supply stocks. The supply shortage has had a negative effect on prices and thus has affected the value that companies could capture through selling their product or supply price rises have also increased the price of the end-product, which has reduced the size of the value segment. An interesting effect of the COVID-19 pandemic is that while companies might have experienced problems in their small domestic-market value segment, in some of their big foreign markets the value segment might have been enlarged to compensate for the lost value capture in the domestic or other small foreign markets.

The critical jolt has made companies employ coping mechanisms by acting quickly to the changes in their ecosystem with solutions ranging from diversifying suppliers, using complementary value chains, or dual sourcing from alternative sourcing channels, or adopting product import substitution, which effectively meant a reconfiguration addressing the balance between efficiency and risk or rather security. Stockpiling has increased and larger investments in raw materials have been used to secure continuity of operations and value capture. Such an approach has an impact on the balance between product inventory and sales, i.e., when sales were reduced and inventory grew, delays or inability to capture value has threatened the cash flow of some companies, albeit logistics has been diversified in search of alternative ways to ensure product delivery.

Value networks have also been tested with suppliers and producers experiencing severe problems. Hence, soft issues such as mutual support, commitment, long-term agreements, strategic partnerships and delayed payments based on trust and good will have also surfaced as coping mechanisms.

One of the key changes brought by the critical jolt is product component changes to reduce supplier dependency, as well as greater focus on the domestic market and pivoting to markets that are somewhat similar in terms of value segments and securing a level-playing field (economically and politically similar). This has led to an enhanced understanding of geographic, socio-cultural and geopolitical distance and a drive towards regionalisation that is still difficult to implement as global decoupling is still in process. Moreover, while in sectors that were negatively affected by COVID-19, business models have become more focused on core value proposition and supported by lean organisational architecture, in strategic industries new business models have emerged or value propositions have been diversified and value capture has increased (for more discussion, see Arslan et al., 2021). For example, Tesar (2021) suggests that companies in the health sector did not suffer from lockdowns as they were essential in dealing with the pandemic. Moreover, firms such as Netflix, Zoom, Amazon and Alibaba, gained a competitive advantage by expanding their value proposition, value segment and value networks and captured greater value as they did not rely on complex value chains (Schwab & Malleret, 2020).

Thus overall, the critical jolt of COVID-19 has led to reconfiguration of all value constituent parts (see the 5V model; Taran et al., 2016), but more so it has driven substantive reconfiguration of the value networks, value segments and value capture, and less so in the value proposition of the firms. Moreover, companies have been diversifying their participation in value chains and defining new relationships with customers, as well as new approaches to agency, choice and action to create a new balance between efficiency and security.

124   *Svetla T. Marinova et al.*

The Challenge of Great Uncertainty

The reality of the business environment as of to-date with exponentially increased uncertainty under which companies and ecosystems face many risks, some of which are frequently experienced but not having the potential to affect business model configurations and relationships in them, while another risk might be so serious that it can challenge the very existence of the firm. The latter is the unrecognised abrupt risk triggered by a black swan event that is critical with its effect. Under such conditions, past cannot be a reliable indicator of the future, which forces companies into resilience thinking that can mitigate critical junctures of a black swan nature. We might suggest that resilience is often used in inflationary terms to indicate that companies are trying to find solutions for issues that have not existed in the past, albeit looking in the past is something that is critically needed, but it does not provide directly (ready-made) new solutions. This is very different from the types of risk when past is a reliable predictor of the future being associated with direct causality, probability that can be calculated, and predictions made based on correlations as in systemic risk – those are risks that you companies can measure or at least managers think they can measure, to make predictions of their effects for the future. Under the current decoupling of production, supply, relationships, exchange, markets and knowledge flows, whatever "measurement" is out of question.

In recent years, critical junctures have accelerated – the 2003 SARS Hong Kong, the 2007 financial crisis originating in the United States with its spill over effects causing the 2008 European sovereign crisis, the over-looked 2016 introduction of tariffs and trade restrictions, which favoured US companies and ecosystems, in 2019 the start of the COVID pandemic, in 2021 regional wars and the 2022 war in Europe that was not expected. It has a special significance with unprecedented sanctions leading to massive decoupling processes forcing major business model reconfiguration of firms all over the world.

To-date we see sudden and non-transitory inflation that is on the supply side; it is inflation that is different from the one in overheated markets which is driven by consumption. The cause of inflation can be found in the disrupted supply-demand relationships, in decoupled supply and value chains; it is demonstrated in financial and monetary aspects, but not caused by them. Inflation is a monetary phenomenon and central banks have to take action, but they are currently powerless to control inflation. Thus, companies in their ecosystems are faced with unprecedented supply chain complexities, economic cooling down coupled with stagflation, which means that whatever central banks do – increase or decrease interest rates – will be wrong. At the same time, China's Zero-COVID policy and de-coupling of global value chains initially driven by the COVID-19 pandemic have increased the cost of supplies, putting further inflationary pressure on the price of company inputs. In addition, interest rates are back in action, the military conflicts and threats are rising, sanctions, trade and investment barriers are continuously erected. It could be argued that this unprecedented inflationary pressure is somewhat artificially created – initially via COVID-19 and the subsequent policy decisions underpinned by a strive for economic supremacy and control of limited resources. While in 2020, there was still a positive effect of the energy sector that helped to reduce inflation by reducing energy prices, in 2021 – even before the war in Ukraine – and especially in 2022 energy prices have soared to unprecedented levels and continue to rise unstoppably further increasing inflation. Food prices are still to take the negative effect of energy price rise and are still contributing little to inflation, but they will be key in the next round effects to increase inflation in the future. Among the European countries, only Switzerland is in a special position with just 2.4% inflation. The strong Swiss Franc is increasing and melting away the effects of the higher energy prices, as energy prices are denominated in Euro or USD. This allows Swiss companies and their ecosystems to face the challenges in a more tempered manner and remain competitive.

Huge liquidity has been accumulated in the central and commercial banks in Europe – throughout 2020–2022 government debt has become enormous, which means that there is a lot of money around, a lot of liquidity in the markets and this money is looking for profitable investments, nevertheless investments are being inadequate. This is a direct result of the excessively low and even negative interest rates introduced by central banks across the world. Meanwhile, the picture is complemented by the cases of ships piling up at the ports of China, thus inflating the price of cargo and overall costs of logistics and production inputs. All of these create a rather poisonous system for companies that is coupled with interest rate hike. However, a hike in interest rates is not a solution as indicated earlier, as no borrower will want to take money on credit and although lenders could be willing to lend money. Financing for companies will become more expensive not only in terms of loans, but the risk premiums will also go up. The unique thing during the last decade is that the real interest has never since the last major war been so low as today, which means that even the increase of interest is outperformed by the existing inflation. The current situation with interest rates, lending and borrowing will only increase its severity for company operations

The question is how to use all this information on inflation, interest rates and the problems with supply and what this means for business models? Based on the above described, the answer to this question is a billion dollar one. Consumer price inflation is increasing now across the world, including Europe. But producer price inflation is even higher and is yet to spill over consumer price inflation as a second-round effect – the real effect is yet to be felt. Some companies with big market power will be able to pass on this inflation to customers, but the majority of companies have no or limited market power to pass on the producer inflation onto the customer. This can be called a snowball effect of ever-increasing significance. The latter firms will face an enormous problem, as 15–20% increase of the price of raw materials and other production inputs and the inability to put this inflation onto the customer will force many companies to face serious existential problems as not many profit margins can hold long onto that. At the same time, customers who can pay will do so – the rest might need to survive as they can – and this is especially valid for big multinationals and firms offering unique products.

Currently, we see that products and services are not growing in their volume and variability or if growing they do it at a very slow pace – we have trade and supply restrictions, sanctions, tariffs, while the quantity of money in circulation is high and central banks are trying to reduce the amount of money in circulation. If the velocity of consumption now increases, people will buy more as they try to pre-empt the future inflationary pressure that is eminent, companies and consumers alike will face a new round of inflationary effects that shall be seen more on the production side than on services, as the latter are mostly produced on demand. As a result, production will continuously shrink in volume – not so much in financial terms, consequently, mostly markets for goods will be massively reconfigured. So, the result will be that goods will be stored, and storage stock will temporarily increase with goods not being able to sell – and consequently we see a huge demand for increase in storage areas. The duration of this situation will be regulated quickly – this is based on the major principle of production/operations management in its part of logistics and supply chain management securing the material flows from producers to consumers.

Inflation and interest rates will progressively reduce available household income. Inflation combined with the debt has to be paid back at a higher interest rate, so banks need to think more carefully how to work with customers, although they have really very limited choices, if any – what products they have and probably they need to become more selective in terms of customers. For those with real assets – shares, real estate and debts, in the long-term inflation works well, for people on salaries or savings inflation does not work well being a form of unjust taxation – so governments will be looking at how to re-allocate and re-distribute value and assets, so the regulatory and redistributive power of government will increase, although many governments are not interested in doing that. This situation sets limits on the economy, free trade and exchange.

During the era of hyper-globalisation (Pels, 2021), many companies have invested in emerging markets in search for efficiency gains, natural resource access or market development. However, under the current environmental conditions, emerging markets are experiencing great uncertainty as they are impacted by increasing inflation and instability. The first frontier market that has already defaulted (i.e., Sri Lanka) has been under the pressure of the mix of inflation, energy and food shortages, skyrocketing costs of imports and the increase in interest rates. Previously, it was the less costly imports and inflow of US dollars that acted as a type of a booster shot allowing them to function. In addition to this, household and public sector indebtedness in emerging markets is high, which together with the aforementioned factors will create a highly impactful toxic area acting as a source of inflationary pressure coming up. Thus, business models and ecosystems that originate from or have invested in emerging markets will also be challenged to adopt major reconfiguration actions.

Geopolitics and energy resource price and availability are an immense force that will be putting a huge demand for business model reconfiguration – gas, oil and electricity are fundamental resources used by companies to operate and their unprecedented price jumps are a major problem that may drive many companies and whole ecosystems to re-think the geographical location of activities, their value networks, value segments, value configuration, value proposition and severely diminish the ability of firms for value capture. Together with the amassing pressure coming from inputs, the process of deglobalisation is forcing companies to make choices for changes in their business models, mostly impacting value segments, geographical market dispersion of activities and value networks.

What does this mean for companies?

First and foremost, companies should assume risk identification in a bigger context as any business model can only survive the above-described pressures only, if management could better comprehend and foresee, at least to an extent, what happens next. This is complicated to be dealt with, but at best there some niche knowledge exists. Mitigating risk has become a must and any business model should be reconfigured by focusing on what firms do best, their core value creating networks and value segments, and business model simplification – getting rid of those activities, processes, value segments and value networks that do not contribute to value capture.

One key approach is management to start thinking in scenarios, even in those scenarios that they may not like to happen, but they have to identify risk mitigating mechanisms. For example, what would happen in a state-interventionist war economy? Probability may be low, but if it comes true, then the business model can have the agility to absorb such an unlikely situation, be prepared and have a plan how to act.

The focus on true assets is becoming paramount for any company – a focus on core competences, digitalisation processes, staff trainings, discussion seminars on key issues and forecasted changes, training modes related to IT and digitalisation as these reduce costs, simplifies processes and control, and focuses efforts on what a company can do best. Financial approaches are now becoming less relevant, instead the business model should address the need for a strategic balance between inputs and outputs towards value segments that can afford to pay in order to secure value capture and ensure profit or at least survival.

128 *Svetla T. Marinova et al.*

Resilience means to withstand critical jolts. In this environment, it is not a rubber ball that just jumps back. True resilience is the one that bounces back and up the previous position, based on enhanced learning. This may be fostered by true diversity in organisations – a diversity allowing for strange opinions, assessments of environmental threats, opinions that really address fundamental issues calling for unconventional views on issues that could put the business model at risk. Such a diversity of thinking can allow companies see wonderful business opportunities out there and new possibilities will arise that will require firm-level availability of cash for future investments.

The post-globalisation era calls for companies to take risk by exploring negative areas of market developments and in these proactively define opportunities for business model innovation will arise. This recent development will certainly have an effect on business model choice and configurational elements, in so far as business model design was predominantly driven by positive opportunity and using money that was almost free. Scenario thinking in firms with sound business models should be based on questions of how the firm is coping with restrictions, operating in areas where others may find it difficult to operate, capturing value where others cannot, make decisions on engaging in ecosystems influenced by geopolitical changes, focus on ecosystems with level-playing field. Moreover, learning from the Russian investment experience, big multinational firms have started thinking how to isolate their Chinese ecosystem from their other ecosystem in order to increase overall resilience. Thus, linking business model reconfiguration with the contextual specificity of ecosystem development can be the right way to develop strategic directions in the firm.

Global value chains have worked well for 20 years or so for the companies orchestrating them. The changing environment has confronted firms with immediate operational risk, and they have become a lot more creative in finding new suppliers. In the long run, value network changes in the business model related to distribution and supply are helping them create strategic alternatives and minimise strategic risk. Relationship development with strategic suppliers to achieve reliability of factor inputs will be essential for ensuring company operations.

Companies should better define the relationship between organisation and business model as organisations evolve under the pressure of internal or ecosystemic changes, and their context-specific – national or regional business models, must be reconfigured to ensure value capture in the long term.

Instead of Conclusion: Action Points for Managers

Here are the critical factors that firms need to consider when facing critical jolts of great magnitude, which affect their business models and ecosystems:

- Allow alternative views to enable a deep comprehension of what really happens in the environment and the consequences of the environmental changes for all elements of the business model.
- Revise the traditional strategic approaches to all aspects of the business – redefine strategic goals and priorities to markets, suppliers and institutional players of key significance.
- The universal characteristics of the critical jolts are critical, but never forget and underestimate the specificity of various contexts and make business models reflect this specificity.
- Reconfigure the business model and its positioning in the ecosystem or change the ecosystem to which a firm with its business model belongs (e.g., this is what happened with actors in the Danish mink ecosystem after its collapse – some players managed to successfully reposition themselves in other ecosystems, while others simply stopped their business activities altogether).

References

Arslan, A., Khan, Z., Kontkanen, M., & Tarba, S. (2021). "Perception of strategic industries: Implications for international business", in M.A. Marinov & S.T. Marinova (Eds.), *COVID-19 and International Business: Change of Era*. London and New York: Taylor and Francis, 89–97.

Capoccia, G. (2015). "Critical junctures and institutional change", in J. Mahoney & K. Thelen (Eds.), *Advances in Comparative-Historical Analysis: Strategies for Social Inquiry*. Cambridge: Cambridge University Press, 147–179.

Capoccia, G. & Kelemen, R.D. (2007). "The study of critical junctures: Theory, narrative, and counterfactuals in institutional analysis", *World Politics*, vol. 59(3), pp. 341–369.

Child, J., Lu, Y., & Tsai, T. (2007). "Institutional entrepreneurship in building an environmental protection system for the People's Republic of China", *Organization Studies*, vol. 28, pp. 1013–1034.

Davenport, T., Leibold, M., & Voelpel, S. (2006). *Strategic Management in the Innovation Economy. Strategy Approaches and Tools for Dynamic Innovation Capabilities*. New York: John Wiley and Sons.

Demil, B. & Lecocq, X. (2010). "Business model evolution: In search of dynamic consistency", *Long Range Planning*, vol. 43(2), pp. 227–246.

Gassmann, H., Frankenberger, K., & Csik, M. (2014). The St. Gallen business model navigator. *Working Paper*, University of St. Gallen: ITEM-HSG.

Johnson, M.W., Christensen, C.M., & Kagermann, H. (2008). "Reinventing your business model", *Harvard Business Review*, vol. 86(12), pp. 57–68.

Marinov, M. (2021). "COVID-19 challenges to international business", in M.A. Marinov & S.T. Marinova (Eds.), *COVID-19 and International Business: Change of Era*. London and New York: Taylor and Francis, 27–34.

Marinova, S., Freeman, S., & Marinov, M. (2019). "Value creation in context: A value chain locus perspective", in M.A. Marinov (Ed.), *Value in Marketing: Retrospective and Perspective Stance*. London and New York: Routledge, 180–210.

Moore, J. (1993). "Predators and prey: A new ecology of competition", *Harvard Business Review*, vol. 71(3), pp. 75–86.

Moore, J. (1996). *The Death of Competition - Leadership and Strategy in the Age of Business Ecosystems*. New York, NY: Harper Business.

Nielsen, C., Lund, M., Montemari, M., Paolone, F., Massaro, M., & Dumay, J. (2018). *Business Models: A Research Overview*. London and New York: Routledge.

Nielsen, C., Marinova, S.T., & Marinov, M.A. (2022). *Business Models and Firm Internationalisation*. New York and London: Taylor and Francis.

Odum, E. (1953). *Fundamentals of Ecology*. Philadelphia, PA: W.B. Saunders Company.

Osterwalder, A., Pigneur, Y., & Tucci, C.L. (2005). "Clarifying business models: Origins, present and future of the concept", *Communications of the Association for Information Systems*, vol. 16(1), pp. 1–25.

Pels, J. (2021). "Change of era or era of changes", in M.A. Marinov & S.T. Marinova (Eds.), *COVID-19 and International Business: Change of Era*. London and New York: Taylor and Francis, 19–25.

Rothschild, M. (1992). *Bionomics: Economy as Ecosystem*. New York: Henry Holt & Company.

Schwab, K. & Malleret, T. (2020). *COVID-19: The Great Reset*. Geneva and Washington, DC: World Economic Forum.

Shapiro, I. & Bedi, S. (2006). *Political Contingency: Studying the Unexpected, the Accidental, and the Unforeseen*. New York: New York University Press.

Soifer, H. (2012). "The causal logic of critical junctures", *Comparative Political Studies*, vol. 45(12), pp. 1572–1597.

Taleb, N. (2007). *The Black Swan: The Impact of the Highly Improbable*, 1st ed. London: Penguin.

Tansley, A. (1947). "The early history of modern plant ecology in Britain", *Journal of Ecology*, vol. 35(1), pp. 130–137.

Taran, Y., Nielsen, C., Montemari, M., Thomsen, P., & Paolone, F. (2016). "Business model configurations: A five-V framework to map out potential innovation routes", *European Journal of Innovation Management*, vol. 19(4), 492–527.

Tesar, G. (2021). "Effects of COVID-19 on the export operations of smaller manufacturing enterprises", in M.A. Marinov & S.T. Marinova (Eds.), *COVID-19 and International Business: Change of Era*. London and New York: Taylor and Francis, 268–277.

Webb, A. (2008). "Taking improbable events seriously: An interview with the author of The Black Swan", *Corporate Finance, McKinsey Quarterly*, p. 3, available at: web.archive.org/web/20120907061933/; http://www.wrap20.com/files/The_Black_Swan.pdf (Accessed: 30 June 2022).

Wirtz, B.W., Pistoia, A., Ullrich, S., & Göttel, V. (2015). "Business models: Origin, development and future research perspectives", *Long Range Planning*, vol. 49(1), pp. 36–54.

Zott, C., Amit, R., & Massa, L. (2011). "The business model: Recent developments and future research", *Journal of Management*, vol. 37(4), pp. 1019–1042.

9 Tensions of Coopetition and Integration into the Multiplatform Ecosystems in Digital Care

Mahmoud Mohamed, Petri Ahokangas, and Minna Pikkarainen

Introduction

Platforms have recently gained business prominence and are profoundly changing the dynamics of the digital economy landscape (Tiwana, Konsynski & Bush, 2010; Hein et al., 2020; Jia, Cusumano & Chen, 2019; Rietveld, Schilling & Bellavitis, 2019; Cusumano, Yoffie & Gawer, 2020). The multisided platform is an ecosystem that incorporates the platform hub "core infrastructure" and complementary applications (Tiwana, 2013; Gawer, 2014). The platform ecosystem uses complementary capabilities to incorporate new functionalities that reside behind the scope and scale of the central platform (Cusumano & Gawer, 2002). Furthermore, it grants the central platform the power to orchestrate value creation and capture for the entire platform ecosystem (Wen & Zhu, 2019; Isckia, De Reuver & Lescop, 2020; Tiwana, Konsynski & Bush, 2010). Given the standardised structure of the multisided platform ecosystem, three main key stakeholder roles influence the ecosystem dynamics: Platform leader, complementors and end users (Tiwana, 2013). The platform leader is the owner of the platform core infrastructure, who orchestrates the dynamics of the platform ecosystem and grants the access rights to the complementors (Cusumano & Gawer, 2002; Williamson & De Meyer, 2012; Teece, 2018; Rietveld, Schilling & Bellavitis, 2019). Complementors are the stakeholders who provide the complementary offering and expand the scope of the platform (Tiwana, 2013). Depending on the platform leader's governance roles that defines who does what (Williamson & De Meyer, 2012), complementors have heterogeneous incentives to join the platform ecosystem that affect their ability to contribute to the platform ecosystem (Boudreau & Jeppesen, 2015). Nevertheless, the complementor's value creation activities are the key indicator of platform success (Cusumano & Gawer, 2002; Tiwana, 2013).

Coopetition – the strategic alignment of parallel competition and collaborative dynamics – is the building block for aggregating platforms into the multiplatform ecosystems (MPEs). Nevertheless, tensions often arise when platform leaders manage value creation activities and coordinate the

DOI: 10.4324/9781003326731-9

inter-platform relations between complementors in the platform ecosystem (Zhang et al., 2022). The extant research has found that tensions may arise because complementors have heterogeneous motivations in joining the platform ecosystem (Boudreau & Jeppesen, 2015) that influence their decisions and activities within the ecosystem (McIntyre & Srinivasan, 2017), because there are no roles to control the relationship between platform leaders and complementors, and complementors are not under the platform leader's direct control in designing a knowledge-sharing framework (Zhang et al., 2020). It becomes challenging for the platform leader to manage these tensions, especially when developing a cooperative value creation framework including a wide range of platform complementors (Tura, Kutvonen & Ritaa, 2018; Zhang et al., 2022).

The extant strategic management research has examined these tensions from three perspectives: (I) Strict governance roles imposed by the platform leader on complementors (Tiwana, 2013; O'Mahony & Karp, 2022; Zhang et al., 2020); (II) the competition between platform owner and complementors (Wen and Zhu, 2019); and (III) the competition between complementors in the platform ecosystem (Hein et al., 2020; Zhang et al., 2020). Yet platform ecosystems today are evolving as meta-organisations (Gulati, Puranam & Tushman, 2012; Kretschmer et al., 2022), enabling the architectural design to incorporate a diverse set of platforms to work together where each platform may share part of the main infrastructure with others (Cusumano, Yoffie & Gawer, 2020; Kretschmer et al., 2022; Zhang & Williamson, 2021). The platform leader decides on the openness of the overall ecosystem by easing the restriction of joining the platform and developing complementary offerings (Eisenmann, Parker & Van Alstyne, 2009).

Strategic management research has addressed tensions when developing an inter-platform cooperative framework for the single multisided platform (e.g., gatekeeping tensions between platform leader and complementors) but has yet to address the inter-platform tensions in MPEs (Zhang et al., 2020; Zhang & Williamson, 2021). However, there is some knowledge related to integration stages into MPEs (Kretschmer et al., 2022), complementarity, governance and leadership roles between platforms (Tura, Kutvonen & Ritala, 2018; O'Mahony & Karp, 2022). As well as the contextual factors that influence the inter-platform competition (Kretschmer et al., 2022) and platforms' decision to integrate into MPEs (Gawer & Henderson, 2007; Miller & Toh, 2022). However, there is still a lack of research about the knowledge sharing between complementors and gatekeeping, affecting their ability to share knowledge in the MPEs.

This study addresses the gap by focusing on the coopetition and inter-platform tensions that arise when integrating into MPEs. Therefore, we aim to explore the coopetition-related tensions when complementing entrant and incumbent platforms integrate into MPEs. To approach this, we implemented qualitative case study research (Yin, 2003) backed with the platform ecosystem (Isckia, De Reuver & Lescop, 2020), coopetition dynamics

Tensions of Coopetition and Integration   133

(Khanna, Gulati & Nohria, 1998; Tsai, 2002; Tiwana, 2013; Zhu & Iansiti, 2012; Ritala, 2019; Zhang et al., 2020) and knowledge-sharing literature alongside competition and governance from the multisided platform context (Zhu & Liu, 2018; Kretschmer et al., 2022; O'Mahony & Karp, 2022; Zhang et al., 2020).

The rest of the chapter is structured as follows. The next part discusses the inter-platform tensions and constructs the study's theoretical background. We then explain the empirical study setting and the study's findings. This chapter is concluded with the theoretical and managerial implications of the study and recommendations for future research.

Related Literature

Strategic management scholars have addressed tensions of inter-platform complementarity in the multisided platform ecosystems stemming from the unbalanced dynamics of coopetition and competition between complementors and platform leaders. On the one hand, coopetition originates from the alignment of common benefits between all complementors, regardless of their heterogeneous incentives and the private benefits of joining the platform (Zhang et al., 2020). Building a coopetition framework therefore requires all complementors to emphasise collaborative ties with other complementors over competitive ones (Ritala, 2019; Tsai, 2002). On the other hand, competition arises either through platform leader pressure on complementors via vertical integration (Zhu & Liu, 2018; Wen & Zhu, 2019) or between complementors in the platform ecosystem (Boudreau & Jeppesen, 2015; McIntyre & Srinivasan, 2017; Zhang et al., 2020; Zhang & Williamson, 2021). The unbalanced dynamics of cooperative and competitive powers create tensions between platform leaders and complementors that affect the value creation and capture of the overall platform ecosystem. The extant strategic management literature has addressed these tensions from the platform leader-to-complementor relations perspective. However, the tensions that are likely to arise while integrating into a complex MPEs ecosystem are relatively scant (Zhang & Williamson, 2021). With the current technological advances in which ecosystems built around platforms expand to include multiple platforms working together, this paradox is becoming a significant challenge when transitioning to MPEs as a multi-layered coopetition-based ecosystem.

Platform leaders may establish competitive pressure on complementors through vertical integration when they enter the complementor's product space and compete against them (Zhu & Liu, 2018). Scholars investigated vertical integration as a platform leader's approach to handling product areas in which complementors are underperforming (Wen & Zhu, 2019) and improving customer satisfaction with the overall platform ecosystem (Cusumano & Gawer, 2002). Furthermore, vertical integration is likely to occur when the platform leader decides to enter areas where complementors perform well, because complementors lack the resources to form strict governance mechanisms to prevent platform leaders from undertaking vertical integration (Zhu & Iansiti, 2012). Vertical integration may affect the platform's overall performance and survival (Leiblein & Miller, 2003; Iansiti & Levien, 2004). Meanwhile, inter-platform competition arises from prioritising the complementor's heterogenous private benefits over the commonly shared benefits (Boudreau & Jeppesen, 2015; Ritala, 2018) that influence platform governance roles (Tiwana, 2013; O'Mahony & Karp, 2022) and knowledge-sharing incentives between complementors (Tsai, 2002; Zhang et al., 2020).

Extant research has found that complementors become more willing to cooperate with other complementors when they are less impacted by competitive pressure (Ritala et al., 2018; O'Mahony & Karp, 2022; Zhang et al., 2020). Inter-platform collaborative relations contribute to extensive knowledge-sharing mechanisms and leveraging the platform's overall quality (Tsai, 2002; Gnyawali & Park, 2011). Scholars argue that value creation is unlikely to happen unless complementors build an interconnected win–win relationship with other complementors and platform leaders (Ritala, 2018; Zhu & Liu, 2018). Nevertheless, inter-platform competition is associated with platform leaders' willingness to orchestrate the ecosystem and foster the platform's competitiveness (Kretschmer et al., 2022). Depending on the degree of knowledge sharing and openness, the platform ecosystem expands to include multiple complementors, who aim to increase their opportunities in the ecosystem (Isckia, De Reuver & Lescop, 2020; Zhang & Williamson, 2021). However, openness gives the platform ecosystem a considerable competitive advantage over its rivals. Yet it raises competitive tensions between complementors concerning future collaborations that may influence some complementors' future strategies (Zhu & Iansiti, 2012). For this, competition originates between platforms through direct or indirect network effects when they compete to control the competitive landscape of specific markets (Economides & Katsamakas, 2006; Tiwana, Konsynski & Bush, 2010).

Coopetition between complementors alters the excessive competition dynamics between platforms in the platform ecosystem (Zhang et al., 2020). Coopetition is the strategic approach of building collaborative linkages with competitors to efficiently utilise resources, achieve market growth, create new market opportunities and enhance the overall competitive dynamics in the platform ecosystem (Lepak, Smith & Taylor, 2007; Ritala, 2019). The balance of coopetition dynamics at the platform ecosystem level is the wheel for managing the value creation between all platforms in MPEs (Gnyawali et al., 2016). However, previous research has highlighted coopetition from building a collaborative framework in the single organisation platform, which included building a knowledge-sharing framework between all complementors within the platform ecosystem (Ritala & Hurmelinna-Laukkanen, 2019; Ritala, 2019;

Zhang et al., 2020). Coopetition establishes routine knowledge when information is repeatedly shared among all stakeholders in the platform ecosystem (Wong, 2004). For this, control of the platform ecosystem is granted to the central technological hub to facilitate the complementarity between stakeholders in the platform ecosystem, especially when platforms enter new markets and attempt to convince complementors to join under a degree of uncertainty (Tiwana, Konsynski & Bush, 2010; Valkokari, 2015). The hierarchy and establishment of the incumbent firms can create huge obstacles to the platform entering specific markets unless the platform leader grants complementors the flexibility and autonomy to design their offerings (Kretschmer et al., 2022; Zhang et al., 2020). Strategic management scholars have investigated the tensions of platform complementarity to arise from platform leaders' own resources, which gives platform leaders the authority to grant access to the external complementors (Gawer & Cusumano, 2002; Eisenmann, Parker & Van Alstyne, 2006; Gawer, 2014).

The dynamics of complementarity in MPEs can exist between platforms operating in different markets rather than interacting on different sides of a single market (Zhang & Williamson, 2021). The extant research has examined modularity as a platform strategy to manage complexity, boost innovation and scale the platform's business scope (Baldwin & Clark, 2002; Kretschmer et al., 2022; Yrjölä, Ahokangas & Matinmikko-Blue, 2021). In this study, we follow Tiwana's (2013) definition of the stakeholder roles in the platform ecosystem. The stakeholder roles define individual platforms' tendency to integrate into MPEs, whether they expand their business scope or build new cooperative relations and allow other complementors, because the end user of one platform could be the same end user of multiple other platforms. Likewise, the complementor of one platform could be the complementor of other platforms included in the same ecosystem. It becomes complex to either build a coopetition framework between multiple platforms in the same ecosystem or coordinate their heterogenous private benefits to serve the overall common platform goal. The empirical evidence that coopetition can drive platform-to-platform openness and collective governance is lacking (O'Mahony & Karp, 2022), especially in the context of MPEs, where the coopetition dynamics can be multi-layered and complex, which may lead to tensions rather than collective governance (Ritala & Hurmelinna-Laukkanen, 2019; Zhang & Williamson, 2021).

By combining the coopetition and knowledge-sharing framework and the platform-to-platform openness literature, we aim to deepen our understanding of the tensions in managing coopetition while integrating into MPEs. The extant platform literature focuses on the dynamics between the platform leader and complementors in regard to platform openness with its complementors. However, we seek to contribute to the theoretical discussion of MPEs through the digital care ecosystem as a study context for two reasons. First, the extant literature refers to the digital care ecosystem as connected health platforms that act as a pre-existing ecosystem on which platforms integrate (Niemelä et al., 2019). Second, all the case companies participating in this study aimed to develop platforms and integrate them with other solutions into Stroke-Data MPEs. To that end, coopetition and competition dynamics define individual platform integration strategies into MPEs.

Methodology

Research Design

This study opts for a qualitative research approach through a case study setting aligned with an open-ended research question (Eisenhardt, 1989; Yin, 2003). The existing platform theories are developed around the complementarity and competition between platform leaders and complementors in the intra-platform setting. Nevertheless, the empirical evidence on inter-platform complementarity and coopetition dynamics is limited, with multiple demand and multiple supply sides existing around the focal platform (Kretschmer et al., 2022; Zhang & Williamson, 2021). Due to the scant evidence of the inter-platform complementarity dynamics (Kretschmer et al., 2022; Zhang et al., 2020), we chose an exploratory case study approach to analyse our case (Patton, 2002; Yin, 2003). We started by formulating the theoretical background to gain a comprehensive understanding of the existing theories and formulate a pre-understanding of the research phenomenon (Miller & Toh, 2022; Yin, 2003).

We then followed the purposeful sampling approach in selecting case companies integrating into MPEs (Patton, 2002). In general, purposeful sampling justifies the selection of participant case companies that meet the study's aim and purpose (Collingridge & Gantt, 2008). In doing so, the case companies included in this study are Finnish High-Tech companies operating in the healthcare domain. All the case companies are part of the Stroke-Data consortium, part of Business Finland's Smart Life programme, which facilitates innovation and technology deployment for health tech companies. The programme aimed to co-create a decision-support system for stroke prevention and diagnosis. Each company had their own platform to integrate into the overall Stroke-Data MPEs or technology patent to complement the other case companies' platforms integrating into the Stroke-Data MPEs. Table 9.1 summarises the case companies and their offering in MPEs.

Research Context

The digital stroke care pathway is the contextual framework for this study that comprises multiple multisided platforms working together. The digital care ecosystem requires platforms to have an overall integration into a parenting platform to unify the user interface for the end user. The necessity for platforms to build on each other and intersect at one or more

Table 9.1 Summary of the case companies and interview rounds

Case	Case company's background	Interview rounds and duration in minutes			Number of interviewees
		First	Second	Third	
A	Medical technology provider. The company has two platform roles in the Stroke-Data platform: (I) Building a platform for a preventive solution to be used by patients and healthcare experts; and (II) a regulatory expert role for making the developed solutions certifiable for medical use. The company aims for Stroke-Data MPEs to help carry out initial R&D projects related to new software prototypes as medical devices for patients at risk of a stroke. Furthermore, conducting R&D for a new solution for remote patient examination supports clinical decision-making.	85	80	100	4
B	Rehabilitation service provider. The company is developing a big data platform to integrate sleep and rest period data. The platform will be integrated into all points across the Stroke-Data platform.	168	–	–	3
C	Cloud service and data analytics provider. It is a small and medium-sized enterprise (SME) company, with its core business around a platform specialising in business intelligence and data reporting and warehousing, reporting, planning and budgeting sub-domains.	61	–	–	1
D	IT and service-oriented software provider. The company has an empathic building solution to visualise the building of all data collection points and analyses them together. Through visualisation, the information gets to be accessible through the data, which can be used to develop preventive solutions on the Stroke-Data platform. The company aims for new international business opportunities from the Stroke-Data platform.	66	–	–	2

Table 9.1 (Continued)

Case	Case company's background	Interview rounds and duration in minutes			Number of interviewees
		First	*Second*	*Third*	
E	AI solution provider which used to develop the rehabilitation platform for stroke patients to be used in the rehabilitation homes or hospitals. The rehabilitation solution will be integrated within the Stroke-Data platform.	56	80	101	2
F	Healthcare technology provider. The company is providing sensors for other platforms involved in the Stroke-Data platform. The sensors can be used in the rehabilitation part of the co-developed solution.	99	–	–	1
G	The case company has a Brain status sensor that measures the ECG. The aim is to make use of the sensor as a data source for the Stroke-Data platform. The developed platform will be used in intensive care units and ambulances to deliver real-time data of the patient status. In addition, the company intends to come up with a physician decision support system linked to their platform solution. The company aims to study how to bring AI-driven analytics to Stroke diagnostics and decision-making.	–	–	113	4
H	Fundus cameras and software solution provider. The company plans to integrate their cameras in the Stroke-Data platform to prevent cardiovascular diseases related to stroke detection, treatment and rehabilitation.	–	–	18	1

Source: The authors.

points in the ecosystem therefore existed alongside this study. In this study, each case company had its platform infrastructure "focal incumbent platform" or technology patent "complementing platform". All the participating platforms joined the Stroke-Data consortium to leverage their capabilities, integrate their platforms and jointly co-develop a solution for stroke prevention, diagnostics and rehabilitation. Every platform planned to integrate its solution into the planned Stroke-Data MPEs (Figure 9.1).

Stroke-Data MPE is the target solution to build from this study (Figure 9.1). In addition, the case companies "platform stakeholders" were conceptualised as individual multisided platforms that complemented each other in MPEs. Figure 9.1 depicts the Stroke-Data MPEs. The Stroke-Data MPEs consist of four intersecting platforms. Depending on the degree of complementarity and data ownership, each platform has a certain degree of platform-to-platform openness, where part of an individual company's platform infrastructure or technology patent is shared with another company's platform. The four intersecting platforms are (I) a back-end solution platform; (II) an expert solution platform; (III) a patient solution platform; and (IV) a patient's family care-related solution platform that focuses on updating the patient's family about the patient's status during and after stroke treatment.

Data Collection and Case Companies' Background

Based on the exploratory nature of this study (Eisenhardt, 1989), we conducted three data collection rounds between the spring of 2020 and the autumn of 2021 to understand how the process unfolded and achieve the study's aim. The semi-structured interviews were the primary source of data collection (Dearnley, 2005). As the data collection proceeded to the third round, we reached data saturation, where no significant insights could develop from collecting further data (Morse, 1995; Guest, Bunce & Johnson, 2006). We interviewed managerial-level and decision-making experts from eight case companies integrating their platforms into Stroke-Data MPEs. The fundamental role of the interviewees selected for this study was that they directly affected their case company's strategic choice. We conducted 14 interviews for this study in three rounds based on the integration phase in the Stroke-Data MPEs. We did not reveal interviewees' names or case companies' names for data anonymisation purposes (Table 9.1). General interview themes and questions were sent in advance if the interviewees asked for them. We provided some illustrations during the interviews to clarify the theme if required or to guide the conversation towards the business context rather than the engineering focus.

Data Analysis

This study started by formulating what we know about coopetition and competition in the single multisided platform, then progressed to what we

140 *Mahmoud Mohamed et al.*

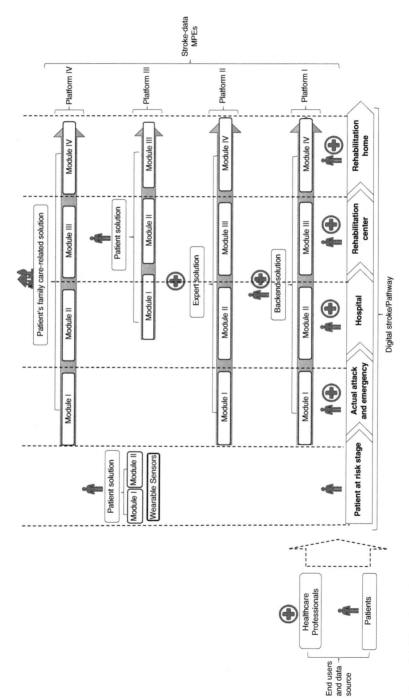

Figure 9.1 The planned integrations into the digital care pathway.

Source: The authors.

know and do not about MPEs. The study aimed to identify the tensions of cooptition that arise when platforms integrate into MPEs. In doing so, we recorded all the interviews after obtaining all the participants' approval, then transcribed interviews immediately after conducting them. During the interviews, we took some sidenotes to highlight interesting themes emerging from the discussion and guide through further data collection rounds (Miles & Huberman, 1994; Eriksson & Kovalainen, 2008). We followed the thematic analysis approach to analyse our data (Braun & Clarke, 2006). We started analysing the data through in-depth reading of interview transcripts for each case company. We then started the coding using the NVIVO software in three coding rounds. The open coding round (Corley & Gioia, 2004) gives the study a purpose and direction for conducting in-depth qualitative analysis (Yin, 2003). We started by assigning codes emerging from the literature background corresponding to this study's main themes to categorise the enormous amount of data into sub-categories and ease and guide the process for further analysis (Miles & Huberman, 1994). As the study progressed, new data were collected, and multiple codes emerging from the data and corresponding quotes were added to the initial coding list (Corley & Gioia, 2004). Accordingly, more new themes have emerged in the study than expected during the initial planning for the early data collection rounds (Miles & Huberman, 1994). For example, the platform's opportunistic behaviour and dropouts from MPEs arose in the study, which was not planned in the original study setting. Similar codes from the open coding rounds were then merged into sub-groups in the second axial coding round. The main themes for the study were then categorised in the final coding round (Strauss & Corbin, 1997; Corley & Gioia, 2004).

Findings

In the analysis of the Stroke-Data MPEs (Figure 9.2), we considered the scarcity of literature related to the platform-to-platform openness and integration into MPEs. This helped us expand our scope beyond the integration stages and identify the causes of inter-platform tensions in MPEs.

Building on the three interview rounds, we defined the targeted integration into Stroke-Data MPEs, the integration requirements for joining the ecosystem and the tensions that arose during the integration. Despite all the benefits driven by cooptition and platform-to-platform openness in MPEs, the existence of multiple leading platforms, "incumbent platforms" and multiple complementing "entrant platforms" triggers tensions in managing the overall cooptition dynamics between stakeholders in MPEs, regarding who does what, and who dominates a particular part/function of the overall ecosystem offering or even dominates a specific market entry. In the Stroke-Data MPEs, the tensions between ecosystem stakeholders arise

142 *Mahmoud Mohamed et al.*

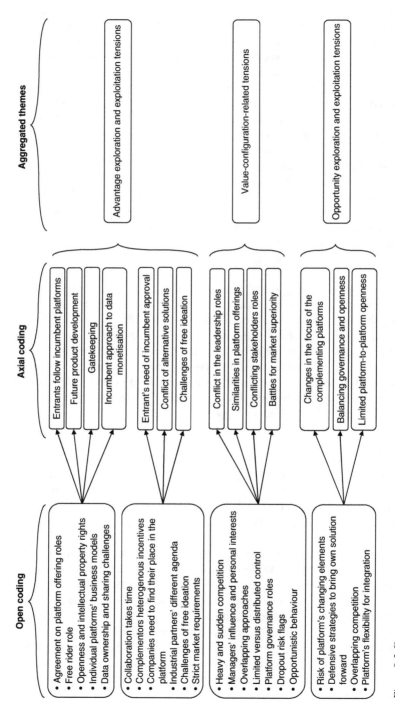

Figure 9.2 Data structure.
Source: The authors.

from an imbalance between (I) platform gatekeeping versus knowledge sharing, (II) competition for market superiority versus coopetition and (III) governance versus platform-to-platform openness.

Platform Gatekeeping Versus Knowledge Sharing

While integrating into Stroke-Data MPEs, the lack of monetised data required to develop further AI algorithms was the primary key element to stimulate tensions between platforms. All the cases involved in the integration into Stroke-Data MPEs appeared to have data-sharing limitations. They lacked an extensive knowledge-sharing framework with other platforms involved in MPEs. Due to the nature of the Stroke-Data MPEs operating in the healthcare domain, hospitals come first as the processor of the anonymised patients' data. We conceptualised hospitals as the central data hub that complements all the platforms involved in Stroke-Data MPEs. Hospitals refuse to monetise anonymised patients' data with entrant platforms involved in platform development unless they are associated with a trustworthy incumbent. In some cases, they managed to obtain an anonymised patient's data. However, the extensive anonymisation of data prevented the development of further algorithms in the later stages, limiting the platforms' capacity for further development.

All the interviewees argued that they would benefit from the coopetition if hospitals "as the primary data source in the stroke-data MPEs" tried not to strategically manoeuvre companies' trials in developing new services by limiting/or prohibiting access to anonymised patient data. Case G is an incumbent platform that participates in the Stroke-Data platform's patient and expert solutions. Interviewee 3 questioned the data owner's attitude towards sharing and enabling companies to do the research and development work because any development work for their platform depended on hospitals' views of data access. Interviewee 2 commented:

> Hospitals believe that companies would not be doing research work if they shared monetised patient data. They will be doing product development work and utilising the fruits they already have [referring to the anonymised patient's data], and I disagree.

Interviewee 3 also disagreed with the hospital's view of data access by explaining,

> We are in many cases conducting similar research cases to those universities are doing in algorithm development and various sources. There may be room for improvement in the hospital's attitude as the data owner. Of course, companies will do a product development if there is a market opportunity, but yes, we currently have a big R and a small D for future product development.

144   *Mahmoud Mohamed et al.*

Interviewee 1 from case E commented on the same discussion, explaining that it takes 5–6 years to get the technology to the market.

"We conduct extensive research before the development, but hospitals delay the process", Interviewee 1 concluded.

As a response to the requirements related to data-sharing mechanisms hospitals place on the entrants, entrant platforms may initiate gate-keeping when an incumbent platform starts developing a broader product portfolio using the monetised data from the entrant platform's side. We found that platforms were willing to collectively establish a knowledge-sharing framework unless it was not used to expand the product umbrella of the complementing platform. Interviewee 1 from case E commented:

Once platforms start working on the data sharing, they need to be/or positively forced to be trustworthy every second when you are sourcing sensitive data, then analysing and sharing these data afterwards.

The new entrant platforms in the Stroke-Data MPEs were extensively developing platform solutions, while incumbent platforms were negotiating higher terms of data sharing. Interviewee 1 continued:

We are [referring to case E] currently in the process of developing our company and solution, so we're not yet at the stage where we could share the data and negotiate more terms.

Meanwhile, interviewee 1 from case A believed that "personal relations and trust between platform managers" were the basic elements for building a successful knowledge-sharing framework. Interviewee 3 from case G argued that

initiating data-sharing partnerships between stakeholders in Stroke-Data are crucial for the success of the whole ecosystem.

The business reality is that every platform wants to retain its dominance in the market and negotiate higher terms from the complementing platforms.

Another tension arises when two or more platforms build their knowledge-sharing framework as a sub-set of the central one in MPEs. Cases A and E have built their knowledge-sharing framework to develop the rehabilitation platform in the Stroke-Data MPEs. During one joint interview discussion with the two companies, Interviewee 1 from case E explained that both companies shared many of society and business values. Furthermore, from the rehabilitation part of the Stroke-Data MPEs, both companies shared the same interest in developing our solution to create interaction between patients and healthcare professionals. Interviewee 1 from case A specifically described their coopetition dynamics with case E, saying:

We're not working as a whole [referring to Stroke-Data stakeholders] – we're working as a sub-set. But if we reach mutual agreements, we will have a communication relationship with the rest.

Market Superiority Versus Coopetition

Incumbent platforms tend to establish a coopetition framework with entrant platforms if the dynamics of coopetition guarantee their market dominance will be maintained. For this, Interviewee 3 from case A highlights the necessity of defining each platform's role and then proceeding with the market agreements for all the ecosystem's stakeholders. Interviewee 3 noted:

It is not very clear which consortium members are supposed to do what – at the end of the day, this is something we need to have.

Stakeholders in MPEs need to clarify and agree the market leadership roles to make coopetition happen. To reach these agreements, Interviewee 1 highlights *"the conflict of platform leadership roles that arise"*, because the only way to keep incumbent platforms dominant in their area is to negotiate higher terms from entrant platforms to fully/or partly open their platform to the entrant platforms. As discussed in the previous chapter, entrant platforms in complex domains (e.g., the healthcare domain) seek the approval of incumbent platforms to get recognised in those domains where the requirement for innovation is rather complex. This becomes the bargaining power for the incumbent platforms when discussing the perks of competition for each stakeholder involved in MPEs, because case E wanted approval for their new technology in the healthcare domain. Interviewee 1 from case D said:

We want Stroke-Data to help us open the doors and discuss with other stakeholders, but we will have several safety issues that we have to go through.

Interviewee 1 from case A highlighted *"personal relations between managers"* to come first while building a coopetition framework. Additionally, Interviewee 1 from case C disappointedly pointed out that coopetition with the incumbent platform was time-consuming for growth companies with high aims to expand in the market. He mentioned:

It takes time to build the collaboration and reach the kind of coopetition we're aiming for.

Regardless of the stakeholder's position in MPEs, platform-to-platform openness is associated with the fear of sudden competition from opportunistic stakeholders. Interviewee 3 from case A justifies the incumbent platform approach in creating their defensive mechanism before initiating any coopetition framework with other stakeholders in MPEs as the burden of protecting their competitive advantage and market dominance. Interviewee 3 from case A does not see it as a bargaining advantage from the incumbents' perspective over the new entrants:

> *It is important to discuss the competitive advantage of companies with new stakeholders; like decide what is the right process to admit new stakeholders ..., that we are not just suddenly bringing some competitor in there without discussing and agreeing together about it somehow.*

The role of designing and evaluating coopetition dynamics and aligning who is going to do what is privileged to the incumbent platforms, as Interviewee 4 explained:

> *If a big competitor suddenly appeared sort of wanting to do the same things, then, there could be some kind of conflict.*

Designing a coopetition agreement that specifies each stakeholder's role in MPEs thus prevents the rise of overlapping/conflicting interests. Interviewee 3 highlights the *"consortium agreement proposal from each stakeholder"* as the way to cover any significant risks that may arise on the establishment of the coopetition framework. To overcome the threat of sudden competition from stakeholders with different agendas, Interviewee 3 highlighted that the coopetition agreement must specify the conditions that governed each stakeholder's competitive advantage developed in MPEs.

Incumbent platforms tend to create a defensive mechanism before initiating any coopetition framework with other platforms in MPEs. Interviewee 3 from case A specifically mentioned *"the free-rider role"* as the condition to consider before granting other incumbents or new entrant platforms access to the focal platform's infrastructure; Interviewee 3 concluded:

> *We don't want to end up specifying the whole requirement domain for the whole solution, so we cannot do like ... work for them, or we cannot do ... work for them, and that is part of our share of responsibility in this discussion as well.*

Respectively, incumbent platforms negotiate higher authority in the decision-making related to further product development or research activities. Then, if the new entrant platform has no opportunity to get a large enough share of the coopetition framework pie, they drop out of MPEs. In the case of Stroke-Data, the negotiation of coopetition dynamics between an incumbent platform and entrant platform led one new entrant platform to drop out of the Stroke-Data MPEs. The dropout occurred during the early stages of formulating the proposal for a coopetition agreement between all stakeholders participating in the Stroke-Data MPEs.

Interviewee 3 from case A believed that *"similarities in the platform offerings"* caused tensions between stakeholders in MPEs. The case A proposal for their participatory role in the data analysis part was similar to the case D proposal for the Stroke-Data platform. As case company A successfully had built a similar system in the Swedish hospitals, they planned to develop it in the Stroke-Data. Meanwhile, case D already specialised in data analytics; the company planned to build a big data platform to aggregate data from all possible data collection points across the whole digital care stroke treatment and rehabilitation ecosystem. As Interviewee 3 from case A noted:

We need to reach an agreement about who is supposed to do what.

A special agreement was needed between cases A and D to plan what they were doing and prevent the overlapping conflicts of interest to avoid the *"overlapping competition"*, Interviewee 1 from case A highlighted. The proposal for coopetition discussion between cases A and D opened the way to a collaboration between cases A and G, because case G can use the data from case A servers to develop the brain status solution.

Similarly, case company C provides a video solution for case company D to be used on the big data platform. Interviewee 1 from case C explained that they had to study the big data of case D first, then explore how to align their big data concept capabilities to proceed with the implementation and pilot cases. However, there was an overlapping similarity between case C and F platforms, especially if case F felt that case C was their competitor on the Stroke-Data platform. Interviewee 1 from case C said:

We need to discuss and agree with them [referring to case F], because they have their platform, and I don't know if they feel we are their competitor.

The overlapping/or similarity of platform offerings between stakeholders in MPEs creates the challenge of coopetition versus competition. If stakeholders do not reach a fair agreement for the coopetition framework, it can lead to MPE dropouts. Interviewee 2 from case E highlighted that *"stakeholders' heterogenous incentives to join the platform ecosystem"* might create a conflict between stakeholders in MPEs. Interviewee 1 described their fears when they decided to join the Stroke-Data platform:

At first, it seemed we might have some minor conflict with case A once they started developing a clear solution. However, we needed to be quiet with all parties and sharp in our area to protect and support others.

Some stakeholders tend to build partnership agreements if there is an overlapping approach between stakeholders in MPEs. From the partnership

148 *Mahmoud Mohamed et al.*

perspective, two or more stakeholders decide to co-develop their platform. Case E is building the rehabilitation solution on the Stroke-Data platform. However, they partnered with case A to build the patient solution platform by monetising the data from the case E platform, because case A needed the patient/end-user data to develop the patient solution platform. Interviewee 1 from case E explained:

> *The cooperation with case A is built on the basis that we provide data for their solution and on having the kind of set-up in which we support them and vice versa.*

Interviewee 2 mentioned that if stakeholders did not reach partnership agreements when platform solution overlapped, incumbent platforms might try to acquire the new entrants *"to avoid the conflict of overlapping solutions that will become competition in the future"*.

Meanwhile, to keep the dynamics of coopetition working, the new entrant platform must face *"the risk of changing elements"*, Interviewee 1 concluded. As much as opportunity, coopetition put new entrants under continuous pressure to change the context of their platform/complementary offering. As Interviewee 1 said:

> *We have to leave space for the additional actors we need in the project to be able to deliver those things.*

New entrants therefore needed to have flexible configuration models to meet the integration requirements of the incumbent platforms. Interviewee 1 viewed their transition to the Stroke-Data platform as an opportunity that introduced future uncertainties to their current model. Interviewee 1 continued:

> *We do not know patient needs yet, and all the stakeholders involved at the moment know it. They know that actor X or potential competitor X needs to be involved in reaching the project's target. For example, now we're talking about getting involved in Sweden. Everybody [referring to Stroke-Data stakeholders] would say yes, we want to expand to Sweden and have Swedish partners, but we're doing this with our resources. However, it's nice to get involved there, but they do not need to touch our current model.*

Balancing Governance and Platform Openness

The challenge of balancing between governance and platform openness driven by the fear of the product imitation or development of further innovations by other platforms. The tensions of governance activities may constrain any further integrations into MPEs. Despite having a knowledge-sharing framework, we found that platforms tended to anonymise data to share it extensively with other platforms. For example, in the Stroke-Data MPEs, the knowledge-sharing framework had anonymised data that constrained the development of any further AI algorithms. We found that the development of long-term visions for the governance practices between platforms was a huge challenge. Platforms often tended to avoid open discussions of their intended data-sharing policies. It was also challenging to discuss individually planned governance mechanisms between all the platforms.

In the Stroke-Data MPEs the incumbent platforms were ready to engage in coopetition with new entrants if it would guarantee their market dominance (e.g., dominance in data analytics and visualisation). Our finding indicates that incumbents tend to negotiate bigger terms from small businesses/new entrants integrating into MPEs, because they cannot do it alone due to their limited financial resources and the market's maturity level (e.g., healthcare domain). Interviewee 1 from case D argued:

> *If you give something to us, we will also give something to you. We research and collaborate on this because that is our intention as well. But in Stroke-Data, we'd like to organise more discussion with [mentioning company name] to find out to build up this collaboration.*

To that end, platforms tend to engage in the coopetition framework if it does not affect their position in the market. They tend to negotiate bigger terms from other complementing/small platforms. The variations and contradictions of individual goals of each platform create a considerable challenge that leads to some MPE dropouts.

From this, case G, as an incumbent platform, focused on their brain status solution and did not wish to initiate competition with new entrant platforms. However, they wanted the data for their server to build further algorithms and integrate their solution across the whole care pathway. This was challenging without reaching an agreement for platform-to-platform openness with the hospitals and other platforms involved in Stroke-Data MPEs. Platform-to-platform openness was challenging in this situation. If case G started developing further algorithms generated through platform-to-platform openness, this would drive direct competition with case E. To prevent direct competition with case E, case G tried to implement limited platform-to-platform openness to keep the coopetition dynamics and avoid direct competition with their complementor.

Another coopetition tension occurred between case G as an incumbent platform and case D, because case D had its big data platform to integrate into the hospital and home environment within Stroke-Data MPEs. There was an opportunity for case G to integrate its brain status platform into the big data platform, generating further data for the case E platform. However, case G argued that their solution was intended for hospital use and was not targeted at use in the home environment (referring to rehabilitation homes). Participant 1 from case G noted:

150   *Mahmoud Mohamed et al.*

> *We saw the trust among business ecosystem members related to the technical data integration and quality, which still needs initial investment in data linking, depending on hospitals and service providers. But if the ecosystem didn't work out well this time, it may be a key learning opportunity for other business modelling ideas.*

Case G did not want to expand their business scope to home environments through coopetition and a high level of data sharing with case D. Their current solution targeted the hospital and ambulance environments. Expanding to home environments would intensify competition with case E. This would also change the platform's current focus:

> *"We aren't planning to go in that direction at all"*, Interviewee 3 concluded.

Another similar tension happened between case D and cases E and A, which hindered Norway's global reach. As per the Norwegian system, the big data platform developed by case D required comprehensive integration with the rehabilitation platform jointly developed by cases E and A. If the integration had happened, it would have been implemented in Norway if all the stakeholders in the Stroke-Data MPEs approved the use of the case D big data platform. However, cases D, E and A did not reach a coopetition agreement with all the stakeholders in the Stroke-Data MPEs. Accordingly, the big data platform within the rehabilitation part of the Stroke-Data platform did not meet the Norwegian hospitals' requirements.

Discussion

This study explores how coopetition-related tensions emerge when platforms integrate into MPEs, and how platforms deal with these tensions. Each case company in the studied MPES has its own platform that contributes to the MPE either as a focal "incumbent platform" to integrate other platforms into/or as a complementary platform for the focal platforms. We focused on the coopetition between entrants and incumbent platforms rather than the contextual factors for platforms' integration into MPEs. Our findings indicate that tensions of coopetition emerge in MPEs because of the ecosystem requirement for higher levels of integration and knowledge sharing between all platforms. Incumbent platforms implement full integrations into the new entrant platforms to overcome the threat of competition from new entrant platforms. This is the opposite of competition dynamics in the multisided platform setting, in which new entrant platforms come with radical innovations to disrupt market dynamics for incumbent platforms. We categorised the coopetition-related tensions into three main phases (Figure 9.3). In the following sub-chapters, we discuss

Tensions of Coopetition and Integration 151

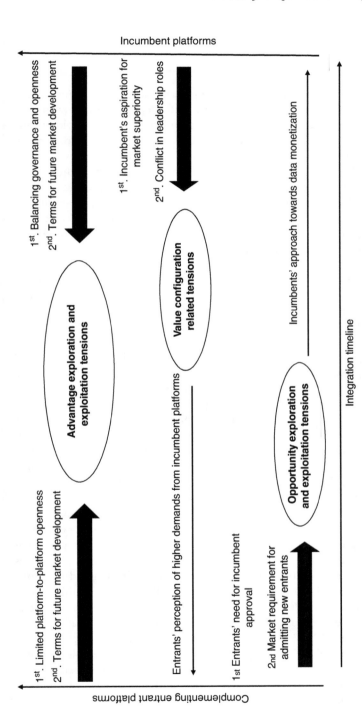

Figure 9.3 Coopetition-related tensions in MPEs.

Source: The authors.

our findings by emphasising the coopetition-related tensions that arise during integration into MPEs.

Opportunity Exploration and Exploitation Tensions

Our analysis reveals that higher complementarity levels may stimulate incumbent platforms' tendency to establish gatekeeping with new entrant platforms as a precaution against sudden competition or technology imitation. The market requirement establishes a strong drive for coopetition from the entrant platform's side, seeking their competitors' approval. In the Stroke-Data MPEs, healthcare as a complex domain constrains the entrant platform's ability to access the data unless they are part of the incumbents' offering. Furthermore, the accreditation and licensing requirements for admitting new technology are rather strict and are difficult to achieve with the entrant platform's resources. The integration requirements placed by the healthcare domain emerged as the bargaining power for incumbents to negotiate the terms of the coopetition agreement, which stimulates gatekeeping tensions between all the platforms integrating into MPEs. Gatekeeping may perform well as a platform strategy to shape the ecosystem's requirements built around platform sides (Boudreau & Jeppesen, 2015; Zhang et al., 2020). Incumbent platforms therefore try to maintain market dominance by applying centralised control models to safeguard their platform's technical core (Den Hartigh et al., 2016). In contrast, we find that gatekeeping in MPEs hinders the individual platform's motivation to share data with other platforms and innovate if they are threatened by technology imitation or admitting rival platforms to MPEs. We observed a bottleneck in the gatekeeping when all the platforms integrating into MPEs tended to utilise data to get a more significant market share, with each platform tending to constrain the others from winning the battle for significant market shares. Furthermore, incumbent platforms may initiate gatekeeping as a defensive mechanism when new entrant platforms threaten further product development.

The ecosystem built around MPEs evolves when new stakeholders decide to join the ecosystem. Nevertheless, the leadership and control in MPEs undergo multiple transitions between centralised and collective control deciding whom to admit to the ecosystem. Incumbent platforms prefer to keep their centralised control to maintain their market dominance and guarantee equal market opportunities for all platforms within MPEs (Gawer & Cusumano, 2002; Den Hartigh et al., 2016). Nevertheless, entrant platforms eager for opportunity exploration and exploitation drive integration into MPEs and collaborate with incumbents. We find that entrant platforms fail to integrate into MPEs if they lack a flexible platform design that meets the incumbent's integration requirements, because the platform flexibility refers to the ability to build sub-systems around the platform's technical core (Tiwana, Konsynski & Bush, 2010).

We argue that tensions arise with integrations into MPEs from co-ordinating coopetition dynamics between incumbent and new entrant platforms, especially when opportunistic behaviour tends to prioritise private benefits – i.e., the platform may realise greater value added outside MPE boundaries, then threaten/or decide to drop out instead of collaborating for greater collective benefits – and therefore triggers competition between stakeholders in MPEs – i.e., the gatekeeping effect arising between platforms limiting the amount of shared knowledge and thereby preventing other platforms from developing further dependent innovations.

Tensions Associated with Value Configuration

MPEs provide a mediating ecosystem to enable the multi-layered complementarity between multiple platforms to enrich the value proposition for the whole field/industry more than can be created by an individual multisided platform working independently. The complexity of the multi-layered ecosystem drives these layers to shape the ecosystem's overall goal (Teece, 2018). Our findings indicate that competition on the inter-platform level arises from individual platforms' tendency to add new complementary offerings to the existing ones to expand their market base and reach the global market. This may result in platforms' tendency to implement a transparent knowledge-sharing framework with other platforms in MPEs. We found that incumbent platforms joined MPEs as part of their battle for market dominance; cooperating with the new entrant platforms guaranteed their market dominance. For this, tensions happen during the transition to extensive knowledge-sharing mechanisms as a requirement for integration into MPEs.

In MPEs, the incumbent platforms' aspiration for market superiority justifies their control and leadership rights through their share of the research and development costs incurred during the risky stages of the battle for market dominance. Nevertheless, the incumbent platforms use it as a strategic manoeuvre for designing the governance roles for the whole ecosystem. This leads incumbents to anonymise data before sharing them with entrant platforms; the anonymisation is done to an extent that hinders further innovation. Tensions in agreeing governance roles may constrain the configuration of MPEs or hinder further innovations driven by the fear of losing market dominance.

Regardless of the ecosystem's enabling role in creating the network between multiple platforms to work together holistically, the ecosystem establishes a boundary role for all the stakeholders in the ecosystem. The ecosystem governance role places some boundaries that differ, depending on the stakeholder role in the platform. For example, the leading platforms consider knowledge sharing a limitation for their future market expansions. For this, platform leaders will get complementors to develop similar innovations that stimulate sudden competition in certain markets or technical

154   *Mahmoud Mohamed et al.*

domains. Furthermore, each stakeholder in the platform of the platform's ecosystem aims for a winning market share role (Figure 9.3).

Advantage Exploration and Exploitation Tensions

Like the distributed platform leadership roles enabled by collective governance in a multisided platform setting (O'Mahony & Karp, 2022), we find that inter-platform coopetition in MPEs intensifies data sharing. However, it increases tensions when the platform's opportunistic behaviour becomes visible. We therefore claim that collective governance emerges between platforms in MPEs when they fully agree on the coopetition terms in response to the appearance of sudden competition in MPEs. The incumbent platforms retain their dominant leadership role in deciding whom to admit to MPEs and the conditions for granting access to new stakeholders. The entrant platforms' dependency on incumbents for entering complex domains like healthcare originates the unbalanced leadership roles in MPEs. For this, platforms integrating into MPEs need to be opportunistically aligned (O'Mahony & Karp, 2022); otherwise, opportunistic dropouts will occur if unbalanced leadership roles pressurise the new entrant platforms' autonomy to grant access to new possible partners/stakeholders. Complementary relationship and competition are closely intertwined and are needed to grow the MPEs. Despite competitive pressure through the unbalanced coopetition dynamics, it stimulates the R&D trials in each platform. We found that the balanced cooperative and competitive dynamics are the enablers of platform innovations that go beyond the scope of each platform and find new ways to retain their presence in the market.

Implications for Theory

This study makes three main contributions in exploring how coopetition-related tension arises when complementing entrant and incumbent platforms integrate into MPEs.

First, it addresses the gap in the platform coopetition literature by building a foundation for platform research when multiple platforms are integrated into MPEs. The extant coopetition literature highlights the need to address the role of coopetition in relation to the competitiveness and emergence of the ecosystem (Choi, Garcia & Friedrich, 2010; Ritala, Golnam & Wegmann, 2014; Ritala, 2019). In doing so, we analysed the integration of individual platforms into MPEs until the coopetition agreement between participating platforms is reached. Moreover, we tracked the platform-to-platform openness and governance roles and conditions. As much as the opportunity that coopetition between platforms in MPEs brings to the platforms, we argue that coopetition-related tensions may hinder the integration process by causing a dropout in the middle of the integration process, especially when platforms attempt to grant or hinder access to its infrastructure in trade and the broader market share of new product development. This finding resonates with findings related to the platform's decision to choose the control mode, either by allowing the centralised or controlled control of the platform's technical core to maintain a certain degree of market dominance (Den Hartigh et al., 2016). Furthermore, our study highlights that the competition for market dominance in a particular field remains the constraint for developing the practical coopetition framework between multiple platforms in MPEs. The coopetition becomes a wise strategic choice for entrant platforms operating in complex domains that need huge initial investments to bring novel solutions to the market. This finding resonates with the collective value creation literature through coopetition (Gnyawali & Park, 2011; Ritala & Hurmelinna-Laukkanen, 2019; Zhang et al., 2020). The extant literature focuses on studying the platform leadership, governance strategies, and complementarity between platform owners and complementors who add value on the supply side of the platform during the battles for market dominance (Gawer & Cusumano, 2015; Den Hartigh et al., 2016). Furthermore, scholars have examined the competition situations between platform owners and complementors (Zhu & Liu, 2018), following the recommendations of Zhang et al. (2020) that the complementor's interaction in relation to knowledge sharing and platform openness should be explored. This study identifies the collective governance mechanism between complementing entrant and incumbent platforms. Especially when single platforms integrate into MPEs, each platform will revise its access and control role in accordance with the new platform setting. We argue that platforms integrate into MPEs to expand their business scope and create value by building a collaborative relationship with their competitors. Platform-to-platform openness is the key to integrating and establishing the coopetition dynamics.

Second, we conclude that the value proposition in MPE ecosystems depends on the degree of end-user centricity and dual knowledge sharing between complementors and platform leaders. However, when platforms integrate into MPEs, their old governance models initiate the tensions with the new collective value creation-based model. This enables the rivalry power between platforms to influence their ability to share information with other complementing platforms, which leads to fragmented innovations and inside-the-box untapped opportunities (Zhang et al., 2020). This view is consistent with Koo and Eesley's (2021) view of the platform owner's right to orchestrate the platform design rules to govern value creation dynamics between stakeholders. Our research suggests another consequence in MPEs: A knowledge-sharing framework to be integrated within the platform's architecture as a condition for the integration into MPEs. This intensifies the cooperative initiatives between all the stakeholders in the ecosystem and reduces the likelihood of gatekeeping initiated by the incumbents as a defensive strategy against technology imitation or hijacking.

156 *Mahmoud Mohamed et al.*

Third, our study concludes that knowledge sharing at the ecosystem level is very important, because it influences the formation of the coopetition framework between platforms in MPEs. We argue that coopetition is likely to form when competing actors realise that the collective benefits driven by the cooperative strategy are greater than the individual actor's private benefits. Gatekeeping tensions hinder the achievement of collective governance agreements, challenging the expansion of collaborative dynamics between platforms integrating into MPEs. This finding complements the extant discussion around platform governance and complementary dynamics in the platform ecosystem (Iansiti & Levien, 2004; Gawer & Cusumano, 2015; Zhang et al., 2020; Broekhuizen et al., 2021). Since platform governance remains the most critical feature in the integration into MPEs, the power of control is based on the ownership of the platform's technical infrastructure (Rietveld, Schilling & Bellavitis, 2019; Kretschmer et al., 2022). Our study shows that platform leadership roles grant leading platforms the "owner of the technical core" right to define the goals of the entire ecosystem and guide the value creation and capture activities between all the platforms involved in MPEs. This is consistent with the view that grants incumbents "as platform leaders" the right to design the governance mechanisms for the platform ecosystem and establish the communication linkages between all complementors (Zhang et al., 2020). We also suggest another consequence: The gatekeeping of the complementing entrant platforms hinders knowledge sharing and the retraining of complementors' innovation when a platform's innovation becomes dependent on incumbent governance roles.

Based on this exploratory study, we found that creating multi-layered coopetition in MPEs is possible from the theoretical perspective. However, building the collaborative framework tends to be challenging when several platforms that integrate into the ecosystem appear to have competing market goals. The process of opening the platform infrastructure and establishing a knowledge-sharing framework with other platforms in the ecosystem embodies multiple challenges. Platforms tend to retrain the information if other platforms utilise it for further product development efforts outside the platform ecosystem.

Implications for Practice

Our study proposes several recommendations for platform managers and practitioners when platforms consider integrating into MPEs an opportunity to expand their business scope and market share. First, we encourage platform managers to consider the contextual factors for their platforms to integrate into MPEs in defining the goals of their integrations. The in-depth analysis of our case indicates that coopetition comes as a risky strategic decision for the incumbent platforms to undertake, especially when they collaborate with competing entrants who bring disruptive innovation to the market. Incumbents risk collaborating with entrants associated with the fear of technology imitation and losing the aspiration for market superiority. Nonetheless, the integration into MPEs and collaboration with competing platforms enriches the individual platform's ability to conduct R&D projects on a larger scale beyond the individual platform's ability. By highlighting the coopetition-related tensions, we hope to encourage platform managers and decision-makers to define the coopetition framework in terms of the choice of leadership and governance roles, whether centralised or collective models. We propose that well-defined contextual factors for platforms' integration into MPS reduce the likelihood of tensions that cause dropouts in the advanced stages of integrations. The agreement of the coopetition framework that is made during the early stages of integration into MPEs can also influence the control of the tensions that may arise in later phases.

Second, we argue that high levels of platform-to-platform openness do not prevent the inter-complementarity tensions when some platforms realise significant opportunities outside the scope of MPEs. However, when platforms operate in complex domains like healthcare, a balanced coopetition dynamics between incumbent and new entrant platform works well in MPEs if it guarantees the incumbent platforms' dominance in the market and enables new entrant platforms to get their own share of the market. We conclude that collective governance models are needed to integrate new entrants and incumbent platforms into MPEs. Otherwise, tensions will arise from controlled governance; opportunistic behaviour then hinders the collective value creation between platforms. This study may encourage platform managers and decision-makers to achieve a collective governance model within their coopetition agreement.

Limitations and Directions for Future Research

Our study runs into several limitations that could be investigated by future research. First, this study holistically investigates coopetition-related tensions in MPEs. Furthermore, empirical evidence is needed to examine how the organisational structure of MPEs can coordinate coopetition tensions between complementors and facilitate knowledge sharing between competing platforms. Second, this study examines inter-platform complementarity as a tension rather than an intensifier of further innovations. Building on Cusumano and Gawer's (2002) study, we find that keeping complementors with similar goals in one management hub improves collaborative relations. Otherwise, the opportunistic behaviour disrupts inter- and intra-platform collaborative dynamics (Kretschmer et al., 2022). Additional studies are needed to validate the framework for managing the complementor's conflict of interest in MPEs when their complementary relationship threatens competition. Third, we use the digital care ecosystem as the contextual framework for our study, favouring the collaborative settings of MPEs. Studying

158 *Mahmoud Mohamed et al.*

similar platform settings in other contexts, including a wide range of complementors, is needed to examine cross-industry complementary relationships between platforms and the contextual motives for joining the MPE ecosystem.

Our study's empirical setting did not allow a direct analysis of the stages of the complementors' disputes for two reasons. On the one hand, this study was conducted as part of the Stroke-Data project that aimed to integrate platforms into Stroke-Data MPEs. On the other hand, it was challenging to collect further data on the complementing platforms' response to the incumbents' demands, especially when we tried to navigate the platform's future market strategies and aims of the coopetition. We believe further longitudinal studies are needed to analyse the complementors' interactions during advanced stages, especially the post-integration stage, including knowledge sharing versus gatekeeping between platforms in MPEs. In addition, it will be beneficial to propose strategies for managing inter-platform tensions when complementors realise benefits outside ecosystem boundaries. Our current findings categorise that tension in the scope of the complementors' opportunistic behaviour, which leads to dropouts from the platforms.

Nevertheless, we suggest further research to investigate the strategic framework for managing these tensions. In addition, further research will be beneficial for investigating the technological versus institutional conditions, *"government legislation versus technological and market requirements"*, which may affect MPEs' overall dynamics. Finally, our study is based on eight Finnish technology-oriented platforms operating in the healthcare domain. All the case companies had to meet the integration and hospital requirements to implement their technology. It is therefore challenging to generalise this study's findings for other domains/industries. Nevertheless, this study opens future research avenues for analysing coopetition-related tensions in other MPEs settings.

Acknowledgement

This research received funding as part of the Stroke-Data Project. We also acknowledge generous research grants from the Foundation for Economic Education – Liikesivistysrahasto and the Finnish Cultural Foundation – The Northern Ostrobothnia Regional Fund.

References

Baldwin, C.Y. & Clark, K.B. (2002). "The option value of modularity in design", *Harvard NOM Research Paper*, vol. 1, pp. 1–14.

Boudreau, K.J. & Jeppesen, L.B. (2015). "Unpaid crowd complementors: The platform network effect mirage", *Strategic Management Journal*, vol. 36(12), pp. 1761–1777.

Tensions of Coopetition and Integration 159

Braun, V. & Clarke, V. (2006). "Using thematic analysis in psychology", *Qualitative Research in Psychology*, vol. 3(2), pp. 77–101.

Broekhuizen, T.L., Emrich, O., Gijsenberg, M.J., Broekhuis, M., Donkers, B., & Sloot, L.M. (2021). "Digital platform openness: Drivers, dimensions and outcomes", *Journal of Business Research*, vol. 122, pp. 902–914.

Choi, P., Garcia, R., & Friedrich, C. (2010). "The drivers for collective horizontal coopetition: A case study of screwcap initiatives in the international wine industry", *International Journal of Strategic Business Alliances*, vol. 1(3), pp. 271–290.

Collingridge, D.S. & Gantt, E.E. (2008). "The quality of qualitative research", *American Journal of Medical Quality*, vol. 23(5), pp. 389–395.

Corley, K.G. & Gioia, D.A. (2004). "Identity ambiguity and change in the wake of a corporate spin-off", *Administrative Science Quarterly*, vol. 49(2), pp. 173–208.

Cusumano, M.A. & Gawer, A. (2002). "The elements of platform leadership", *MIT Sloan Management Review*, vol. 43(3), p. 51.

Cusumano, M., Yoffie, D., & Gawer, A. (2020). "The future of platforms", *MIT Sloan Management Review*, vol. 61(3), pp. 46–54.

Dearnley, C. (2005). "A reflection on the use of semi-structured interviews", *Nurse Researcher*, vol. 13(1), pp. 19–28.

Den Hartigh, E., Ortt, J.R., Van de Kaa, G., & Stolwijk, C.C. (2016). "Platform control during battles for market dominance: The case of Apple versus IBM in the early personal computer industry", *Technovation*, vol. 48, pp. 4–12.

Economides, N. & Katsamakas, E. (2006). "Two-sided competition of proprietary vs. open-source technology platforms and the implications for the software industry", *Management Science*, vol. 52(7), pp. 1057–1071.

Eisenhardt, K.M. (1989). "Building theories from case study research", *Academy of Management Review*, vol. 14(4), pp. 532–550.

Eisenmann, T., Parker, G., & Van Alstyne, M.W. (2006). "Strategies for two-sided markets", *Harvard Business Review*, vol. 84(10), p. 92.

Eisenmann, T.R., Parker, G., & Van Alstyne, M. (2009). "Opening platforms: How, when and why", *Platforms, Markets and Innovation*, vol. 6, pp. 131–162.

Eriksson, P. & Kovalainen, A. (2008). "Research philosophy", in *Qualitative Methods in Business Research*. London: SAGE Publications Ltd., 4–10, available at: http://0-dx.doi.org.oasis.unisa.ac.za/10.4135/9780857028044.d3 (Accessed: 23 April 2022).

Gawer, A. (2014). "Bridging differing perspectives on technological platforms: Toward an integrative framework", *Research Policy*, vol. 43(7), pp. 1239–1249.

Gawer, A. & Cusumano, M.A. (2015). "Platform leaders", *MIT Sloan Management Review*, vol. 56(2), pp. 68–75.

Gawer, A. & Cusumano, M.A. (2002). *Platform Leadership: How Intel, Microsoft, and Cisco Drive Industry Innovation*. Boston, MA: Harvard Business School Press.

Gawer, A. & Henderson, R. (2007). "Platform owner entry and innovation in complementary markets: Evidence from Intel", *Journal of Economics & Management Strategy*, vol. 16(1), pp. 1–34.

Gnyawali, D.R., Madhavan, R., He, J., & Bengtsson, M. (2016). "The competition–cooperation paradox in inter-firm relationships: A conceptual framework", *Industrial Marketing Management*, vol. 53, pp. 7–18.

Gnyawali, D.R. & Park, B.J.R. (2011). "Co-opetition between giants: Collaboration with competitors for technological innovation", *Research Policy*, vol. 40(5), pp. 650–663.

Guest, G., Bunce, A., & Johnson, L. (2006). "How many interviews are enough? An experiment with data saturation and variability", *Field Methods*, vol. 18(1), pp. 59–82.

Gulati, R., Puranam, P., & Tushman, M., (2012). "Meta-organisation design: Rethinking design in interorganizational and community contexts', *Strategic Management Journal*, vol. 33(6), pp. 571–586

Hein, A., Schreieck, M., Riasanow, T., Setzke, D.S., Wiesche, M., Böhm, M., & Krcmar, H. (2020). "Digital platform ecosystems", *Electronic Markets*, vol. 30(1), pp. 87–98.

Iansiti, M. & Levien, R. (2004). *Keystones and Dominators: Framing Operating and Technology Strategy in a Business Ecosystem*. Boston, MA: Harvard Business School Press.

Isckia, T., De Reuver, M., & Lescop, D. (2020). "Orchestrating platform ecosystems: The interplay of innovation and business development subsystems", *Journal of Innovation Economics Management*, vol. 2, pp. 197–223.

Jia, X., Cusumano, M.A., & Chen, J. (2019). "An analysis of multisided platform research over the past three decades: Framework and discussion", in *MIT Sloan Working Paper number 5891-19*. Cambridge, MA: MIT Sloan School of Management.

Khanna, T., Gulati, R., & Nohria, N. (1998). "The dynamics of learning alliances: Competition, cooperation, and relative scope", *Strategic Management Journal*, vol. 19(3), pp. 193–210.

Koo, W.W. & Eesley, C.E. (2021). "Platform governance and the rural–urban divide: Sellers' responses to design change", *Strategic Management Journal*, vol. 42(5), pp. 941–967.

Kretschmer, T., Leiponen, A., Schilling, M., & Vasudeva, G. (2022). "Platform ecosystems as meta-organisations: Implications for platform strategies", *Strategic Management Journal*, vol. 43(2), pp. 405–424.

Leiblein, M.J. & Miller, D.J. (2003). "An empirical examination of transaction- and firm-level influences on the vertical boundaries of the firm", *Strategic Management Journal*, vol. 24(9), pp. 839–859.

Lepak, D.P., Smith, K.G., & Taylor, M.S. (2007). "Value creation and value capture: A multilevel perspective", *Academy of Management Review*, vol. 32(1), pp. 180–194.

McIntyre, D.P. & Srinivasan, A. (2017). "Networks, platforms, and strategy: Emerging views and next steps", *Strategic Management Journal*, vol. 38(1), pp. 141–160.

Miles, M.B. & Huberman, A.M. (1994). *Qualitative Data Analysis: An Expanded Sourcebook*. London: SAGE Publication.

Miller, C.D. & Toh, P.K. (2022). "Complementary components and returns from coordination within ecosystems via standard setting", *Strategic Management Journal*, vol. 43(3), pp. 627–662.

Miller-Young, J. & Yeo, M. (2015). "Conceptualising and communicating SoTL: A framework for the field", *Teaching and Learning Inquiry*, vol. 3(2), pp. 37–53.

Morse, J.M. (1995). "The significance of saturation", *Qualitative Health Research*, vol. 5(2), pp. 147–149.

Niemelä, R., Pikkarainen, M., Ervasti, M., & Reponen, J. (2019). "The change of paediatric surgery practice due to the emergence of connected health technologies", *Technological Forecasting and Social Change*, vol. 146, pp. 352–365.

O'Mahony, S. & Karp, R. (2022). "From proprietary to collective governance: How do platform participation strategies evolve?", *Strategic Management Journal*, vol. 43(3), pp. 530–562.

Patton, M.Q. (2002). "Two decades of developments in qualitative inquiry: A personal, experiential perspective", *Qualitative Social Work*, vol. 1(3), pp. 261–283.

Rietveld, J., Schilling, M.A., & Bellavitis, C. (2019). "Platform strategy: Managing ecosystem value through selective promotion of complements", *Organization Science*, vol. 30(6), pp. 1232–1251.

Ritala, P. (2019). "Coopetition and market performance", in *The Routledge Companion to Coopetition Strategies*. London and New York, NY: Routledge, 317–325.

Ritala, P., Golnam, A., & Wegmann, A. (2014). "Coopetition-based business models: The case of Amazon.com", *Industrial Marketing Management*, vol. 43(2), pp. 236–249.

Ritala, P. & Hurmelinna-Laukkanen, P. (2019). "Dynamics of coopetitive value creation and appropriation", in *The Routledge Companion to Coopetition Strategies*. London and New York, NY: Routledge, 58–67.

Ritala, P., Husted, K., Olander, H., & Michailova, S. (2018). "External knowledge sharing and radical innovation: The downsides of uncontrolled openness", *Journal of Knowledge Management*, vol. 22(5), pp. 1104–1123.

Strauss, A. & Corbin, J.M. (1997). *Grounded Theory in Practice*. London: SAGE Publications.

Teece, D.J. (2018). "Profiting from innovation in the digital economy: Enabling technologies, standards, and licensing models in the wireless world", *Research Policy*, vol. 47(8), pp. 1367–1387.

Tiwana, A. (2013). *Platform Ecosystems: Aligning Architecture, Governance, and Strategy*. London: Morgan Kaufmann.

Tiwana, A., Konsynski, B., & Bush, A.A. (2010). "Platform evolution: Coevolution of platform architecture, governance, and environmental dynamics (research commentary)", *Information Systems Research*, vol. 21(4), pp. 675–687.

Tsai, W. (2002). "Social structure of "coopetition" within a multiunit organisation: Coordination, competition, and intraorganizational knowledge sharing", *Organization Science*, vol. 13(2), pp. 179–190.

Tura, N., Kutvonen, A., & Ritala, P. (2018). "Platform design framework: Conceptualisation and application", *Technology Analysis & Strategic Management*, vol. 30(8), pp. 881–894.

Valkokari, K. (2015). "Business, innovation, and knowledge ecosystems: How they differ and how to survive and thrive within them", *Technology Innovation Management Review*, vol. 5(8), pp. 17–24.

Wen, W. & Zhu, F. (2019). "Threat of platform-owner entry and complementor responses: Evidence from the mobile app market", *Strategic Management Journal*, vol. 40(9), pp. 1336–1367.

Williamson, P.J. & De Meyer, A. (2012). "Ecosystem advantage: How to successfully harness the power of partners", *California Management Review*, vol. 55(1), pp. 24–46.

Wong, S.S. (2004). "Distal and local group learning: Performance trade-offs and tensions", *Organization Science*, vol. 15(6), pp. 645–656.

Yin, R.K. (2003). "Designing case studies", *Qualitative Research Methods*, vol. 5(14), pp. 359–386.

Yrjölä, S.I., Ahokangas, P., & Matinmikko-Blue, M. (2021). "Platform-based ecosystemic business models in future mobile operator business", *Journal of Business Models*, vol. 9(4), pp. 67–93.

Zhang, M.Y. & Williamson, P. (2021). "The emergence of multiplatform ecosystems: insights from China's mobile payments system in overcoming bottlenecks to reach the mass market", *Technological Forecasting and Social Change*, vol. 173, p. 121128.

Zhang, Y., Li, J., & Tong, T.W. (2022). "Platform governance matters: How platform gatekeeping affects knowledge sharing among complementors", *Strategic Management Journal*, vol. 43(3), pp. 599–626.

Zhu, F. & Iansiti, M. (2012). "Entry into platform-based markets", *Strategic Management Journal*, vol. 33(1), pp. 88–106.

Zhu, F. & Liu, Q. (2018). "Competing with complementors: An empirical look at Amazon.com", *Strategic Management Journal*, vol. 39(10), pp. 2618–2642.

10 Customer Orientation: The Case of Creating Value in Ecosystems

Mika Yrjölä, Aleksi Niittymies, and Abdollah Mohammadparast Tabas

Introduction

Scholars have been increasingly turning attention to customer value created in ecosystems instead of individual competing companies (Adner, 2006; Clarysse et al., 2014; Gyrd-Jones & Kornum, 2013). The ecosystem perspective on value creation is concerned with the interrelated and interconnected firms or entities that collaborate with each other to create value (Kapoor, 2018; Frow et al., 2014). The ecosystems consist of multiple actors, such as customers, partners, suppliers and other stakeholders (Iansiti & Levien, 2004), specialising in specific parts in the value production chain (Gyrd-Jones & Kornum, 2013). To make the ecosystem work, the actors adopt different interrelated and overlapping roles in which firms can simultaneously be competitors and complementors while also being in a customer–supplier relationship. The underlying premise is that in the modern world, firms lack the resources and capabilities to provide up-to-date customer value individually (Frow et al., 2014).

However, due to the multiple interrelated and overlapping roles firms have to adopt within the ecosystem, the traditional understanding of the customer has become outdated. In such circumstances, managers face considerable challenges in identifying who the customer is and how value is being created. This is problematic because the added value of an ecosystem can be hampered by its inability to effectively foster and manage customer relationships and value creation processes. Inadequate understanding of the customer increases the risk that the organisation will become irrelevant in the eyes of its customers, miss important external threats and opportunities and ultimately lose its ability to operate in the ecosystem (Day & Moorman, 2013). Conversely, organisations that achieve a customer orientation tend to be rewarded with superior financial performance (Hortinha, Lages & Lages, 2011; Narver & Slater, 1990; Shah et al., 2006). Despite the highlighted role of customer orientation in ecosystems, we know relatively little about how managers make sense of customer value creation within ecosystems.

In this chapter, our purpose is to explore the ways in which managers understand customer value creation within ecosystems and how managers

DOI: 10.4324/9781003326731-10

164   *Mika Yrjölä et al.*

foster customer orientation in their organisational contexts. We address this question by drawing from iterative and abductive research approaches and examining the managerial understanding of customer value creation within 34 companies embedded in ecosystems or networks. Based on our analyses, we identify four ways managers view customer orientation: (1) As culture, (2) as a strategy, (3) as a mental model and (4) as customer intimacy. Thereafter, we further explicate the different managerial ways of understanding customer orientation as well as their interrelations based on their structural composition and whether they emphasise individual- or organisational-level aspects of customer orientation.

The rest of this chapter is organised as follows. First, we review the literature on customer orientation and value creation in ecosystems, which is followed by an explication of our methodological choices. Thereafter, the findings are explained and supported with empirical case data. Finally, we conclude by discussing our contributions and their implications.

Theoretical Background: Customer Orientation, Customer Value and Ecosystems

Customer Orientation

The customer orientation of companies and managers has spurred much research and discussion (Morgan et al., 2018). Multiple definitions and conceptualisations exist. Authors have used the concepts of customer orientation (Angulo-Ruiz et al., 2014; Bettencourt & Brown, 2003; Deshpandé, Farley & Webster, 1993; Hartline, Maxham Iii & McKee, 2000; Homburg, Workman & Jensen, 2000; Hortinha, Lages & Lages, 2011; Kohli & Jaworski, 1990; Narver & Slater, 1990; Schwepker, 2003), customer-centricity (Chang, Park & Chaiy, 2010; Gurau, Ranchhod & Hackney, 2003; Lamberti, 2013; Shah et al., 2006; Sheth, Sisodia & Sharma, 2000; Trainor et al., 2014), demand orientation (Morash, Droge & Vickery, 1996), customer intimacy (Treacy & Wiersema, 1993) and customer focus (Lindic & da Silva, 2011; Said et al., 2009; Zhao, Dröge & Stank, 2001).

Customer orientation has been studied in terms of information gathering and sharing, cultural values and norms, and customer perceptions of an organisation's service and interaction (Deshpandé, Farley & Webster, 1993; Korunka et al., 2007). Moreover, customer orientation can be analysed from the perspective of individuals or the organisation (Whelan et al., 2010). On an individual level, customer orientation refers to individual employees' or managers' tendency to think and act in ways that recognise and meet individual customer needs (Brown et al., 2002). On an organisational level, customer orientation refers to the organisations' atmosphere, culture, and practices that contribute to meeting customer needs (Grizzle et al., 2009).

Organisational-level customer orientation, therefore, is thought to promote individuals' customer-oriented attitudes and behaviours (Grizzle et al., 2009).

In this chapter, we define customer orientation as an organisational tendency to emphasise the importance of customers with the implicit or explicit assumption that creating customer value is a priority for organisational success in the long term (Korunka et al., 2007; Grizzle et al., 2009; Morgan et al., 2018). This tendency can be visible in various organisational elements, such as attitudes, norms, processes, routines and decision-making. Instead of focusing our attention on individual elements, our focus in this chapter is to uncover how managers understand customer orientation in their own contexts. The managerial perspective is important because previous studies have shown that adopting a customer orientation is difficult and complex (Yrjölä, 2020) and that managers are key to its success (Lamberti, 2013). For instance, managers show a systematic tendency to fail in their efforts to take customer preferences into consideration (Hattula et al., 2015) and to overestimate customer satisfaction and loyalty. Implementing a customer orientation puts great pressure on the organisation and its members, which is why top management involvement is crucial (Lamberti, 2013). Moreover, implementation is likely to fail without the adequate support and training of frontline personnel (Reich & Benbasat, 1990). Managerial involvement and actions are crucial in the implementation of a customer orientation because the implementation process might otherwise lead to conflict in employees' roles and role ambiguity, which, in turn, can lead to a decrease in customer-oriented behaviours (Bettencourt & Brown, 2003).

Through an emphasis on customers, the objective of a customer orientation is to create a competitive advantage for the business or to ensure long-term profitability in general (Deshpandé, Farley & Webster, 1993; Narver & Slater, 1990; Shah et al., 2006; Reich & Benbasat, 1990). Studies have shown that customer orientation improves the financial performance of companies (Shah et al., 2006). The logic behind customer orientation is that a better understanding of customer needs enables organisations to better customise offerings to individual customers or customer segments, which in turn means that these organisations can create superior value for customers (Kohli & Jaworski, 1990; Korunka et al., 2007; Lamberti, 2013; Lindic & da Silva, 2011; Morash, Droge & Vickery, 1996; Narver & Slater, 1990; Sheth, Sisodia & Sharma, 2000; Slater & Narver, 2000; Zhao, Dröge & Stank, 2001; Treacy & Wiersema, 1993; Zhou & Li, 2010).

Customer orientation has been found to affect multiple aspects of organisations. First, it affects organisational processes directed towards customers, especially the gathering and analysing of customer or market information (Hult, Ketchen & Slater, 2005) and customer relation management processes (Trainor et al., 2014). For example, customer orientation allows the organisation to maintain more durable customer relationships (Rapp, Trainor & Agnihotri, 2010). Customer orientation has also been found to improve service quality (Said et al., 2009) and innovation capabilities (Hortinha, Lages & Lages, 2011). Second, customer orientation affects and manifests itself in organisational culture, including organisational members' shared beliefs and ways of acting in relation to the customers (Chang, Park & Chaiy, 2010; Hult, Ketchen & Slater, 2005; Narver & Slater, 1990; Slater & Narver, 2000; Strong & Harris 2004). Third, customer orientation can also be visible in the organisational structure (Homburg, Workman & Jensen, 2000; Mukerjee, 2013). A customer-oriented organisation is one that is structured around the needs of different customer groups or segments (instead of being organised around product categories) (Homburg, Workman & Jensen, 2000), and all functional activities are integrated and aligned in the delivery of superior customer value, enabling a firm to overcome functional barriers and share customer information (Wang & Feng, 2012).

In summary, managers, as actors that shape organisational processes, culture and strategies, are critical in the implementation of customer orientation. Customer orientation involves the assumption that creating customer value is a priority for organisational success in the long term, but how this priority is operationalised in different contexts is the responsibility of management. Although customer orientation can involve multiple aspects, such as individual, cultural, structural and informational considerations, we know very little about how individual managers understand customer orientation in an ecosystem context.

Customer Value Creation in Ecosystems

In recent years, there has been an increase in the popularity of the ecosystem metaphor among industry practitioners, research scholars and politicians (Audretsch et al. 2019; Spigel, 2017). The ecosystem idea, derived from the natural sciences, examines the interdependence and interconnection of entities involved in the value creation process (Frow et al., 2014; Kapoor, 2018). The term ecosystem is a mix of two terms: "eco" refers to the natural environment, and "system" refers to the degree of complexity (Cavallo, Ghezzi & Balocco, 2019). Moore (1996) was the first to introduce the notion of ecosystems into the realm of management. The management ecosystem comprises numerous participants, including customers, partners, suppliers and other stakeholders (Iansiti & Levien, 2004).

Each company in an ecosystem specialises in supplying a certain good or service component, and value is co-created through the intricate interplay of a network of stakeholders (Gyrd-Jones & Kornum, 2013). This contrasts with the typical linear approach to business and customer value creation, in which a company offers value directly to the customer (Vargo & Lusch, 2004). Adner (2006) claimed that no single company can deliver value alone; companies must collaborate to create value for customers (Clarysse et al., 2014). Frow et al. (2014) emphasised that no single company possesses all the necessary resources to operate autonomously. There is a mix of collaboration to create value and competition to capture value inside the ecosystem's firms (Bremner et al., 2017). As a result, businesses form an ecosystem and become reliant on one another for survival (Overholm, 2015).

Companies are interconnected and interdependent, and the activities of one company affect the performance of other companies (Amit & Zott, 2012). The ecosystem is dynamic and ever-changing (Mack & Mayer, 2016), with companies' roles and positions continually changing (Adner, 2017). This requires supply-side companies to align their objectives with the ecosystem (Zahra & Nambisan, 2011). Actors in the ecosystem are tasked with connecting value creation to customers (Overholm, 2015). Customers are increasingly becoming the primary focus of businesses in which companies collaborate with customers to create value (Grönroos, 2011; Prahalad & Ramaswamy, 2004).

Customers exert a significant amount of control over the environment, even though they do not consciously control it (Voima et al., 2011). Customer involvement in the value co-creation process increases the efficiency and effectiveness of the value creation process (Agrawal & Rahman, 2015). According to Füller, Hutter and Faullant (2011), involving customers in value co-creation results in higher product quality. Feng et al. (2019) asserted that businesses can gather and disseminate information that enables them to provide enhanced services to their clients. Similarly, Tether and Tajar (2008) claimed that high-tech companies could enhance service/product development and innovation. In general, consumer involvement in value co-creation increases consumer satisfaction (Marzocchi & Zammit, 2006).

Synthesising Framework

Figure 10.1, based on a synthesis of the literature, illustrates the preliminary framework of this chapter.

Methodology

Our purpose is to develop a better understanding of how managers understand customer value creation while operating within ecosystems and networks – a context in which the boundaries between customer, collaborator and complementors can easily become blurred. Studying managerial perceptions and different ways of understanding customer value is challenging, as it requires capturing mental representations of the managers, which are notoriously hard to observe (Huff, 1990). To meet this challenge, we adopted a case study approach due to its suitability for addressing the perceptions and representation of managers (Maitland & Sammartino, 2015).

We collected data from 34 companies heavily embedded in networks and ecosystems by utilising semi-structured interviews as our primary means of enquiry. One top manager from each of the case companies was

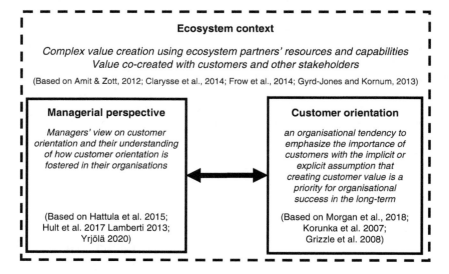

Figure 10.1 Preliminary framework for customer orientation in ecosystems.
Source: The authors.

interviewed, resulting in 34 interviews. The interviews were audio-recorded and transcribed. The transcribed interviews totalled 377 pages.

The companies were selected for the sample as they all operate within networks or ecosystems, thus providing access to a setting where firms in the ecosystem have multiple different roles simultaneously (i.e., customer, collaborator, complementor). We pursued breadth instead of depth in our sampling because we observed that how managers perceive customer value creation becomes quickly apparent, but a certain breadth is required to create convincing categorisation (Table 10.1).

In our analysis, we drew from iterative and abductive research logic, which provided a coherent backdrop for our study while enabling flexibility to utilise features from multiple different qualitative approaches instead of committing to any structured "template" of qualitative enquiry (Eisenhardt, 1989; Gioia et al., 2013). The abductive logic allowed the interplay and back-and-forth movement between existing theory and emergent empirical insights to guide our research process instead of rigid methodological procedures (Piekkari & Welch, 2017). Indeed, the redirections and changes in our research process were the source of the theoretical insights and allowed us to explicate the structures and interdependent relationships (Dubois & Gadde, 2014). This was an especially suitable approach for our purposes because customer value creation has been studied from multiple perspectives and the existing theoretical understanding provides a solid starting point, but the complexities of customer

Customer Orientation   169

Table 10.1 Participants in the study

Participant	Position/title	Industry	Revenue in million euros	Number of employees
1	CEO	Health services	9	48
2	CMO	Software	2	20
3	Executive VP of international sales	Health services	8	53
4	CEO	Healthcare	30	50
5	CEO	Health services	13	30
6	Chairman of Board	Construction	30	80
7	CEO	Health services	11	32
8	CMO	Healthcare	30	130
9	Managing Director	MedTech	11	50
10	CMO	Interior textile	5	30
11	CEO	MedTech	7	18
12	CEO	Media	350	2000
13	CEO	MedTech	3	9
14	CEO and Founder	Software	2	20
15	Quality and Regulatory specialist	Health services	2	7
16	Chairman of Board	Construction	30	100
17	CEO	MedTech	5	15
18	Founder	Services/Franchising	20	300
19	CEO	MedTech	4	10
20*	Business Area Director	Construction	150	1000
21*	Business Area Director	Construction	150	1000
22	CEO	MedTech	12	27
23	CEO	Machine industry	25	100
24	CEO	MedTech	17	38
25	International inquiries	Software	50	500
26	CEO	MedTech	5	12
27	VP of Sales and Marketing	MedTech	35	109
28**	COO	Food industry	80	80
29**	CFO	Food industry	80	80
30	CEO	Health services	6	25
31	CEO	Health services	5	23
32	CEO	MedTech	4	20
33	CEO	Health services	6	28
34	CEO	Health services	25	95

Source: The authors.

Notes

* Participants from the same firm who were interviewed separately.
** Participants from the same firm who were interviewed together.

170   *Mika Yrjölä et al.*

value creation within ecosystems and networks are not covered by the existing theoretical understanding.

Based on our analysis, we uncovered four ways managers can understand customer orientation while operating in networks and ecosystems: (1) customer orientation as culture, (2) customer orientation as a strategy, (3) customer orientation as a mental model and (4) customer orientation as customer intimacy. We then turned these four emergent categorisations into a fourfold table illustrating the interdependent relationships between the themes based on their structural composition and whether they emphasised individual- or organisation-level aspects of customer orientation.

Findings

Our findings illustrate four ways in which managers view customer orientation: As culture, as a strategy, as a mental model, and as customer intimacy (Figure 10.2). These views differ in their assumptions regarding the sources of competitive advantage as well as in perceptions of how customer orientation is fostered in organisations. Two of the views on customer orientation involve an organisational focus, whereas two depict a focus on the individual. Moreover, two of the approaches involve a more abstract view of customer orientation (psychological or cultural), whereas the two others involve a more concrete one (strategic or operational).

Customer Orientation as Culture

The first view of customer orientation considered it inherent in the organisational culture. According to the managers, a customer-oriented culture would be the best way to create a competitive advantage because the advantage lies in the customer service and experiences created by the company's personnel. Customer service or customer support could mean, for example, "*tools and processes where we very quickly kind of respond to whatever question of concern the customer has*" (Participant 3). Further, it involved the idea of being flexible towards customers: "*Making everything easy way for our customers. We are very flexible, as we are small companies*" (Participant 13). Participant 8 summarised this view:

> Our competitive advantage comes from the processes and operations; for example, how things are operating, how quickly we can ship products from the factory, and, of course, price is nowadays the baseline from which we start planning. But in my view, the service and the processes are where competitive advantages come from. ... Now that our situation is changed after acquiring a competitor, we are starting strategy work. And I plan on making a statement regarding how we shouldn't forget the customer and the core ... We must not forget the customer or be too self-confident. (Participant 8)

Customer Orientation   171

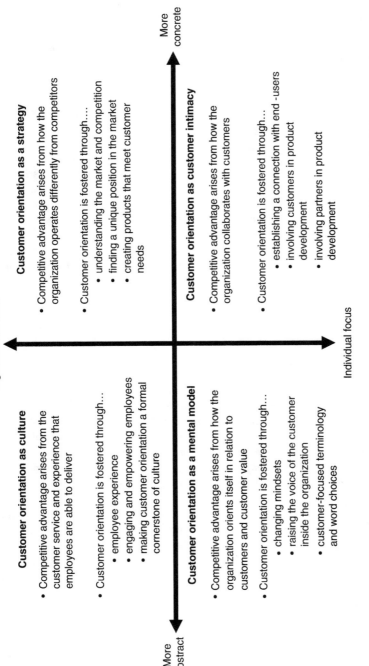

Figure 10.2 How managers understand customer value creation in the ecosystem context and activities through which managers advance customer orientation in their organisational contexts.

Source: The authors.

172 *Mika Yrjölä et al.*

Customer-oriented culture can be fostered through improving employee experience, engaging and empowering employees, and making customer orientation a formal cornerstone of culture. First, managers underlined how the personnel working with customers are critical to success: *"I like to think that the salespeople working at the grass roots level also have a surprisingly large impact. The quality of their sales work matters, which can be seen in certain ways, such as ... how they are able to translate our products into value for the customer"* (Participant 8). This creates an imperative to make sure they are satisfied and motivated to deliver excellent customer experiences. Participant 18 used the term employee experience:

> *In our thinking today, it is quite clear for us that the individual service person is the most important piece of the puzzle. ... The customer experience is totally reliant on that person. Even if everything else is excellent, it won't matter if the customer encounter isn't good. And in the other case, even if everything else is lacklustre, the individual service person can save the experience by being a wonderful person, the happiest person in the world, and delivering the best experience imaginable. ... The same way we have customer experiences, we talk about employee experiences. ... As I said, employees are even more important than customers.* (Participant 18)

Second, the managers fostered a customer-oriented culture by engaging and empowering employees in customer-related tasks and activities. For example, Participant 25 explained how their organisation involved employees in defining target customer groups:

> *We have made strategic choices regarding which markets we want to operate in and which types of customers we want to work with. ... Together with employees, we have these discussions so that we can all agree on these choices and that we could all understand, for example, why we're trying to get certain types and certain sizes of customers from specific markets. ... So, when a customer relationship has begun, we try to evaluate at a certain point that should we invest more in this relationship, is this aligned with our strategy.* (Participant 25)

Third, the managers used a more formal means of fostering a customer-oriented culture. For instance, Participant 21 indicated that in their organisation, customer orientation was made a formal part of culture:

> *We have defined the cornerstones of our culture. ... 'Customer is king', meaning that we operate close to the customer, understand customer needs, and, importantly, who we define as our customer. The end user can be seen as the customer but also the company delivering that final solution.* (Participant 21)

In summary, the first view of customer orientation involves paying attention to organisational members' shared beliefs and routines regarding customers. Viewed in this way, customer orientation as an organisational culture could be fostered by focusing on the experiences and involvement of employees, as well as signaling the importance of customer orientation in formal company documents relating to culture.

Customer Orientation as a Strategy

The second view of customer orientation perceived it as a strategy or strategic choice for the company. Here, the managers underlined the need to understand how the markets, especially competitors, operate. By operating differently from competitors, companies can be perceived as unique and attractive choices by customers. The goal is to stand out from competition, whether established through a unique operational model or a compelling customer experience:

> The world has changed compared to how it was when we started twelve years ago. When we launched, our competitive advantage was that we had such a unique operating model; we stood out from the competition very strongly. ... But in the last five years, I think it all comes down to the customer experience. Previously, we focused on our unique concept because the industry was so fragmented at the time. ... So, currently I believe that our competitive advantage now and in the future lies in customer experience, customer insight, and technology. I dare say there are not many companies that are as tech-oriented as ours. We know very much about our customers and how our personnel are operating; we know everything in real time; and we have multiple metrics, such as average service times for each service and what are the waiting times. We are very data-oriented, which is not typical in our industry. (Participant 18)

> At the heart of the strategy is getting an answer to the question of what the business's purpose is. Why could we grow, and what allows us to internationalise? What is the added value that we can produce for the market and customers? ... [In creating a competitive advantage], it is important to understand customer needs. What creates value for the customer? Competitive advantage is best built around things that are meaningful to customers. (Participant 20)

Moreover, some of the interviewees talked about challenging industry standards. For instance, Participant 25 remarked that their company was profiled as a challenger in the industry:

> Our industry is growing so fast that even without competitive differentiation, we can achieve a ten percent yearly growth. In terms of competitive advantage, an advantage can arise from even very small nuances. What we perceive our advantage to be is that we're challenging the large incumbents with more agile operating models ... Our advantage is based on agile software development methods and user-centred operations. ... We've made a conscious choice of doing

174 *Mika Yrjölä et al.*

things differently ... In the customers' eyes, the differentiation comes from the fact that we develop software very differently from our competitors; we have profiled ourselves as challengers in the industry. (Participant 25)

Customer orientation as a strategy can be developed further by analysing and understanding the market and competitors, finding a unique positioning in the market, and creating products that meet the needs of customers. Relating to the first method, managers highlighted the need for market research: *"This is a fundamental question: you have to know the market, conduct market research, visit the market, and thoroughly figure out what the best way of entering the market is and what we offer as solution"* (Participant 6). Participant 10 added:

The first thing to do is market research and getting to know and understand the market. ... It would have been impossible for us to grow without knowing the market well. For example, we went to the main trade fairs in Europe so that we could understand our competitors, you know, who are offering similar products. We should know what they are manufacturing and what they are capable of producing. That's how we found our own segment. I am a firm believer in doing your own thing, not trying to copy what others are doing. ... We have to know who the market leader is, who is operating in the market, and try to spot some good and bad things in what others are doing, and eventually find our own way of doing things and our own clientele. (Participant 10)

As the aforementioned quotations highlight, "market research" included both structured and non-structured ways of analysing the market. Using this intelligence, the managers were able to create unique value propositions, as illustrated in the following quotation:

We've really tried to find what kind of unique customer value we can produce for our customers ... What could be the unique element that we could produce to create customer value? That's what we were defining. We were also testing out our value proposition very broadly to home in on how to best communicate that customer value. (Participant 2)

Moreover, the interviewees highlighted that customer orientation is successful if the products match customer needs. For instance, Participant 3 informed us that their company tried to offer a *"superior product that fulfils the explicit and implicit needs and wants that our customers have. I would say that would be our main and key advantage"* (Participant 3). Participant 5 offered a similar opinion, reporting that their company was *"making sure that the product is competitive, and we meet the customer expectations"* (Participant 5). Participants 4 and 23 both emphasised that customer orientation should create products that are favourably different from competition in the eyes of customers:

> *There's no point in entering a market if the product does not have a demonstrated competitive advantage. The advantage doesn't have to be remarkable, but there has to be real demand for the product.* (Participant 4)

> *You can't enter a market with a "product-first" orientation. Without a good product, it is useless to go there, no matter your entry strategy.* (Participant 23)

To summarise, customer orientation as a strategy emphasises the need to understand the competitive reality in the market. Such an understanding is achieved through various market research methods that enable companies to identify a unique position in the market and develop products that meet customer needs in a way that is superior to competition.

Customer Orientation as a Mental Model

The third way of viewing customer orientation involved perceiving it as an individual-level phenomenon, a mental model. This involved sharing the belief in the importance of being customer-oriented, as Participant 13 stated: "*We have nothing but customers. If we do not have customers, we have nothing. It is the key element and nothing else than customers*" (Participant 13). Here, the interviewees described how changes in the way organisational actors think about customers can open up possibilities for improving competitive advantage. For instance, Participant 2 described how to orient the organisation towards creating customer value:

> *Our [competitive advantage] lies in how we are orienting ourselves to building growth and producing unique customer value. … It is not common in our industry. … We think about both short- and long-term customer value creation, which in turn affects customers' willingness to pay. For example, if we add this feature, will it improve conversion now and will it increase customer-perceived value in the long term, thus improving customer lifetime value. …? A key strength for us is that we only add features to our product that create more value for customers in the long term.* (Participant 2)

Participant 21 agreed about the importance of mental models by referring to "a kind of a mindset question". "Flipping the situation around", their organisation changed their product development to a more customer-oriented model:

> *No, we've started investigating the end users' needs in more detail. We ask more specific questions, and, for example, open up our product development to customers to specify the specific usage for the products, the problem that the customer wants solved, whether it's a general problem or a niche need. This is opposed to starting from our product portfolio and trying to sell what we already have. So, it is a kind of mindset question. We flip the situation around.* (Participant 21)

176　*Mika Yrjölä et al.*

The interviewees recognised multiple ways to foster customer-oriented mental models. First, they underlined the need to change organisational mindsets and decision-making processes (as indicated in Participant 21's quotation given earlier). Second, the interviewees referred to their own roles in bringing the voice of the customer to the boardroom: "... *to raise the voice of customers inside the organisation and drive changes to be done are most according to the customer needs that sometimes can be challenging*" (Participant 13). Finally, Participant 20 highlighted that a change in thinking can be achieved by focusing on word choices and terminology regarding customers. For their organisation, the key to moving away from product orientation was to adopt the terminology of value propositions:

> *When I started in this post three years ago, the first impression or the first observation I made was that thinking in terms of value for customers wasn't as widespread as it could have been in the organisation. I mean that we should think in terms of value propositions to start the thinking from what creates value for customers and how we could make it concrete, turn it into euros, and translate our activities into added value for customers. My first impression was that the organisation had a product-oriented way of thinking and acting back then. I hired a partner to hold an internal two-day workshop with me and our international sales personnel to develop a value proposition. That's how we managed to adopt this terminology – this sort of philosophy.* (Participant 20)

Thus, customer orientation as a mental model involves managers paying attention to how organisational actors think about and make decisions regarding customers. The participants believed that changing thinking and decision-making to being more outside-in rather than inside-out would be the key to building competitive advantages. According to this view, managers can foster customer-oriented mental models by changing mindsets, ensuring that the customers' voice is present in discussions, and introducing customer-oriented terminology (e.g., customer value and value propositions).

Customer Orientation as Customer Intimacy

The fourth view of customer orientation viewed it as customer intimacy: close relations and collaboration with customers. Some interviewees equated customer orientation with customer information collecting: "*We are all time going towards more customer orientation in that sense that we get more and more customer feedback*" (Participant 7). According to the interviewees, competitive advantage arises from how closely the organisation works with its customers. The interviewees clearly saw value in this. For example, Participant 12 observed that the best customer knowledge and capabilities reside at the customer interface:

The personnel can decide what they do. We here at the conglomerate level don't implement anything. The people [at the customer interface] design and implement everything because they are in the know about the customer interface and the technologies there. ... I don't micromanage them; they can design the timetables and required personnel and how they are going to pull it off. It's our company principle that decisions are made where they will be implemented. There are no top-down orders. (Participant 12)

Customer intimacy can be employed, according to the managers, by establishing and maintaining direct contact with the end users of the product or service. It can also be strengthened by involving customers and partners in product development to ensure that the products meet customer needs. The importance of establishing a connection with the end user is illustrated in the following quotation by Participant 16:

Our goal is to always have contact with the end user of our products, but in our industry, it is now always possible. There's often a middleman, which means that the competition will likely be purely on price. That is not our strength ... We aim for projects where we can design, produce, and build everything ourselves. (Participant 16)

According to the interviewees, a connection to end users is important to ensure that the company can remain relevant in the market by gaining access to data and information regarding customers. The following quotation illustrates this: *"... companies want to get in position where they have their own customers. That there is no one between the company and its customers"* (Participant 3). Similarly, Participant 19 reflected:

Every operation, every product, and every idea start from customers. The best idea is that you hear about the need from customers. Then you turn it around as a product and solution. Then you start a project to create it. And then you need to have your whole organisation think for customers. Everything comes from customers. The customer is the king. (Participant 19)

The companies used various means of gathering customer intelligence; for instance: *"Every time we meet the customers, we try to have short memos of the meeting. It could be something something short memo or something like that"* (Participant 11) and *"Our customers are teaching us. We have various customer contacts every single day. We have happy customers and some unhappy ones, as well. We want to learn from both every single day. Different stories"* (Participant 15). The gathered customer insight is then used to improve the offerings:

We actually directly and indirectly always try to listen to our customers to try to understand how to further develop our offering, because today, from certain perspectives, our offering is superior to the competition. (Participant 3)

178 *Mika Yrjölä et al.*

> *First, you need to listen to customers. You need to have an understanding once thinking about continuous products and how we can improve our products over time. That is, listening to and discussing with the customers. Then customer orientation is now building up. This is what we are talking about accessibility to customers.* (Participant 17)

The second way to improve customer intimacy is through collaborating with customers and end users. As one interviewee put it, *"It is very important to develop in close relation with the customers. [The product] needs to meet the customers' expectations"* (Participant 17).

> *[In creating customer insight], our basic method is talking to customers and listening to them. As a recent example, we have started using a service design approach, so we are involving them right at the beginning ... – even before we make an offering, we involve the customer in defining what kind of service would fit them. There's usually a product involved, but very often, service elements as well. This process secures a better chance of success for us when the customer is already involved in the solutions we are about to offer.* (Participant 20)

> *As a goal, we must follow the amount of time product developers have visited our customers. It's one indicator. ... Our product development works very close to the customer and the commercial side, as it should. ... I adhere to the school of thought that the balance between product development projects that come from the customer versus those that come from in-house should be something like 80–20 or 75–25. In my view, it is more fruitful in generating sales.* (Participant 20)

The final way in which the interviewees reported fostering customer intimacy was through collaboration with partnering companies. As Participant 1 put it, cooperation with customers and partnering companies should be done by thinking *"what is the best for customer"* and they went on to share that this was relatively easy because *"I think everybody respects the customer"* (Participant 1). Participant 3 added: *"Because by yourself, you will ever never be able to build the complete solutions that satisfy the customer needs, what you need to do is partner up. You should collaborate with companies"* (Participant 3).

> *... if we recognise a potential customer and we are engaging conversation with the potential customers, we need to create a joint offering. We need to create that documentation in such a manner that it has all the products in the ecosystem and some sort of integration and that it appears as one brand, etc. Something we need to generate together.* (Participant 5)

One reason for partnering up is to improve the credibility of the offering in the eyes of customers:

... if you are partnering with some well-established companies that give you very much credibility rather than you go by yourself as alone, as a small company. And, in relation to the customer base, I think as a small Finnish company we need to have help of the big guy to get access to the customers. It is a bit easy and kind of through the established partnership. (Participant 5)

As the following quotations highlight, partnering is more successful when all the companies working together understand how they can jointly improve customer value or the customer experience:

We try to convince them that we have something that does not compete with their existing portfolio. We try to convince them that we care about complementing their own portfolios and bringing value to their customers. (Participant 9)

We analyse the actors in the target market to understand which ones have the most potential for us. In international markets, I've noticed that there is a lot of competition. For example, in [the market], there is a lot of competition, and these actors are very keen on finding product features that increase their competitive advantages. ... They are very interested in investing in a better customer experience. ... They have figured out that a better customer experience will be more profitable in the long run. (Participant 14)

In summary, the fourth view on customer orientation involves perceiving it in terms of how closely the company operates with its customers and how deep the cooperation between the company and its customers and/or end users. According to the interviewees, customer orientation as customer intimacy could be improved through establishing and maintaining contact with end users as well as collaborating with customers and other companies in the ecosystem.

Discussion and Conclusion

This chapter sets out to explore the ways in which managers understand customer value creation within ecosystems and how managers believe they can foster customer orientation in their organisational contexts. We identified four ways in which managers view customer orientation: (1) as culture, (2) as a strategy, (3) as a mental model, and (4) as customer intimacy. These ways of viewing customer orientation can be organised according to their focus on the individual- or organisational-level aspects of customer orientation. As explained in the theoretical chapter background on customer orientation, some authors have made this distinction between individual and organisational levels in research (Brown et al., 2002; Grizzle et al., 2009; Whelan et al., 2010). Thus, it is interesting to observe how the managerial views of customer orientation in this study exhibited a similar

180 *Mika Yrjölä et al.*

distinction. Moreover, these managerial views on customer orientation could also be categorised based on how abstract or concrete the approach to customer orientation was.

The chapter was motivated by the theoretically interesting problem of how customer orientation should be understood and managed in an ecosystem context, where organisations can take multiple, simultaneous and even conflicting roles (e.g., competitors can also be suppliers, partners and customers). The four views on customer orientation provide a tentative answer to this problem. First, they demonstrate that there is no single right answer to how organisations should orient themselves towards customers in ecosystems. For some managers, customer orientation is visible in concrete ways, such as in new product development activities or product features (customer orientation as customer intimacy). For others, customer orientation is present in more strategic considerations, such as in the organisation's competitive profile. Second, being customer-oriented in an ecosystem context will likely require balancing these four views as situations change. We hope that managers will find it useful to use Figure 10.2 as a starting point for changing their views. For instance, they could attempt to change perspectives from the organisation to the level of individual employees or from concrete aspects to more conceptual ones. Third, the four views uncovered in this research might reflect different roles in the ecosystem. For example, customer orientation as customer intimacy emphasises collaboration with customers and partners, which can reflect the ecosystem role of the complementor or value co-creator. As another example, customer orientation as a strategy is very competitor-focused, likely reflecting a different role in the ecosystem.

As explained in the theoretical background section, there are multiple interpretations of customer orientation in the literature. Some of these interpretations are close to the views of the interviewed managers. For instance, customer orientation can be understood in terms of information, culture or interaction. The interpretation of customer orientation as a culture or business philosophy was also present in our findings, especially the notion that customer orientation should be visible in the organisation's culture, values and norms (Deshpandé, Farley & Webster, 1993). Nonetheless, this study is among the first to investigate how managers view customer orientation. We hope our findings will spark further research into customer orientation from a managerial perspective. We especially want to highlight that customer orientation is not a unidimensional concept; instead, it should be analysed as a multidimensional concept.

References

Adner, R. (2006). "Match your innovation strategy to your innovation ecosystem", *Harvard Business Review*, vol. 84(4), p. 98.

Adner, R. (2017). "Ecosystem as structure: An actionable construct for strategy", *Journal of Management*, vol. 43(1), pp. 39–58.

Agrawal, A.K. & Rahman, Z. (2015). "Roles and resource contributions of customers in value co-creation", *International Strategic Management Review*, vol. 3(1–2), pp. 144–160.

Amit, R., & Zott, C. (2012). "Creating value through business model innovation", *MIT Sloan Management Review*, vol. 53(3), pp. 41–49.

Angulo-Ruiz, F., Donthu, N., Prior, D., & Rialp, J. (2014). "The financial contribution of customer-oriented marketing capability", *Journal of the Academy of Marketing Science*, vol. 42(4), pp. 380–399. doi:10.1007/s11747-013-0353-6

Audretsch, D. B., Cunningham, J. A., Kuratko, D. F., Lehmann, E. E., & Menter, M. (2019). Entrepreneurial ecosystems: economic, technological, and societal impacts. *The Journal of Technology Transfer*, vol. 44(2), pp. 313–325.

Bettencourt, L.A. & Brown, S.W. (2003). "Role stressors and customer-oriented boundary-spanning behaviors in service organizations". *Journal of the Academy of Marketing Science*, vol. 31(4), pp. 394–408.

Bremner, R., Eisenhardt, K.M., & Hannah, D. (2017). "Business ecosystems", in L. Mesquita, J. Reuer, & R. Ragozzino (Eds.), *Collaborative Strategy: A Guide to Strategic Alliances*. Northampton, MA: Edward Elgar.

Brown, T.J., Mowen, J.C., Donavan, D.T., & Licata, J.W. (2002). "The customer orientation of service workers: Personality trait effects on self-and supervisor performance ratings", *Journal of Marketing Research*, vol. 39(1), pp. 110–119. doi:10.1509/jmkr.39.1.110.18928

Cavallo, A., Ghezzi, A., & Balocco, R. (2019). "Entrepreneurial ecosystem research: Present debates and future directions", *International Entrepreneurship and Management Journal*, vol. 15(4), pp. 1291–1321.

Chang, W., Park, J.E., & Chaiy, S. (2010). "How does CRM technology transform into organizational performance? A mediating role of marketing capability", *Journal of Business Research*, vol. 63, pp. 849–855.

Clarysse, B., Wright, M., Bruneel, J., & Mahajan, A. (2014). "Creating value in ecosystems: Crossing the chasm between knowledge and business ecosystems", *Research Policy*, vol. 43(7), pp. 1164–1176.

Day, G. & Moorman, C. (2010). *Strategy from the Outside In: Profiting from Customer Value*. New York: McGraw-Hill.

Day, G., & Moorman, C. (2013). "Regaining customer relevance: The outside-in turnaround", *Strategy & Leadership*, vol. 41(4), pp. 17–23. doi:10.1108/sl-04-2013-0021

Deshpandé, R., Farley, J., & Webster, J.F. (1993). "Corporate culture, customer orientation, and innovativeness in Japanese firms: A quadrad analysis", *Journal of Marketing*, vol. 57(1), pp. 23–37. doi:10.1177/002224299305700102

Dubois, A. & Gadde, L.-E. (2014). "'Systematic combining' – A decade later", *Journal of Business Research*, vol. 67(6), pp. 1277–1284.

Eisenhardt, K.M. (1989). "Building theories from case study research". *Academy of Management Review*, vol. 14(4), pp. 532–550.

Feng, T., Wang, D., Lawton, A., & Luo, B.N. (2019). "Customer orientation and firm performance: The joint moderating effects of ethical leadership and competitive intensity", *Journal of Business Research*, vol. 100, pp. 111–121.

Frow, P., McColl-Kennedy, J.R., Hilton, T., Davidson, A., Payne, A., & Brozovic, D. (2014). "Value propositions: A service ecosystems perspective", *Marketing Theory*, vol. 14(3), pp. 327–351.

182   *Mika Yrjölä et al.*

Füller, J., Hutter, K., & Faullant, R. (2011). "Why co-creation experience matters? Creative experience and its impact on the quantity and quality of creative contributions", *R&D Management*, vol. 41(3), pp. 259–273.

Gioia, D., Corley, G., & Hamilton, A. (2013). "Seeking qualitative rigor in inductive research: Notes on the Gioia methodology", *Organisational Research Methods*, vol. 16(1), pp. 15–31.

Grizzle, J.W., Zablah, A.R., Brown, T.J., Mowen, J.C., & Lee, J.M. (2009). "Employee customer orientation in context: How the environment moderates the influence of customer orientation on performance outcomes", *Journal of Applied Psychology*, vol. 94(5), p. 1227.

Grönroos, C. (2011). A service perspective on business relationships: The value creation, interaction and marketing interface. *Industrial Marketing Management*, vol. 40(2), pp. 240–247.

Gurau, C., Ranchhod, A., & Hackney, R. (2003). "Customer-centric strategic planning: Integrating CRM in online business systems", *International Technology and Management*, vol. 4, pp. 199–214.

Gyrd-Jones, R.I. & Kornum, N. (2013). "Managing the co-created brand: Value and cultural complementarity in online and offline multi-stakeholder ecosystems", *Journal of business research*, vol. 66(9), pp. 1484–1493.

Hartline, M.D., Maxham Iii, J.G., & McKee, D.O. (2000). "Corridors of influence in the dissemination of customer-oriented strategy to customer contact service employees", *Journal of Marketing*, vol. 64(2), pp. 35–50. doi:10.1509/jmkg.64.2.35.18001

Hattula, J.D., Herzog, W., Dahl, D.W., & Reinecke, S. (2015). "Managerial empathy facilitates egocentric predictions of consumer preferences", *Journal of Marketing Research*, vol. 52(2), pp. 235–252.

Homburg, C., Workman Jr, J.P., & Jensen, O. (2000). "Fundamental changes in marketing organisation: The movement toward a customer-focused organisational structure", *Journal of the Academy of Marketing Science*, vol. 28(4), pp. 459–478. doi:10.1007/978-3-322-81525-5_4

Hortinha, P., Lages, C., & Lages, L.F. (2011). "The trade-off between customer and technology orientations: Impact on innovation capabilities and export performance", *Journal of International Marketing*, vol. 19(3), pp. 36–58. doi:10.1509/jimk.19.3.36

Huff, A.S. (1990). *Mapping Strategic Thought*. Chichester: John Wiley and Sons Ltd.

Hult, G.T.M., Ketchen, D.J., & Slater, S.F. (2005). "Market orientation and performance: An integration of disparate approaches", *Strategic Management Journal*, vol. 26(12), pp. 1173–1181. doi:10.1002/smj.494

Iansiti, M. & Levien, R. (2004). *The Keystone Advantage: What the New Dynamics of Business Ecosystems Mean for Strategy, Innovation, and Sustainability*. Cambridge, MA: Harvard Business Press.

Kapoor, R. (2018). "Ecosystems: Broadening the locus of value creation", *Journal of Organization Design*, vol. 7(1), pp. 1–16.

Kohli, A.K. & Jaworski, B.J. (1990). "Market orientation: The construct, research propositions, and managerial implications", *Journal of marketing*, vol. 54(2), pp. 1–18.

Korunka, C., Scharitzer, D., Carayon, P., Hoonakker, P., Sonnek, A., & Sainfort, F. (2007). "Customer orientation among employees in public administration: A transnational, longitudinal study", *Applied Ergonomics*, vol. 38(3), pp. 307–315.

Lamberti, L. (2013). "Customer centricity: The construct and the operational antecedents", *Journal of Strategic Marketing*, vol. 21(7), pp. 588–612. doi:10.1080/0965254x.2013.817476

Lindic, J. & da Silva, C.M. (2011). "Value proposition as a catalyst for a customer focused innovation", *Management Decision*, vol. 49(10), pp. 1694–1708. doi:10.1108/00251741111183834

Mack, E. & Mayer, H. (2016). "The evolutionary dynamics of entrepreneurial eco-systems", *Urban Studies*, vol. 53(10), pp. 2118–2133.

Maitland, E. & Sammartino, A. (2015). "Decision making and uncertainty: The role of heuristics and experience in assessing a politically hazardous environment", *Strategic Management Journal*, vol. 36(10), pp. 1554–1578.

Marzocchi, G.L. & Zammit, A. (2006). "Self-scanning technologies in retail: determinants of adoption". *The Service Industries Journal*, vol. 26(6), pp. 651–669.

Moore, J.F. (1996). *The Death of Competition: Leadership and Strategy in the Age of Business Ecosystems*. New York: Harper Business.

Morash, E.A., Droge, C.L., & Vickery, S.K. (1996). "Strategic logistics capabilities for competitive advantage and firm success", *Journal of Business Logistics*, vol. 17(1), pp. 1–26.

Morgan, N.A., Whitler, K.A., Feng, H., & Chari, S. (2018). "Research in marketing strategy", *Journal of the Academy of Marketing Science*, vol. 47 (1), pp. 4–29. doi:10.1007/s11747-018-0598-1

Mukerjee, K. (2013). "Customer-oriented organizations: A framework for innovation", *Journal of Business Strategy*, vol. 34(3), pp. 49–56.

Narver, J.C. & Slater, S.F. (1990). "The effect of a market orientation on business profitability", *Journal of Marketing*, vol. 54(4), pp. 20–35. doi:10.4135/9781452231426.n3

Overholm, H. (2015). "Collectively created opportunities in emerging ecosystems: The case of solar service ventures", *Technovation*, vol. 39, pp. 14–25.

Prahalad, C.K. & Ramaswamy, V. (2004). "Co-creation experiences: The next practice in value creation". *Journal of Interactive Marketing*, vol. 18(3), pp. 5–14.

Piekkari, R. & Welch, C. (2017). "The case study in management research: Beyond the positivist legacy of Eisenhardt and Yin?", in C. Cassell, A.L. Cunliffe, & G. Grandy (Eds.), *Sage Handbook of Qualitative Business and Management Research Methods: History and Traditions*. London: Sage Publications, 345–358.

Rapp, A., Trainor, K.J., & Agnihotri, R. (2010). "Performance implications of customer-linking capabilities: Examining the complementary role of customer orientation and CRM technology", *Journal of Business Research*, vol. 63(11), pp. 1229–1236. doi:10.1016/j.jbusres.2009.11.002

Reich, B.H. & Benbasat, I. (1990). "An empirical investigation of factors influencing the success of customer-oriented strategic systems", *Information Systems Research*, vol. 1(3), pp. 325–347.

Said, J., Hui, W.S., Taylor, D., & Othman, R. (2009). "Customer-focused strategies and information technology capabilities: Implications for service quality of Malaysian local authorities", *International Review of Business Research Papers*, vol. 5(3), pp. 241–256.

Schwepker, C.H. Jr (2003). "An exploratory investigation of the relationship between ethical conflict and salesperson performance", *Journal of Business & Industrial Marketing*, vol. 18(4/5), pp. 435–446. doi:10.1108/08858620310480313.

184   *Mika Yrjölä et al.*

Shah, D., Rust, R.T., Parasuraman, A., Staelin, R., & Day, G.S. (2006). "The path to customer centricity", *Journal of Service Research*, vol. 9(2), pp. 113–124.

Sheth, J.N., Sisodia, R.S., & Sharma, A. (2000). "The antecedents and consequences of customer-centric marketing", *Journal of the Academy of Marketing Science*, vol. 28(1), pp. 55–66. doi: 10.1177/0092070300281006

Slater, S.F. & Narver, J.C. (2000). "The positive effect of a market orientation on business profitability: A balanced replication", *Journal of Business Research*, vol. 48(1), pp. 69–73. doi: 10.1016/s0148-2963(98)00077-0

Spigel, B. (2017). "The relational organization of entrepreneurial ecosystems", *Entrepreneurship Theory and Practice*, vol. 41(1), pp. 49–72.

Strong, C. A., & Harris, L. C. (2004). The drivers of customer orientation: an exploration of relational, human resource and procedural tactics. *Journal of Strategic Marketing*, vol. 12(3), pp. 183–204.

Tether, B.S. & Tajar, A. (2008). "The organisational-cooperation mode of innovation and its prominence amongst European service firms", *Research Policy*, vol. 37(4), pp. 720–739.

Trainor, K.J., Andzulis, J.M., Rapp, A., & Agnihotri, R. (2014). "Social media technology usage and customer relationship performance: A capabilities-based examination of social CRM", *Journal of Business Research*, vol. 67(6), pp. 1201–1208.

Treacy, M. & Wiersema, F. (1993). "Customer intimacy and other value disciplines", *Harvard Business Review*, vol. 71(1), pp. 84–93.

Vargo, S.L. & Lusch, R.F. (2004). "Evolving to a new dominant logic for marketing", *Journal of Marketing*, vol. 68(1), pp. 1–17. doi: 10.1509/jmkg.68.1.1.24036

Voima, P., Heinonen, K., Strandvik, T., Mickelsson, K.J., & Arantola-Hattab, L.J. (2011). "A customer ecosystem perspective on service". *Proceedings QUIS 12: Advances in Service Quality, Innovation and Excellence*, 1015–1024. International Research Symposium on Service Excellence in Management (QUIS), Ithaca, United States, 2 June 2011.

Wang, Y. & Feng, H. (2012). "Customer relationship management capabilities", *Management Decision*, vol. 50(1), pp. 115–129.

Whelan, S., Davies, G., Walsh, M., & Bourke, R. (2010). "Public sector corporate branding and customer orientation", *Journal of Business Research*, vol. 63, pp. 1164–1171.

Yrjölä, M. (2020). "Eye on the customer: Breaking away from the inside-out mindset", *Journal of Business Strategy*, vol. 42(3), pp. 206–214.

Zahra, S.A. & Nambisan, S. (2011). "Entrepreneurship in global innovation ecosystems", *AMS Review*, vol. 1(1), pp. 4–17.

Zhao, M., Dröge, C., & Stank, T.P. (2001). "The effects of logistics capabilities on firm performance: Customer-focused versus information-focused capabilities", *Journal of Business Logistics*, vol. 22(2), pp. 91–107.

Zhou, K.Z., & Li, C.B. (2010). "How strategic orientations influence the building of dynamic capability in emerging economies", *Journal of Business Research*, vol. 63(3), pp. 224–231.

11 How Global Virtual Teams Are Innovating the Business Models of MNEs and Higher Education Institutions

Ernesto Tavoletti

Introduction

It is known that exogenous environmental factors such as technological change, changing customer behaviours and economic change can trigger the development of business model innovation (BMI) (Teece, 2018), while internal resistance to change, path dependency and managers' cognitive limitations restrain BMIs (Gilbert, 2005). Furthermore, the founding team (Beckman & Burton, 2008), the initial imprinting of business models (BMs; Marquis & Tilcsik, 2013), the individual interest and socialised agency in promoting innovation all have a persisting influence on the ability to innovate the BMs at a later stage (Anand, Gardner & Morris, 2007).

The literature has investigated why not all organisations influenced by the same environmental factors develop BMIs so as the necessary conditions under which BMI emerges (Snihur & Zott, 2020). However, some disruptive environmental factors trigger BMIs across most organisations. COVID-19 is one of them as it has produced widespread disruptive changes in international business (IB): In the level of globalisation, business expectations, corporate strategy, international finance, internationalisation, global supply chains, sustainability, export operations, FDIs, management of expatriates, talent management and human resource management to cite just a few (for a comprehensive picture, see Marinov & Marinova, 2021).

With special reference to human resource management, remote working has become both more popular and more effective due to lockdowns enforced in many countries across the globe, while international travel has become difficult and expensive; many physical meetings have been replaced by the usage of tools such as Microsoft Teams or Zoom (Arslan, Gölgeci & Larimo, 2021). This phenomenon has boosted an organisational setting already well-known and studied in IB under the label of global virtual teams (GVTs) (Stahl et al., 2010; Stahl & Maznevski, 2021).

The term "virtual team" appeared in the literature in the mid–1980s (Miles & Snow, 1986) and became popular in the early 1990s as the advent of the world wide web made online communication tools ubiquitous (Davidow & Malone, 1992). However, the first article on the Web of

DOI: 10.4324/9781003326731-11

Science adopting the term is a study exploring the challenges of creating and maintaining trust in a GVT whose members transcend time, space and culture (Jarvenpaa, 1999).

The GVTs are now ubiquitous in business, education, government and NGOs, with a long-lasting transformative effect on BMs. This chapter will explore the enhanced role of GVTs in the post-COVID-19 era. The second section focuses on how GVTs have been affecting BMI in multinational enterprises (MNEs). The third section addresses the role of GVTs in higher education institutions (HEIs) and business schools. The fourth section concludes and highlights future research paths.

How GVTs Are Changing the BMs of MNEs

The Neo-Global Corporation and GVTs

GVTs have been triggering BMIs in both SMEs and MNEs, but in the second ones, the implications on activities and structures are far more complex and worth investigating than in SMEs. Understanding the BMs of MNEs requires understanding their structures and activities operating practice. The structure of MNEs can be described according to a set of well-known archetypes: The centralised exporter, the international projector, the international coordinator and the multi-centred MNE (Verbeke & Lee, 2021).

However, structures do not fully describe the coordination activities of an MNE. Some path setting studies conducted in the 1980s tried to capture the changing nature of MNEs, elaborating the "transnational solution", with its core idea of a network of differentiated national subsidiaries and a global headquarters with a "matrix mindset" (Bartlett, 1981; Doz, Bartlett & Prahalad, 1981; Doz & Prahalad, 1981, 1984; Bartlett & Ghoshal, 1989). Since then, the rise of global value chains and extended innovative supply networks even in mature industries (Kazemargi et al., 2022) and the Internet have transformed the way MNEs carry on their activities, but the transnational idea had remained the most popular till very recently when the idea of a "neo-global" corporation (NGC) emerged (Mees-Buss, Welch & Westney, 2019).

The NGC idea emerged from a case study on Unilever, the same corporation that had been at the base of the transnational idea and adopted the transnational model explicitly (Maljers, 1992). The main change that produced the idea of the NGC was observed in the early 2000s and is the progressive vanishing of the central role of the multi-function country subsidiary, substituted by centrally controlled and highly specialised sub-units (Birkinshaw, 2001). This process of labour specialisation produced a "fine-slicing" of outsourced "back-end" activities (Buckley, 2009), and improved technologies allowed progressively virtual rather than geographical headquarters, with top and middle management organised in GVTs dispersed across the globe (Baaij & Slangen, 2013).

The idea of a virtual corporation is not new, but what was little more than a pioneer trend of some particular MNEs or a futuristic imagination (Davidow & Malone, 1992). In the case of large MNEs such as Unilever, this transformation was already evident in 2005, when decision making for the back end of the value chain was moved from regional to global teams, dispersed across the world and located wherever it was most efficient for them to operate, as enhanced technologies allowed local responsiveness to be achieved remotely, without local category and brand development teams (Mees-Buss et al., 2019). However, only recently, thanks to enhanced technology and COVID-19 induced changes in working behaviours, GVTs widespread in top management teams and across the entire organisation.

The research on GVTs was already consistent and growing: there is a more than tenfold increase in articles on the subject from 1999 to 2020, as recorded by Web of Science, Scopus and Google Scholar; the number of citations of the GVT literature has also increased rapidly, and from the 175 articles about GVTs published between 1999 and 2020 on Web of Science, there are 6,822 citations in total, growing rapidly since 1999 but only after COVID-19, there has been a full awareness that GVTs are not a marginal working environment but an ordinary one with a far-reaching impact on BMs (Tavoletti & Taras, 2021).

Even before the COVID-19 pandemic, GVTs were becoming commonplace in MNEs. In March 2018, CultureWizard invited executives of major organisations worldwide to participate in its fifth biennial GVT survey. The survey had 1,620 respondents from 90 countries who testified to the preponderance and importance of GVTs: 89% of respondents stated that they are on at least one team, 88% that the teams are critical to conducting daily work and 62% that they work on teams with three or more cultures, but only 22% reported they had received training for intercultural virtual work and only 15% said they had been effective as a leader in a GVT (CultureWizard, 2018).

Therefore, the phenomenon of GVTs in MNEs is both huge, growing and permanent. However, its implications on BMs are often underestimated, and training is missing in most cases despite the extensive literature investigating the organisational implications. Team members that are not adequately prepared in online intercultural dynamics when working in GVTs lament "lack of participation", "lack of engagement", "lack of ownership" and "low-context communication". Cross-cultural misunderstandings concerning deadlines or frustration with some team members who say "yes" when they mean "no", or the enforcement of a "hegemonic" culture by the project managers or team leaders are often reported (CultureWizard, 2018).

Workers use multiple senses and forms of communication. When some of them are made impossible in GVTs, the importance of the remaining ones intensifies and amplifies due to the language differences, time zones, expectations regarding leadership, management of meetings and different cultural backgrounds in general. For instance, there is evidence that in the

188 *Ernesto Tavoletti*

absence of full information on teammates, the level of socio-economic development of the country the person comes from (country-of-origin effect) has a lasting effect on how peers evaluate the person, and this effect is stronger than objectively measured language skills or technical skills or cultural intelligence (CQ; Tavoletti et al., 2022). These results have strong implications as they confirm that cross-national conflicts, country stereotypes, prejudices and evaluation biases have especially fertile ground in GVTs.

The Nature and Peculiarities of GVTs Operating in MNEs

The literature has investigated these phenomena extensively (Stahl & Maznevski, 2021). For instance, concerning the widely discussed relationship between diversity and creativity, a recent meta-analysis provides evidence that deep-level diversity is associated with more creativity, and surface-level diversity, which can raise social identity threats, is negatively related to creativity and innovation for simple tasks but unrelated for complex tasks (Wang et al., 2019). In addition, we know that language, language fluency and accents influence the dynamics of power in teams (Hinds, Neeley & Cramton, 2014) and working together online increases the challenges faced by any team and international teams (Jimenez et al., 2017). Working in GVTs reduces the amount of non-verbal communication and decreases the amount of information available to build trust, cohesion and commitment (Reiche et al., 2017).

Time zones are very relevant for global virtual cooperation, but their impact on GVTs is mixed. On the one hand, GVTs can work around the clock and access different local resources and networks across the globe (Wildman & Griffith, 2015), but on the other hand, the coordination costs increase significantly (Jonsen, Maznevski & Davison, 2012). The time zones mixed results are in line with other sections of the literature reporting that GVTs may offer not just obstacles but significant benefits through workers' positive appraisal of the challenge and learning opportunity that, in turn, can improve engagement, satisfaction and innovation (Nurmi & Hinds, 2016). Global virtual work can also quickly leverage remote and diversified human resources, producing huge cost savings (Cummings, 2004). However, to work effectively in GVTs, CQ is essential and empirical results are unequivocal in showing that CQ positively moderates the relationship between expectations of challenges and team-level effort, improving team performance (Magnusson, Schuster & Taras, 2014). Furthermore, culture and the cultural values to which team members subscribe influence how decisions are made and communicated in GVTs, and intercultural online communication styles are context-based depending on the purpose, roles, situation and people (Zakaria, 2017).

The dispersion of individuals can also be across the nation, city, buildings or floors of the same building, so even a "small distance" can impact team performance unless efficient online communication is provided. For example, Siebdrat, Hoegl and Ernst (2009), based on 80 software development teams from 28 labs worldwide (including labs in Brazil, China, Denmark, France, Germany, India and the United States), show that dispersion across floors of the same building is more damaging to team performance, in terms of effectiveness (that is, the quality of team output) and efficiency (in terms of time and cost) than dispersion across a country or continent. The apparent paradox is explained by the fact that team members dispersed on different floors of the same building do not consider themselves geographically dispersed and do not take online countermeasures, despite that distance is big enough to impede face-to-face communication; the opposite happens for team members located in different continents. Therefore, the traditional approach suggests that team performance suffers from high geographical dispersion, and managers typically view dispersion (even just across the city or the floors of the same building) as a liability rather than an opportunity. On the opposite, the dispersion can be an asset if companies have effective global virtual communication networks that utilise geographically dispersed team members' diversity and varied expertise. On the other hand, assembling a globally dispersed and talented team is not enough to reap the benefits of GVT collaboration without socio-emotional and task-related processes, teamwork skills, "self-leadership" due to the lack of a locally present leadership, some periodical face-to-face meetings to build trust, CQ and an understanding of the peculiarities of global virtual work (Siebdrat, Hoegl & Ernst, 2009).

An important aspect of managing GVTs collaboration is establishing a psychologically safe communication climate starting from the first messages in the early stage of team formation due to the anchoring effect of the first communications (Glikson & Erez, 2020). Zakaria and Mohd Yusof (2020) refer to "swift trust formation", a rapidly developed form of trust that arises during a GVT's inception stage and formulate prescriptions for promoting high-trust behaviours in GVTs. In fact, the ad hoc, short-term nature of most GVTs makes swift trust important. Along a similar line of thinking is the construct of "expeditious cohesion" in GVTs (Tavoletti et al., 2022). Trust-building in a virtual and fast-changing environment has been at the centre of GVTs literature since the first article in which the concept appeared (Jarvenpaa & Leidner, 1999) as national stereotypes find fertile ground online and within structures that are temporary and geographically dispersed. ore sophisticated visual communication tools developed by online programme providers are used to moderate trust-building in GVTs. Nevertheless, Klitmøller, Schneider and Jonsen (2015), through ethnographic research on GVTs of a Finnish MNE, report that verbal communication, as opposed to written communication, is more likely to generate social categorisation, negative stereotypes and reduced trust in GVTs, and confirm that GVT collaboration is highly exposed to evaluation biases and national stereotypes (Tavoletti et al., 2019).

190   *Ernesto Tavoletti*

GVTs in Action in MNEs

Despite working in GVTs being common for knowledge workers in MNEs, there is still little awareness about the implications on BMs. In order to carry on complex functions, corporations such as General Electric, IBM and SAP have been relying for years on competencies very geographically dispersed but solidly connected in international corporate networks of operations: for instance, SAP Aktiengesellschaft is headquartered in Walldorf, Germany, but has strategic R&D centres in China, India, Israel and the United States to reduce costs and leverage global know-how in software engineering (Siebdrat et al., 2009). That way, a manager located anywhere can organise a GVT that is entirely geographically dispersed, leveraging the best competencies available globally. The advantages for MNEs of resorting to GVTs include the following: (1) Working potentially 24 hours a day thanks to time zones; (2) heterogeneous and diversified knowledge resources and databases; (3) not being limited by distance and travelling; (4) access to the best skills and expertise globally; (5) access to distant upstream and downstream market knowledge; (6) cost-saving. The disadvantages for MNEs of resorting to GVTs include the following: (1) More cross-cultural issues; (2) limited face-to-face communications; (3) difficult to build trust online due to the lack of any social interaction; (4) the challenge of developing common cultural ground; (5) teamwork is more difficult to manage online; (6) language differences becoming more challenging in online communication.

All the aforementioned issues force MNEs to rethink themselves not as a network of national subsidiaries with boots on the ground that are progressively disappearing in fragmentation of outsourced activities but as a network of GVTs in need of best practices and procedures to function efficiently and effectively. One of them is the presence of multicultural "knowledge brokers" who transcend different cultural boundaries and help bridge differences among colleagues in different GVTs subgroups of MNEs' managers (Eisenberg & Mattarelli, 2017). In fact, as a typical procedure, MNEs have been offshoring work to emergent countries using GVTs with an "onsite-offshore model", where a subgroup of the team is located onsite (such as the headquarters of the MNE or the client site) and another one "off-shore", often in an emergent country (Mattarelli & Gupta 2009). Therefore, knowledge sharing is an important outcome for GVTs involved in knowledge-intensive activities inside MNEs, such as top-management activities (Mees-Buss, Welch & Westney, 2019), marketing and human resource management (Pereira & Anderson, 2012), information systems consultancy (van Oshri, van Fenema & Kotlarskyj, 2008), product development (McDonough, Kahnb & Barczaka, 2001), software development (Herbsleb & Moitra, 2001) and innovation management (Gibson & Gibbs, 2006).

Through a sample of 56 aerospace engineering GVTs working on a state-of-the-art next-generation military aircraft, Gibson and Gibbs (2006) went deeper into the hurdles of global virtual collaboration and provided qualitative and quantitative support for the following hypotheses: (1) Geographic dispersion is negatively related to team innovation; (2) electronic dependence is negatively related to team innovation; (3) dynamic structural arrangements (licencing, project-based relationships, outsourcing or consortia, frequently changing the roles of participants and their relationships) are negatively related to team innovation; (4) nationality diversity is negatively related to team innovation. In addition, all the relationships were moderated by a psychologically safe communication climate (characterised by support, openness, trust, mutual respect and risk-taking), and the strongest moderating effect occurred for the relationships between national diversity and innovation and geographic dispersion and innovation, which are the defining aspects of GVTs. The results highlight that the massive adoption of GVTs in MNEs to pursue innovation requires a rethinking of the overall structure and BMs.

Maznevski and Chudoba (2000) investigated the communication incidents in GVTs, their rhythms and patterns. They showed that the temporal rhythm is structured by a defining beat of regular, intense face-to-face meetings, followed by less intensive, shorter interaction incidents using various media. Furthermore, the length of time required between the face-to-face meetings depended on the level of interdependence required by the task and the degree of shared view and strength of relationships among members.

GVTs have become the micro-foundations of NGCs (Mees-Buss, Welch & Westney, 2019), so understanding their peculiarities is critical for their efficiency and effectiveness and, as a result, the creation and sharing of knowledge inside MNEs.

Much literature has been produced since Hinds, Liu and Lyon (2011) solicited a more contextual and dynamic view of culture in social networks and technology use in response to a decade of increasingly prevalent collaboration across national boundaries. However, in the meantime, MNEs' activities, under the push of the COVID-19 pandemic, have been accelerating the shift to virtual and geographically dispersed configurations across the globe, and till the very micro-foundations of work, changing their BMs deeply. The knowledge we have accumulated about the GVTs is waiting to be transferred to a new generation of global managers.

Universities, business schools and HEIs play a critical role as they are where the new generations of managers and knowledge workers should become aware of online cross-cultural barriers and GVTs potential.

How GVTs Are Changing the BMs of HEIs: Towards a Global Virtual University

BMI in HEIs: The Antecedents

The debate about BMI in HEIs in the last two decades has been mainly about the shifting from the traditional preparing for critical thinking to

192 *Ernesto Tavoletti*

preparing for careers, the transformation of the student body into customers, and the consequential lessening of curricula, teaching methods and standards (Carlson & Fleisher, 2002). That has led to a shift from the traditional university–industry linkages literature (Etzkowitz, 1998; D'Este & Patel, 2007) to exploring how multiple stakeholders should have a say and directly influence BMI in HEIs in order to enhance national and regional innovation systems (Miller, McAdam & McAdam, 2014; McAdam, Miller & McAdam, 2017). However, especially in business schools, teaching and research have remained very similar to 30 years ago (Trkman, 2019).

The second line of research on BMI in HEIs has been the impact of online learning on the traditional business model of higher education, starting from the rise and limits of massive open online courses (MOOCs) and the threats they pose to the model of paid online courses offered by distance teaching universities and to a lesser extent to traditional on-campus ones (Kalman, 2014). MOOCs have been analyzed in relation to their teaching model, revenue model and role in less economically developed counties (Daniel, Vázquez Cano & Gisbert Cervera, 2015), highlighting both benefits for students, in terms of reduced education costs and global access, and the challenge to the traditional dominance of brick-and-mortar institutions as providers of quality higher education (Burd, Smith & Reisman, 2015). However, online learning and MOOCs still refer to brick and mortar institutions providing services to individual remotely located students and do not bring the triple complexity of global, virtual, and teamwork-based activities that characterise GVTs and involve faculty, students and staff. As a result, the effects of GVTs on the BMs of HEIs are far greater than the traditional offering of online learning to a restricted or unlimited number of students.

Within the business literature on GVTs, the focus has been on the corporate context (Nurmi & Hinds, 2016) rather than the educational institutions, but GVTs have been part of management learning and education for a decade (Taras & Gonzalez-Perez, 2015) and in the post-COVID-19 scenario are shaking the BMs of HEIs.

The X-Culture Project and Its Impact on BMI in HEIs

For certain, the most important and recognised experiential learning project in GVTs in IB and international management is the X-Culture Project (http://x-culture.org), a major collaborative project launched in 2010 as a multi-lateral initiative that each semester involves around 5,000 graduate and undergraduate students from more than 150 universities in more than 75 countries on six continents. The Academy of International Business has recognised the project (Stahl & Maznevski, 2021, p. 12) not just as a successful experiential learning teaching initiative for students (Gonzalez-Perez, Lynden and Taras 2019) but as an early-stage research lab providing tests of hypotheses for GVTs studies before taking them to more complex field settings (Jang et al., 2017; Jimenez et al., 2017) as students work on consulting projects for clients and it reproduces a real business consulting activity (Taras et al., 2013). In addition, some of these studies, based on the X-Culture database, have explored the relationship between academic pedigree and individual performance in the workplace (Taras et al., 2021), team diversity and team performance (Taras et al., 2019), team cohesiveness and performance (Tavoletti et al., 2022), CQ and performance (Richter et al., 2021).

The project involves international teams of between five and eight undergraduate and graduate IB or international management students. Each student in the team from a different university and nation (except for the United States, which due to the numerosity of US students, can have two representatives in each team) employs Internet-based technology to collaborate on an IB proposal for an X-Culture corporate partner or self-selected corporate client. The project lasts ten weeks and comprises ten milestones: (1) Pre-project readiness test to assess required skills and knowledge of the project; (2) establish contact with teammates; (3) meet teammates; (4) select client organisations and project (they can choose, as a team, the challenge company among around ten challenges); (5) identify market success factors (industry and competition analysis; market selection and analysis); (6) marketing (promotional channels, message, promotional materials, pricing); (7) management (entry modes and logistics (shipping, trade Regulations, certification)); (8) submission of draft team report for plagiarism check; (9) final team report; (10) post-project survey. The project was designed to replicate a typical GVT corporate setting with teams asked to complete a detailed sequence of tasks according to centrally provided guidelines and specific deadlines. During the ten weeks of the project, the students are supplemented with teaching materials and webinars with managers of challenge companies and experts about the different milestones and business plan drafting.

Therefore, in the pre-pandemic period, the X-Culture students were both parts of a traditional IB or international management in-person course, unfolding in parallel to X-Culture, and part of a GVT in X-Culture. However, the COVID-19 pandemic, with courses and teaching activities moving online or being provided in blended forms, has multiplied the virtual level of interactions: (1) The lecturer being out of campus and online on Teams or Zoom or other platforms (in another city, region or nation due to travel restrictions or quarantines), providing synchronous or asynchronous lectures, and the students on campus while working in X-Culture GVTs; (2) the lecturer being on campus, providing synchronous or asynchronous lectures on Teams or Zoom or other platforms, and some students being in person on campus and some students being online cooperating among themselves, while all working in X-Culture GVTs; (3) both the lecturers and the students being online while all working in X-Culture GVTs.

194   *Ernesto Tavoletti*

BMI in HEIs in the Post-pandemic World

Due to the trajectory and development of the COVID-19 pandemic investing Italy first among western countries, Italian universities have been leading the world in moving all their activities online (Zubascu, 2020). Multiple success stories have been reported concerning the adoption of online learning globally and the implications it had for GVTs' collaboration in 900-plus-year-old institutions:

> the 900-plus-year-old University of Bologna ... reached out to Microsoft at the end of February 2020 to ask for support in bringing their classes online to help create learning continuity for the students. In its first week, the university went live with 50% of the classes, and by the second week, they were at 100%, reaching out to 87,000 students with more than 3,600 courses online, with positive feedbacks from IT, faculty, and the students. (Spataro, 2020)

The rest of the world followed with rapid decision-making and pivots atypical of universities (Greenberg & Hibbert, 2020). The success stories extend to both students and faculty throughout the developed world. A random selection of 26 HEIs in different US states, identifying 4,892 faculty that taught a 100% online course within the previous year, provided solid evidence that faculty are satisfied with online teaching (Marasi, Jones & Parker, 2022).

Moreover, in developing countries, where due to the absence of advanced digital learning management systems, public universities resorted to social networks (e.g., Facebook and WhatsApp) and/or digital communication platforms (e.g., Microsoft Teams and Zoom), overall positive learning experiences of students have been reported, despite limited support by educators and peers (Sobaih et al., 2021). As a result, students in developing countries would like to continue adopting online learning after the COVID-19 pandemic, had no problems using online learning platforms, and were greatly facilitated in their daily commuting, with a favourable impact on student's academic achievement in practical-related courses: "Surprisingly, 73.9% regarded online learning platforms to be more convenient than conventional learning since they can attend classes from the comfort of their own homes and have complete control over course material" (Adeyeye et al., 2022, p. 878).

Virtuality did not limit itself to teaching and research activities but extended to the governance of universities. For example, board councils and coordination activities went entirely online. They did not go entirely back to the previous traditions once the cost and time-saving, the environment-saving potentiality of online meetings became apparent to an already geographically dispersed and on the move academic community (across floors, buildings, cities, nations and continents; Fitzgerald, 2022). The

COVID-19 was a great acceleration for already existing trends and in a sequence of past and looming grand crises, going from the 2007/2008 global economic meltdown to the expected environmental crises of the "Anthropocene" in which we entered – the Earth's geological epoch in which humanity is altering Earth on a planetary scale (Laasch, Ryazanova & Wright, 2022).

All of that has been giving substance to the idea of a cost-saving, environmentally friendly global virtual university (GVU) in the post-COVID-19 "new normal". The idea of technology-driven GVU has been present for a couple of decades in a geographically isolated and advanced society such as New Zealand and in response to the crisis produced by the burst of the bubble in the dot-com world, which had catalyzed a growing critical reexamination of the fundamental political economy of online learning (Gunn & Recker, 2001). It was considered a "not utopian vision" already 20 years ago, in the aftermath of the gloomy vision that followed the 11 September attack on the United States as a response to those events, in order to build a more peaceful and prosperous world and transform the human energies mobilised for violence into human efforts for peace trough global virtual learning (Tiffin & Rajasingham, 2003). The experience and terminology have their origins in the University of North Carolina, that by no coincidence, is coordinating the X-Culture project today (Thompson, 2000).

Nonetheless, after 20 years of debates, GVUs are not a reality, and most universities are still rooted in a city or region and most of the time, they adopt the location's name. The oldest western university, the University of Bologna, has the name of the city in which it was founded and is currently located (de Ridder-Symoens & Rüegg, 2003). The first ranked universities in all the major ranking refer to a place, despite faculty and students, and most of their linkages have a truly global nature and compete at the global level. Should a significant part of their teaching and research activities stay online, with most of their stakeholders, students and staff being global, the reality of a GVU is not entirely unimaginable. It would still require labs and buildings, but they should be in a single place for no reason, and each activity might be in the best place, according to efficacy and efficiency criteria. As for the NGCs, the back-office activities of universities might be outsourced according to cost-saving criteria, while the research activities might combine GVTs, and labs spread in the best possible locations. After all, if GVTs managed the engineering of a state-of-the-art next-generation military aircraft (Gibson & Gibbs, 2006) and if the production of a military aircraft is spread across the globe, why should this not be possible for higher education activities after more than twenty years of technological progress since the idea of a GVU was first conceived?

The GVU of the future would probably have the form of a closed platform with superior technology, functioning as a gate to physical labs and activities across the globe that global students and faculty could access to pursue their objectives. It would not be linked to any nation-state, and like

196 *Ernesto Tavoletti*

some global cities, it would enjoy the privilege of global status (King, 1990). Probably, what has impeded the emergence of a GVU is not a lack of technology but the presence of national institutions that have been regulating universities and have been linking them to national policy objectives and the local stakeholders financing them so that the possible emergence of a real GVU is dependent on the decline of the national state and the emergence of a new global order. As the western concept of *universitas* (de Ridder-Symoens & Rüegg, 2003) was born in the Middle Ages, at a time of great mobility of scholars in Europe and in absentia of national states, the GVU might flourish if the national states further released their steering governance model upon universities, that is the system of instruments and institutional arrangements which seek to govern organisational and academic behaviours within HEIs (Ferlie, Musselin & Andresani, 2008). That is because universities largely depend on the national states or regional governments for financing.

Consequently, they are heavily regulated to benefit national, regional and even local needs (Tavoletti, 2009) while pursuing global excellence in knowledge development, generating a constant tension between local and global (Lazzeretti & Tavoletti, 2005). Therefore, GVUs might blossom only if national and regional governments' financing and steering role diminished in an increasingly global and borderless higher education environment. If globalisation should reverse its course, so would the popularity of GVUs, as the global reach allowed by virtuality only makes sense if a thriving global educational, research, and labour markets still exist. In the scenario of diminished globalisation, we would still have thriving distance learning and virtual universities, but they would serve regional and national needs, and the global dimension would be lost or greatly diminished.

Conclusion

The COVID-19 pandemic made popular to the many what was already an emerging phenomenon for some of the most talented knowledge workers in academia and MNEs: Working from home or personally inspiring locations under objectives, combining families and personal well-being while being empowered to do their best work – and at the same time being totally and socially connected in GVTs, thanks to improved information technology and matured virtual work culture. Of course, not all knowledge workers can enjoy the opportunity, depending on their work, but a consistently growing number can (or could) if the old cultural habits and the old BMs are adapted to the new circumstances.

Many old corporate bosses will not renounce easily to the habit of leaving home and family in the morning and reaching by car the top floor of a building while being surrounded by in-person collaborators, and "for many ages to come the old Adam will be so strong in us" (Keynes, 1930), demanding traditional work habits but, "thanks to" the global COVID-19 pandemic, it has become evident to many that very often international teamwork can be done even more effectively through GVTs. It has become self-evident to MNEs and our international students, faculty, and staff. Also, the linkages between universities and corporations can follow the same paths with stage and work moving online whenever this is more efficient and effective.

Global managing consulting firms (MCFs) are especially important as they are the key change agents for other MNEs in motivating, inventing, implementing, theorising and labelling management innovation and BMI (Birkinshaw, Hamel & Mol, 2008). MCFs have been adopting new digital BMs under the pressure of digital transformation, moving from the traditional *solution-shop* (that means diagnosing and solving problems whose scope is undefined, using high-paid consultants' judgement rather than through repeatable processes) to the digitally based *value-added process business* (that means addressing problems of defined scope with standard, repeatable and controllable software-based processes) and the *facilitated network* models (that is enabling the exchange of products and services, where customers pay fees to the network manager, who, in turn, pays the service provider), and they will be transferring these digital BMs to MNEs worldwide (Tavoletti et al., 2022). These new digital BMs demand the ability to work efficiently and effectively in GVTs. MCFs and GVUs offering GVTs training can play a leading role in transferring practice to the MNEs still rooted in old and less efficient practices.

New digital BMs relying on GVTs also contribute to more sustainable cities and societies, and MNEs used to allure talents by offering exclusive office amenities, such as the famous Googleplex or Apple Park, might resort to unrivalled home-working flexibility producing new and unexplored virtual organisational settings (Megahed & Ghoneim, 2020).

On 7 May 2022, reportedly, Apple's Director of machine learning, Ian Goodfellow, resigned in part due to his opposition to Apple's plan to return partially to in-person work. A group of employees took a similar position in the summer of 2021 in a letter to the CEO Tim Cook:

> Without the inclusivity that flexibility brings, many of us feel we have to choose between either a combination of our families, our well-being, and being empowered to do our best work, or being a part of Apple. This is a decision none of us takes lightly, and a decision many would prefer not to have to make. (Fathi, 2022)

As the "war for talent" is one of the greatest concerns in the global competitive arena, this is not something that MNEs can underestimate concerning their most strategic resources (Kane et al., 2017). On the opposite, they must design new digital BMs in an increasingly digital world to retain and attract the best talents.

198 *Ernesto Tavoletti*

References

Adeyeye, B., Ojih, S. E., Bello, D., Adesina, E., Yartey, D., Ben-Enukora, C., & Adeyeye, Q. (2022). "Online learning platforms and covenant university students' academic performance in practical related courses during COVID-19 pandemic", *Sustainability*, vol. 14(2), p. 878. doi: 10.3390/su14020878

Anand, N., Gardner, H.K., & Morris, T. (2007). "Knowledge-based innovation: Emergence and embedding of new practice areas in management consulting firms", *Academy of Management Journal*, vol. 50(2), pp. 406–428. doi: 10.5465/amj.2007. 24634457

Arslan, A., Gölgeci, I., & Larimo, J. (2021). "Expatriates, rise of telecommuting, and implications for international business", in M.A. Marinov & S.T. Marinova (Eds.). *COVID-19 and International Business: Change of Era.* London and New York: Taylor and Francis, 156–166.

Baaij, M.G. & Slangen, A.H. (2013). "The role of headquarters–subsidiary geographic distance in strategic decisions by spatially disaggregated headquarters", *Journal of International Business Studies*, vol. 44(9), pp. 941–952. doi: 10.1057/jibs.2013.41

Bartlett, C.A. (1981). "Multinational structural change: Evolution versus reorganization", in L. Otterbeck (Ed.), *The Management of Headquarters–Subsidiary Relationships in Multinational Corporations.* London: Gower, 121–146.

Bartlett, C.A. & Ghoshal, S. (1989). *Managing Across Borders: The Transnational Solution.* Boston, MA: Harvard Business School Press.

Beckman, C.M. & Burton, M.D. (2008). "Founding the future: Path dependence in the evolution of top management teams from founding to IPO", *Organization Science*, vol. 19(1), pp. 3–24. doi: 10.1287/orsc.1070.0311

Birkinshaw, J. (2001). "Strategy and management in MNE subsidiaries", in A.M. Rugman & T.L. Brewer (Eds.), *The Oxford Handbook of International Business.* Oxford, UK: Oxford University Press, 380–401. doi: 10.1093/oxfordhb/9780199234257.003. 0014

Birkinshaw, J., Hamel, G., & Mol, M.J. (2008). "Management innovation", *Academy of Management Review*, vol. 33(4), pp. 825–845. doi: 10.5465/amr.2008.34421969

Buckley, P.J. (2009). "The impact of the global factory on economic development", *Journal of World Business*, vol. 44(2), pp. 131–143. doi: 10.1016/j.jwb.2008.05.003

Burd, E.L., Smith, S.P., & Reisman, S. (2015). "Exploring business models for MOOCs in higher education", *Innovative Higher Education*, vol. 40(1), pp. 37–49. doi: 10.1007/ s10755-014-9297-0

Carlson, P.M. & Fleisher, M.S. (2002). "Shifting realities in higher education: Today's business model threatens our academic excellence", *International Journal of Public Administration*, vol. 25(9–10), pp. 1097–1111. doi: 10.1081/PAD-120006127

CultureWizard (2018). "Trends in high-performing global virtual teams by RW3". Retrieved on 5 April 2022 from: https://content.ebulletins.com/hubfs/C1/Culture %20Wizard/LL-2018%20Trends%20in%20Global%20VTs%20Draft%2012%20and %20a%20half.pdf

Cummings, J. N. (2004). "Work groups, structural diversity, and knowledge sharing in a global organization", *Management Science*, vol. 50(3), pp. 352–364. doi: 10.1287/ mnsc.1030.0134

Daniel, J., Vázquez Cano, E., & Gisbert Cervera, M. (2015). "The future of MOOCs: Adaptive learning or business model?" *International Journal of Educational Technology in Higher Education*, vol. 12(1), pp. 64–73. doi: 10.7238/rusc.v12i1.2475

Davidow, W.H. & Malone, M.S. (1992). *The Virtual Corporation. Structuring and Revitalizing the Corporation for the 21st Century.* New York: Harper Collins.

de Ridder-Symoens, H. & Rüegg, W. (Eds.). (2003). *A History of the University in Europe: Volume 1, Universities in the Middle Ages.* Cambridge: Cambridge University Press.

D'Este, P. & Patel, P. (2007). "University–industry linkages in the UK: What are the factors underlying the variety of interactions with industry?" *Research Policy*, vol. 36(9), pp. 1295–1313. doi:10.1016/j.respol.2007.05.002

Doz, Y.L., Bartlett, C.A., & Prahalad, C.K. (1981). "Global competitive pressures vs. host country demands: Managing tensions in multinational corporations", *California Management Review*, vol. 23(3), pp. 63–74. doi:10.2307/41172603

Doz, Y. & Prahalad, C.K. (1981). "Headquarters influence and strategic control in MNCs", *Sloan Management Review*, vol. 23(1), pp. 15–29.

Doz, Y. & Prahalad, C.K. (1984). "Patterns of strategic control within multinational corporations", *Journal of International Business Studies*, vol. 15(2), pp. 55–72. doi:10.1057/palgrave.jibs.8490482

Eisenberg, J. & Mattarelli, E. (2017). "Building bridges in global virtual teams: The role of multicultural brokers in overcoming the negative effects of identity threats on knowledge sharing across subgroups", *Journal of International Management*, vol. 23(4), pp. 399–411. doi:10.1016/j.intman.2016.11.007

Etzkowitz, H. (1998). "The norms of entrepreneurial science: cognitive effects of the new university–industry linkages", *Research Policy*, vol. 27(8), pp. 823–833. doi:10.1016/S0048-7333(98)00093-6

Fathi, S. (2022). "Apple's director of machine learning resigns due to return to office work", *MacRumors*, 7 May 2022, available at: https://www.macrumors.com/2022/05/07/apple-director-of-machine-learning-resigns/ (Accessed: 9 May 2022).

Ferlie, E., Musselin, C., & Andresani, G. (2008). "The steering of higher education systems: A public management perspective", *Higher Education*, vol. 56(3), pp. 325–348. doi:10.1007/s10734-008-9125-5

Fitzgerald, M. (2022). "How online learning is reshaping higher education", *US News*, 15 February, available at: https://www.usnews.com/news/education-news/articles/2022-02-15/how-online-learning-is-reshaping-higher-education

Gibson, C.B. & Gibbs, J.L. (2006). "Unpacking the concept of virtuality: The effects of geographic dispersion, electronic dependence, dynamic structure, and national diversity on team innovation", *Administrative Science Quarterly*, vol. 51(3), pp. 451–495. doi:10.2189/asqu.51.3.451

Gilbert, C.G. (2005). "Unbundling the structure of inertia: Resource versus routine rigidity", *Academy of Management Journal*, vol. 48(5), pp. 741–763. doi:10.5465/amj.2005.18803920

Glikson, E. & Erez, M. (2020). "The emergence of a communication climate in global virtual teams", *Journal of World Business*, vol. 55(6), p. 101001. doi:10.1016/j.jwb.2019.101001

Gonzalez-Perez, M.A., Lynden, K., & Taras, V. (Eds.). (2019). *The Palgrave Handbook of Learning and Teaching International Business and Management.* Cham, Switzerland: Palgrave Macmillan.

Greenberg, D. & Hibbert, P. (2020). "From the editors—Covid-19: Learning to hope and hoping to learn", *Academy of Management Learning & Education*, vol. 19(2), pp. 123–130. doi:10.5465/amle.2020.0247

Gunn, C. & Recker, M.M. (2001). "New Zealand higher education in the age of the global virtual university", *Educational Technology Research and Development*, vol. 49(2), pp. 106–116. https://www.jstor.org/stable/30220314

Herbsleb, J.D. & Moitra, D. (2001). "Global software development", *IEEE Software*, vol. 18(2), pp. 16–20. doi:10.1109/52.914732

Hinds, P., Liu, L., & Lyon, J. (2011). "Putting the global in global work: An intercultural lens on the practice of cross-national collaboration", *Academy of Management Annals*, vol. 5(1), pp. 135–188. doi:10.5465/19416520.2011.586108

Hinds, P.J., Neeley, T.B., & Cramton, C.D. (2014). "Language as a lightning rod: Power contests, emotion regulation, and subgroup dynamics in global teams", *Journal of International Business Studies*, vol. 45(5), pp. 536–561. doi:10.1057/jibs.2013.62

Jang, S. (2017). "Cultural brokerage and creative performance in multicultural teams", *Organization Science*, vol. 28(6), pp. 993–1009. doi:10.1287/orsc.2017.1162

Jarvenpaa, S.L. & Leidner, D.E. (1999). "Communication and trust in global virtual teams", *Organization Science*, vol. 10(6), pp. 791–815. doi:10.1287/orsc.10.6.791

Jimenez, A., Boehe, D.M., Taras, V., & Caprar, D. V. (2017). "Working across boundaries: Current and future perspectives on global virtual teams", *Journal of International Management*, vol. 23(4), pp. 341–349. doi:10.1016/j.intman.2017.05.001

Jonsen, K., Maznevski, M., & Davison, S.C. (2012). "Global virtual team dynamics and effectiveness", in G.K. Stahl, I. Bjorkman, S. Morris (Eds.), *Handbook of Research in International Human Resource Management*, 2nd ed. Cheltenham: Edward Elgar Publishing, 363–392. doi:10.4337/9781849809191.00024

Kalman, Y.M. (2014). "A race to the bottom: MOOCs and higher education business models", *Open Learning: The Journal of Open, Distance and e-Learning*, vol. 29(1), pp. 5–14. doi:10.1080/02680513.2014.922410

Kane, G.C., Palmer, D., Phillips, A.N., & Kiron, D. (2017). "Winning the digital war for talent", *MIT Sloan Management Review*, vol. 58(2), pp. 17–19.

Kazemargi, N., Tavoletti, E., Appolloni, A., & Cerruti, C. (2022). "Managing open innovation within supply networks in mature industries", *European Journal of Innovation Management*. doi:10.1108/EJIM-12-2021-0606

Keynes, J.M. (1930). "Economic possibilities for our grandchildren", in *Essays in Persuasion*. New York: Harcourt Brace, 358–373. https://www.aspeninstitute.org/wp-content/uploads/files/content/upload/Intro_and_Section_I.pdf

King, A. (1990). *Global Cities*. London and New York: Routledge.

Klitmøller, A., Schneider, S.C., & Jonsen, K. (2015). "Speaking of global virtual teams: Language differences, social categorization and media choice", *Personnel Review*, vol. 44(2), pp. 270–285. doi:10.1108/PR-11-2013-0205

Laasch, O., Ryazanova, O., & Wright, A.L. (2022). "Lingering COVID and looming grand crises: Envisioning business schools' business model transformations", *Academy of Management Learning & Education*, vol. 21(1), pp. 1–6.

Lazzeretti, L. & Tavoletti, E. (2005). "Higher education excellence and local economic development: The case of the entrepreneurial University of Twente", *European Planning Studies*, vol. 13(3), pp. 475–493. doi:10.1080/09654310500089779

Magnusson, P., Schuster, A., & Taras, V. (2014). "A process-based explanation of the psychic distance paradox: Evidence from global virtual teams", *Management International Review*, vol. 54(3), pp. 283–306. doi:10.1007/s11575-014-0208-5

Maljers, F.A. (1992). "Inside Unilever: The evolving transnational company", *Harvard Business Review*, vol. 70(5), pp. 46–52.

Marasi, S., Jones, B., & Parker, J.M. (2022). "Faculty satisfaction with online teaching: a comprehensive study with American faculty", *Studies in Higher Education*, vol. 47(3), pp. 513–525. doi:10.1080/03075079.2020.1767050

Marinov, M.A. & Marinova, S.T. (2021). *COVID-19 and International Business: Change of Era*. London and New York: Francis and Taylor.

Marquis, C. & Tilcsik, A. (2013). "Imprinting: Toward a multilevel theory", *Academy of Management Annals*, vol. 7(1), pp. 195–245. doi:10.5465/19416520.2013.766076

Mattarelli, E. & Gupta, A. (2009). "Offshore-onsite subgroup dynamics in globally distributed teams", *Information Technology & People*, vol. 3(22), pp. 242–269. doi:10.1108/09593840910981437

Maznevski, M.L. & Chudoba, K.M. (2000). "Bridging space over time: Global virtual team dynamics and effectiveness", *Organization Science*, vol. 11(5), pp. 473–492. doi:10.1287/orsc.11.5.473.15200

McAdam, M., Miller, K., & McAdam, R. (2017). "University business models in disequilibrium–engaging industry and end users within university technology transfer processes", *R&D Management*, vol. 47(3), pp. 458–472. doi:10.1111/radm.12265

McDonough, E.F., Kahnb, K.B. & Barczaka, G. (2001). "An investigation of the use of global, virtual, and colocated new product development teams", *Journal of Product Innovation Management: An International Publication of the Product Development & Management Association*, vol. 18(2), pp. 110–120. doi:10.1016/S0737-6782(00)00073-4

Mees-Buss, J., Welch, C., & Westney, D.E. (2019). "What happened to the transnational? The emergence of the neo-global corporation", *Journal of International Business Studies*, vol. 50(9), pp. 1513–1543. doi:10.1057/s41267-019-00253-5

Megahed, N.A. & Ghoneim, E.M. (2020). "Antivirus-built environment: Lessons learned from Covid-19 pandemic", *Sustainable Cities and Society*, vol. 61, p. 102350. doi:10.1016/j.scs.2020.102350

Miles, R.E. & Snow, C.C. (1986). "Organizations: New concepts for new forms", *California Management Review*, vol. 28(3), pp. 62–73. doi:10.2307/41165202

Miller, K., McAdam, M., & McAdam, R. (2014). "The changing university business model: a stakeholder perspective", *R&D Management*, vol. 44(3), pp. 265–287. doi:10.1111/radm.12064

Nurmi, N. & Hinds, P.J. (2016). "Job complexity and learning opportunities: A silver lining in the design of global virtual work", *Journal of International Business Studies*, vol. 47(6), pp. 631–654. doi:10.1057/jibs.2016.11

Pereira, V. & Anderson, V. (2012). "A longitudinal examination of HRM in a human resources offshoring (HRO) organization operating from India", *Journal of World Business*, vol. 47(2), pp. 223–231. doi:10.1016/j.jwb.2011.04.009

Reiche, B.S., Bird, A., Mendenhall, M.E., & Osland, J.S. (2017). "Contextualizing leadership: A typology of global leadership roles", *Journal of International Business Studies*, vol. 48(5), pp. 552–572. doi:10.1057/s41267-016-0030-3

Richter, N.F., Martin, J., Hansen, S.V., Taras, V., & Alon, I. (2021). "Motivational configurations of cultural intelligence, social integration, and performance in global virtual teams", *Journal of Business Research*, vol. 129, pp. 351–367. doi:10.1016/j.jbusres.2021.03.012

Siebdrat, F., Hoegl, M., & Ernst, H. (2009). "How to manage virtual teams", *MIT Sloan Management Review*, vol. 50(4), pp. 63–68.

Snihur, Y. & Zott, C. (2020). "The genesis and metamorphosis of novelty imprints: How business model innovation emerges in young ventures", *Academy of Management Journal*, vol. 63(2), pp. 554–583. doi:10.5465/amj.2017.0706

Sobaih, A.E.E., Salem, A.E., Hasanein, A.M., & Elnasr, A.E.A. (2021). "Responses to Covid-19 in higher education: Students' learning experience using Microsoft teams versus social network sites", *Sustainability*, vol. 13(18), p. 10036. doi:10.3390/su131810036

Spataro, J. (2020). "Learning from our customers in Italy", 8 April 2020, available at: https://www.microsoft.com/en-us/microsoft-365/blog/2020/04/08/learning-from-customers-italy/ (Accessed: 8 May 2022).

Stahl, G.K. & Maznevski, M.L. (2021). "Unraveling the effects of cultural diversity in teams: A retrospective of research on multicultural work groups and an agenda for future research", *Journal of International Business Studies*, vol. 52(1), pp. 4–22. doi: 10.1057/s41267-020-00389-9

Stahl, G.K., Maznevski, M.L., Voigt, A., & Jonsen, K. (2010). "Unravelling the effects of cultural diversity in teams: A meta-analysis of research on multicultural work groups", *Journal of International Business Studies*, vol. 41(4), pp. 690–709. doi:10.1057/jibs.2009.85

Taras, V., Caprar, D., Rottig, D., Sarala, R., Zakaria, N., Ordenana, X., Minor, M., Jimenez, A., Bryla, P., Lei, C., Wankel, C., Zhao, F., Froese, F., Bode, A., Schuster, A., Vaiginiene, E., Bathula, H., Yajnik, N., Baldegger, R., & Huang, V.Z. (2013). "A global classroom? Evaluating the effectiveness of global virtual collaboration as a teaching tool in management education", *Academy of Management Learning and Education*, vol. 12(3), pp. 414–435. doi:10.5465/amle.2012.0195

Taras, V., Baack, D., Caprar, D., Dow, D., Froese, F., Jimenez, A., & Magnusson, P. (2019). "Diverse effects of diversity: Disaggregating effects of diversity in global virtual teams", *Journal of International Management*, vol. 25(4), p. 100689. doi:10.1016/j.intman.2019.100689

Taras, V. & Gonzalez-Perez, M.A. (Eds). (2015). *The Palgrave Handbook of Experiential Learning in International Business*. Basingstoke: Palgrave Macmillan.

Taras, V., Gunkel, M., Assouad, A., Tavoletti, E., Kraemer, J., Jiménez, A., Svirina, W., Si Lei, & Shah, G. (2021). "The predictive power of university pedigree on the graduate's performance in global virtual teams", *European Journal of International Management*, vol. 16(4), pp. 555–584. doi:10.1504/EJIM.2021.10031657

Taras, V., Shah, G., Gunkel, M., & Tavoletti, E. (2020). "Graduates of elite universities get paid more. Do they perform better?" *Harvard Business Review*, 4 September 2020, available at: https://hbr.org/2020/09/graduates-of-elite-universities-get-paid-more-do-they-perform-better

Tavoletti, E. (2009). *Higher Education and Local Economic Development*. Firenze: Firenze University Press.

Tavoletti, E., Florea, L., Taras, V., Sahin, F., Çetin, F., & Askun, D. (2022). "Cohesion and performance in global virtual teams: The moderating role of technical skills", *European Journal of Innovation Management* (forthcoming).

Tavoletti, E., Kazemargi, N., Cerruti, C., Grieco, C., & Appolloni, A. (2022). "Business model innovation and digital transformation in global management consulting firms", *European Journal of Innovation Management*, vol. 25(6), pp. 612–636. doi:10.1108/EJIM-11-2020-0443

Tavoletti, E., Stephens, R.D., & Dong, L. (2019). "The impact of peer evaluation on team effort, productivity, motivation and performance in global virtual teams", *Team Performance Management*, vol. 25(5/6), pp. 334–347. doi:10.1108/TPM-03-2019-0025

Tavoletti, E., Stephens, R.D., Taras, V., & Dong, L. (2022). "Nationality biases in peer evaluations: The country-of-origin effect in global virtual teams", *International Business Review*, vol. 31(2), p. 101969. doi:10.1016/j.ibusrev.2021.101969

Tavoletti, E. & Taras, V. (2021). "A systematic review of global virtual teams. European International Business Academy (EIBA)". 47th Annual Conference: Firms, Innovation and Location: Reshaping International Business for Sustainable Development in the Post-Pandemic Era.

Teece, D.J. (2018). "Business models and dynamic capabilities", *Long Range Planning*, vol. 51(1), pp. 40–49. doi:10.1016/j.lrp.2017.06.007

Thompson, H.E. (2000). Global virtual university: An experiment between the university of North Carolina at Wilmington and the digital communities of Japan. *Proceedings of the 24th Annual International Computer Software and Applications Conference.* COMPSAC 2000, IEEE, 288–289. doi:10.1109/CMPSAC.2000.884736

Tiffin, J. & Rajasingham, L. (2003). *The Global Virtual University*. London and New York: Routledge.

Trkman, P. (2019). "Value proposition of business schools: More than meets the eye", *International Journal of Management Education*, vol. 17(3), p. 100310. doi:10.1016/j.ijme.2019.100310

van Oshri, I., van Fenema, P., & Kotlarskyj, J. (2008). "Knowledge transfer in globally distributed teams: The role of transactional memory", *Information Systems Journal*, vol. 18, pp. 593–616. doi:10.1111/j.1365-2575.2007.00243.x

Verbeke, A. & Lee, I. (2021). *International Business Strategy*. Cambridge: Cambridge University Press.

Wang, J., Grand, H.-L. C., Chen, T., & Leung, K. (2019). "Team creativity/innovation in culturally diverse teams: A meta-analysis", *Journal of Organizational Behavior*, vol. 40(6), pp. 693–708. doi:10.1002/job.2362

Wildman, J.L. & Griffith, R. (2015). *Leading Global Teams: Translating Multidisciplinary Science to Practice*. New York: Springer.

Zakaria, N. (2017). "Emergent patterns of switching behaviors and intercultural communication styles of global virtual teams during distributed decision making", *Journal of International Management*, vol. 23(4), pp. 350–366. doi:10.1016/j.intman.2016.09.002

Zakaria, N. & Mohd Yusof, S.A. (2020). "Crossing cultural boundaries using the internet: Toward building a model of swift trust formation in global virtual teams", *Journal of International Management*, vol. 26(1), p. 100654. doi:10.1016/j.intman.2018.10.004

Zubascu, F. (2020). "Italian universities scramble to move teaching and research online during coronavirus lockdown", *Science Business*, 10 March 2020, available at: https://sciencebusiness.net/news/italian-universities-scramble-move-teaching-and-research-online-during-coronavirus-lockdown (Accessed: 9 May 2022).

12 Healthcare Ecosystems and Business Models Reconfiguration: Decoupling and Resilience in the Context of Data-Driven Technologies: A Systematic Literature Review

Anna Żukowicka-Surma, Magnus Holmén, Jeaneth Johansson, and Svante Andersson

Introduction

New data-driven technologies such as artificial intelligence (AI) and internet-of-things (IoT) are introduced to different sectors. Digitalisation may lead to disruptive changes in any industry, including creating or entering new business models, lowering or changing entry barriers into the market and enabling the breakup of sectorial silos. Although digitalisation is not a novel phenomenon, data–driven related research has recently received increased attention. Previous studies in the management domain deal with digitalisation in various fields such as high-tech, automotive industry, retail, fintech and healthcare. A significant aspect of digitalisation is the increased abundance of data, increased role of automatic or semi–manual data analysis approaches and the associated value potential. For healthcare, digital transformation brings enormous opportunities for quality improvement and efficiency.

However, while digitalisation or data-driven technologies may be critically important, their efficiency and effectiveness depend on connecting systems, data and people, bringing about new challenges at different levels, i.e., macro societal, meso industrial or organisational micro individual level. The nature of digitalisation and performance at different levels are not well understood. There are various gaps in the literature in understanding digitalisation challenges for healthcare and the sector's strengths and weaknesses. Although the COVID-19 pandemic significantly accelerated the healthcare sector's digitisation, innovation adoption in the sector proceeds slower than in many other industries (Truong et al., 2019) as five core explanations for this are identified. First, healthcare professionals are reluctant to adopt changes in their patient care practice mainly due to the "Do No Harm" Oath, causing organisational decoupling between new ways of working with established routines and processes. The micro-level habitus of mental models involving

DOI: 10.4324/9781003326731-12

cognitive dissonance and the meso-level organisational inertia hinder changes in the sector governed by evidence-based practice (Dryden-Palmer, Parshuram and Berta, 2020). Second, technological and institutional development proceeds at different speeds; therefore, innovative practices and digital transformation strategies cannot directly be copied from industry to healthcare. The healthcare sector is not as digital mature as the industry (Dreger et al., 2021; Kulkov, 2021). The third barrier to adoption is that the healthcare sector faces tensions because of the expectation to maximise public value over business profit to fulfil the increasing demand of contradictory human needs resulting from social development. Such values are often difficult to capture. Fourth, data-driven solutions and systems are becoming more complex and less predictable, which is difficult for healthcare leaderships as their core activities are far from the decision-making relevant for exploiting the potential of new data and analysis methods outside smaller domains (e.g., radiology imaging). Digital competence in the industry is relatively low so far. As a follow-up, the fifth problem is that much of the existing research about data-driven solutions tackle specific technological problems in the computer science domain relating to the cross-fields of medical informatics and medical data engineering. It does not explicitly involve the healthcare professionals and their everyday practice (Ashfaq & Nowaczyk, 2019; Blom et al., 2019; Cui & Zhang, 2021; Heyman et al., 2021; Johnson et al., 2021; Scott, Carter and Coiera, 2021). Altogether, there is scarcity of research on data-driven management in healthcare, implying a lack of consensus on how to handle the challenges of data-driven technologies in healthcare practice. Although researchers, practitioners and policymakers are paying attention to digitalisation issues in healthcare, a systematic overview of the implications of data-driven use in healthcare is still lacking. We will address if and how the literature has analysed changes in healthcare-related business models and ecosystems. Although the study is grounded in the management field, we decided to explore the broader context of healthcare and data-driven technology application by describing the big picture and explaining the research problems across the management, engineering and healthcare domains.

The study's motivation was to explore the emerging digital healthcare landscape to identify the sector's processes and problems and formulate research gaps for further investigation. After an initial screening, our purpose was to identify potential opportunities for data-driven technology value (co)creation, particularly concerning business model innovation and ecosystems. The chapter systematically reviews the literature to identify and understand knowledge gaps in the digital healthcare landscape. It develops a research agenda to answer the research question: Whether and how do healthcare actors explore new business opportunities in the context of digitalisation?

The chapter is structured as follows. First, the authors discuss the research background and the design of the systematic literature review, followed by the results from the analysis of research articles. Finally, conclusions are drawn from the study.

206   *Anna Żukowicka-Surma et al.*

Methods and Data

A systematic literature review (SLR) methodology was applied to answer the research question. It allows a transparent and relevant assessment of the current research supported by documented evidence to provide insights, critical reflections, managerial implications and a road map for future research. It framed and systematised the analysis of digital healthcare innovation and adoption by drawing on studies from innovation management, healthcare implementation and medical data engineering journals.

The work was done in the following way: decision on definitions, systematic search in databases by using predefined words and concepts, study selection and screening and data extraction and analysis. We followed the Preferred Reporting Items for Systematic Reviews and Meta-Analyses (PRISMA) method, initially defining key concepts and formulating search terms relating to the digital healthcare landscape approach and data-driven-related components. The definitions of the key concepts are found in Table 12.1.

The keywords and concepts were identified to explore three main research domains: innovation management, healthcare implementation and medical data engineering (see Table 12.2).

The web-based Scholar Google search engine was used, allowing access to publications by providing full text, bibliographic information and metadata of electronic documents, which may include too many publications of poor quality. The main obstacle of the Scholar Google search engine is the absence

Table 12.1 Operational definitions for the key concepts

Term	Operational Definition
Digitalisation	"The process of digital technologies use to change a business model and provide new revenue and value-producing opportunities" (Gartner.com∗)
Digital healthcare landscape	a new dimension of healthcare activities (sphere) that deploys data-driven processes
Data-driven	"Utilization big data analytics to capture more value from traditional business activities" (Lager & Sun, 2021: 1) or "AI systems capable of processing different types of data in supporting clinical decision-making" (Shamout et al., 2021: 8)
Ecosystem	"Community of interdependent yet hierarchically independent heterogeneous participants who collectively generate an ecosystem value proposition—often emerge through collective action, where ecosystem participants interact with each other and the external environment" (Thomas & Ritala, 2022: 1)

Source: The authors.

Healthcare Ecosystems and Business Models Reconfiguration   207

Table 12.2 Interdisciplinary keywords and key concepts used to construct search queries

Field	Key Concepts
Business (management)	• Health innovation • Collaboration for integration of data-driven healthcare innovation • Data integration in data-driven healthcare • Collaboration/integration of labour/digital entrepreneurship • Business model innovation – data strategy in use (data-driven innovation) • OB (cognition/decision-making/routines/behavioural change) • Development process (scaling and utilisation/distribution AI solutions: AI new services, AI new products) • Information/data-driven business models/(legitimacy) • Internationalisation of MedTech to new business models • AI sustainable transitions
IT (Data engineering)	• AI/ML • Transferability of AI models • Enculturation
Implementation (Healthcare)	• Change management • Security/ethics • User involvement

Source: The authors.

of functionality to refine the search results based on the research discipline. Nevertheless, Scholar Google allows avoiding retrieval errors in mapping the relevant sources. Moreover, it uses citation counts, which supported evaluating the importance of scientific work during the bibliometric analysis.

Relevance and quality assessment search criteria such as a paper written in English, full text available and relevance of the title, were applied during the theoretical and practical sources screening. The research investigated recent peer-reviewed journal articles (from the last and present year – from January and February 2022). However, it was necessary to broaden the timeframe to older sources to complement the findings by most cited sources having origins in the journals with high IF. Consequently, 90% of the resources originate between 2018 and 2022.

Inconsistent terminology was a critical barrier to the progress of the research (Au-Yong-Oliveira et al., 2021); therefore, 178 peer-reviewed journal articles were supplemented with the grey literature search (Enticott, Johnson and Teede, 2021). The general Internet search with Google Scholar resulted in 18 non-peer-reviewed sources such as OECD and WHO reports, conference papers, dissertation thesis and book chapters, which stated for 9% of the total sources set. The final database for SLR has 196 sources from interfields of innovation management, healthcare implementation and medical engineering from 2006 to 2022, of which 75% come from 2021 to 2022 years and 20% from 2013 to 2020 (the majority come from 2020).

The data analysis was supported by NVivo 10 (type of CAQDAS – computer-assisted qualitative data analysis software) to provide reliable and credible results. Spreadsheets were used to extract data from the literature sources and record each article's metadata such as references, abstracts or keywords.

Data Coding

Article data were categorised based on keywords from the included papers, presenting the overarching digital healthcare landscape and aiming to define a central structure of the research theme grounded in organisational theory. It followed iterations to clarify and classify codes, create categories and sort the data to explore and develop the dataset structure. The next steps aimed to identify patterns and construct thematic conclusions to gather evidence on the effects of digitalisation on healthcare at different dimensions.

Results

The narrative synthesis method systematically reviewed the entire studies relating to the digital healthcare landscape and collated the findings into a coherent structure due to the heterogeneity of research concepts. The two broad "complementary" approaches were used for the literature analysis: a subjective approach based on a qualitative analysis of the literature and an objective approach based on quantitative bibliometric analysis (Acedo and Casillas, 2005).

The Characteristics of Published Literature

The following section presents the bibliometric analysis of the contributions made by authors and journal sources from innovation management, healthcare implementation and medical data engineering domains. Tables illustrate the results and a narrative description of the references analysis and the findings related to the emerging trends. To explain the logic across all the datasets, the main actors, the timeline and the critical events deciding on the domains' dynamics were identified to create the conceptual framework described in section B.

Research on Digital Healthcare Landscape Distribution among Three Interdisciplinary Domains

A   Bibliometric Approaches

The search identified 196 studies from innovation management, healthcare implementation and medical data engineering. The main finding is that

Healthcare Ecosystems and Business Models Reconfiguration 209

Table 12.3 Distribution of interdisciplinary articles published between 2001 and 2022

	Before 2013	2013–2020	2021–2022
Management articles ($\sum 92$)	6	14	72
Healthcare articles ($\sum 70$)	4	21	45
Engineering articles ($\sum 34$)	0	4	30

Source: The authors.

data-driven technology influences the healthcare landscape at different levels of analysis. The main challenge was the complexity of the field, epitomised in a variety of perspectives indicated in the introduction and subsequently identified through the investigation, which might be a consequence of the accelerated conceptualisation evolution of the digital healthcare landscape. The papers were differentiated according to the logic of the journal profile as Business/economy and social sciences; Healthcare implementation/medicine; and Engineering/ Medical data engineering. The management domain is represented by 92 articles published between 2001 and 2022. Seventy papers have origin in the healthcare domain journals, and 34 sources relate to engineering.

The time frame was divided into three periods to show the evolution of digital healthcare literature. Most articles come from the current period (2021–2022) – 72 from the management domain, the healthcare domain is represented by 45, and less – 30 provide engineering domain. The previous period (2013–2020) offers relevant fewer sources: respective management – 14, healthcare – 21, engineering – 4 and the least represented is the period before 2013, which gives only a handful but relevant and essential for the research development papers coming from two domains – management and healthcare. The articles' distribution is illustrated in Table 12.3 and following Figure 12.1.

Citation Analysis

Citation analysis is a widely used bibliometric method supporting empirical investigations of academic disciplines' structure and research activity (Coombes & Nicholson, 2013). However, it only provides an indirect representation of the research's influence on science because there are many reasons for citing or not citing an antecedent paper. Nevertheless, the citation counts analysis identified the most influential research from the earlier two periods, which helps extend the understanding of the evaluation of the domains' performance. The most cited studies (2445 and 1857 citations) come from 2010 and 2012 related to digital innovation's organizing logic (Yoo, Henfridsson and Lyytinen, 2010; Yoo et al., 2012). The third research in the ranking refers to data analytics capabilities in healthcare (1034 citations) (Wang, Kung and Byrd, 2018). Between 2021 and 2022 the

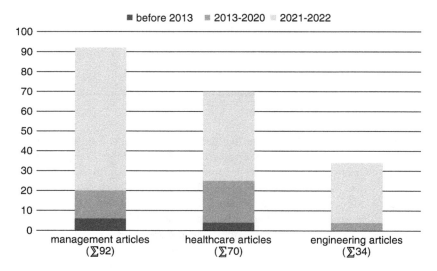

Figure 12.1 Distribution of the published articles.
Source: The authors.

research gathered 1655 references cited from 147 journal articles, representing a reduction compared to the previous periods. This reduction is explained as these articles have had less time to be cited by other authors since publication. Moreover, the year 2022 is underrepresented because the inclusion process in the analysis ended on 28 February 2022.

The ten most cited articles were published in management or healthcare domains journals such as *Information Systems Research, Organization Science, Technological Forecasting and Social Change, Academy of Management Journal, Implementation Science, Nature Reviews Microbiology, Journal of Organizational Behavior, Organization Science, BMC Health Services Research* and *The Lancet Digital Health*. However, the top places take the management domain with conceptual papers, where healthcare is only superficially referred. Table 12.4 presents the ranking of the most cited study.

Citations per article in each period show 508 citations before 2013; 87 later period 2013–2020; and 11 citations in the current period 2021–2022. The latter is not surprising that the highest value is in the oldest period because they had more time to gather citations. The results are summarised in Table 12.5.

Citation Analysis in the Three Journals Domains

Citations distribution in domains and periods is presented in Table 12.6 and following Figure 12.2.

Table 12.4 The top 10 cited articles

Ranking	Reference	Journal	Journal if 2021	$\sum$ Citations (on 21/03/2022)	Journal Domain	Research Method*
1	Yoo, Henfridsson and Lyytinen, 2010	Information systems research	5,207	2445	management	C
2	Yoo et al., 2012	Organization science	5,000	1857	management	C
3	Wang, Kung and Byrd, 2018	Technological Forecasting and Social Change	8,593	1034	management	C
4	George et al., 2016	Academy of management journal	10,194	965	management	C
5	Gagliardi et al., 2015	Implementation science	7,327	399	healthcare	C
6	Vandenberg et al., 2021	Nature Reviews Microbiology	60,633	329	healthcare	E qual.
7	Ramanujam and Rousseau, 2006	Journal of Organizational Behavior	8,174	286	management	C
8	Dougherty and Dunne, 2012	Organization Science	5,000	203	management	E qual.
9	Barnett et al., 2011	BMC health services research	2,655	198	healthcare	E qual.
10	Gasser et al., 2020	The Lancet Digital Health	N/A	143	healthcare	C

Source: The authors.

Notes: N/A = scientific level placement 2022 and Norwegian HEIs as 1.
* Research method: C-conceptual, E qual-empirical qualitative.

Table 12.5 Citation distribution analysis in the three periods

	Before 2013	2013–2020	2021–2022
∑ articles (196)	10	39	147
∑ citations in the period	5080	3408	1655

Source: The authors.

Table 12.6 Citations distribution between domains in the three periods

	Before 2013	2013–2020	2021–2022
Management domain 92 articles (∑ citations 7739)	4803	2207	729
Healthcare domain 70 articles (∑ citations 2029)	277	1064	688
Engineering 34 articles (∑ citations 375)	0	137	238

Source: The authors.

The extended analysis of citations in each domain illustrated by the figure indicates that the most citations came from the management domain (4803) research before 2013 (represented only by six articles). In contrast, the healthcare domain produced the most citations (1064) in the later period

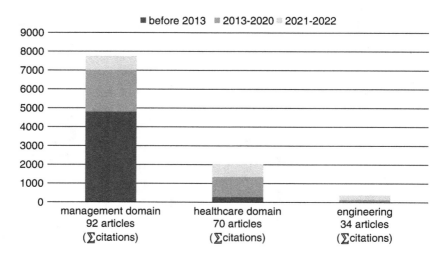

Figure 12.2 Citations distribution in the three domains.
Source: The authors.

Healthcare Ecosystems and Business Models Reconfiguration 213

Table 12.7 Citations and (citations per article) distribution (in each domain and period)

	Before 2013 (10 Articles)	2013–2020 (39 Articles)	2021–2022 (147 Articles)
Management domain 92 articles citations $\sum$ (citations/article)	4803 (800)	2207 (158)	729 (10)
Healthcare domain 70 articles citations $\sum$ (citations/article)	277 (69)	1064 (51)	688 (15)
Engineering 34 articles citations $\sum$ (citations/article)	0	137 (34)	238 (8)

Source: The authors.

2013–2020 (from 21 articles). Moreover, the last period (from 2021.01.01 to 2022.02.28) already produced 688 citations (out of 45 sources). The most surprising result refers to the engineering domain, where the most citations (238) come from the current period (2021–2022) from 34 articles showing an increase of interest in this research domain (where the oldest articles come from 2019). However, citation analysis does not show the healthcare landscape development. In summary, citation per article in each domain in the whole period shows the values: for management (84), healthcare (29) and engineering (11), illustrated in Table 12.7.

The citation analysis of the most impactful research in each journal domain will be presented in the following sections.

Journals' Citation Impact Analysis

Based on the findings from the previous section, the journals' impact factor analysis was performed to identify the most impactful studies on the digital healthcare landscape. The ranking is based on the currently available on the Web of Science journals' Impact Factor (IF) 2021. The 196 articles have appeared in 127 journals in innovation management, healthcare implementation and medical data engineering. Table 12.8 presents 25 journals with the highest IF.

The top-10 IF journals are medical, engineering and management domains as follows: *The Lancet* (IF – 79,321), *Nature Reviews Microbiology* (IF – 60,633), *Diabetes Care*, *Nature Machine Intelligence* (the only engineering journal in the ranking with IF 15,508), *JAMA Surgery*, *International Journal of Management Reviews* (IF – 13,419 the highest place among management journals in the hierarchy), *NPJ digital medicine*, *The Journal of Strategic Information Systems*, *Business Strategy and the Environment*, and *Academy of management journal*. The

Table 12.8 Top 25 journals' citation impact and productivity

Ranking	Journal	Journal if 2021*	Articles ∑	Citations ∑ (on 21/03/2022)	Journal Domain
1	The Lancet	79,321	1	34	Healthcare
2	Nature Reviews Microbiology	60,633	1	329	Healthcare
3	Diabetes Care	19,112	1	35	Healthcare
4	Nature Machine Intelligence	15,508	1	4	Engineering
5	JAMA surgery	14,766	1	98	Healthcare
6	International Journal of Management Reviews	13,419	1	0	Management
7	NPJ digital medicine	11,653	1	41	Healthcare
8	The Journal of Strategic Information Systems	11,022	1	0	Management
9	Business Strategy and the Environment	10,302	1	71	Management
10	Academy of management journal	10,194	1	965	Management
11	Journal of Cleaner Production	9,297	1	36	Management
12	BMC medicine	8,775	1	91	Healthcare
13	Journal of manufacturing systems	8,633	1	31	Management
14	Technological Forecasting and Social Change	8,593	5	1119	Management
15	Journal of World Business	8,513	1	2	Management
16	JAMA Network Open	8,483	2	10	Healthcare
17	Journal of Organizational Behavior	8,174	1	286	Management
18	Research policy	8,110	1	11	Management
19	Journal of Sustainable Tourism	7,968	1	38	Management
20	International Journal of Production Economics	7,885	1	12	Management
21	Neuropsychopharmacology	7,853	1	21	Healthcare
22	Rheumatology	7,580	1	1	Healthcare
23	Journal of Business Research	7,550	3	89	Management
24	Information Systems Journal	7,453	1	7	Management
25	Implementation Science	7,327	3	486	Healthcare

Source: The authors based on impactforjournal.com/jcr-2021/.

Note

* IF2021 = (Citation in 2020 + Citations in 2019)/ (Papers Published in 2020+ Papers Published in 2019).

three journals with the highest IF come from the healthcare domain with the following papers: *The Lancet* (IF: 79,321) with the paper: "Digital health nation: Israel's global big data innovation hub" (Balicer & Afek, 2017); *Nature Reviews Microbiology* (IF: 60,633) with the paper: "Considerations for diagnostic COVID-19 tests" (Vandenberg et al., 2021); and *Diabetes Care* (IF: 19,112) with the article: "From Hong Kong Diabetes Register to JADE Program to RAMP-DM for data-driven actions" (Chan et al., 2019).

However, the most cited articles were published in the management journals (*Technological Forecasting and Social Change* – IF 8,593) with 1119 citations coming from five articles and *Academy of Management Journal* (IF 10,194) with 965 citations coming from the conceptual paper: "Understanding and tackling societal grand challenges through management research" (George et al., 2016).

The citation analysis presented in the previous section (A) attempted to analyse the influence of interdisciplinary theory on the current digital healthcare landscape and evaluate how scholarship assimilates and contributes to the fields' development. The analysis and evaluation of the knowledge transfer processes involved the characteristics of the critical references, the analysis of citing behaviour and the citation impact and productivity of the top-cited journals.

Summarising the findings: the most impactful research (assessed by journal IF and the article citations analysis) comes from the management journals, while journals from the healthcare domain (with higher IF than management and engineering journals) illustrate the most current challenges of the sector. The engineering journals (with the lowest IF) deliver research on the technology with the potential to be implemented in healthcare.

B *Findings – The Digital Landscape Structure*

The following section reveals the structure of the digital healthcare landscape by analysing the references and the emerging trends. First, it focuses on the heart of the three domains. As explained at the beginning of the section, the knowledge about data-driven healthcare solutions is spread across management, healthcare and engineering journals. Second, links between the domains across the timeline are established.

Conclusions on Healthcare Sources and Interpretations of the Trends across the Timeline

The first paragraph relates to the healthcare domain represented by 70 macro-oriented studies dedicated to the global population's attempts to improve health outcomes (public health) connected to an (eco) system perspective. Therefore, the research tackled difficulties in identifying specific examples of healthcare business models. However, it provided the source for exploration and definition of the sector's problems to be solved (identified as the domain's strengths and weaknesses). The overview of the dataset provides conceptual and empirical examples from diverse areas of the clinical practice relating to data-driven decision-making or prognostic and prediction support capabilities (Au-Yong-Oliveira et al., 2021; Dreger et al., 2021; Scott, Carter and Coiera, 2021). The conceptual streams of the research refer to ophthalmology (Camara et al., 2022; Gunasekeran et al., 2021), digital tools used in generating real-world evidence in rheumatology (Kataria & Ravindran, 2022) or AI application in precision medicine (Johnson et al., 2021).

The empirical evidence refers to the decision-making augmented by automated AI models in surgery (Loftus et al., 2020) or empowering geriatrics patients with a mobile assessment app (Tan et al., 2021). Some examples from the emergency are machine learning models supporting 30-day patients' mortality prediction (Blom et al., 2019; Heyman et al., 2021) or deep learning for the deterioration of COVID-19 patients (Shamout et al., 2021). Other empirical research is dedicated to psychiatric or mental health (Chu et al., 2022), pathology, and laboratory medicine (diagnostic – Huddy et al., 2021, or microbiology – Vandenberg et al., 2021) and blood chains supply (Nagurney & Dutta, 2021). The empirical evidence also refers to the capability to share health-related data among general practitioners within the innovative technological infrastructure based on interoperability specifications (Frontoni et al., 2019); and conceptualising other technical and organisational changes in the primary care accelerated by the COVID-19 pandemic (Pagliari, 2021).

The research tackles multidisciplinary teams of frontline clinicians, researchers and community members, embedded in healthcare in integrated systems and eHealth (Chan et al., 2019; Enticott, Johnson and Teede, 2021; Jurkeviciute et al., 2021). The multi-stepped protocol for accelerating the adoption of AI that emphasises the organisational change factors at the national level, including creating awareness and capacity building framed by the Knowledge-to-Action framework (Wiljer et al., 2021). The conceptual research highlights the advantages and disadvantages of integrating AI into community-based primary health care, which facilitates diagnosis and disease management but brings doubts concerning its unintended harmful effects (Rahimi et al., 2021). Although data processing and learning promote the advancement of medicine by unlocking innovative approaches for patient care, nevertheless, the integration of raw data from different sources; limitation of hardware processing capacity; a lack of supporting training programs, as well as issues on ethics and larger societal acceptable practices are challenging for computational pathology (Cui & Zhang, 2021).

After a brief overview of the research types, the studies were analysed across the timeline. Most elements identified in the healthcare papers corresponded to macro-outcomes that finally affect micro-levels (as coordinating building capacity in the ecosystem of people, projects and systems required if the volume of data collected during routine healthcare is to be used to benefit patients in the form of health promotion and prevention). The earliest research from the dataset addressed a profound need for information (in the form of medical informatics for quality data) to improve the quality of health care and health care systems (WHO report, 2001); and factors (barriers and facilitators) of implementation and diffusion of healthcare service innovations to improve organisational efficiency (Barnett et al., 2011). The research also provided evidence of professional collaboration and knowledge sharing as Communities of Practices (cross-disciplinary professional teams sharing knowledge across intra-organisational and inter-organisational boundaries) to provide good quality medical services (Kislov, Walshe, and Harvey, 2012) also as healthcare interdisciplinary professional teams empowered by medical informatics for evidence-based performance improvement (Willis, Pulliam and Bacon, 2004). Also, later research (2013–2020) provided an evidence-based innovation framework based on Rogers' Diffusion of Innovations theory, revealing the impact of power and authority in healthcare teams on the change implementation (Dryden-Palmer, Parshuram, and Berta, 2020).

The empirical evidence related to integrated healthcare at the macro-level trends presented successful examples of global big-data innovation sharing hub in Israel (Balicer & Afek, 2017) or dedicated healthcare research information regional platform in Sweden (Ashfaq et al., 2020). However, such technological innovation introduces more complexity to the healthcare systems (Reed et al., 2018; Reed, Green and Howe, 2019; Reed et al., 2019). To overcome this weakness is considered support from innovative technological data-driven tools such as AI (Blom et al., 2019; Loftus et al., 2020; Shaw et al. in 2019; Truong et al., 2019) or quality management methods such as Deming's Quality circle (Dryden-Palmer, Parshuram and Berta, 2020) for sustainable improvement through Interactive Simulation (Antonacci et al., 2018).

The current and previous years (2021–2022) provided a rich set of innovation-related stream research on the digital technology applications in healthcare, which might be explained by the severe need to solve the COVID-19 pandemic-related problems, as expressed by the highly cited (329) article (Vandenberg et al., 2021) about the successful diagnostic tests published in *Nature Reviews Microbiology* (the journal among highest with IF − 60,633). Other research related to pandemic management referred to the acceleration of innovative integrated data-driven solutions (Sheng et al., 2021), data-driven pandemic space modelling (Chu et al., 2021); and adoption of digital health solutions such as telehealth, AI decision support for triaging and clinical care and home monitoring (Gunasekeran et al., 2021). The other stream of the current research emphasised the ethical challenges related to big data (Ferretti et al., 2022), health data poverty (Ibrahim et al., 2021), privacy, and data protection (Tuazon, 2021) and responsible AI (Siala & Wang, 2022).

Finally, the analysis of the top 10 cited articles from the healthcare domain presented in Table 12.9 summarises the most impactful factors in

Table 12.9 The top 10 cited articles from the healthcare domain

Ranking	Reference	Journal	Journal if 2021	$\sum$ Citations (on 21/03/2022)
1	Gagliardi et al., 2015	Implementation science	7,327	399
2	Vandenberg et al., 2021	Nature Reviews Microbiology	60,633	329
3	Barnett et al., 2011	BMC health services research	2,655	198
4	Gasser et al., 2020	The Lancet Digital Health	N/A	143
5	Loftus et al., 2020	JAMA surgery	14,766	98
6	Shaw et al., 2019	Journal of medical Internet research	5,428	92
7	Reed et al., 2018	BMC medicine	8,775	91
8	Kislov, Walshe and Harvey, 2012	Implementation Science	7,327	79
9	Cui and Zhang, 2021	Laboratory Investigation	5,662	49
10	Gunasekeran et al., 2021	The Lancet Digital Health	N/A	46

Source: The authors.

Note: N/A = scientific level placement 2022 and Norwegian HEIs as 1.

Healthcare Ecosystems and Business Models Reconfiguration 219

healthcare implementation research. It refers to evidence and knowledge (Gagliardi et al., 2015; Reed et al., 2018) within communities of practice (Kislov, Walshe and Harvey, 2012); and challenges according to AI (Cui & Zhang, 2021; Loftus et al., 2020; Shaw et al., 2019) specifically emphasised in the research tackling healthcare sector remedies to mitigate COVID-19 pandemic (Gasser et al., 2020; Gunasekeran et al., 2021; Vandenberg et al., 2021).

In summary, healthcare research analysis identified the potential for data-driven prediction and decision-making in improving health outcomes at the macro-level, facilitated by cross-sectoral multidisciplinary collaboration. Which, however, needs to consider challenges coming from technology elaborated in the coming section.

Conclusions on Engineering Sources and Interpretations of the Trends across the Timeline

The following section presents the analysis of the 34-engineering research papers, which provides the most current research from the concise period 2019–2022 on the implications for the healthcare sector (as opportunities or threats). Most elements corresponded to empirical research on innovative data-driven physical and virtual solutions applications for the healthcare sector relating to data and data analytics, AI, machine learning (ML), deep learning (DL), virtual reality (VR), metaverse, mathematical algorithms, Industry 4.0, wearables and IoT, cloud, and blockchains. Some papers also emphasised ethical challenges related to AI.

The earliest papers in the collection that attracted relatively high scholarly attention (expressed by the number of citations) presented practical examples of ML and DL use based on electronic health records (EHR) in the complex healthcare system (Ashfaq et al., 2019). The research from 2020 provided ML application for life prediction (Fan, Nowaczyk and Rögnvaldsson, 2020) or digitally empowered managing supply chains during the pandemic (macro-level) (Baveja, Kapoor and Melamed, 2020). The studies from the current period (2021–2022) (that did not have time to gather enough citations to be ranked among the top 10) emphasised the role of connectivity of data-driven technology (blockchain, Industry 4.0) (Dimitrievski et al., 2021; Hussain et al., 2021; Paul et al., 2021), and the ethical concerns of the innovative technology (Fosch-Villaronga et al., 2021; Jobin et al., 2021; Wang, Xie and Rodrigues, 2022; Wehrens et al., 2021). Conceptual articles also referred to Industry 4.0 applications for medical/healthcare services (Paul et al., 2021) and IoT for smart healthcare (Hussain et al., 2021), IoT for sustainable healthcare (Dimitrievski et al., 2021), human-centred design in industry 4.0 (Nguyen Ngoc, Lasa and Iriarte, 2022) or Quality 4.0 (Javaid et al., 2021). Moreover, an empirical article from 2021 examined the impact of data-driven culture on organisational innovation and performance (Chatterjee, Chaudhuri and Vrontis, 2021). The most cited paper from 2022 (already 76 citations on 21 March 2022) presented a survey on blockchain for big data

220   *Anna Żukowicka-Surma et al.*

(Deepa et al., 2022). Other empirical articles referred to big data analytics in healthcare (Jayasri & Aruna, 2022) and the applicability of data-driven responses to monitor and forecast the COVID-19 spread (Amaral et al., 2021).

The analysis of top-10 cited articles from the engineering domain presented in Table 12.10 summarises the most impactful research from engineering journals. It emphasised explicitly the studies on digital technology supporting efforts against the COVID-19 pandemic (Amaral et al., 2021; Baveja, Kapoor and Melamed, 2020).

To summarise, engineering research like healthcare orients more on the macro-level (system) than the business (models)-level. It provides a source of innovative data-driven solutions with the potential to be implemented in healthcare. However, it needs consideration of technology-related opportunities and threats. Therefore, the following section elaborates on appropriate managerial methods for technology implementation, answering the needs to improve the quality of healthcare services and healthcare systems.

Conclusions on Management Sources and Interpretations of the Trends across the Timeline

The factors identified in 92 management articles relate to managerial methods and solutions bridging healthcare with engineering (actions, means of scientific investigation and experiences, such as business models and ecosystems) that respond to specific challenges in implementing technological solutions articulated in the healthcare research domain. First, the types of digitalisation related to the healthcare policy and service were examined in the articles' strategies, methods, experiences or actions. This variety is a sign of the dynamism of research on digital technology applications at the intersection of several existing fields. Therefore, the opportunities or threats for the healthcare sector were identified. Since many trends were identified, only a few crucial examples will be elaborated.

Over the timeline, the earliest research provided examples of increased system complexity (emphasised in the healthcare journals) resulting from the technology introduction (Dougherty & Dunne, 2012). Therefore, management research proposed system simplification allowing communication between actors, which affected the need to leave a holistic perspective and create a new business model – as a source for creativity, entrepreneurship and empowerment. Tucker, Hendy and Barlow (2012) emphasised the role of sensemaking and social accounts of middle managers in hospitals through change agents at the micro-level. This new business model might work as a cognitive instrument for a system heuristic logic connecting technological potential with the realisation of economic value (=good) through innovation at the macro-level (Barlow, 2015; Cisnetto & Barlow, 2020). Moreover, the current period 2021–2022 provided rich research on multiple innovative methods to manage healthcare digitalisation. The coordination-building

Table 12.10 The top 10 cited articles from the engineering domain

Ranking	Reference	Journal	Journal if 2021	$\sum$ Citations (on 21/03/2022)
1	Deepa et al., 2022	Future Generation Computer Systems	7,187	76
2	Ashfaq et al., 2019	Journal of biomedical informatics	6,317	59
3	Baveja, Kapoor and Melamed, 2020	Annals of Operations Research	4,854	44
4	Fan, Nowaczyk and Rögnvaldsson, 2020	Reliability Engineering & System Safety	6,188	29
5	Balakrishnan and Dwivedi, 2021	Annals of Operations Research	4,854	29
6	Chatterjee, Chaudhuri and Vrontis 2021	Annals of Operations Research	4,854	21
7	Ahsan et al., 2021	Technologies	N/A	15
8	Javaid et al., 2021	Sensors International	*	15
9	Amaral et al. 2021	Sensors	3,576	14
10	Yahaya Lotfi and Mahmud, 2021	Pattern Recognition Letters	3,756	14

Source: The authors.

Notes: N/A = scientific level placement 2022 and Norwegian HEIs as 1.

* = no IF.

capacity in the ecosystem of people, projects and systems is the source of the data-driven value for patients at the macro-level.

The citation analysis identified the most impactful research referring to the digital healthcare landscape challenges, such as the emerging organising logic of digital innovation architecture of devices, networks, services and contents created by digital technology (Yoo, Henfridsson and Lyytinen, 2010), or strategic implications of big data analytics in healthcare (Wang, Kung and Byrd, 2018). The healthcare industry's fundamental challenge refers to organisational learning and employee involvement, known as the "knowledge-doing gap" at the micro-level (Ramanujam & Rousseau, 2006) and cross-sectoral integrative knowledge (Dougherty & Dunne, 2012). The current empirical, highly cited research examined impacting factors for healthcare professionals to adopt an AI-based medical diagnosis support system (Fan et al., 2020). Moreover, the most cited paper (80 citations) in the current period discussed the principles of trustworthy AI (Thiebes, Lins and Sunyaev, 2021). Table 12.11 summarises the top 10 cited management articles.

The empirical research from the management journals with the high IF referred to the factors mentioned already in the above summary, such as big data analytics capability for operational flexibility and resilience in the integrated hospital supply chains (Yu et al., 2021a – published in *Technological Forecasting and Social Change* – IF 8,593) or the critical factors of AI for value formation and market performance in healthcare (Kumar, Dwivedi and Anand, 2021 – published in *Information Systems Frontiers* – IF 6,191) and data-driven hospital operations effects on operational performance (Yu et al., 2021b – published in *IEEE Transactions on Engineering Management* – IF 6,146). Moreover, the research published in the *International Journal of Information Management* (scientific level placement 2022 and Norwegian HEIs as 2) provided evidence of learning healthcare system ensuring quality, safety and value based on the secondary data from electronic health records (EHR) (Hausvik, Thapa and Munkvold, 2021).

The following section summarises other opportunities and challenges healthcare management encounters in the digital landscape. Apell & Eriksson's (2021) study identified the system-blocking mechanisms for AI healthcare technology innovations resulting from limited resources and healthcare professional leaders' poor communication. The socio-technical framework analysis indicated the need for vision and mission statements to improve healthcare. Especially facing the need to increase responsiveness to exceptional disruptions in supply and value chains such as the COVID-19 pandemic, healthcare executives were challenged with how to orchestrate digital medical resources (Yu et al., 2021b) for operational performance improvements such as cost, delivery and quality (Margherita, Elia and Klein, 2021). Therefore, AI-affected automation impacting labour demand and equilibrium employment triggered changing business models and restructuring of the industry, the technical standards and the ethical framework for AI use (Sena & Nocker, 2021).

Table 12.11 The top 10 cited articles from the management domain

Ranking	Reference	Journal	Journal if 2021	∑ Citations (on 21/03/2022)
1	Yoo, Henfridsson and Lyytinen, 2010	Information systems research	5,207	2445
2	Yoo et al., 2012	Organization science	5,000	1857
3	Wang, Kung and Byrd, 2018	Technological Forecasting and Social Change	8,593	1034
4	George et al., 2016	Academy of management journal	10,194	965
5	Ramanujam and Rousseau, 2006	Journal of Organizational Behavior	8,174	286
6	Dougherty and Dunne, 2012	Organization Science	5,000	203
7	Fan W. et al., 2020	Annals of Operations Research	4,854	94
8	Thiebes, Lins and Sunyaev, 2021	Electronic Markets	4,765	80
9	Kraus et al., 2021	Journal of Business Research	7,550	72
10	Awan, Sroufe and Shahbaz, 2021	Business Strategy and the Environment	10,302	71

Source: The authors.

Moreover, considering the transition from "Industry 4.0" to "Industry 5.0", where humans – smart systems collaboration will get priority, Mondal & Samaddar (2022) explored the motivational, regulation and supporting integrational factors for data-driven supply chain performance and high-quality healthcare services. Current research also emphasised the strategic impact of employee behaviour factors at the micro-level such as commitment to organisational change or change readiness among cross-functional healthcare professional teams (Fournier, Chênevert and Jobin, 2021; Harrison et al., 2022); and reducing organisational (Dussart, van Oortmerssen and Albronda, 2021) or institutional powers (Keegan, Canhoto and Yen, 2022) across healthcare silos structure for strengthening knowledge integration in information networks and systems.

Finally, the research indicated the success factors at the micro-level as an agile response, especially in the case of cybersecurity (He et al., 2022), and entrepreneurship's role in creating shared value from data by developing social innovation across meta-organisations (Battisti, Agarwal and Brem, 2022). This small number of elements that did not align with the existing mainstream subdomains revealed fields for further development also expressed in the following section as future research recommendations identified in the management journals.

Future Research Directions

The sources provided a foundation for continued research emerging from the analysis that may stimulate new avenues of research in the following fields:

- engagement and collaboration of multiple actors (stakeholders) demanding new design strategies (Elia et al., 2021; Fosch-Villaronga et al., 2021; Ibáñez et al., 2021; Ibrahim et al., 2021; Keegan, Canhoto and Yen, 2022; Rana et al., 2021; Shvetsova and Lee, 2021) that needs considering different business, social, political, institutional, environmental contexts (George et al., 2016; Secundo et al., 2021);
- resources and capabilities orchestration through meta-organisations that enable new business models supporting entrepreneurs in extracting value from data (Battisti, Agarwal and Brem, 2022);
- responsible and ethical entrepreneurship (Battisti, Agarwal and Brem, 2022; Ibáñez et al., 2021; Secundo et al., 2021; Wang, Kung and Byrd, 2018);
- the data-driven culture (digital mindset) (Cao et al., 2021, 13; Chatterjee, Chaudhuri and Vrontis, 2021; Wang, Kung and Byrd, 2018; Yu et al., 2021b);
- the need for the main logic of digital transformation to integration (Huang, Chou and Liu, 2021; Lager & Sun, 2021);

Healthcare Ecosystems and Business Models Reconfiguration   225

- understanding and defining AI capabilities and new context for business model innovation (Sjödin et al., 2021; Zuiderwijk, Chen and Salem, 2021).

The main patterns among the recommended future streams of empirical investigation refer to value (co)creation through entrepreneurial collaboration among all actors at the ecosystem dimension for data-driven resources and capabilities (from innovative business models) transformation.

The Summary – SWOT Frame

As elaborated in the previous section, challenges might be translated by the healthcare sector as opportunities or threats depending on other coexisting situational factors. Therefore, SWOT (Strengths, Weaknesses, Opportunities and Threats) approach was used to identify internal and external factors involved in the strategic planning of data-driven technology applications in healthcare. The analysis of the articles from different domains identified challenges and opportunities coming from the sector's technological context and healthcare sectoral strengths and weaknesses summarised in Table 12.12.

The pooled analysis of technology implementation factors in the healthcare system allowed identifying patterns for **data-driven value (co) creation** based on communication between different systems and cross-disciplinary actors' involvement and collaboration for innovative resources re-combination (Ciasullo, Cosimato and Pellicano, 2017), enabling standardisation to decrease systems complexity.

Table 12.12 Digitalisation in healthcare

EXTERNAL FACTORS: CONTEXT (TECHNOLOGY AND SYSTEM)	OPPORTUNITIES: • Technological acceleration (affected by, e.g., COVID-19 pandemic) • Informatics/digital capabilities (innovation) • Resources (e.g., quality data as a source for knowledge-building)	THREATS: • Ethics/regulations/ jurisdictions • Interoperability issues (data governance – from different sources or within a silo)
INTERNAL FACTORS: HEALTHCARE SECTOR (SKILLS, RESOURCES AND CAPABILITIES)	STRENGTHS: • Knowledge-sharing hubs (interdisciplinary cross-sectoral communication and collaboration)	WEAKNESSES: • Systems complexity (silo structure) • Power tensions in the change management process (at the micro-level: leadership, employee involvement and "knowledge-doing gap" issues)

Source: The authors.

226 *Anna Żukowicka-Surma et al.*

Discussion

The Big Picture of the Digital Landscape

This section summarises the scope used in the analysis of the selected articles, including the type of digitalisation aspects, the system's dimension and the types of healthcare implications, that collectively aimed to answer the research question: Whether and how do healthcare actors explore new business opportunities in the context of digitalisation?

First, the types of digitalisation aspects were examined in the selected articles by exploring the new digital landscape in which the healthcare sector is situated to understand its processes and problems and then define the research gaps for further investigation. The study provided evidence that many studies cover broad (general) digital transformation application perspectives. At the same time, only a few identified factors relate specifically to healthcare (such as AI-related ethical concerns). It concluded the need to develop the empirical studies relating to healthcare because the specificity of the sector in the current research has not been substantially addressed. Second, the dimension (macro societal, meso industrial or organisational level, and micro individual level) at which the studies addressed implications resulting from digitalisation. According to the subjective qualitative analysis, most studies addressed this topic globally, while some are scoped towards the institutional or local organisational levels. Third, the implications for the practice and recommendations for future studies were discussed (such as challenges or opportunities management). It encompasses all the rules and actions related to healthcare policy and service. The research identified four digitalisation implications for the healthcare practice and theory from the reviewed articles. Factors at the micro-level relate to the organisational data-driven culture positively impacting digital technology orientation such as professional teams' knowledge-sharing collaboration. At the meso-level are institutional (policy, strategy, processes, measures, legislation and regulation) and ethical challenges. Examples identified at the macro-level include innovative big-data sharing hubs and platforms related to the (eco)system approach.

The SLR provided a nuanced interdisciplinary and multidimensional picture of the digital healthcare landscape because knowledge about data-driven healthcare solutions is spread across management, healthcare and data engineering. The analysis of 196 articles from the three fields revealed that despite the convergence at the surface level of each discipline, there is substantive divergence across domains related to the specific types of research conducted by each field. Based on SWOT analysis, the investigation resulted in the identification of potential opportunities for value (co)creation by appropriate managerial methods (actions, means or scientific study identified in the management domain journals) for data-driven technology (placed in engineering journals) application in the healthcare sector to cope

Healthcare Ecosystems and Business Models Reconfiguration   227

with the digital landscape treats and opportunities (by managing healthcare sectors strengths and weaknesses) to answer sector's needs to improve health outcomes at the macro-level (identified in the healthcare domain). Therefore, the study draws on the idea of building bridges between management researchers, healthcare practitioners, and scientists (from the life science field – medicine) and the technical professions (engineering, computer science) to examine the opportunities for interdisciplinary collaboration in the process of identifying challenges and creating innovative solutions specific for the digitalisation in healthcare in the future research agenda.

Contribution

As a contribution to the book on *Reconfiguration of Business Models and Ecosystems: Decoupling and Resilience,* this chapter presents a systematic review of literature on the digital healthcare landscape to identify potential opportunities for data-driven technology value (co)creation, particularly concerning business model innovation and ecosystems; and develops a research agenda.

The authors carried out an SLR identifying relevant and high-quality research using the web-based Scholar Google search engine, eventually selecting 196 articles for the study. Most papers were published in the current and past 2021 years, showing the topicality of healthcare innovation management research in the digital age. The studies in the selection concerned qualitative research, literature reviews or conceptual papers. The qualitative analysis identified the potential benefits of data-driven technology use in healthcare at organisational, institutional, ethical and macro-dimensions elaborated in the findings section. Most of the examined studies apply a broad and inclusive interdisciplinary use of the digital healthcare landscape. Based on the literature review and the bibliometric analysis of articles included in this chapter, the authors propose a research agenda concerning digitalisation's process-related and content-related implications for healthcare.

Because the knowledge from resources about digital solutions in healthcare is spread out between interdisciplinary fields of management, healthcare and engineering, the authors propose the development of the integrative conceptual framework for digital healthcare (for the data-driven value (co) creation through coordinating building capacity in the ecosystem of people, projects and systems) in the future research agenda.

As implications for practice and research, the chapter provides a foundation for continued research emerging from the analysis, emphasising aspects that may stimulate new avenues of research elaborated in the section related to the management sources. The future research agenda calls for the development of multidisciplinary, theoretical foundations for data-driven technology for healthcare and investigations of its practical implementation, engagement and communication plans for government strategies on data-driven technology use. Furthermore, the research agenda calls for studies on risk management,

228   *Anna Żukowicka-Surma et al.*

performance and impact measurement, and evaluation of scaling-up data-driven technology use in the healthcare sector (its weaknesses and challenges).

Limitations (Methodological Considerations)

The first limitation concerns the qualitative data analysis. The classification of different categories of presented challenges can be partly affected by subjective bias in interpreting the data obtained from the articles. Nevertheless, to minimise this limitation, a well-consolidated protocol for coding the analysed data was adopted (Strauss & Corbin, 1998), drawing on Kast and Rosenzweig's contingency intra- and inter-organisational relations system model rooted in the organisational theory (Morgan, 1997). Moreover, although the study was conducted in a structured and systematic manner, the qualitative approach limits the statistical generalisation of the findings to other contexts. However, ensuring credibility and reliability of data analysis supported by NVivo 10 software resulted in identification patterns for further investigation.

Another limitation refers to the terminology heterogeneity, the lack of structured descriptions of the healthcare landscape approach and data-driven related components; therefore, the main operational definitions were constructed to minimise this limitation at the initial step of the research. The other limitation is the Scholar Google search engine, which does not differentiate the research disciplines, resulting in difficulties classifying the articles into narrow domains. Moreover, some of the shortlisted articles did not refer to healthcare specifically. However, these articles did refer to a type of digital landscape criteria that suits the inclusive, broad interdisciplinary definition of the digital healthcare landscape used in this study. The last constraint relates to the citation analysis of the retrospective sources, which only provides an indirect representation of the research's influence on science, specifically if the study is based on the newest sources from the years 2021–2022.

Conclusions

The SLR provided a nuanced multidimensional picture of the digital healthcare landscape. The chapter addresses the healthcare reconfiguration in the context of innovative data-driven technology by investigating and describing the current state of the interdisciplinary research and tendencies. The chapter discusses adopting digitalisation and healthcare management practices to enhance data-driven outcomes. The chapter showed that data-driven technology influences healthcare at the macro, meso and micro levels. However, it also demonstrates that the research on data-driven technologies in healthcare is in the early stage of development. Therefore, the authors propose developing the integrative conceptual framework for digital healthcare in the future research agenda.

References

Acedo, F.J. & Casillas, J.C. (2005). "Current paradigms in the international management field: An author co-citation analysis", *International Business Review*, vol. 14(5), pp. 619–639.

Ahsan, M.M., Mahmud, M.A., Saha, P.K., Gupta, K.D., & Siddique, Z. (2021). "Effect of data scaling methods on machine learning algorithms and model performance", *Technologies*, vol. 9(3), pp. 52–69.

Amaral, F., Casaca, W., Oishi, C.M., & Cuminato, J.A. (2021). "Towards providing effective data-driven responses to predict the Covid-19 in São Paulo and Brazil", *Sensors*, vol. 21(2), pp. 540–565.

Antonacci, G., Reed, J.E., Sriram, V., & Barlow, J. (2018). "Quality improvement through interactive simulation", *International Journal for Quality In Health Care*, vol. 30, pp. 29–30.

Apell, P. & Eriksson, H. (2021). "Artificial intelligence (AI) healthcare technology innovations: The current state and challenges from a life science industry perspective". *Technology Analysis & Strategic Management*, pp. 1–15. 10.1080/09537325.2021. 1971188

Ashfaq, A. & Nowaczyk, S. (19 Jan2020). "Machine learning in healthcare – a system's perspective", *arXiv preprint, arXiv:1909.07370*. https://arxiv.org/pdf/1909.07370.pdf

Ashfaq, A., Lönn, S., Nilsson, H., Eriksson, J.A., Kwatra, J., Yasin, Z.M., ... & Lingman, M. (2020). "Data resource profile: Regional healthcare information platform in Halland, Sweden, a dedicated environment for healthcare research", *International Journal of Epidemiology*, pp. 738–739. 10.1093/ije/dyz262

Ashfaq, A., Sant'Anna, A., Lingman, M., & Nowaczyk, S. (2019). "Readmission prediction using deep learning on electronic health records", *Journal of Biomedical Informatics*, vol. 97, p. 103256.

Au-Yong-Oliveira, M., Pesqueira, A., Sousa, M.J., Dal Mas, F., & Soliman, M. (2021). "The potential of big data research in healthcare for medical doctors' learning", *Journal of Medical Systems*, vol. 45(1), pp. 1–14.

Awan, U., Sroufe, R., & Shahbaz, M. (2021). "Industry 4.0 and the circular economy: A literature review and recommendations for future research", *Business Strategy and the Environment*, vol. 30(4), pp. 2038–2060.

Balakrishnan, J. & Dwivedi, Y.K. (2021). "Conversational commerce: Entering the next stage of AI-powered digital assistants", *Annals of Operations Research*, pp. 1–35. 10.1007/s10479-021-04049-5 (Accessed on 10 May 2022).

Balicer, R.D. & Afek, A. (2017). "Digital health nation: Israel's global big data innovation hub", *The Lancet*, vol. 389(10088), pp. 2451–2453.

Barlow, J.G. (2015). "Changing the innovariton landscape in the UK's National Hedalth Service to meet its future challenges", *Innovation and Entrepreneurship Health*, vol. 2(8), pp. 59–67.

Barnett, J., Vasileiou, K., Djemil, F., Brooks, L., & Young, T. (2011). "Understanding innovators' experiences of barriers and facilitators in implementation and diffusion of healthcare service innovations: a qualitative study", *BMC Health Services Research*, vol. 11(1), pp. 1–12.

Battisti, S., Agarwal, N., & Brem, A. (2022). "Creating new tech entrepreneurs with digital platforms: Meta-organizations for shared value in data-driven retail ecosystems", *Technological Forecasting and Social Change*, vol. 175, p. 121392.

230 *Anna Żukowicka-Surma et al.*

Baveja, A., Kapoor, A., & Melamed, B. (2020). "Stopping Covid-19: A pandemic-management service value chain approach", *Annals of Operations Research*, vol. 289(2), pp. 173–184.

Blom, M.C., Ashfaq, A., Sant'Anna A., Anderson, P.D. & Lingman, M. (2019). "Training machine learning models to predict 30-day mortality in patients discharged from the emergency department: A retrospective, population-based registry study", *British Medical Journal*, vol. 9(8), p. e028015.

Brozović, D. & Tregua, M. (2022). "The evolution of service systems to service eco-systems: A literature review". *International Journal of Management Reviews*, vol. 24(4), pp. 459–479. 10.1111/ijmr.12287 (Accessed on 12 May 2022).

Camara, J., Neto, A., Pires, I.M., Villasana, M.V., Zdravevski, E. & Cunha, A. (2022). "Literature review on artificial intelligence methods for Glaucoma screening, segmentation, and classification", *Journal of Imaging*, vol. 8(2), pp. 19–47.

Cao, G., Duan, Y., Edwards, J.S. and Dwivedi, Y.K. (2021). "Understanding managers' attitudes and behavioral intentions towards using artificial intelligence for organizational decision-making", *Technovation*, vol. 106, p. 102312.

Chan, J.C., Lim, L.L., Luk, A.O., Ozaki, R., Kong, A.P., Ma, R.C. … . & Lo, S.V. (2019). "From Hong Kong Diabetes Register to JADE Program to RAMP-DM for data-driven actions", *Diabetes Care*, vol. 42(11), pp. 2022–2031.

Chatterjee, S., Chaudhuri, R., & Vrontis, D. (2021). "Does data-driven culture impact innovation and performance of a firm? An empirical examination", *Annals of Operations Research*, pp. 1–26. 10.1007/s10479-020-03887-z

Chu, A.M., Chan, T.W., So, M.K., & Wong, W.K. (2021). "Dynamic network analysis of COVID-19 with a latent pandemic space model", *International Journal of Environmental Research and Public Health*, vol. 18(6), p. 3195.

Chu, W., Becker, K.D., Boustani, M.M., Park, A.L., & Chorpita, B.F. (2022). "Is it easy to use and useful? Mental health professionals' perspectives inform development of a novel treatment engagement system for youth mental health services", *Cognitive and Behavioral Practice*. (in press).

Ciasullo, M.V., Cosimato, S., & Pellicano, M. (2017). "Service innovations in the healthcare service ecosystem: a case study", *Systems*, vol. 5(2), pp. 37–56.

Cisnetto, V. & Barlow, J. (2020). "The development of complex and controversial innovations. Genetically modified mosquitoes for malaria eradication", *Research Policy*, vol. 49(3), p. 103917.

Coombes, P.H. & Nicholson, J.D. (2013). "Business models and their relationship with marketing: A systematic literature review", *Industrial Marketing Management*, vol. 42(5), pp. 656–664.

Cui, M. & Zhang, D.Y. (2021). "Artificial intelligence and computational pathology", *Laboratory Investigation*, vol. 101(4), pp. 412–422.

Deepa, N., Pham, Q.V., Nguyen, D.C., Bhattacharya, S., Prabadevi, B., Gadekallu, T.R. … . & Pathirana, P.N. (2022). "A survey on blockchain for big data: Approaches, opportunities, and future directions", *Future Generation Computer Systems*, vol. 131, pp. 209–226.

Dimitrievski, A., Filiposka, S., Melero, F.J., Zdravevski, E., Lameski, P., Pires, I.M. … . & Trajkovik, V. (2021). "Rural healthcare iot architecture based on low-energy lora", *International Journal of Environmental Research and Public Health*, vol. 18(14), p. 7660.

Dougherty, D. & Dunne, D.D. (2012). "Digital science and knowledge boundaries in complex innovation". *Organization Science*, vol. 23(5), pp. 1467–1484.

Dreger, M., Eckhardt, H., Felgner, S., Errmann, H., Lantzsch, H., Rombey, T. .... & Panteli, D. (2021). "Implementation of innovative medical technologies in German inpatient care: Patterns of utilization and evidence development", *Implementation Science*, vol. 16(1), pp. 1–17.

Dryden-Palmer, K.D., Parshuram, C.S., & Berta, W.B. (2020). "Context, complexity and process in the implementation of evidence-based innovation: A realist informed review", *BMC Health Services Research*, vol. 20(1), pp. 1–15.

Dussart, P., van Oortmerssen, L.A., & Albronda, B. (2021). "Perspectives on knowledge integration in cross-functional teams in information systems development", *Team Performance Management: An International Journal*, vol. 27(3/4), pp. 316–331.

Elia, G., Margherita, A., Ciavolino, E., & Moustaghfir, K. (2021). "Digital society incubator: Combining exponential technology and human potential to Build resilient entrepreneurial ecosystems", *Administrative Sciences*, vol. 11(3), pp. 96–112.

Enticott, J., Johnson, A., & Teede, H. (2021). "Learning health systems using data to drive healthcare improvement and impact: A systematic review", *BMC Health Services Research*, vol. 21(1), pp. 1–16.

Fan, W., Liu, J., Zhu, S., & Pardalos, P.M. (2020). "Investigating the impacting factors for the healthcare professionals to adopt artificial intelligence-based medical diagnosis support system (AIMDSS)", *Annals of Operations Research*, vol. 294(1), pp. 567–592.

Fan, Y., Nowaczyk, S., & Rögnvaldsson, T. (2020). "Transfer learning for remaining useful life prediction based on consensus self-organizing models", *Reliability Engineering and System Safety*, vol. 203, p. 107098.

Ferretti, A., Ienca, M., Velarde, M.R., Hurst, S., & Vayena, E. (2022). "The challenges of big data for research ethics committees: A qualitative Swiss study", *Journal of Empirical Research on Human Research Ethics*, vol. 17(1–2), pp. 129–143.

Fosch-Villaronga, E., Chokoshvili, D., Vallevik, V.B., Ienca, M., & Pierce, R.L. (2021). "Implementing AI in healthcare: An ethical and legal analysis based on case studies. Data protection and privacy", *Volume 13: Data Protection and Artificial Intelligence*, vol. 13, pp. 187–216.

Fournier, P.L., Chênevert, D., & Jobin, M.H. (2021). "The antecedents of physicians' behavioral support for lean in healthcare: The mediating role of commitment to organizational change", *International Journal of Production Economics*, vol. 232, p. 107961.

Frontoni, E., Mancini, A., Baldi, M., Paolanti, M., Moccia, S., Zingaretti, P. ... ., & Misericordia, P. (2019). "Sharing health data among general practitioners: The Nu. Sa. project", *International Journal of Medical Informatics*, vol. 129, pp. 267–274.

Gagliardi, A.R., Berta, W., Kothari, A., Boyko, J., & Urquhart, R. (2015). "Integrated knowledge translation (IKT) in health care: A scoping review", *Implementation Science*, vol. 11(1), pp. 1–12.

Gasser, U., Ienca, M., Scheibner, J., Sleigh, J., & Vayena, E. (2020). "Digital tools against COVID-19: Taxonomy, ethical challenges, and navigation aid", *The Lancet Digital Health*, vol. 2(8), pp. e425–e434.

George, G., Howard-Grenville, J., Joshi, A., & Tihanyi, L. (2016). "Understanding and tackling societal grand challenges through management research", *Academy of Management Journal*, vol. 59(6), pp. 1880–1895.

Gunasekeran, D.V., Tham, Y.C., Ting, D.S., Tan, G.S., & Wong, T.Y. (2021). "Digital health during COVID-19: Lessons from operationalising new models of care in ophthalmology", *The Lancet Digital Health*, vol. 3(2), pp. e124–e134.

Harrison, R., Chauhan, A., Minbashian, A., McMullan, R.. & Schwarz, G. (2022). "Is gaining affective commitment the missing strategy for successful change management in healthcare?" *Journal of Healthcare Leadership*, vol. 14, pp. 1–4.

Hausvik, G.I., Thapa, D., & Munkvold, B.E. (2021). "Information *quality life cycle in secondary use of EHR data*", *International Journal of Information Management*, vol. 56, p. 102227.

He, Y., Zamani, E.D., Lloyd, S., & Luo, C. (2022). "Agile incident response (AIR): Improving the incident response process in healthcare", *International Journal of Information Management*, vol. 62, p. 102435.

Heyman, E.T., Ashfaq, A., Khoshnood, A., Ohlsson, M., Ekelund, U., Holmqvist, L.D., & Lingman, M. (2021). "Improving Machine *Learning 30-Day Mortality Prediction by Discounting Surprising Deaths*", *The Journal of Emergency Medicine*, vol. 61(6), pp. 763–773.

Huang, C.H., Chou, T.C., & Liu, J.S. (2021). "Understanding the intrinsic nature of the trends of digital innovation: A main path analysis". Hawaii International Conference on System Sciences (*HICSS*), pp. 5912–5921. 10.24251/HICSS.2021.715

Huddy, J.R., Ni, M.Z., Barlow, J., & Hanna, G.B. (2021). "Qualitative analysis of stakeholder interviews to identify the barriers and facilitators to the adoption of point-of-care diagnostic tests in the UK". *BMJ open*, vol. 11(4), p. e042944.

Hussain, F., Abbas, S.G., Shah, G.A., Pires, I.M., Fayyaz, U.U., Shahzad, F. ... & Zdravevski, E. (2021). "A framework for malicious traffic detection in IoT healthcare environment", *Sensors*, vol. 21(9), pp. 3025–3044.

Ibáñez, M.J., Guerrero, M., Yáñez-Valdés, C., & Barros-Celume, S. (2021). "Digital social entrepreneurship: The N-Helix response to stakeholders' COVID-19 needs", *The Journal of Technology Transfer*, pp. 1–24.

Ibrahim, H., Liu, X., Zariffa, N., Morris, A.D., & Denniston, A.K. (2021). "Health data poverty: An assailable barrier to equiTable digital health care", *The Lancet Digital Health*, vol. 3(4), pp. e260–e265.

Javaid, M., Haleem, A., Singh, R.P., & Suman, R. (2021). "Significance of Quality 4.0 towards comprehensive enhancement in manufacturing sector", *Sensors International*, vol. 2, p. 100109.

Jayasri, N.P. & Aruna, R. (2022). "Big data analytics in health care by data mining and classification techniques", *ICT Express*, vol. 8(2), pp. 250–257.

Jobin, A., Man, K., Damasio, A., Kaissis, G., Braren, R., Stoyanovich, J. ... ., & Luengo-Oroz, M. (2021). "AI reflections in 2020", *Nature Machine Intelligence*, vol. 3(1), pp. 2–8.

Johnson, K.B., Wei, W.Q., Weeraratne, D., Frisse, M.E., Misulis, K., Rhee, K. ... . & Snowdon, J.L. (2021). "Precision medicine, AI, and the future of personalized health care", *Clinical and Translational Science*, vol. 14(1), pp. 86–93.

Jurkeviciute, M., Enam, A., Torres-Bonilla, J., & Eriksson, H. (2021). "Planning a holistic summative eHealth evaluation in an interdisciplinary and multi-national setting: A case study and propositions for guideline development", *BMC Medical Informatics and Decision Making*, vol. 21(1), pp. 1–13.

Kataria, S. & Ravindran, V. (2022). "Harnessing of real-world data and real-world evidence using digital tools: utility and potential models in rheumatology practice", *Rheumatology*, vol. 61(2), pp. 502–513.

Keegan, B.J., Canhoto, A.I., & Yen, D.A.W. (2022). "Power negotiation on the tango dancefloor: The adoption of AI in B2B marketing", *Industrial Marketing Management*, vol. 100, pp. 36–48.

Healthcare Ecosystems and Business Models Reconfiguration   233

Kislov, R., Walshe, K., & Harvey, G. (2012). "Managing boundaries in primary care service improvement: A developmental approach to communities of practice", *Implementation Science*, vol. 7(1), pp. 1–14.

Kraus, S., Schiavone, F., Pluzhnikova, A., & Invernizzi, A.C. (2021). "Digital transformation in healthcare: Analyzing the current state-of-research", *Journal of Business Research*, vol. 123, pp. 557–567.

Kulkov, I. (2021). "Next-generation business models for artificial intelligence start-ups in the healthcare industry", *International Journal of Entrepreneurial Behavior & Research*. 10.1108/IJEBR-04-2021-0304

Kumar, P., Dwivedi, Y.K., & Anand, A. (2021). "Responsible artificial intelligence (AI) for value formation and market performance in healthcare: The mediating role of Patient's cognitive engagement", *Information Systems Frontiers*, pp. 1–24. https://link.springer.com/article/10.1007/s10796-021-10136-6 (Accessed 8 April 2022)

Lager, D. & Sun, Y. (2021). *The Role of IP in a Data-Driven Business Model. A Case Study in a Healthcare Company.* (Master thesis) Gothenburg: Sweden: Chalmers University of Technology.

Loftus, T.J., Tighe, P.J., Filiberto, A.C., Efron, P.A., Brakenridge, S.C., Mohr, A.M., ... , & Bihorac, A. (2020). "Artificial intelligence and surgical decision-making", *JAMA Surgery*, vol. 155(2), pp. 148–158.

Margherita, A., Elia, G., & Klein, M. (2021). "Managing the COVID-19 emergency: A coordination framework to enhance response practices and actions", *Technological Forecasting and Social Change*, vol. 166, p. 120656.

Mondal, S. & Samaddar, K. (2022). Reinforcing the significance of human factor in achieving quality performance in data-driven supply chain management. *The TQM Journal.* (in print)

Morgan, G. (1997). *Images of Organization.* Thousand Oaks, CA: Sage Publications Inc.

Nagurney, A. & Dutta, P. (2021). "A multiclass, multiproduct Covid-19 convalescent plasma donor equilibrium model", *Operations Research Forum*, vol. 2(3), pp. 1–30.

Nguyen Ngoc, H., Lasa, G. & Iriarte, I. (2022). "Human-centred design in industry 4.0: Case study review and opportunities for future research", *Journal of Intelligent Manufacturing*, vol. 33(1), pp. 35–76.

Pagliari, C. (2021). "Digital health and primary care: Past, pandemic and prospects", *Journal of Global Health*, vol. 11, p. 01005.

Paul, S., Riffat, M., Yasir, A., Mahim, M.N., Sharnali, B.Y., Naheen, I.T., ... & Kulkarni, A. (2021). "Industry 4.0 applications for medical/healthcare services", *Journal of Sensor and Actuator Networks*, vol. 10(3), pp. 43–75.

Rahimi, S.A., Légaré, F., Sharma, G., Archambault, P., Zomahoun, H.T.V., Chandavong, S., ... & Légaré, J. (2021). "Application of artificial intelligence in community-Based primary health care: Systematic scoping review and critical appraisal", *Journal of Medical Internet Research*, vol. 23(9), p. e29839.

Ramanujam, R. & Rousseau, D.M. (2006). "The challenges are organizational not just clinical", *Journal of Organizational Behavior: The International Journal of Industrial, Occupational and Organizational Psychology and Behavior*, vol. 27(7), pp. 811–827.

Rana, J., Gaur, L., Singh, G., Awan, U., & Rasheed, M.I. (2021). "Reinforcing customer journey through artificial intelligence: A review and research agenda", *International Journal of Emerging Markets*, vol. 17(7), pp. 1738–1758.

Reed, J.E., Green, S., & Howe, C. (2019). "Translating evidence in complex systems: A comparative review of implementation and improvement frameworks", *International Journal for Quality in Health Care*, vol. 31(3), pp. 173–182.

Reed, J.E., Howe, C., Doyle, C., & Bell, D. (2018). "Simple rules for evidence translation in complex systems: A qualitative study", *BMC Medicine*, vol. 16(1), pp. 1–20.

Reed, J.E., Howe, C., Doyle, C., & Bell, D. (2019). "Successful healthcare improvements from translating evidence in complex systems (SHIFT-Evidence): Simple rules to guide practice and research", *International Journal for Quality in Health Care*, vol. 31(3), pp. 238–244.

Scott, I., Carter, S., & Coiera, E. (2021). "Clinician checklist for assessing suitability of machine learning applications in healthcare", *BMJ Health and Care Informatics*, vol. 28(1), p. e100251.

Secundo, G., Gioconda, M., Del Vecchio, P., Gianluca, E., Margherita, A., & Valentina, N. (2021). "Threat or opportunity? A case study of digital-enabled redesign of entrepreneurship education in the COVID-19 emergency", *Technological Forecasting and Social Change*, vol. 166, p. 120565.

Sena, V., & Nocker, M. (2021). "AI and business models: The good, the bad and the ugly", *Foundations and Trends in Technology, Information and Operations Management*, vol. 14(4), pp. 324–397.

Shamout, F.E., Shen, Y., Wu, N., Kaku, A., Park, J., Makino, T., … & Geras, K.J. (2021). "An artificial intelligence system for predicting the deterioration of COVID-19 patients in the emergency department", *NPJ Digital Medicine*, vol. 4(1), pp. 1–11.

Shaw, J., Rudzicz, F., Jamieson, T., & Goldfarb, A. (2019). "Artificial intelligence and the implementation challenge", *Journal of Medical Internet Research*, vol. 21(7), p. e13659.

Sheng, J., Amankwah-Amoah, J., Khan, Z., & Wang, X. (2021). "COVID-19 pandemic in the new era of big data analytics: Methodological innovations and future research directions", *British Journal of Management*, vol. 32(4), pp. 1164–1183.

Shvetsova, O.A. & Lee, S.K. (2021). "Living labs in university-industry cooperation as a part of innovation ecosystem: Case study of South Korea", *Sustainability*, vol. 13(11), pp. 5793–5816.

Siala, H. & Wang, Y. (2022). "SHIFTing artificial intelligence to be responsible in healthcare: A systematic review", *Social Science and Medicine*, p. 114782. 10.1016/j.socscimed.2022.114782

Sjödin, D., Parida, V., Palmié, M., & Wincent, J. (2021). "How AI capabilities enable business model innovation: Scaling AI through co-evolutionary processes and feedback loops", *Journal of Business Research*, vol. 134, pp. 574–587.

Strauss, A. & Corbin, J., 1998. *Basics of Qualitative Research Techniques*. New York, NY: Sage Publications.

Tan, L.F., Chan, Y.H., Tay, A., Jayasundram, J., Low, N.A., & Merchant, R.A. (2021). "Practicality and reliability of self vs administered rapid geriatric assessment mobile app", *The Journal of Nutrition, Health and Aging*, vol. 25(9), pp. 1064–1069.

Thomas, L.D. & Ritala, P. (2022). "Ecosystem legitimacy emergence: A collective action view", *Journal of Management*, vol. 48(3), pp. 515–541.

Thiebes, S., Lins, S., & Sunyaev, A. (2021). "Trustworthy artificial intelligence", *Electronic Markets*, vol. 31(2), pp. 447–464.

Truong, T., Gilbank, P., Johnson-Cover, K., & Ieraci, A. (2019). "A framework for applied AI in healthcare", *Studies in Health Technology and Informatics*, vol. 264, pp. 1993–1994.

Tuazon, M.J.D. (2021). *To Protect Lives or Personal Data?* (Master thesis) Lund: Sweden: Faculty of Law Lund University.

Tucker, D.A., Hendy, J., & Barlow, J. (2012). "Sensemaking and social accounts of middle managers", *Academy of Management Proceedings*, vol. 1, pp. 14017–14017.

Vandenberg, O., Martiny, D., Rochas, O., van Belkum, A., & Kozlakidis, Z. (2021). "Considerations for diagnostic COVID-19 tests", *Nature Reviews Microbiology*, vol. 19(3), pp. 171–183.

Wang, K., Xie, S., & Rodrigues, J. (2022). "Medical data security of wearable tele-rehabilitation under internet of things", *Internet of Things and Cyber-Physical Systems*, vol. 2, p. 1–11.

Wang, Y., Kung, L., & Byrd, T.A. (2018). "Big data analytics: Understanding its capabilities and potential benefits for healthcare organizations", *Technological Forecasting and Social Change*, vol. 126, pp. 3–13.

Wehrens, R., Stevens, M., Kostenzer, J., Weggelaar, A.M., & de Bont, A. (2021). "Ethics as discursive work: The role of ethical framing in the promissory future of data-driven healthcare technologies", *Science, Technology, and Human Values*, p. 01622439211053661. 10.1177/0162243921105366

Wiljer, D., Salhia, M., Dolatabadi, E., Dhalla, A., Gillan, C., Al-Mouaswas, D., ... & Tavares, W. (2021). "Accelerating the appropriate adoption of artificial intelligence in health care: Protocol for a multistepped approach", *JMIR Research Protocols*, vol. 10(10), p. e30940.

Willis, S.E., Pulliam, T.J., & Bacon, T.J. (2004). "Educating a new generation of healthcare professionals with a lifelong commitment to quality of care", *North Carolina Medical Journal*, vol. 65(5), pp. 292–294.

World Health Organization (WHO) (2001). *Health and Medical Informatics in the Eastern Mediterranean Region* (No. EM/RC48/6). Washington, DC: WHO.

Yahaya, S.W., Lotfi, A., & Mahmud, M. (2021). "Towards a data-driven adaptive anomaly detection system for human activity", *Pattern Recognition Letters*, vol. 145, pp. 200–207.

Yoo, Y., Boland Jr, R.J., Lyytinen, K., & Majchrzak, A. (2012). "Organizing for innovation in the digitized world", *Organization Science*, vol. 23(5), pp. 1398–1408.

Yoo, Y., Henfridsson, O., & Lyytinen, K. (2010). "Research commentary – the new organizing logic of digital innovation: An agenda for information systems research", *Information Systems Research*, vol. 21(4), pp. 724–735.

Yu, W., Zhao, G., Liu, Q., & Song, Y. (2021a). "Role of big data analytics capability in developing integrated hospital supply chains and operational flexibility: An organizational information processing theory perspective", *Technological Forecasting and Social Change*, vol. 163, p. 120417.

Yu, W., Liu, Q., Zhao, G., & Song, Y. (2021b). Exploring the effects of data-driven hospital operations on operational performance from the resource orchestration theory perspective. *IEEE Transactions on Engineering Management*, doi: 10.1109/TEM.2021.3098541.

Zuiderwijk, A., Chen, Y.C., & Salem, F. (2021). "Implications of the use of artificial intelligence in public governance: A systematic literature review and a research agenda", *Government Information Quarterly*, vol. 38(3), p. 101577.

13 IT Entrepreneur Resilience in Geopolitical Turbulence

Liubov Ermolaeva and Daria Klishevich

Introduction

The current business climate worldwide is characterised with extreme velocity, uncertainty and volatility. The COVID-19 pandemic has led to a drastic environmental jolt that altered the pathways of economies, institutions and the strategies of companies worldwide (Hitt et al., 2021). It posed existential questions to firms. Large, small and medium enterprises alike have experienced exogenous shocks resulting from lockdowns that have led to disruption of economic and social life. There has been no other equivalent to such a major systemic disruption in entrepreneurial literature so far. The impact of the pandemic on entrepreneurship worldwide has been documented in the research literature (Shepherd, 2020; Zahra, 2020; Marinov & Marinova, 2021). Scholars often underline the role of entrepreneurs in responding to major disruptions such as the COVID-19 pandemic. Their ability to find entrepreneurial opportunities even at a time of crisis manifests innate resilience, whereas their innovative solutions produce novel ways of company operations and organisation (Meyer et al., 2021). In the period 2020–2022, entrepreneurs have been faced with a variety of disruptive challenges that forced them to adopt radical business model reconfiguration (Korsgaard et al., 2020).

The pandemic resulted in a renewed interest of how companies respond to crises and transform their business models and strategies. Crises are salient, unpredictable and potentially disruptive, harmful to pre-defined company goals and to company-stakeholder relationships (Bundy et al., 2017). The chances of firms to survive crises depend on the entrepreneurial ability to respond to environmental jolts and make the best use of the new opportunities created by a crisis (Cucculelli & Peruzzi, 2020). Embracing opportunities that open up in times of crisis is one of the strategic responses that entrepreneurs demonstrate (Wenzel et al., 2021). Moreover, under economic and societal disruptions, small and medium enterprises (SMEs) are those expected to provide benefits to society that are unavailable otherwise, yet their ability to do so can be seriously challenged by a crisis (Thukral, 2021).

The literature on the impact of crises on entrepreneurship has been growing in the last couple of decades (Doern, Williams & Vorley, 2019).

DOI: 10.4324/9781003326731-13

Entrepreneurs act differently in response to a crisis. Davidsson and Gordon (2016) identified four types of survival behaviour: (a) *disengagement* that happens when a company exits from the market and entrepreneurs cancel their entrepreneurial activity; (b) *delay* is related to the postponement of company establishment or of the introduction of new operations/business activities to a better day; (c) *compensation* is associated with an increase in the amount of invested resources in developing the business, including human and resource capital and (d) *adaptation*, i.e., the reconfiguration of the initial business model in response to market changes.

Scholars note that crisis management literature is mostly focused on the negative aspect of a crisis, namely on avoiding or mitigating the detrimental effects of disruptions, yet every crisis brings both threats and opportunities (Pedersen & Ritter, 2022).

Start-ups face challenges as they have to respond to various crises, as well as other economic actors do, yet their strategic responses have been somewhat neglected in the management literature (Kuckertz et al., 2020). As Kuckertz et al. (2020) note, innovative start-ups have the characteristics that enable them to cope with crises better than other types of firms, since innovativeness leads to greater company resilience and innovative start-ups usually anticipate crises and adjust to them. Nevertheless, start-ups are also considered to be vulnerable due to their small size and young age (Guckenbiehl & de Zubielqui, 2022).

The Russian start-up market has attracted a lot of attention in the last decade, being a vibrant business area with its hub set in Moscow and receiving significant government support. The Skolkovo Innovation Center has been largely financed by government funds and state corporations started its activities in 2010 and became the playground for testing new policies on entrepreneurial activities in Russia (Melkadze, 2021). Since 2006, the Russian government allocated more than 500 billion rubles (approximately USD 810 million) to the development of innovative projects, including technoparks, and to the direct funding of innovative companies. The Russian start-up market is an interesting case of one in an emerging market with a lot of highly qualified specialists with technical backgrounds, yet the venture capital investment market is considered underdeveloped (Guseva & Stepanova, 2021). According to data from 2022, there are 647 start-ups, which places the country in the 21st place worldwide (Startup Ranking, 2022).

According to Startup Barometer which monitors the Russian start-up industry, as a result of the pandemic crisis, only 3% of start-up founders considered closing the project as an option. 45% identified new opportunities for development, 40% had to adapt only their product to the changing environment, while 24% reconfigured their business model. The survey was conducted following the first month of the protective measure introduction (Startup Barometer, 2020). Founders moved from a focus on the product to a focus on sales and funds acquisition, while more than 50% of the respondents could not use the government support measures since the start-up industry was not considered as much affected by COVID-19 (Startup Barometer, 2020).

The jolt in 2022 has so far had an extraordinary effect on all businesses. Scholars note that high-tech industries are especially threatened as a result of the severe sanctions imposed against companies, institutions and state-affiliated individuals. Along with the formal sanctions, the informal pressure forced many large foreign companies to leave the Russian market (Markus, 2022). As a result, high-tech export to Russia – that was predominantly from the United States and Europe (66% altogether) – was restricted leaving Russia to rely mostly on China and other friendly states. Yet, there are doubts that they will be able to fully compensate for the substantial volume of high-tech imports that is still needed (Markus, 2022).

According to interviews with entrepreneurs conducted by the authors of this chapter, the pandemic crisis was a very easy rehearsal prior to the current crisis due to the magnitude of disruption, decoupling and required changes in global value chains. All sanctions imposed on Russia after February 2022 have affected directly small entrepreneurs and start-ups. Among some of the major problems are financial restrictions, disconnection from SWIFT, ban on investment in any projects related to Russia, currency volatility, ban on import of many categories of items and refusal to work with Russian firms from many Western partners because of reputational risks. Altogether, these have created systemic risks and a huge uncertainty.

IT firms are a special group of companies as they do not depend too much on imports, but they do depend on payments in USDs and euros, as most of their clients are abroad and most of the investments in them come from abroad. That was one of the reasons why many IT firms relocated to other countries since the military operation in Ukraine began (Babkin, 2022). Even though many IT specialists left Russia, a lot of IT entrepreneurs stayed and adapted to the current environmental situation and the major ecosystemic disruption. The new conditions for doing business pushed firms to adapt their operations and change their strategies while reconfiguring their business models. One distinct opportunity for IT start-ups is the huge demand for local IT solutions in the country after the market exit of IT giants such as SAP, Microsoft and IBM (Podtserob, 2022). Delay as a strategy cannot work in such a situation when changes are fast and the disruption is of such a magnitude that it leads to breakdown and replacement of value chains (Streeck & Thelen, 2005). Moreover, in a situation of total uncertainty, it does not make much sense to delay because tomorrow seems completely different from today. Compensation is not a strategy either. Fast changes and unpredictable future do not allow to invest money in anything, which is not your core business that you must save. The only survival strategy suggested by Davidsson and Gordon (2016) which would work in the current crisis seems to be an adaptation. Thus, further in our study, we explore how IT firms have been adapting to the crisis and what makes them resilient to the new harsh conditions in which they unexpectedly found themselves.

Literature Review

Entrepreneurship and Crisis

International entrepreneurship literature focuses on two main research questions related to crisis: first, how a crisis can influence the intention of people to start new ventures, and second, how a crisis can affect existing entrepreneurial projects. The first question is typically dealt with by international entrepreneurship studies, while the second one has been examined by scholars of international business, strategy and general management fields of research.

Scholars usually consider starting a new business in the taxonomy of necessity-driven and opportunity-driven approaches. In the case of countries where opportunity entrepreneurship prevails, a crisis leads to a decline of the wish to open a new enterprise, mainly due to the lack of funds (Goschin, Antonia & Tigau, 2021). Parallel to this, when there is a crisis, the positive image of being an entrepreneur has a much weaker effect on the intention to start a new venture since people become entrepreneurs to deal with a complicated financial situation and not because of the vital social role entrepreneurs play (Pinho & de Lurdes Martins, 2020).

At a time of crisis, people tend to start a business out of necessity more often than because of new opportunities and therefore, the initial development of business projects is affected negatively by the market entry regulations in the country where they operate and by the educational environment. The latter can lie in the necessity to swiftly adapt education to the fast-changing environmental conditions (Pinho & de Lurdes Martins, 2020).

Start-ups, especially IT ones, as recently SMEs, are considered more entrepreneurial than large companies. They are predominantly niche players that internationalise fast, which makes most of them born-global at birth (Etemad, Gurau, and Dana, 2022; Hennart, 2014). Major crises open up opportunities for digitalisation and business model transformation of other firms and thus, create new market niches (Seetharaman, 2020) that start-ups may either identify or create, but in both cases, they can fill in these market gaps quickly.

Deep, disruptive crises force companies to change quickly in order to survive (Roux-Dufort, 2007). However, start-ups are supposed to have liabilities such as the liability of newness and smallness, along with sometimes constrained financial resources (Guckenbiehl & de Zubielqui, 2022). Yet, scholars underline that the adverse effect of a crisis results in different consequences for start-ups that demonstrate various strategic responses to it (Kuckertz et al., 2020). Supposedly, younger firms are more likely to invest in innovation at times of a crisis (Archibugi, Filippetti & Frenz, 2013). Along with that, entrepreneurial opportunity recognition is considered a vital growth driver of new ventures at a time of crisis (Devece, Peris-Ortiz & Rueda-Armengot, 2016).

Resilience

External shocks, like the financial crisis of 2008, have substantially disrupted the existing economic foundations for doing business and created the need for identifying new growth opportunities. This is where the concept of resilience comes into play (Bishop, 2019). The attention of scholars to the resilience phenomenon has been connected mostly to the health system crisis in 2020, as a result of the pandemic (Thukral, 2021). Resilience is a concept that has a crucial place in the literature in relation to how entrepreneurs tackle crises (Kuckertz et al., 2020; Doern et al., 2019). It refers to the ability of entrepreneurs to resume work in a situation of disruptions and accounts for the resources they can use for this. Resources that entrepreneurs have accumulated prior to a crisis are usually used during a crisis and after it (Williams et al., 2017). Resilience is a multidimensional construct that embraces a variety of attributes, behaviours and traits (Thukral, 2021).

Entrepreneurship literature identifies some personal characteristics of individuals that are associated with entrepreneurship, such as the wish to have autonomy, status, wealth or power (Thukral, 2021), yet one of the main traits that characterise entrepreneurs is considered to be a natural openness to the environment and its opportunities, ability to take risks and use the chances that any situation creates (Peris-Ortiz, Fuster-Estruch & Devece-Carañana, 2014). These personal characteristics enhance the entrepreneurial ability to recognise or create opportunities and are considered essential in entrepreneurship (Thukral, 2021).

Resilience also includes the ability to pivot business activity in a creative and innovative way to meet the changing needs of customers (Thukral, 2021) and hence, it is vital for organisations' strategic agility and business continuity (Herbane, 2019). Innovative firms are found to survive more than less innovative ones, according to the results of Guerzoni, Nava and Nuccio (2021) who studied the evidence of companies surviving after the 2008 financial crisis. Resilience helps individuals see chances in chaos, survive the uncertainty around them and turn the opportunities into real benefits (Thukral, 2021).

As Herbane (2019) notes, scholars draw attention to engineering, ecosystem and socio-ecological research that addresses various manifestations of resilience. Engineering and ecosystem perspectives underline the "bouncing back" from the impact of stress and coming back to the prior state or reformation that stems from robustness (de Bruijne, Boin & van Eeten, 2010; Johnson & Elliott, 2011). Alternatively, the social-ecological perspective on resilience focuses on the dynamic learning, adaptation and transformation (Herbane, 2019). Herbane (2019) identifies the two themes that characterise the debate on resilience. These are responsiveness (response, recovery and adaptation following a sudden shock) and reinvention in the sense that resilience is inseparable from strategic planning (Burnard & Bhamra, 2011; Herbane, 2019).

Kuckertz et al. (2020) highlight the fact that existing studies mostly focus on how entrepreneurs accumulate and develop resources that they subsequently use to tackle crisis (Bullough et al., 2014; Doern et al., 2019) and do not specifically focus on start-ups that have some unique traits.

Born-Globals

International entrepreneurs act to innovate and seek sometimes seemingly risky opportunities in their cross-border activities aiming to create and capture value for their firms (McDougall & Oviatt, 2000). Yet, even before the pandemic started, scholars debated the future of globalisation in the light of rising populist movements, geopolitical upheaval and protectionist measures that posed some crucial questions on the role of the nature and extent of internationalisation, its benefits and those who take advantages of it. The pandemic intensified these discussions and heated the debate on the future of international firms (Marinov & Marinova, 2021; Zahra, 2020). Along with the threats and challenges, international entrepreneurs enacted the opportunities that appeared during the pandemic. Adjustment to the pandemic consequences provided an interesting laboratory to study the resilience of international entrepreneurs to crises.

There is a growing interest in the research literature to a particular phenomenon, born globals that have clear entrepreneurial and international aspiration from the outset (Oviatt & McDougall, 2005). Such companies favour opportunities in the global market, despite of their newness, limited size and lack of foreign experience, which are argued to lead to their limited ability to produce new market knowledge and sustain operations in international competition (Monferrer Tirado et al., 2021).

Research on international entrepreneurship has highlighted the fact that only a limited number of firms can achieve substantial growth and born globals constitute a vital group of high-growth young firms (Moen, Falahat & Lee, 2022). However, newly formed firms that compete domestically and internationally differ significantly (McDougall, 1989), and the crucial distinction is the ability of born globals to succeed in their international aspirations (Langseth et al., 2016). Even though research on born globals is 20 years old, there is still a lack of understanding and empirical knowledge on what determines the international performance of such firms compared to other firms that operate internationally (Moen, Falahat & Lee, 2022).

What helps born globals survive the international competition and succeed? Monferrer Tirado et al. provide three answers. First, the international entrepreneurship approach highlights the entrepreneurial nature of such firms. Second, the resource and capabilities approach focuses on the access of born globals to knowledge-based resources and capabilities. Third, the relational approach points to strategic behaviours shared in network contexts (Monferrer Tirado et al., 2021).

The importance of networks for a company's successful activities is especially important for born globals since they have limited resources and foreign market knowledge, and have to develop them rapidly and in an unknown and potentially hostile or at least competitive environment. Thus, the necessity to complement their internal knowledge with knowledge from other sources reinforces the need to organise spaces for sharing knowledge and experience (Monferrer Tirado et al., 2021). The authors note that especially at a time of crisis it is vital for such firms to create stronger formal ties with partners, to cooperate with those who have the same values and be proactive in networks, as well as initiate and/or participate in the joint use, development and transformation of common resources (Monferrer Tirado et al., 2021).

Business Model Change as a Result of Crisis

Business models are considered a structured management tool that is associated with securing competitive advantage. They are vital not only in research literature but in the real practice of companies (Wirtz et al., 2016). Manolova et al. (2020) state that there is a consensus that business models encompass customer-focused value creation, profit formula, crucial resources and processes. Business model is also considered as a source of innovation, yet it does not stay still, and is therefore subject to change and adjustment. Business model change is one of the adaptation or reconfiguration scenarios that companies use in response to crises (Davidsson & Gordon, 2016). Kuckertz et al. (2020) argue that a start-up may be better equipped to tackle crises than any other economic actor because of their small size, flexibility, agility and innovativeness. Business model change usually includes transformation in terms of resources, offerings, clients and finances, and the process usually includes adaptation or pivoting (Osterwalder & Pigneur, 2010).

There is an emerging research stream that deals with business model change that companies experience as a result of a crisis (Ritter & Pedersen, 2020). Companies do it in order to accommodate their activities to the changing environment (Manolova et al., 2020). The above-mentioned authors state that companies implement changes along the three dimensions of their business model: value proposition, value creation, and value capture (Guckenbiehl & de Zubielqui, 2022). This results in business model adaptation and innovation. Scholars highlight the scarcity of research on business model change related to small and medium enterprises in crises, yet there is a lot of potential in studying such firms. As Guckenbiehl and de Zubielqui (2022) note, there is a need to study how SMEs survive crises and change their business model in response to environmental shocks (Miller et al., 2020). Guckenbiehl and Corral de Zubielqui (2022) analyse Australian start-ups and reveal six types of start-up strategies, labelled as stable beneficiaries, business-as-usual continuers, digital adjusters, adversity survivors, opportunity graspers and lemonade makers. The authors state that most start-ups changed their business model in response to a crisis because of the crisis-induced opportunities and adversity.

Kuckertz et al. (2020) provide empirical evidence of the business model change of start-ups as a result of the COVID-19 pandemic when many

Figure 13.1 Resilience model of start-ups.
Source: The authors.

start-ups redirected their activities rapidly to where it was possible under the new environmental conditions. The study of Manolova et al. (2020) examines the response of women entrepreneurs to crisis, and it can relate to start-ups that generally lack resources due to their small size and newness, and moreover as women entrepreneurs are believed to be a vulnerable group. The study reveals that women pivoted their businesses and changed the business models of their start-ups.

As a result of the literature review, we developed a resilience model of start-ups (Figure 13.1).

Methodology

A multiple case-study method has been used in this study. This method allows to study complex phenomena in difficult external conditions (Doz, 2011). The analysis of selected cases enhances the understanding of some common features and differences between the cases. For the case selection, we applied the following criteria: first, a firm is considered a start-up and has Russian origin; second, it operates in the IT field, and third, it operates internationally. Four of the selected cases corresponded to all criteria although their IT products or services are applicable in various industries and their international presence is rather diverse. We conducted several interviews with IT start-ups' representatives in April 2022. To triangulate the data, we also studied media materials, interviews with experts and the start-ups' websites, as well as social media.

Research Context

All interviews with start-up representatives took place in April 2022, two months after the beginning of the major geopolitical crisis. Starting from February 2022, Russia has been severely sanctioned by most Western countries. Among the harshest consequences are the disconnection of the

244 *Liubov Ermolaeva and Daria Klishevich*

national financial system from the global financial system, meaning that it became almost impossible either to transfer or to get money from abroad. This affected import and export significantly. Over the first two months import decreased, and according to estimations of the Central Bank of Russia, the decrease may be at the level of 32.5–36.5% (Tkachev, 2022). Another issue that has further deepened Russia's isolation from the world economy was the reaction of multinational firms (MNCs). Many companies suspended their operations and investments, several companies exited the market altogether. Among the IT giants that suspended their activities are Microsoft, Adobe and many others. The political, economic and moral pressure resulted in the migration of thousands of qualified specialists, including IT specialists, and in the end of March 2022, the reported number of IT specialists that left the country ranged from 50 to 70 thousand (Polyakova, 2022). In this very uncertain and critical situation, every enterprise faced the need to react strategically on such a huge external shock. For IT start-ups major problems were the ban on their financial operations with Western countries, reputational risks and the outflow of IT specialists.

Description of Cases

Case 1. Group of Start-ups (Mobile Developers, Platform, Venture Fond)

Ivan (anonymised name) is an IT entrepreneur owning several high-tech businesses in Russia. The youngest start-up is mobile game development, which is at its early stage of development and does not earn money yet. One incumbent business is a study platform connecting students and tutors. It has been operating in Russia and the United States. The venture fund has been investing in IT projects from all over the world. In the new geopolitical situation, all companies went through different transformations. The platform business had to register in Russia because it could not access money (finance and payments) from abroad. The management team though was relocated to Cyprus. With this project, the entrepreneur applied for government support, which was announced early on. For that purpose, the entrepreneurs split up the business and registered it as a start-up in Skolkovo (the business incubator hub in Moscow). One start-up, which is at an early stage of its development (mobile games) was relocated to Armenia. The reason was the team's concerns of working as a Russian firm (reputational risk), financial risks (some of the investors are foreigners) and the moral beliefs of the team. Armenia offers favourable taxation for IT start-ups and thus, the start-up benefited from this relocation, as well as from the ruble appreciation. The new start-up is still funded by a Russian firm and therefore, the exchange rate has been rather beneficial for paying in USD. To enable the further investments of the venture fund in IT projects, the founders registered several firms in Dubai, Ireland and Cyrpus.

IT Entrepreneur Resiliencein Geopolitical Turbulence   245

Case 2. Start-up – Blockchain Developer (Decentralised Finance)

Two entrepreneurs from Russia and Germany, being experts in the cryptocurrency market, started their project 1.5 years ago. Since then, they attracted several million USD of investments from all over the world. Now, nine people are working for the start-up, and they are mostly Russian by origin. The specifics of decentralised finance is that the start-up exists in a virtual space, all team members are individual entrepreneurs, and it is not required to be formally registered as a company under any legislation. That is why the Russian roots can be revealed only if the entrepreneurs want to claim that. Nevertheless, some of the team moved to Dubai. The reason to be in a safer environment without the risk to be drafted in the army. There was not any other risk for the start-up. However, some changes occurred, e.g., due to the appreciation of the ruble, the entrepreneurs had to reconsider their contracts that were nominated in USD. Dubai proved to be a more comfortable environment for cryptocurrency start-ups because of its legislation and networks, as a new world hub for IT entrepreneurs, including blockchain developers. Thus, the start-up sees new opportunities on the world market. According to the entrepreneurs, the start-up has ambitious plans, including attracting global talent from all over the world.

Case 3. Start-up Producing Software and Hardware for Special Devices Targeting Blind People

The start-up develops and produces special devices for blind people to make the environment around them more accessible. Their main markets are the United States, Japan and partly Europe. Russia is not a sufficient market in terms of market size for their invention. However, all developers and engineers are based in Russia. The start-up has a branch in the United States, which is responsible for marketing and sales on the American market, as well as investment attraction. Since the geopolitical crisis began the start-up has had many problems with American clients. The major problem is that they refuse working with a company of Russian origin. Moreover, payment impediments appeared. The founder of the start-up arranged several face-to-face meetings with the main clients and partners in the United States to discuss how these challenges could be overcome. The start-up is splitting the United States and Russian branches so that developers and engineers stay in Russia, but sales, marketing and investor relations remain in the United States. The start-up keeps producing their unique devices and presenting them at international events despite the new very complicated circumstances.

Case 4. Software for Geological Mining

The company develops information systems for geological exploration. The geography of its operations is quite broad in its scope, yet mostly within the

CIS countries: Russia, Kazakhstan, Kyrgyzstan, Georgia, Armenia, but including also Turkey and Algeria. The partners in Kyrgystan, Georgia and Armenia suspended contracts with the Russian firm. The major problem was payment because of the sanctions imposed on most Russian banks. As the company has its branch in Kazakhstan, a solution was found quickly. All payments in USD were made to the Kazakh branch account. The company had to make new contracts with its clients in different countries. To date, the company is going to launch its branch in Uzbekistan, where a new geological field is opening. Moreover, it is close to Kazakhstan and is not under sanctions.

Data Analysis

The interviews were analysed using the following codes: "problems" (identifying problems which the start-ups faced), "opportunities" (identifying whether the entrepreneurs saw opportunities at the time of the unprecedented crisis), "enhancer" (resources or capabilities that helped to overcome the severe challenges posed by the crisis), "liability" (barriers to overcoming the crisis), "response" (what actions the start-ups undertook to handle the situation), "business model change" (how the start-ups' response to the environmental change influenced their business model). For data triangulation, we also related the interviews to the information in secondary sources, such as social media and webpages. The results of data analysis can be seen in Table 13.1.

Findings

Response

Almost all start-ups faced similar problems: difficulties with payments from and to overseas and refusal of partners to continue the cooperation. Two out of four start-ups solved these problems by relocating part of the business in other countries or rearranging the contracts and moving their USD-nominated financial operations into existing foreign branches. Thus, start-up developing software for geology transferred all international contract to its Kazakhstan branch, the mobile game-developing start-up registered its office in Armenia and moved 70% of team to Georgia. The producer of devices for blind people however didn't relocate his company to foreign market but tried to run two separate businesses – one in Russia and one in the United States. And for the fourth company developing blockchain the current situation didn't turn out a very harmful. As an entrepreneur said: "*We depend only on crypto-currency market, nothing else*". That was the only start-up which didn't have a liability of "Russianness", because as an entrepreneur said: "*No one cares about your origin in crypto world*". For all the rest, the liability of

Table 13.1 Data analysis results

Case	Problems	Opportunities	Enhancer	Liability	Business model transformation	Response
Mobile games development **Study world: platform for students and professors** **Investment in different start-ups worldwide**	Employees want to be in safe environment, not thinking about drafting to the war *"We can't invest from Russia"*	More specialists on the job market, because large companies either seize their operations or relocating to other countries. New project in finance marketing – to provide service for payment of foreign subscriptions.	*"We search for new locations gathering information from our friends, partners (networks)"* Group of companies: synergy effect + diversification Russian-speaking countries (Armenia, Georgia) Experience of working on different projects Entrepreneurial spirit and optimism	Russian residence (difficulties to hire people)	Value creation Value capture	Relocation to Armenia, officially we are Armenian company. Business operations do not change much. *"Our costs on the one hand increased on the other hand decreased because salaries were fixed in dollars (dollars dropped down relatively to ruble)"* *"We transfer company back to Russia because we couldn't get money. We registered our firm in Skolkovo to minimise taxes. We relocated part of our team to Cyprus".* *"Our investment's portfolio consists of foreign assets. Therefore, we registered one company in Dubai, another in Cyprus and one more in Ireland. So far no one asked us to leave the project".*

Table 13.1 (Continued)

Case	Problems	Opportunities	Enhancer	Liability	Business model transformation	Response
Blockchain developers	"We were worried about drafting, that's way we moved to Dubai". "Our main problem crypto currency devaluation at the moment, we don't depend on current context"	"In Dubai everything is easier with crypto currency – you may exchange crypto currency on real currency for example. Dubai is world hub of crypto projects". "Currency devaluation is also an opportunity to develop infrastructure for the future"	Innovativeness Independence from real financial market Ambitiousness Agility "Our money are in stable coins" (meaning that they don't depend on currency volatility) "DAO – it's a team of people who can vote with their tockens. We don't need registered firm to work in cryptocurrency market" "We set our salaries lower than crypto market, because we want to save stable cash flow" "'Crypto people' do not care where you are from"	Newness	No changes in value proposition Slight changes in value creation and value capture	Audit "We are ready to offer free accommodation for team members. But most of our team is in Russia" "The only thing changed we raised salary because it is in dollars and dollars dropped down whereas inflation increased"
Software for geology	International payments are impossible "Our current and potential partners do not work to sign contracts with us because of political and business risks"	New field in Uzbekistan More government's projects	Diverse portfolio of international projects – risks diversification Agility		Changes in value creation and value capture	Audit of resources Rearranged all international contracts to Kazakhstan branch

Devices for blind people (software and hardware)			Value creation
Devices for blind people (software and hardware)	"We need to save our clients in the United States. Our clients are scared to work with us". "Russian market has never been interesting for us"	Talented engineers and developers A lot of partners worldwide Thinking of crisis as a task	"I talked to everyone in the United States personally. We explained them how we gonna work further. We plan to separate the two businesses. In Russia we keep developers and engineers, in the US sales office will be launched". "There are two options for us: first to sign a contract with a person you trust but with no-Russian citizenship (management buy-out); second is to launch start-up in accelerator in the United States". "I'm flying to Europe, get money there and come back to Russia with cash (this is how we deal today with money)"
		"Russianness" Nich product, Russian market is limited "This is not a problem, this is a task which you have to complete".	

Source: The authors.

250 Liubov Ermolaeva and Daria Klishevich

"Russianness" became the major barrier for continuing its business, especially for those who operated in Western markets. None of the identified in the literature problems was revealed in our cases: neither liability of smallness or newness, or lack of resources or experience.

Enhancers

We identified "enhancers", which were introduced by scholars earlier. The "enhancer" typical for all start-ups is agility. Ability to react quickly to the situation and adjust the business processes was revealed in every case. "*Within one month we relocated on company to Armenia, registered another company in Skolkovo and applied for subsidies, moved part of our staff to Cyrpus and Georgia and registered a few new companies abroad*" (Ivan, founder of group of IT firms). This quick reaction to the external turmoil demonstrates the resilience of entrepreneurs themselves. "*I look at this crisis as at a task, which I need to complete*" (Dima – anonymised name, devices for blind people). Moreover, the IT community very quickly created a lot of resources helping to find information on different locations, taxation systems, visa issues etc. The availability of information was extraordinary, literally everyone could easily get all the information he or she needed with tips and lifehacks. Besides agility and fast reactions our start-ups relied on different resources and capabilities. The group of companies leveraged their resources by using the synergy of all start-ups in a group. The geology software start-up relied on its international assets; their diverse international portfolio helped them to rearrange all the contracts fast. The devices for blind people start-ups benefited from a wide network of international partners. Even during the geopolitical crisis, the start-up continued participating in conferences and other events. Their niche product, on the one hand, was liability because they couldn't operate only on the Russian market (too small for their invention), but on the other hand, it is an "enhancer" because it roots them in a very specific network of enterprises working with blindness.

The only start-up that stands out is blockchain developers. Because of their innovative field of operations, the entrepreneurs do not depend on the real financial market or legislation. They are not only born-global but also born digital what makes them resident of pure digital world – crypto world. The innovativeness and ambitiousness are the main enhancers of their resilience to any external shocks.

Opportunities Recognition

Thukral (2021) argued that resilience helps individuals see the chances in chaos and turn the opportunities into real benefits (Thukral, 2021). In our cases, entrepreneurs revealed opportunities too. The founder of group of companies claimed that more well-qualified and experienced specialists are now available at the job market because of seizing operations of global and local IT giants. Despite media's concern that too many IT specialists left Russia and soon companies will lack those, our respondent didn't acknowledge the problem. In fact, the issue with employees has another aspect. Two of the entrepreneurs said that the reason of relocation was the unwillingness of employees to work for a "Russian" company anymore. *"For some guys it is very important now to be employed in a foreign company, they care about their CV, thus they prefer to work for companies which are not officially registered in Russia"* (Ivan).

The opposite situation occurred in two other cases. The company producing devices for blind people claimed that employees are one of the reasons to stay in Russia. *"We have the best engineers who are smart and can do literally everything. And they are cheap. Why should I leave?"*

Two of the four cases showed clear signs of opportunity-seeking behaviour. The founder of groups of start-ups started developing financial marketing software to address the new problems of Russian citizens' inability to pay for foreign subscriptions. As Visa and Mastercard suspended their operations, the Russians could not use these cards anymore. A lot of users of foreign software and online services cannot pay for them. Several start-ups including our case simultaneously develop special services such as virtual cards. The blockchain developers also see this market decline as an opportunity to develop infrastructure and prepare themselves for future growth.

Business Model Transformation

The scholars argued that during time of global discontinuities and disruptions companies need to adapt their business models rapidly (Doz & Kosonen, 2010). The fast start-up reaction to changes happening in Russia in 2022 resulted in incremental changes in their business models. The value creation dimension experienced most of the changes. The examined start-ups didn't change their value proposition because their products or services were still demanded on the market. What required some transformations is their business operations. Partly those changes in business operations were necessary to survive for example transferring all the international contracts to subsidiary in Kazakhstan (geology software), partly those changes were preventive. For example, relocating management teams in Cyprus (mobile games) or Dubai (blockchain developers) with registration of new legal entities was not required for survival. The entrepreneurs have undertaken these actions for the future – to keep their employees, to secure its financial assets and to anticipate new contracts. Between-cases analysis illustrates that more drastic changes happened to entrepreneurs looking for new opportunities in new circumstances. These cases are geology software and mobile games; entrepreneurs looked at new directions for companies' development outside Russia what encouraged significant changes in value creation. The business model of blockchain developers was innovative itself thus it didn't require any significant transformation. And for start-up producing devices for blind people changes were mostly in formalities because start-up depends on human resources (engineers) who are rooted in Russia. This case back to the time of conducting the interview was in the most uncertain status as they still didn't get compliance from the American partners.

Speaking about the value capture aspect of the business model it was a matter of necessity because of difficulties with payments to and from abroad. The geology software and mobile games developers' start-ups were urged to rearrange their cash flows in order to support new branches abroad. Software development firm used to invest in the Kazakh branch from the Russian head office, however, after all the foreign contracts were linked to the Kazakh branch it obtained its financial independence in terms of costs and sales.

The ruble volatility became an issue for each start-up. First, contracts with IT specialists are usually bounded to USD. That's why some start-ups firstly lose from ruble appreciation in the beginning of the military conflict but then they benefited from ruble appreciation in later months. The relocation process was complicated by this currency volatility what partly affected the value capture aspect of business models of three out of four start-ups which started relocation. Thus, internationalisation provoked quite a significant change in the business models of start-ups what was also acknowledged in the literature (Rissanen et al., 2020). The revised model of start-up's resilience is introduced in Figure 13.2.

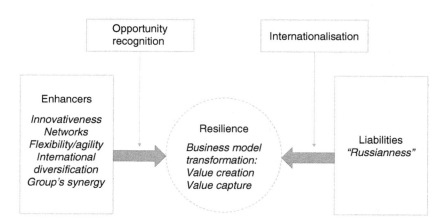

Figure 13.2 Model for resilience of Russian start-ups.
Source: The authors.

Conclusions

In this study, we aimed to answer two research questions – how start-ups in Russia adapt to new circumstances and what makes them resilient to the current crisis. Multiple case study has been conducted. We made interviews with Russian founders of start-ups two months after the major geopolitical crisis took place. The unprecedently taught sanctions imposed on Russia together with distraction and total uncertainty pushed almost every business to reconsider its existence. Start-ups have certain specific determining their reaction. First, they usually target global markets, and their business models are built on this assumption. Second, scholars often emphasised start-up's vulnerability in terms of size, experience and resources. And third, specifically Russian start-ups have grown up thanks to abundance of qualified specialists with a technical background and government support (Guseva & Stepanova, 2021). In the beginning of 2022, Russian start-ups suddenly found themselves isolated from their main market – the global one. We analysed four cases to figure out how start-ups responded to this challenge. We looked at their response from a business model perspective. We found out that the rapid reaction of Russian start-ups resulted in significant changes in the value-creation aspect of their business models. Most of these changes were entailed by relocating part of the business to foreign countries. Thus, we proved once again that internationalisation affects business model transformation significantly. Another although less significant change was observed in the value capture model. That change arose from a necessity, whereas some of the changes in the value creation model took place as opportunity recognition behaviour. Opportunity recognition drove the most drastic transformation of the studied start-ups' business models.

We identified in the literature liabilities and enhancers of start-up's resilience. While studying the cases, we related our analysis results to the literature, and we found some variances determined by context specificity. First of all, we didn't identify any other liability as a liability of "being Russian" or liability of "Russianness". It explains why the value proposition model has not changed – the products or services of Russian start-ups are still demanded by the market. However, to overcome these liabilities start-ups were forced to relocate to other countries.

Second, we revealed a few enhancers of resilience which have not been mentioned in the literature regarding start-ups. These enhancers are international diversification and group's synergy. Nevertheless, we identified same enhancers as scholars did such as agility (Kuckertz et al., 2020), networks (Monferrer Tirado et al., 2021) and innovativeness (Guckenbiehl & de Zubielqui, 2022). One more characteristic typical to all entrepreneurs and revealed by our study is individual resilience and optimism. Thanks to entrepreneurial resilience and optimism business keeps going on and even driving innovations.

References

Archibugi, D., Filippetti, A. & Frenz, M. (2013). "The impact of the economic crisis on innovation: Evidence from Europe", *Technological Forecasting and Social Change*, vol. 80(7), pp. 1247–1260.

Babkin, D. (2022). "Relocation fixes the service", *Kommersant*. https://www.kommersant.ru/doc/5355094 (Accessed: 8 June 2022) [in Russian].

Bishop, P. (2019). "Knowledge diversity and entrepreneurship following an economic crisis: an empirical study of regional resilience in Great Britain", *Entrepreneurship & Regional Development*, vol. 31(5-6), pp. 496–515.

Bullough, A., Renko, M. & Myatt, T. (2014). "Danger zone entrepreneurs: The importance of resilience and self-efficacy for entrepreneurial intentions", *Entrepreneurship: Theory and Practice*, vol. 38(3), pp. 473–499.

Bundy, J., Pfarrer, M.D., Short, C.E. & Coombs, W.T. (2017). "Crises and crisis management: Integration, interpretation, and research development", *Journal of Management*, vol. 43(6), pp. 1661–1692.

Burnard, K. & Bhamra, R. (2011). "Organisational resilience: Development of a conceptual framework for organisational responses", *International Journal of Production Research*, vol. 49(18), pp. 5581–5599.

Cucculelli, M. & Peruzzi, V. (2020). "Post-crisis firm survival, business model changes, and learning: Evidence from the Italian manufacturing industry", *Small Business Economics*, vol. 54(2), pp. 459–474.

Davidsson, P. & Gordon, S.R. (2016). "Much ado about nothing? The surprising persistence of nascent entrepreneurs through macroeconomic crisis", *Entrepreneurship Theory and Practice*, vol. 40(4), pp. 915–941.

de Bruijne, M., Boin, A. & van Eeten, M. (2010). "Resilience: Exploring the concept and its meanings", in L.K. Comfort, A. Boin and C.C. Demchak (Eds.), *Designing Resilience: Preparing for Extreme Events*. Pittsburgh: University of Pittsburgh Press, 13–32.

Devece, C., Peris-Ortiz, M. & Rueda-Armengot, C. (2016). "Entrepreneurship during economic crisis: Success factors and paths to failure", *Journal of Business Research*, vol. 69(11), pp. 5366–5370.

Doern, R., Williams, N. & Vorley, T. (2019). "Special issue on entrepreneurship and crises: Business as usual? An introduction and review of the literature", *Entrepreneurship and Regional Development*, vol. 31(5–6), pp. 400–412.

Doz, Y.L. (2011). "Qualitative research for international business", *Journal of International Business Studies*, vol. 42(5), pp. 582–590.

Doz, Y.L. & Kosonen, M. (2010), "Embedding strategic agility: A leadership agenda for accelerating business model renewal", *Long Range Planning*, vol. 43(2/3), pp. 370–382.

Etemad, H., Gurau, C. & Dana, L.-P. (2022). "International entrepreneurship research agendas evolving: A longitudinal study using the Delphi method", *Journal of International Entrepreneurship*, vol. 20(1), pp. 29–51.

Goschin, Z., Antonia, M. & Tigau, H. (2021). "Entrepreneurship recovery in Romania after the great recession. A dynamic spatial panel approach", *Sustainability*, vol. 13(19), pp. 1–12.

Guckenbiehl, P. & de Zubielqui, G.C. (2022). "Start-ups' business model changes during the COVID-19 pandemic: Counteracting adversities and pursuing opportunities", *International Small Business Journal: Researching Entrepreneurship*, vol. 40(2), pp. 150–177.

Guerzoni, M., Nava, C.R. & Nuccio, M. (2021). "Start-ups survival through a crisis. Combining machine learning with econometrics to measure innovation", *Economics of Innovation and New Technology*, vol. 30(5), pp. 468–493.

Guseva, O.A. & Stepanova, A.N. (2021). "Start-ups in Russia: Ownership and performance", *New Economic Association*, vol. 52(4), pp. 67–97.

Hennart, J.-F. (2014). "The Accidental Internationalists: A Theory of Born Globals", *Entrepreneurship Theory and Practice*, vol. 38 (1), pp. 117–135. 10.1111/etap.12076

Herbane, B. (2019). "Rethinking organizational resilience and strategic renewal in SMEs", *Entrepreneurship and Regional Development*, vol. 31(5–6), 476–495.

Hitt, M.A., Arregle, J.-L. & Holmes, R.M., Jr. (2021). "Strategic management theory in a post-pandemic and non-ergodic world", *Journal of Management Studies*, vol. 58(1), pp. 259–264.

Johnson, N. & Elliott, D. (2011). "Using social capital to organise for success? A case study of public–private interface in the UK Highways Agency", *Policy and Society*, vol. 30(2), pp. 101–113.

Korsgaard, S., Hunt, R.A., Townsend, D.M. & Ingstrup, M.B. (2020). "COVID-19 and the importance of space in entrepreneurship research and policy", *International Small Business Journal: Researching Entrepreneurship*, vol. 38(8), pp. 697–710.

Kuckertz, A., Brändle, L., Gaudig, A., Hinderer, S., Morales Reyes, C.A., Prochotta, A., Steinbrink, K.M. & Berger, E.S.C. (2020). "Start-ups in times of crisis – A rapid response to the COVID-19 pandemic", *Journal of Business Venturing Insights*. Available at: https://www.sciencedirect.com/science/article/pii/S2352673420300251 (Accessed: 7 June 2022).

Langseth, H., O'Dwyer, M. & Arpa, C. (2016). "Forces influencing the speed of internationalization", *Journal of Small Business and Enterprise Development*, vol. 23(1), pp. 122–148.

Marinov, M.A. & Marinova, S.T. (2021). *COVID-19 and International Business: Change of Era*. London and New York, NY: Taylor and Francis.

Markus, S. (2022). "Long-term business implications of Russia's war in Ukraine", *Asian Business and Management*. Available at: https://link.springer.com/article/10.1057/s41291-022-00181-7 (Accessed: 8 June 2022).

Manolova, T.S., Brush, C.G., Edelman, L.F. & Elam, A. (2020). "Pivoting to stay the course: How women entrepreneurs take advantage of opportunities created by the COVID-19 pandemic", *International Small Business Journal*, vol. 38(6), pp. 481–491.

McDougall, P.P. (1989). "International versus domestic entrepreneurship: New venture strategic behavior and industry structure", *Journal of Business Venturing*, vol. 4(6), pp. 387–400.

McDougall, P.P. & Oviatt, B.M. (2000). "International entrepreneurship: The intersection of two research paths", *Academy of Management Journal*, vol. 43(5), 902–906.

Melkadze, A. (2021). "Start-ups in Russia – Statistics and facts". Available at: https://www.statista.com/topics/7574/start-ups-in-russia/ (Accessed: 8 June 2022).

Meyer, K.E., Prashantham, S. & Xu, S. (2021). "Entrepreneurship and the post-COVID-19 recovery in emerging economies", *Management and Organization Review*, vol. 17(5), pp. 1101–1118.

Miller, K., McAdam, M., Spieth, P. & Brady, M. (2020). "Business models big and small: Review of conceptualisations and constructs and future directions for SME business model research", *Journal of Business Research*, vol. 131, pp. 619–626.

Moen, Ø., Falahat, M. & Lee, Y.-Y. (2022) "Are born global firms really a "new breed" of exporters? Empirical evidence from an emerging market", *Journal of International Entrepreneurship*, vol. 20(1), pp. 157–193.

Monferrer Tirado, D., Molinera, M., Irúnb, I. & Estradaa, M. (2021). "Network market and entrepreneurial orientations as facilitators of international performance in born globals. The mediating role of ambidextrous dynamic capabilities", *Journal of Business Research*, vol. 137(C), pp. 430–443.

Osterwalder, A. & Pigneur, Y. (2010). *Business Model Generation: A Handbook for Visionaries, Game Changers and Challengers.* Hoboken, NJ: John Wiley and Sons.

Oviatt, B.M. & McDougall, P.P. (2005). "Defining international entrepreneurship and modeling the speed of internationalization", *Entrepreneurship: Theory & Practice*, vol. 9, pp. 537–553.

Pedersen, C.L. & Ritter, T. (2022). "The market-shaping potential of a crisis", *Industrial Marketing Management*, vol. 103, pp. 146–153.

Peris-Ortiz, M., Fuster-Estruch, V. & Devece-Carañana, C. (2014). "Entrepreneurship and innovation in a context of crisis", in K. Rüdiger, M. Peris Ortiz & A. Blanco González (eds.), *Entrepreneurship, Innovation and Economic Crisis.* Cham: Springer. 10.1007/978-3-319-02384-7_1

Pinho, J.C. & de Lurdes Martins, M. (2020). "The opportunity to create a business: Systemic banking crisis, institutional factor conditions and trade openness", *Journal of International Entrepreneurship*, vol. 18(4), pp. 393–418.

Podtserob, N. (2022). "Digital audit: Searching for technologies", *Harvard Business Review Russia.* Available at: https://hbr-russia.ru/innovatsii/tekhnologii/tsifrovoy-audit-v-poiskakh-tekhnologiy/ (Accessed: 8 June 2022) [in Russian].

Polyakova, V. (2022). "Russian Central Bank forecasted that up to 100 thousand IT specialists will leave in April", *Russian Central Bank*, Available at: https://www.rbc.ru/politics/22/03/2022/6239c48b9a7947da733b01fd. (Accessed: 14 October 2022) [in Russian].

Rissanen, T., Ermolaeva, L., Saarenketo, T., Torkkeli, L. & Ahi, M. (2020). "The role of home market context in business model change in internationalizing SMEs", *European Business Review*, vol. 32(2), pp. 257–275.

Ritter, T. & Pedersen C.L. (2020). "Analyzing the impact of the coronavirus crisis on business models", *Industrial Marketing Management*, vol. 88, pp. 214–224.

Roux-Dufort, C. (2007). "Is crisis management (only) a management of exceptions?" *Journal of Contingencies and Crisis Management*, vol. 15(2), pp. 105–114.

Seetharaman, P. (2020). "Business models shifts: Impact of Covid-19", *International Journal of Information Management.* Available at: https://www.sciencedirect.com/science/article/pii/S0268401220309890 (Accessed: 8 June 2022).

Shepherd, D.A. (2020). "COVID 19 and entrepreneurship: Time to pivot?", *Journal of Management Studies*, vol. 57(8), pp. 1750–1753.

Startup Barometer (2020). "Research on tech entrepreneurship market in Russia". Available at: https://generation-startup.ru/upload/docs/Startup_Barometer_2020.pdf (Accessed: 8 June 2022) [in Russian].

Startup Ranking (2022). "Countries". Available at: https://www.startupranking.com/countries (Accessed: 8 June 2022).

Streeck, W. & Thelen, K. (2005). "Introduction: Institutional change in advanced political economies", in W. Streeck & K. Thelen (eds.), *Beyond Continuity: Institutional Change in Advanced Political Economies.* Oxford: Oxford University Press, 1–39.

Thukral, E. (2021). "COVID-19: Small and medium enterprises challenges and responses with creativity, innovation, and entrepreneurship", *Strategic Change*, vol. 30(2), pp. 153–158.

Tkachev, I. (2022). "Central Bank gave the first official forecast on the depth of recession", *Russian Central Bank*. Available at: https://www.rbc.ru/economics/29/04/2022/626bc2939a7947ebdf90a9f1. (Accessed: 14 October 2022) [in Russian].

Wenzel, M., Stanske, S. & Lieberman, M.B. (2021). "Strategic responses to crisis", *Strategic Management Journal*, vol. 42(2), pp. 016–027.

Williams, T.A., Gruber, D.A., Sutcliffe, K.M., Shepherd, D.A. & Zhao, E.Y. (2017). "Organizational response to adversity: Fusing crisis management and resilience research streams", *The Academy of Management Annals*, vol. 11(2), pp. 733–769.

Wirtz, B.W., Pistoia, A., Ullrich, S. & Göttel, V. (2016). "Business models: Origin, development and future research perspectives", *Long Range Planning*, vol. 49(1), pp. 36–54.

Zahra, S.A. (2020). "International entrepreneurship in the post Covid world", *Journal of World Business*, vol. 56(1). Available at: https://www.sciencedirect.com/science/article/pii/S1090951620300717?via%3Dihub (Accessed: 8 June 2022).

14 Old-School Gender Values in a New Labour Model: A Case Study of Women's Entrepreneurship in Israel

Guy Abutbul-Selinger, Anat Guy, and Avaraham Shnider

Introduction

Recent literature studying new business and organisational models has focused on the advantages and disadvantages of each model in terms of finance, markets, human resources, etc. The assumption implicit in this literature is that business and organisational models are chosen in a rational decision-making process by the managers. This literature, however, has neglected the broad research on social context as integral to decision-making and choice in business and organisations. The aim of this study is to examine the choice of business and organisational models within their social contexts. More specifically, we examine the ways in which women entrepreneurs choose small-entrepreneurship work models as a result of their gender characteristics and motivations.

In recent decades, the Israeli labour market has undergone a revolution. From a centralised market, controlled by the public sector, the Israeli market has become privatised, entrepreneurial, with explicit neo-liberal characteristics. A significant phenomenon in this regard is private entrepreneurship, which is perceived by many as a key financial engine. Yet, studies of entrepreneurship in Israel and abroad focus mainly on the facet of entrepreneurship in the limelight: the characteristics of successful entrepreneurs and the start-up industry. The current study aims to reveal a different facet of entrepreneurship – that of small businesses established by women: afterschool day-cares, clothing stores, a styling business or a sleep consultant. This less-glorious aspect of entrepreneurship has been ignored by the literature to date. This is an exploratory study, which aims to reveal the personal, social and demographic characteristics influencing women's decisions to become small business owners.

The first part of the paper will focus on the Israeli labour market while referring to women and to the market's gender-related aspects. Additionally, this part will review the key changes in the labour market in recent decades, focusing on entrepreneurship in general, and particularly on women entrepreneurs. We will then present the method and initial findings of the current study. Finally, we will discuss the findings and their implications for Israeli society, the Israeli market and the women in it.

DOI: 10.4324/9781003326731-14

The Israeli Labour Market

The level of labour market participation in Israel is one of the highest in the world, with an overall rate of 77.3% (Central Bureau of Statistics, 2019). Over the last two decades, the composition of the working population has changed dramatically. The decline in the rate of men's employment, which started during the 1980s, came to a stop and even reversed, rising up to 84.9% according to the CBS, alongside a significant growth in women's employment rates, from 56.5% in 1995 to 76% in 2019. This trend is particularly apparent among populations that have traditionally been marginalised, like Arab men, ultra-orthodox women, older workers and workers with a lower level of education (Central Bureau of Statistics, 2019).

These changes are the result of several trends: first, a sharp cut in the social security benefits for the unemployed (criteria were added, sums were decreased and the eligibility period was cut short). At the same time, child benefits were reduced, and policies were changed, setting a fixed sum of support for each child, instead of a higher sum from the fourth child onwards. Second, tax reforms encouraged labour market participation, such as zero income tax for people who earn up to 4,000 ILS and a work grant (negative income tax) for people with low wages. Third, designated programmes were established, aimed to integrate welfare-supported populations in the labour market (like *Orot LeTaasuka*) alongside programmes that encourage labour market integration of specific populations (single mothers, Arabs, ultra-orthodox and more). Finally, the dramatic changes in the higher-education world, including the establishment of many regional colleges, increased the accessibility of higher education to various populations. Higher education raised employment rates among all parts of the population and particularly among women (40% of the rise in women's employment was found to be related to higher education) (Ekstein, Lifshitz & Larom, 2018).

Women in the Israeli Labour Market

Israel is characterised by a small gender gap in terms of labour market participation, opportunities and promotion in the labour market. On the other hand, the gender gaps in compensation, number of work hours, wage level and promotion options are much higher (Harari-Kamar, 2014).

Most working women in Israel work full-time, and many continue to work full-time even when their children are young. The percentage of full-time working women is much higher than in other Western countries such as Germany (54.2%), Norway (60%), the United Kingdom (57.7%) and the Netherlands (41.6%). Moreover, unlike in the United Kingdom or the United States, part-time jobs for women are not necessarily characterised by low wages or by limited promotion opportunities. A large proportion of part-time working women in Israel work in white-collar and professional jobs, characterised by high prestige and employment security, and 50% work in the public sector (Fichtelberg-Barmatz & Harris, 2014).

Wide-scale legislation in the field of labour laws and employment regulations has removed part-time jobs from their marginal status, turning them into jobs that allow one to shift into full-time and offering hourly wages comparable to full-time jobs (Stier, 2012). Studies examining the impact of Israeli employment patterns on the wages of women suggest that in Israel, part-time employment is not "fined" compared to full-time employment, so long as the employment is continuous (Steir & Levin-Epstein, 1999). The same studies suggest that women in Israel do not necessarily tend to remain in part-time jobs, and more women move from part-time to full-time jobs than the other way around. Furthermore, in Israel, which is considered a relatively supportive country for working women, the diversion from full-time work patterns does not carry many wage implications (Kimhi, 2012; Aharon, 2017).

The percentage of women who participate in the labour market has increased dramatically over the last decade. This rise is explained by changes in work patterns, legislative changes and changes in the higher education market. The integration of mothers of young children into the labour market is the main reason for the overall rise in the rate of working women (Dagan-Buzaglo, Konor-Atias & Arian, 2014). In 2014, according to CBS data, the participation rate was 77.9% among mothers of one child, 78.6% among mothers of two, and 60.2% among mothers of four or more. The ability of mothers of young children to enter the work market is due in part to technological developments and to the creation of new positions, which are more flexible in terms of time and place (for instance, the option of working from home) (Stier & Herzberg, 2013). The changes in retirement laws (Age of Retirement Law, 2004) are another cause of the dramatic change in women's employment patterns. The number of employed women over 60 doubled with the introduction of the possibility to continue working after the age of 62 (Dagan-Buzaglo, Konor-Atias & Arian, 2014). Finally, higher accessibility to higher education has also transformed women's employment patterns (Steir & Hezberg, 2013). In recent years, higher education has become crucial for senior positions. Many women manage to integrate and move up the corporate scale due to their education, and employers are more inclined to hire women for roles that had been considered masculine in the past, particularly in the public sector (Steir & Hezberg, 2013).

In Israel, as in most developed countries, wage gaps are affected by gender segregation in the labour market. Current literature offers a number of explanations for this segregation. The main focus is the division of the higher education market, and later the labour market, into masculine fields (which are more prestigious and offer more promotion and wage opportunities) versus feminine fields (which guarantee integration in the public sector, committed as it is to substantial benefits for working mothers). Additionally, in most families, women carry the primary responsibility for the household and for raising children (Nabil, Miaari & Stier, 2016).

A Gender-Segregated Labour Market

Gender segregation in the labour market is twofold: masculine vs. feminine professional fields and gender differences in compensation and promotion options between men and women working in the same field.

Berkovitch (1997) argues that Israeli society is characterised by a tension between two main axes – the axis of family and the axis of militarism. The former, she argues, has had dramatic effects on the construction of gender in Israeli society. Furthermore, the ethos of creating the Israeli nation and the role of mothers as part of this national project have constructed Israeli women mainly as mothers, who are expected to bear children. This expectation is based both on religious-*Halachic* orders, and the Israeli fear of being overwhelmed demographically by Arab surroundings (Toren, 2003). The transformations in the labour market and the growth rate of working women (Moore & Guy, 2006), including young mothers, did not change the traditional gender-role division at home. Studies suggest that currently, two-thirds of the families in Israel women carry the sole responsibility for household chores like cooking and cleaning (Mandel & Birgier, 2016).

Women in Israel are expected to contribute their share to the household income, while also being responsible and responsive mothers, without challenging the traditional social order. Hence, many of them search for "family-friendly" work arrangements (Stier, 2005a, b). Under these circumstances, women are often considered to be "secondary providers", whose incomes and careers are less important than those of their husbands. Feminist discourse views this segregation as the result of a social construction process of the labour market, led by men and meant primarily to serve their needs (Fogiel-Bijaoui, 2005). An in-depth analysis of professions in the 20th-century labour market reveals a clear gender division between professions that are considered masculine and those that are considered feminine (often described as "pink-collar professions"). While the vast majority in fields such as education, therapy and beauty are women, men are the large majority in fields such as engineering, transportation or technical services. Based on theories of cultural feminism, Rimlet (2001) argues that these differences are partially the result of natural differences between genders. These differences in themselves are not a problem, she argues. But the professional choices of women are translated into the marginality and inferiority of "feminine" professions because of their gender identification, i.e., feminine professions are considered lower in prestige, status and compensation. The distinction between "feminine" and "masculine" professions creates a hierarchical structure, which positions the former as inferior to the latter in terms of value and importance. Figure 14.1 presents the rate of women in professional sectors.

Moreover, studies suggest that even when women and men choose the same profession, there is an internal gender segregation within each field, visible in terms of wages, promotion and career development opportunities;

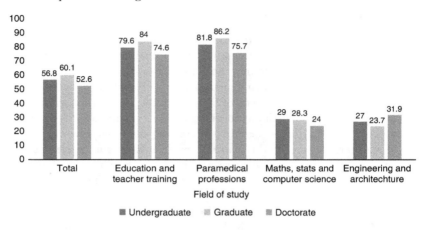

Figure 14.1 Study subject by gender.
Source: The authors, based on data from Central Bureau of Statistics (2019).

these vary between women and men in any field (whether it is considered "feminine" or "masculine"). This phenomenon points to the implicit social prejudices and stereotypes existing in the labour market and affects employers, including perceptions about the "ideal employees" or those who are worthy of promotion, and the automatic association of "masculine" with "more professional" (Rimlet, 2001). By preserving these prejudices, the labour market prioritises hegemonic groups, offering more and better options for their members (Kriesi, Buchmann & Sacchi, 2010). Thus, the figure of the "ideal employee" is deeply rooted in the capitalist perceptions of employees' availability and willingness to work extra hours as a measure of efficiency and dedication. These perceptions favour men, who benefit from higher social legitimation for investing most of their time at work, operating under the assumption that someone else (usually their wife) will take care of the household.

Gender segregation in the labour market begins with similar trends in education. Often, women choose their fields of study based on common social norms, usually focusing on fields like therapy, nursing, education, etc. Hence, while the overall rate of female students is higher than that of men, their studies usually track them toward "feminine" professions, characterised by relatively low wages and limited promotion options (Steir & Yaish, 2014). Research suggests that both women and men choose their studies based on their "interest" in the field: individuals of both genders would like to find an "interesting" job. Yet women tend to focus on human interaction when choosing their careers, while men prioritise other aspects, such as income and social status, in defining the level of their "interest" in a specific profession. These motivational differences are reflected in gender representation in different academic departments – while women tend to choose human-focused

Old-School Gender Values in a New Labour Model   263

subjects such as social work and education, men normally opt for higher-paid professions such as computers, mathematics and physics (Rimlet, 2001). Figure 14.1 presents study subjects as divided by gender.

Gender differences were also found within subjects in the choice of specialisation fields. It seems that even when they study "masculine" professions, women tend to choose the less-prestigious specialisation fields, which have less promotion options. Rahman-Moore and Danziger (2000) reached this conclusion in a study about MBA graduates. Similar findings were presented by Danziger and Eden (2007), who studied accounting students. Different preferences were found in feminine occupations as well, such as preference for education-related occupations.

The last two decades, however, have seen an institutional shift towards including women in the labour market and upgrading their position. Legislative reforms improving women's status in the labour market and protecting their rights are one reflection of this trend. Another is the rise in the number of women in higher-education institutions and a greater diversity in their subject choice. These trends in academia trickle down to the labour market. In recent decades, more women are entering the labour market, and more of them are choosing professions that had been traditionally considered masculine, such as law, high-tech and management positions (Mandel, 2013). Furthermore, Oken and Oliver (2009) found that the rate of married women in the labour market has also risen over the years. This might seem to suggest that the women find it easier to deal with the work-home conflict – yet further data shows that the conflict is still relevant as ever. When a woman becomes a mother, her career is inevitably affected.

Work-Life Balance

As mentioned above, Israeli society is family-oriented, despite its characteristics of modernity and individualism (Fogiel-Bijaoui, 2002). Parenthood is an inseparable part of the normative life path, and Israeli society is a child-centred society. Women are often expected to carry the main burden of raising children, putting working women in an inherent conflict: on one hand, they are expected to carve their professional path, or at the least, make a living – and on the other hand, they are expected to devote most of their resources and abilities to mothering their children.

Almost all women encounter the dilemma of work-life balance. Traditional sociological literature automatically assumes that women are in charge of the family (due to their expressive capabilities), while men are in charge of external tasks (due to their instrumental capabilities) (Parson & Bales, 1995). The introduction of women into the labour market created an inter-role conflict, a collision between the demands and expectations of two different arenas of activity. Under these circumstances, working mothers are required to divide their physiological and psychological resources between the arenas, inevitably privileging one over the other (Greenhaus & Beutell, 1985).

The traditional approach, which assumes limited resources, points out three main criteria for the manifestation of the inter-role conflict: (1) A time-based conflict, whereby there is a time during which a certain role must be accomplished, physically preventing the fulfilment of the other role; (2) an effort-based conflict – whereby a specific effort in one of the roles affects the functioning in the other role; and (3) a behaviour-based conflict – in which the behaviour patterns required in one of the roles contradict those expected in the other role (Greenhaus & Beutell, 1985). When women are expected to fulfil a wider range of roles, their stress level rises due to the resources invested in the effort to balance the different arenas. Furthermore, the struggle to achieve meaningful success in each arena causes frustration and dissatisfaction, which further increases stress (Hobfoll, 1989). Recent studies suggest that gender is a key mediator between work characteristics (like engagement and role), family characteristics (such as familial support, spouse support, family climate, etc.) and the different experiences of work-life conflict (Michel et al., 2011).

Literature of the last decade points to a combination of the traditional approach, which assumes an inherent tension between the arenas, and the enrichment approach, which assumes that the different arenas enrich and empower each other. The combined approach can have four different manifestations: (1) harmful – in which the conflict overcomes enrichment; (2) beneficial – in which enrichment overcomes conflict; (3) active – in which there are similarly high levels of conflict and enrichment; and (4) passive – in which there are similarly low levels of conflict and enrichment (Boz, Martínez-Corts & Munduate, 2016).

Literature points to a number of factors that may affect gender differences in this combined approach of conflict and enrichment. Some argue that men and women operate in different ways: while men erect walls between the different arenas in their lives, women operate all arenas together as a synergetic unit. It was further found that the modes of emotional expression affect the experience of conflict and enrichment, and that the social legitimation of women to externalise emotions and discuss them is also related to conflict and enrichment experiences (Rothbard, 2001).

These subtle distinctions between women and men require us to examine this conflict\enrichment issue through the subjective experiences of individuals. This perspective, which is mainly represented in "boundary work" studies, like those by Sue Clark (2000) and Ashforth, Kreiner and Fugate (2000), tries to examine the practices employed by individuals when they try to blur, combine or distinguish between the two arenas of life and work. These studies, like many others, point out the flexibility of boundaries among women and the great significance of the individual interpretation of roles and their placement within a subjective hierarchy. The interpretive discourse is anchored in the socio-cultural context and is affected by the cultural and ideological discourses of the group to which the individual belongs (Allen, Cho & Meier, 2014).

The boundary theory assumes that three main factors affect the management of boundaries between life and work: the characteristics of the boundaries, the identity of the role, and the organisational climate. The nature of the boundaries refers to the level of flexibility between home and work from a technical aspect (like the ability to work from home) and an emotional perspective (to what extent emotions are being transferred from one arena to another). Role identity refers to the construction of the role as part of the self in terms of its centrality in a person's life (for instance, the centrality of one's parenthood). The centrality of the role serves as an anchor, the focus of negotiation over boundaries. An organisational climate dictates the workplace's position on a spectrum between a standard, collective and personally adapted workplace. Hence, the organisational climate refers to the level of an employee's freedom to dictate their own boundaries and management style (Clark, 2000).

The New Labour Market

In 2013, Frey and Osborn published a comprehensive study with an analysis of professions that are about to become extinct. According to them, the likelihood of a profession's disappearance depends on the amount of repetition and routine required, as opposed to creativity and consideration. Professions that are characterised by repetitive routine tasks will be gradually replaced by computers and robots. According to Frey and Osborne (2013), the occupations of 47% of the American workforce in 2010 are fated to disappear over the next two decades. An analysis of the Israeli market in 2011, conducted by the Taub Institute, yielded similar findings (Madhala-Berik, 2011).

The traditional division of the labour market in the 20th century was based on two main sectors: the core market, composed of institutional corporations offering multiple jobs and promising order and stability to their employees; and the secondary labour market, composed mainly of small organisations offering unstable, short-term jobs (Reich, Gordon & Edwards, 1973). An Israeli study by Steir and Levin-Epstein (1988) added another sector – the public sector – which is similar in its characteristics to the core market.

Recent decades exhibit a shift from traditional employment patterns (a career path planned in advance, with a single employer and a single workplace for life) to new employment patterns (frequent changes, multiple employers, different ways of promotion and more). One of the central changes is the growing popularity of freelance jobs and small entrepreneurship. This form of employment is highly flexible, but it also entails significant questions about employment status and the relevance of employment laws and policies (Van den Born & Van Witteloostuijn, 2013). A survey conducted in the United States in 2017 revealed that freelancers constitute around 34% of the US labour market. In Israel, it was found that contract employees constitute around 25%

of the labour market. Hence, in addition to the two main sectors of core and secondary markets (alongside the Israeli addition of a public sector), there are two other new sectors – freelancers and contract workers.

Another significant change is the higher level of flexibility in work environments. The introduction of communication technology allows remote work, thus enabling employees to work in an organisation without physically being present. The flexibility of boundaries can assist employees in handling work-life balance. On the other hand, it enhances employment instability, reduces the availability of a professional community and requires employees to be highly available 24/7 (Manyika et al., 2011).

There is extensive literature about women in the labour market. Yet the interchanging influences between the gender characteristics of the labour market and the new trends in this market have not been sufficiently examined. A comprehensive theoretical study of the status of women in the new labour market is still required. Empirical work in this field is also scarce (Khallash & Kruse, 2012).

Entrepreneurship and Gender

One of the most prominent trends in the new labour market is the significant growth in the number of entrepreneurs and interest in entrepreneurship. Entrepreneurship is defined as the establishment of a new business. In most cases, the business starts as a small business, offering one service or product, and is managed by a single person, who is defined as the entrepreneur. An entrepreneur is the person who started the business and operates it, usually while taking a financial risk (unlike a salaried employee) (Baron, Markman & Hirsa, 2001).

Current literature suggests that entrepreneurs are usually characterised by qualities such as initiative, management capabilities, organisation, ambition, ability to handle ambivalent and uncertain situations, inner control, strategic thinking, resource management and risk-taking capabilities (Furnham, 1994). Moreover, the decision to open a business is often described as one based on previous knowledge, experience, social connections, available funds and the ability to raise more capital, as well as expectations for profit (Kotchoubey et al., 2013). From a political and socio-economic point of view, entrepreneurship is often described as a field that symbolises progress and as the key to technological innovation and financial progress in the states and regions where it is taking place (Audretsch & Keilbach, 2004; Fritsch & Mueller, 2004).

Traditionally, entrepreneurship was identified with masculine qualities and employment patterns, and the majority of entrepreneurs were men (Stevenson, 1986; Langowitz & Minniti, 2007). The autonomy enabled through entrepreneurship was perceived as more attractive for men, while women tended to look for safer, more secure employment patterns (Wagner, 2004). Yet, recent years have seen a rise in the number of women entrepreneurs and aspiring entrepreneurs (Weiler & Bernasek, 2001). Paradoxically, one of the main reasons for the rise in female entrepreneurship is women's decision to abandon the traditional labour market (Ascher, 2012), which is characterised by a masculine hegemony and is inherently discriminatory. Entrepreneurship allows these women to "invent" their career paths without being committed to social constructs that replicate patriarchal hegemony.

Feminine entrepreneurship is different from masculine entrepreneurship because of the social and cultural constructs at their core. The first difference is motivation: women tend to open businesses in an attempt to achieve a better work-life balance, unlike men, whose motives are mainly financial. Studies suggest that women entrepreneurs explain their choice in terms of self-fulfilment and career-life balance (Bock, 2004). Furthermore, women entrepreneurs are less inclined to take financial risks, and therefore, their businesses are normally characterised as small in size, with limited financial obligations, small risks and no partners (Weiler & Bernasek, 2001).

Often, women's attempts at entrepreneurship are blocked by structural obstacles. Thus, for instance, women entrepreneurs find it harder to raise funds for their businesses, either because they lack the necessary experience or because they are perceived as less trustworthy by financial organisations and banks (Marlow & Patton, 2005). After launching their businesses, women find it harder to maintain and develop them (Glover, 2002). These structural differences are added to the subjective experience of women of the entrepreneurial environment as negative. These subjective perceptions can lead to a mental struggle in developing and maintaining entrepreneurship (Langowitz & Minniti, 2007).

Israel is a powerhouse of high-tech and entrepreneurship. The number of start-up companies, their growth rate, fundraising and percentage of entrepreneurs (GEM, 2019) point to an extraordinary prosperity in this field (De Fontenay & Camel, 2004; Malach-Pines et al., 2005; Syed et al., 2010). Studies of Israeli society suggest that Israelis are willing to take financial risks (Harpaz & Ben Baruch, 2004); Israelis like challenges, and they are particularly independent and creative (De Fontenay & Camel, 2004; Malach-Pines et al., 2005; Syed et al., 2010). A study examining the existence of gender differences found similarities between Israeli men and women in these regards: entrepreneurs of both genders were found to have similar characteristics in terms of demographics, motivations, sense of significance and personal qualities. And yet, men were found to be more confident about their abilities and chances of success. Furthermore, men tended to mention status as a key motivation, while women focused on financial security and self-fulfilment. Malach-Pines and Schwartz (2008) suggested that these differences in motivation may offer an etiological explanation to gender differences in entrepreneurship. Other studies pinned the differences in women entrepreneurs as dependent on geographic location – rural and peripheral (Heilbrunn & Palgi, 2015; Shnider, 2017; Sofer & Saada, 2017).

Studies about women entrepreneurs often distinguish between developing and developed countries. While women entrepreneurs in developing countries choose entrepreneurship as a result of circumstances and necessity, women in developed countries tend to open a business based on considerations of self-fulfilment. Furthermore, entrepreneurship in developed countries is perceived as a masculine skill, which encompasses other masculine and prestigious characteristics such as competitiveness, social and financial prestige, and more (Gupta et al., 2009).

Research Question and Contribution

Our research question centres on the status of women in a specific sector of the new labour market: small entrepreneurship and freelance jobs. We focus on the social characteristics of female entrepreneurs and their motivations to choose this form of employment.

Our aim is to shed some light on the common characteristics of these women, their socio-demographic data and the reasons that brought them to establish small businesses (Warren-Smith, Monk & Parsons, 2001). We strive to understand and describe the characteristics of their work in this new sector and bring out their unique voice – to look at how these women use entrepreneurship to shape their work-life balance and how this discourse is anchored in the socio-cultural Israeli context.

Methodology

There is no official data about the number of entrepreneurs in general or female entrepreneurs in Israel. As we had no sample frame to refer to, a representative sample was impossible to extract. Our study is thus based on a case-study model, which aims to explore a phenomenon, normally a new one, in its natural setting. As the model is not based on a representative sample, we could not make an empirical inference, or argue that the findings are relevant to the entire population. Yet, the case-study methodology does allow us to make an analytic inference – that is, to form a theoretical logical model and present a new theory (Yin, 1994), as we have done in this case.

Our research consisted of 71 women, all members of a group called "mothers' network", intended for women entrepreneurs. The members of the "mothers' network" have a Facebook group, a WhatsApp group chat and weekly meetings. All members are mothers and freelancers, who own and manage their own businesses (which vary in scope and size). Some work full-time while others manage their businesses as a part-time job. Participation was voluntary. In order to examine the motivations of female entrepreneurs in choosing small-business entrepreneurship (Minniti, 2010), we utilised in-depth pilot interviews. We interviewed 18 women entrepreneurs, recruited by snowball sampling in four different locations in

Israel: Jerusalem, Kfar Sirkin, Mevasereth Zion and Rehovot. We encouraged interviewees to reflect on their earlier entrepreneurship experiences, employing open-ended questions which enabled interviewees to move back and forth in time. The result was a body of knowledge that helped us build a questionnaire examining the social characteristics, choices, and key motivations of women entrepreneurs. Group members who agreed to participate were asked to fill out an anonymous self-reporting questionnaire, which included questions about demographic data as well as about their work-life balance and gender-role division at home.

The first part of the questionnaire included questions about the women's businesses and their participation in "mothers' network". This part included questions about the business sector, its management style, location, years of activity, financial success, weekly work hours and the level of active participation in "mothers' network". The answers were all multiple-choice. For the question about the business' location, the options were: in the house, around the house, in your town/village, up to 30-minute drive from your house, more than 30-minute drive from your house. This part also included questions about the women's initial motivation to open a business. Regarding this question, women were asked to rate the following motivations on a scale of 1 (the weakest) to 7 (the strongest): Financial motivation – the need to make a living, business profitability, financial freedom, the opportunity to run one own's business, realisation of one's vision and self-fulfilment – a personal sense of mission, realisation of one's dreams; professional motivation – professional expertise, knowledge and experience; familial motivation – working more comfortable hours that allow me to raise the children; physical motivations – location of business; or other motivations.

The second part of the questionnaire included questions about the women's education and career, including their years of education, field of education, previous work status and employment rates at their previous workplace. This part also included questions about the division of their resources between different aspects of their lives. Participants were asked about the ideal division of their time between different spheres (out of 100% in total) as well as about time division. The spheres enumerated were social status, economic status, self-fulfilment, leisure time, community, work, family, political positions, ethnicity (Mintz & Krymkowski, 2010) and others. The third part referred to the women's positions regarding various dilemmas.

Work-Life Balance

The questions in this part were based on the internationally recognised International Social Survey Programme (ISSP) of the B.I. and Lucille Cohen Institute for Public Opinion Research of Tel-Aviv University. This part included four statements about the mutual "leaks" between home and work. One statement, for instance, was: "You find it difficult to fulfil your familial obligations due to the time dedicated to your work". Participants were asked

270   *Guy Abutbul-Selinger et al.*

to rate the frequency of this statement being true on a 4-point Likert scale: 1 = a few times a week; 2 = a few times a month; 3 = once or twice; 4 = never. A higher rate represents less mutual influence between spheres.

Positions about Women's Integration into the Labour Market

The statements were also based on the ISSP (B.I. and Lucille Cohen Institute, 2019). This part included 15 statements aiming to identify the liberal/conservative positions of the participants toward women's integration in the labour market. One statement, for example, was: "A child at preschool might suffer while their mother is working". The answers were given on a 5-point Likert scale (1 = not at all; 5 = very true). A higher rate represents a more conservative approach.

The Benefits of Taking Care of Children while Managing a Business

This part included three statements dealing with the availability of female entrepreneurs to take care of their children. For example, one such statement asserted: "Being a business owner allows me to be home with my children more often". The answers were given on a 5-point Likert scale (1 = not at all; 5 = very true). A higher rate represents a higher evaluation of the benefits of combining child-raising with managing a business.

Work Satisfaction

This part included five statements about the participants' satisfaction from various aspects of their work, such as the type of work, income, skills, professional development opportunities and general sense whether their decision to open a business was sensible. The answers were given on a 5-point Likert scale (1 = not at all; 5 = very true). A higher rate represents a higher level of satisfaction.

The fourth part of the questionnaire included some socio-demographic questions about the participants' age, familial status, religion, geographic region, number and age of children, type of educational institution attended by young children (if any), religious observance, ethnicity, personal income level and family income level.

Findings

The findings reveal that 59 out of the 71 women (83%) are sole managers of their businesses; 4 (about 6%) run it together with their spouse; 6 (around 8%) manage their business with a partner and 1 (around 1%) manage a business with two partners. Sixty-three (around 89%) of the women manage their business in close proximity of their house: in the house or in its immediate vicinity in their village. Only two of the women (around 3%) manage a business that is located more than 30-minute drive from their home. Six women (8%) did not answer this question.

As we can see in Figure 14.2, around 72% of the entrepreneurs have an academic degree; 32% of them have a master's degree. Hence, this group of entrepreneurs have a slightly higher level of education compared to the general population and the average among women (Fogiel-Bijaoui, 2005).

When analysing the participants' motivations to start a business, we found two distinct clusters: the first includes motivations that are related to the professional aspect: financial independence, management, self-fulfilment and professional development, while the second includes family-related motivations like familial commitments and physical conditions.

A t-test for dependent samples revealed a significant difference between clusters (t (67) = 3.9, $p \leq .001$). Motivations related to self-fulfilment and financial aspects were significantly higher (mean = 2.9, SD = 1.4) compared to familial motivations (mean = 3.8, SD = 1.8).

The participants in this study revealed a relatively egalitarian view about gender roles. The average position on the traditional-liberal scale was 1.8 (out of 5) with a standard deviation of 0.7. Most women did not agree with the statement about children being harmed by their mother's work (mean = 1.9; SD = 0.84). Yet when they were asked about the advantages of being freelancers in terms of taking care of their children (availability, sick days, etc.), the average was much higher – 3.3, with a standard deviation of 1.1. Hence, we can say that the participants are not traditional in their gender views; they do not think that a mother's career harms her children, but they do recognise the significant advantages of being entrepreneurs in terms of their availability for their children.

When asked about previous jobs, it was found that most of the women had been working in fields that required academic education. Most of them had worked in the public sector, in various fields. Figure 14.3 presents the distribution of previous occupations.

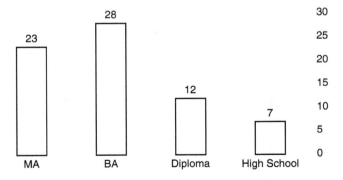

Figure 14.2 Entrepreneurs' education level.

Source: The authors.

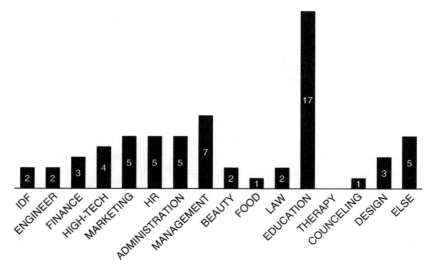

Figure 14.3 The participants' previous occupations.
Source: The authors.

The findings reviewed so far suggest that the participants in this study have higher than average education level, they hold egalitarian gender views and a meritocratic motivation for achievements. So far, it seems that women entrepreneurs in this study reflect the positive transformations in the labour market in terms of positions and education, and they view themselves as professional, educated and leading women. We would expect these positions to be reflected in their field of entrepreneurship and in an egalitarianism in their management of the business, their home and family. Yet a closer look at their work patterns as small business entrepreneurs suggests otherwise.

Fields of Entrepreneurship Compared to Traditional Gender Work Division

Figure 14.4 shows that most of the participants work in fields characterised as "pink collar" jobs, such as design, therapy, beauty, education, food and consultation. In-depth interviews with some participants revealed that even women working in the legal field, which is considered more "masculine", are mostly involved in family law.

This distinct gender rigidity was not found in the analysis of the participants' previous occupations. As we have seen, many of the sampled women had worked in fields considered masculine, such as engineering, high-tech and management. Figure 14.5 presents the varied careers of the participants as salaried employees (in light grey) compared to their gendered

Old-School Gender Values in a New Labour Model 273

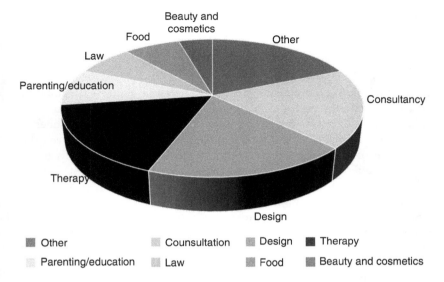

Figure 14.4 Business sector distribution.
Source: The authors.

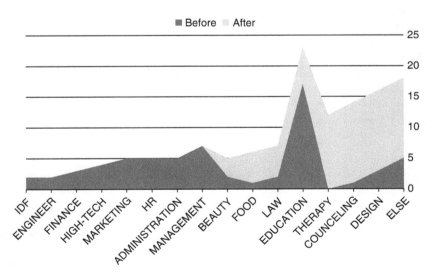

Figure 14.5 Sector division in salaried jobs compared to self-employed businesses.
Source: The authors.

entrepreneurship fields (in dark grey). This difference might suggest that the shift toward entrepreneurship reflects a gender regression – going back to the traditional patterns.

Work-Life Balance

A t-test for difference between dependent samples did not reveal significant differences between the time dedicated by the participants to family life compared to the time dedicated to professional life. The average number of daily hours for each field was around five. Yet, a comparison between the importance of family vs. work (a t-test for dependent samples) revealed a significant difference ($t(63) = 6.9$, $p \leq .001$). The findings suggest that the women attribute greater importance to their family (mean = 8.75, SD = 2.2) compared to their careers (mean = 7.6, SD = 2.2).

Some of the participants did not answer the question about their children's ages. 57% of the women who did answer said they had opened their business when one of their children was born, or when they were about one year old. This finding is in accordance with what we had found in some preliminary interviews conducted before the questionnaire. In these interviews, we learned that often the motivation to open a business originates from the difficulty of returning to the corporate labour market after birth, both in terms of work hours and because of the loss of employment continuity due to maternity leave.

Finally, the findings reveal an income gap between women and their partners. While the spouses' median income was ILS 14,500–16,500, the women's median income was only ILS 6,500–8,000. The income gaps are illustrated in Figure 14.6.

The findings are complex and sometimes contradictory: on the one hand, the participants are highly educated, most of them had worked in the core labour market before starting their own businesses, and they hold egalitarian gender positions; on the other hand, they chose to open businesses in

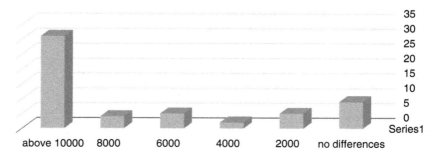

Figure 14.6 Income gaps between women and their spouses.
Source: The authors.

"feminine" fields, their income is low compared to that of their spouses and the timing of their transition is related to a familial development, such as the birth of a child.

The similarity between small entrepreneurship and a "mother-friendly position" is apparent: in both cases, the motivation is mainly familial rather than related to the women's career. Income in both cases is lower, and the schedule is more flexible and adapted to familial needs. Thus, according to the findings of the current study, the new sectors in the work market replicate the gender gap.

Conclusions

Literature about women in the labour market is expanding. Most of it criticises the hidden ways in which the labour market manages to exclude and marginalise women. Yet in recent years, there has been some data showing a rise in women's education and their rate of participation in the labour market, alongside a decrease in the intensity of the home-career conflict. It is possible, though, that this data is based on parameters that were more relevant to the 20th-century labour market. For example, the rate of academically educated women and their fields of study are not necessarily relevant to all sectors of the 21st-century labour market.

The labour market has been transforming itself in recent years, adding new sectors of small entrepreneurs and freelancers. The current study sheds light on a new sector in the labour market: small entrepreneurs.

Examining this new sector through the lens of past analyses is confusing. At first glance, it seems that the patterns of gender discrimination are eradicated by this new sector: the women we sampled are relatively highly educated, they hold "modern" views about meritocracy and gender roles, and they had been working in varied fields with significant options for career advancement.

Yet a closer look at the data reveals a different picture. Despite the demographic characteristics, women who shift to entrepreneurship often represent a new form of segregation in the labour market. Unlike their corporate past jobs, women entrepreneurs often opt for "pink collar" professions (Israeli Institution of Democracy, 2005). The findings reveal that these women invest more time in their families compared to their work, their income is significantly lower than that of their partners, and they are in practice relegated again to the status of "secondary bread earners" in their family. Finally, the timing of their transformation is often linked to the birth of one of their children.

Our conclusions, thus, are twofold: first, the findings suggest that education and perception regarding gender roles are not as effective as they were in the past in predicting women's status in the labour market. The findings suggest that women's status in the labour market, their professional choices and particularly their sector choice are all related to additional

276 *Guy Abutbul-Selinger et al.*

variables. We can see that women's professional choices are still very much related to social perceptions, positioning women as the primary-care givers in their families. The higher rates of women in the labour market did not bring about the revolution in gender perceptions. Despite their higher education, career advancement options and supportive laws, women continue to make career decisions based on familial considerations.

Second, the study presents an interesting portrayal of the small entrepreneurship sector. It seems that within this sector, there is a clear gender division. Women entrepreneurs often choose feminine fields, characterised among other things by a low glass ceiling and limited income. Hence, it seems that gender career patterns are replicated into the new labour market, with its new structure and practices.

This chapter might usefully be named "Reincarnations" – the process in which an old spirit enters a new body. At times, it seemed as if the old labour market had been transformed, becoming less segregated. Our findings suggest that the spirit of gender segregation in the labour market is still alive, entering a new body: the body of a new labour market, with a growing number of entrepreneurs and freelancers.

References

Aharon, G. (2017). "Gendered careers: Career paths of women and men in Israel", *Megamot*, vol. 52(1), pp. 245–285 [in Hebrew].

Allen, T.D., Cho, E. & Meier, L.L. (2014). "Work–family boundary dynamics", *Annual Review of Organizational Psychology and Organizational Behavior*, vol. 1(1), pp. 99–121.

Ascher, J. (2012). "Female entrepreneurship – An appropriate response to gender discrimination", *Journal of Entrepreneurship, Management and Innovation*, vol. 8(4), pp. 97–114.

Ashforth, B.E., Kreiner, G.E. & Fugate, M. (2000). "All in a day's work: Boundaries and micro role transitions", *Academy of Management Review*, vol. 25(3), pp. 472–491.

Audretsch, D.B. & Keilbach, M. (2004). "Entrepreneurship and regional growth: An evolutionary interpretation", *Journal of Evolutionary Economics*, vol. 14(5), pp. 605–616.

Baron, R.A., Markman, G.D. & Hirsa, A. (2001). "Perceptions of women and men as entrepreneurs: Evidence for differential effects of attributional augmenting", *Journal of Applied Psychology*, vol. 86(5), p. 923.

Berkovitch, N. (1997). "Motherhood as a national mission: The construction of womanhood in the legal discourse in Israel". *Women's Studies International Forum*, vol. 20(5–6), pp. 605–619.

Bock, B.B. (2004). "Fitting in and multi-tasking: Dutch farm women's strategies in rural entrepreneurship", *Sociologia Ruralis*, vol. 44(3), pp. 245–260.

Boz, M., Martínez-Corts, I. & Munduate, L. (2016). "Types of combined family-to-work conflict and enrichment and subjective health in Spain: A gender perspective", *Sex Roles*, vol. 74(3-4), pp. 136–153.

Central Bureau of Statistics (CBS) (2019). "Press release", February 25, 2019. https://www.cbs.gov.il/he/mediarelease/DocLib/2019/066/20_19_066b.pdf [in Hebrew] (Accessed: 10 April 2022).

Clark, S.C. (2000). "Work/family border theory: A new theory of work/family balance", *Human Relations*, vol. 53(6), pp. 747–770.

Dagan-Buzaglo, N., Konor-Atias, E. & Arian, O. (2014). *Women aged 60 or more in the labour market: Labour, employment and wages patterns.* Tel Aviv: Adva Center [in Hebrew].

Danziger, N. & Eden, Y. (2007). "Employment ambitions and career style preferences of male and female accounting students: Differences by gender and year of studies", *Megamot*, vol. 45(1), pp. 145–169 [in Hebrew].

De Fontenay, C. & Camel, E. (2004). "Israel's Silicon Wadi: The forces behind cluster formation", in *Building High-Tech Clusters: Silicon Valley and beyond.* Cambridge: Cambridge University Press, 40–77.

Ekstein, T., Lifshitz, O. & Larom, T. (2018). *The Labour Market as an Engine for Growth and the Reduction of Poverty.* Policy paper 03.2018. Herzliya: Reichman University, Aharon Institute for Economic Policy, Inter Disciplinary Center [in Hebrew].

Fichtelberg-Barmatz, O. & Harris, R. (2014). *Commuting Time: Do Mothers of Infants Prefer Working Closer to Their Homes?* Jerusalem: Ministry of Economics [in Hebrew].

Fogiel-Bijaoui, S. (2002). "Familism, postmodernity and the state: The case of Israel", *The Journal of Israeli History*, vol. 21(1–2), pp. 38–62.

Fogiel-Bijaoui, S. (2005). "If it is so good, why is too bad? Gender aspects of neo-liberalism in the Israeli labor market", in A. Bareli, D. Gotwin & T. Firling (eds.), *Society and Economics in Israel: A Historical and Contemporary Outlook.* Jerusalem and Sde Boker, Israel: Yad Yitzhak Ben-Zvi and Ben Gurion Institute, 183–216 [In Hebrew].

Frey, C.B. & Osborne, M. (2013). *The Future of Employment: How Susceptible Are Jobs to Computerisation.* Working Paper, Oxford University, Oxford Martin School, https://www.oxfordmartin.ox.ac.uk/downloads/academic/future-of-employment.pdf (Accessed: 10 April 2021).

Fritsch, M. & Mueller, P. (2004). "Effects of new business formation on regional development over time", *Regional Studies*, vol. 38(8), pp. 961–975.

Furnham, A. (1994). *Personality at Work: The Role of Individual Differences in the Workplace.* Brighton: Psychology Press.

GEM (Global Entrepreneurship Monitor) (2019). https://www.gemconsortium.org/file/open?fileId=50548 (Accessed: 10 March 2021).

Glover, J. (2002). "Women and scientific employment", *Science Studies*, vol. 15(1), pp. 29–45.

Greenhaus, J.H. & Beutell, N.J. (1985). "Sources of conflict between work and family roles", *Academy of Management Review*, vol. 10(1), 76–88.

Greenhaus, J.H. & Powell, G.N. (2006). "When work and family are allies: A theory of work-family enrichment", *Academy of Management Review*, vol. 31(1), pp. 72–92.

Gupta, V.K., Turban, D.B., Wasti, S.A. & Sikdar, A. (2009). "The role of gender stereotypes in perceptions of entrepreneurs and intentions to become an entrepreneur", *Entrepreneurship Theory and Practice*, vol. 33(2), pp. 397–417.

Harari-Kamar, R. (2014). *Gender Gaps in the Labour Market in 2013: Israel vs. Developed Countries.* Jerusalem, Israel: Ministry of Economy [in Hebrew].

Harpaz, Y. & Ben Baruch, D. (2004). "Work and family in Israeli society: 20 years of research", *Human Resources*, vol. 195-6, pp. 36–43 [in Hebrew].

Heilbrunn, S. & Palgi, M. (2015). "Women entrepreneurs in the rural periphery of Israel: Comparing Israeli Palestinians and Israeli Jews", in H.D. Syna & C.E. Costea (eds.), *Women's Voices in Management.* London: Palgrave Macmillan, 216–235.

278 *Guy Abutbul-Selinger et al.*

Hobfoll, S.E. (1989). "Conversation of resources: A new attempt at conceptualizing stress", *Psychologist American*, vol. 44, pp. 524–513.

Israeli Institution of Democracy (2005). "Pink collar" professions. *Parliament*, vol. 47. https://www.idi.org.il/parliaments/11174/11217 [in Hebrew] (Accessed: 12 March 2021).

Khallash, S. & Kruse, M. (2012). "The future of work and work-life balance 2025", *Futures*, vol. 44(7), pp. 678–686.

Kimhi, E. (2012). "Trends in the labor market: Employment and wages gaps", in D. Ben-David (ed.), *State Status Report: Society, Economy and Policy, 2011-2012*. Jerusalem, Isreal: Taub Center [in Hebrew], 107–140.

Kotchoubey, B., Merz, S., Lang, S., Markl, A., Müller, F., Yu, T. & Schwarzbauer, C. (2013). "Global functional connectivity reveals highly significant differences between the vegetative and the minimally conscious state", *Journal of Neurology*, vol. 260(4), pp. 975–983.

Kriesi, I., Buchmann, M. & Sacchi, S. (2010). "Variation in job opportunities for men and women in the Swiss labor market 1962–1989", *Research in Social Stratification and Mobility*, vol. 28(3), pp. 309–323.

Langowitz, N. & Minniti, M. (2007). "The entrepreneurial propensity of women", *Entrepreneurship Theory and Practice*, vol. 31(3), pp. 341–364.

Madhala-Berik, S. (2011). "Endangered professions: Computerizing trends in the Israeli labor market", in A. Weiss & D. Chernihovsky (eds.), *State Status Report – 2015*. Jerusalem, Israel: Taub Center [in Hebrew], 45–80.

Malach-Pines, A. & Schwartz, D. (2008). "Now you see them, now you don't: Gender differences in entrepreneurship", *Journal of Managerial Psychology*, vol. 23(7), pp. 811–832.

Malach-Pines, A., Levy, H., Utasi, A. & Hill, T.L. (2005). "Entrepreneurs as cultural heroes: A cross-cultural, interdisciplinary perspective", *Journal of Managerial Psychology*, vol. 20(6), pp. 541–555.

Mandel, H. (2013). "Winners and losers: Impact of welfare policy on gender wage gaps – international comparison", *Social Security*, vol. 92, pp. 33–73 [in Hebrew].

Mandel, H. & Birgier, D.P. (2016). "The gender revolution in Israel: Progress and stagnation", in *Socioeconomic Inequality in Israel*. New York, NY: Palgrave Macmillan, 153–184.

Manyika, J., Lund, S., Auguste, B.G., Mendonca, L., Welsh, T. & Ramaswamy, S. (2011). *An economy that works: Job creation and America's future*. McKinsey Global Institute. https://www.mckinsey.com/~/media/McKinsey/Featured%20Insights/Employment%20and%20Growth/An%20economy%20that%20works%20for%20US%20job%20creation/MGI_US_job_creation_full_report.pdf (Accessed: 20 May 2021).

Marlow, S. & Patton, D. (2005). "All credit to men? Entrepreneurship, finance, and gender", *Entrepreneurship Theory and Practice*, vol. 29(6), pp. 717–735.

Michel, J.S., Kotrba, L.M., Mitchelson, J.K., Clark, M.A. & Baltes, B.B. (2011). "Antecedents of work–family conflict: A meta-analytic review", *Journal of Organizational Behavior*, vol. 32(5), pp. 689–725.

Minniti, M. (2010). "Female entrepreneurship and economic activity", *The European Journal of Development Research*, vol. 22(3), pp. 294–312.

Mintz, B. & Krymkowski, D.H. (2010). "The intersection of race/ethnicity and gender in occupational segregation: Changes over time in the contemporary United States", *International Journal of Sociology*, vol. 40(4), pp. 31–58.

Moore, D. & Guy, A. (2006). "Combining family and work: Changes in perceptions and preferences of working women", *Social Issues in Israel*, vol. 2, pp. 45–72 [in Hebrew].

Nabil, K., Miaari, S., & Stier, H. (2016). "Introduction". in K. Nabil, S. Miaari, & H. Stier. (eds.). *Socioeconomic Inequality in Israel: A Theoretical and Empirical Analysis*. London: Palgrave Macmillan, pp. 1–12.

Oken, S.B. & Oliver, A.L. (2009). "Salaried work and family structure: A long-term study among Jewish women in Israel", *Israeli Sociology*, vol. 10(2), pp. 307–338 [in Hebrew].

Parson, T. & Bales, R.F. (1995). *Family, socialization, and interaction processes*. Glencoe, IK: Free Press.

Rahman-Moore, D. & Danziger, N. (2000). "Gender differences at the early stages of professional careers of MBA graduates", *Megamot*, vol. 40(2), pp. 262–279 [in Hebrew].

Reich, M., Gordon, D.M. & Edwards, R.C. (1973). "A theory of labor market segmentation", *The American Economic Review*, vol. 63(2), pp. 359–365.

Rimlet, N. (2001). "Between segregation and integration: A call for a feminist reconsideration of equality and gender in the labor market", *Law Research*, vol. 24, pp. 299–342 [in Hebrew].

Rothbard, N.P. (2001). "Enriching or depleting? The dynamics of engagement in work and family roles", *Administrative Science Quarterly*, vol. 46(4), pp. 655–684.

Shnider, A. (2017). "Back to the old village? Pre-modern gender values in the post privatization Moshav", in S. Fogiel-Bijaoui & R. Sharaby (eds.). *Dynamics of Gender Borders Women in Israel's Cooperative Settlements*. Berlin: De Gruyter, 138–145.

Sofer, M. & Saada, M.A.T. (2017). "Entrepreneurship of women in the rural space in Israel: Catalysts and obstacles to enterprise development", *Sociologia Ruralis*, vol. 57, pp. 769–790.

Stier, H. & Levin-Epstein, N. (1988). "Sectorial structure of the Israeli labor market", *Megamot*, vol. 2, pp. 111–132 [in Hebrew].

Stier, H. & Levin-Epstein, N. (1999). "Women's employment pattern: Long-term impact on their wages", *Israeli Sociology*, vol. 1(2), pp. 239–256 [in Hebrew].

Stier, H. (2005a). "Mutual relations between salaried work and family work", *Israeli Sociology*, vol. 7(1), pp. 143–160 [in Hebrew].

Stier, H. (2005b). "Relationships between pay work and work in the family", *Israeli Sociology: A Journal for the Study of Society in Israel*, vol. 7(1), pp. 143–160.

Stier, H. (2012). "Skill-based inequality in job quality: A multilevel framework". *University of Amsterdam, AIAS Working*, 122.

Stier, H. & Herzberg, E. (2013). "Women in the labor market: The impact of education over employment patterns and wages", in D. Ben-David (ed.), *State Status Report: Society, Economy and Policy, 2011-2012*. Jerusalem, Israel: Taub Center [in Hebrew], 185–211.

Stier, H. & Yaish, M. (2014). "Occupational segregation and gender inequality in job quality: A multi-level approach". *Work, Employment and Society*, vol. 28(2), pp. 225–246.

Stevenson, L.A. (1986). "Against all odds: The entrepreneurship of women", *Journal of Small Business Management*, vol. 24(4), pp. 30–36.

Syed, J., Burke, R.J., Pinar Acar, F., Malach Pines, A., Lerner, M. & Schwartz, D. (2010). "Gender differences in entrepreneurship: Equality, diversity and inclusion in times of global crisis". *Equality, Diversity and Inclusion: An International Journal*, vol. 29(2), pp. 186–198.

Toren, N. (2003). "Tradition and transition: Family change in Israel", *Gender Issues*, vol. 21(2), pp. 60–76.

280 *Guy Abutbul-Selinger et al.*

Van den Born, A. & Van Witteloostuijn, A. (2013). "Drivers of freelance career success", *Journal of Organizational Behavior*, vol. 34(1), pp. 24–46.

Wagner, J. (2004). *Are Young and Small Firms Hothouses for Nascent Entrepreneurs? Evidence from German Micro Data.* IZA Discussion Paper No. 989, Bonn, Germany: IZA – Institute of Labor Economics, https://www.econstor.eu/bitstream/10419/20224/1/dp989.pdf (Accessed: 10 May 2021).

Warren-Smith, I., Monk, A. & Parsons, S. (2001). "Women in micro-businesses: Pin money or economic sustainability for rural areas", in *Proceedings of International Conference – The New Challenge of Women's Role in Rural Europe*, Nicosia, Cyprus, 5–7 October 2001, 4–6.

Weiler, S. & Bernasek, A. (2001). "Dodging the glass ceiling? Networks and the new wave of women entrepreneurs", *The Social Science Journal*, vol. 38(1), pp. 85–103.

Yin, R.K. (1994). *Case Study Research Design and Methods: Applied Social Research and Methods Series.* Second ed., Thousand Oaks, CA: Sage Publications Inc.

15 The Emergence of Open Banking and its Implications

Sascha Struwe

The Nature of Open Banking Service

Open banking is nothing less than a revolution in the business model of the existing structures within the financial system. It is poised to disrupt traditional business models of financial service providers and transform the service landscape and its ecosystem. At its core, open banking is concerned with customer data liberation. Simply put, it enables customers to share their financial account data to access advanced financial service experiences. In a traditional banking setting, only banks and their customers could enter those data and provide the financial services to their customers in a trusted manner. Instead of having the direct customer–bank relationship that is to a large extent based on customer–bank trust, in open banking, data can be shared with other unaffiliated financial service and IT providers, and this ability on the one hand undermines the traditional customer–bank relationship, while on the other hand unlocks a variety of new services typically accessed via mobile applications (Harrison, 2021b).

As of now, open banking is mainly associated with two types of service. They include Account Information Services (AIS) and Payment Initiation Services (PIS). AIS allows customers to collect and store financial information across bank accounts in a single place and dashboard, enabling a holistic understanding of the economic situation, potentially making money smarter, while the financial IT service provider can secure the aggregation and thus, get an overview of a client's finances as well. For example, artificial intelligence (AI) may be used to identify services better suited to one's needs (e.g., insurance or subscriptions). Alternatively, it can contribute to better managing rewards, budgets and investments, effectively avoiding overdrafts and improving returns.

PIS facilitate the use of online payments between two actors even if they are not part of the same payment system by creating an interface that bridges both accounts and shares necessary information to enable such transaction. For example, applying for a loan typically requires various actors to share paperwork (e.g., recent financial history, income statements

DOI: 10.4324/9781003326731-15

or credit scores) to evaluate the eligibility of a customer for a credit line. PIS enables this exchange by clicking a button, eliminating manual compilation and accreditation of documents and streamlining the lending process (Harrison, 2021b).

Thus, both types of open banking services aim to enhance financial transparency and effectiveness for the customer by offering integrated and real-time services (BBVA, 2019; Harrison, 2021b).

The emergence of open banking can be generally associated with regulations triggered within Europe. This began in 2007 when the European Union (EU) introduced the Payment Service Directive (PSD), facilitating the development of a single payment market within the EU. Its objective was to promote more competition and innovation and enhance financial service efficiency. Following the PSD, the EU proposed the PSD2 in 2013, which became effective from 2018 to 2019. Based on PSD, PSD2 further enhanced its initial objectives and sought improvement in areas such as customer protection, transaction security and the popularisation of PIS and AIS services. Most notable is the demand for banks to offer application programming interfaces (APIs) to enable the free exchange of financial customer account data across un-affiliated parties (Brodsky & Oakes, 2017; Meichenitsch, 2016). Thus, institutional changes have made banks adopt changes in their business models in terms of financial service provision to customers and redefine their value proposition.

This action is the cornerstone of the disruptive force of open banking. Effectively, this legal innovation discontinued banks' long-lasting monopoly on customer data, liberalising its use. Undoubtfully these actions have implications on value creation for the involved parties.

Value Creation within Closed and Open Banking

Traditional banking is characterised by closed relationships between banks and their customers. Customer data created and captured in this relationship is stored and controlled by the respective bank. Service offerings are mostly standardised one-size-fits-all service packages that more or less fit a wide range of customer needs. To reiterate, a critical aspect of this relationship is that the customer only uses channels (e.g., mobile apps) owned by the bank. Hence, the bank only defines financial services that a customer can enjoy. In such a system, customers are passive recipients of linear service exchange, reducing them to a source of data that has little to no influence on value creation and data usage.

The promotion of the PSD2 showed that regulators were not satisfied with the existing approach to value creation as it encouraged monopolistic behaviour and very little innovative drive. Customers were limited in finding better alternatives due to a lack of competition and disconnect of markets, complicating new market entries. In addition, a continuation of the traditional model may have threatened the viability of EU financial institutions and systems overall as technological developments within global markets would have eventually challenged incumbent actors.

In contrast, open banking opened up the traditional process of value creation by introducing APIs providing access to customer account data, making it significantly easier to develop and launch new financial services for third party providers (TPPs). This action effectively enlarged the value creation potential by introducing more actors and reiterating the customer's role as the essential driver of the value creation process. As customers have control over their data, they can invite other service providers into their service experience. Because of this ability, value creation is much more network-like, and service is formed around the customer instead of being dictated by the bank. Moreover, open banking banks become subject to enhanced competition because now they are one of the potential service providers but not the only ones. This change in the value creation process also shows that value is co-created among several actors.

Figure 15.1 shows the change mentioned above in the value creation process and the potential complexity of multiple actors in the co-creation process.

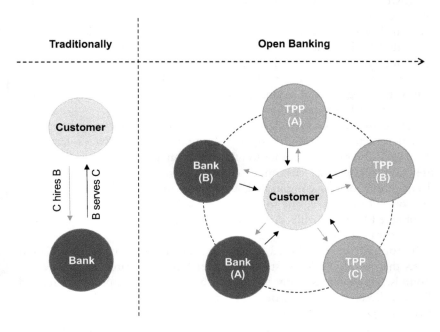

Figure 15.1 Closed vs open banking value chain.
Source: The author.

Implications for Value Creation

Inevitably, these changes within the value creation process have implications for the actors involved. For example, incumbent banks will need to overcome the limitations of siloed developments and legal systems. They will need to develop capabilities for creating compelling and secure APIs and services, and their respective marketing. In addition, building and maintaining potentially coopetitious partnerships at scale with diverse banking and non-banking actors will become necessary. Following, we will discuss these and other related issues through the lens of the changing sources of value in business models.

Source of Value

Traditionally, establishing a customer relationship was the primary source of value for incumbent banking players such as retail banks. This approach was associated mainly with the fact that people tended to stay with one bank due to the lack of differentiation across banks and the involved complexity of change. Often banks exploited these circumstances to generate profits by upselling more expensive and supposedly higher-value services such as credit cards.

However, within an open banking service system, the traditional source of value has become eroded as regulative and technological developments have made it substantially more convenient for customers to change service providers. In this new context, other factors have become more significant for value creation. First is the access to customer data and the associated ability to analyse and offer advanced value propositions. Second is the ability to integrate and connect unaffiliated actors and service offerings across financial services and around the customer needs.

Before any service provider can offer customers open banking services, they need data access. Within open banking, this process always starts with the permission of the customer to utilise its financial data for specific service use cases. Despite the customer's consent, gaining access to the required data is more or less complicated, depending on the individual legal framework. For example, due to the PSD2, banks within the EU are obliged to offer APIs that enable unaffiliated TPPs to access customer data with their permission free of charge.

In contrast, in the United States (US), as of now, no such regulation exists that forces TPPs to establish partnerships with banks or find workarounds. However, as many incumbent banks consider open banking and TPPs a direct threat to their ability to create value, establishing formal relationships can be complicated. Therefore, many TPPs rely on a technological workaround. Screen scraping (SS) is a practice that enables TPPs to utilise customer login data, pretending to be the customer and use automated scripts to retrieve customer data from incumbent bank databases.

The Emergence of Open Banking and its Implications 285

What is problematic with SS is that it holds risks such as privacy infringements, data breaches or accountability concerns. In addition, it is considered an inefficient and costly process as it requires constant modification to keep up with any alteration in the bank's customer interface to avoid process failure.

Yet, having access to data alone does not offer significant value. What creates value is the ability to provide customers with financial services beyond the traditional service of brick-and-mortar banking or disconnected online banking environments. Successful open banking actors emphasise customer-centricity by offering convenient and personalised solutions such as AIS or PIS. Yet, to provide these advanced services, firms need profound capabilities and a particular mindset. For example, data science capabilities such as the application of artificial intelligence (e.g., machine or deep learning) increasingly become the backbone of effective service design to identify customer needs and offer technical solutions. Moreover, cross-functional and agile project management practices have established themselves as standard to address the fast-paced and diverse nature of technological and societal developments.

In addition, so far, most open banking actors have been establishing themselves as specialised service providers. However, to create most value in open banking, it makes sense to combine and re-bundle various specialised service offerings or modules into one more holistic service offering. Therefore, collaborative and orchestration capabilities are essential to use system resources efficiently. This also implies a need for modified business model configurations. Actors must identify new ways of sharing revenues and costs fairly across involved actors considering potential aspects of competition in other service settings (i.e., coopetition).

Business Model Configurations

It is becoming increasingly clear that traditional modes of value creation will not work well in open banking systems, which has implications for bank business models. Banking as a Platform and Banking as a Service are popular choices to address the demands of open banking systems (Bracket et al., 2018; Mallick, 2020).

In the Banking as a Platform business model, banks can aggregate existing traditional banking services and combine these with new and digital services from TPPS to offer new services on their channels. Banks utilise external services to strengthen their core offerings, making the bank a consumer of TPP APIs and services. Arguably this is a suitable model for banks that aim to swiftly expand their service offering and potentially capture new market opportunities through strategic partnerships. In addition, it enables banks to offer services that go beyond traditional financial services, promoting cross and up-selling opportunities with relatively low costs. From a TPP perspective, this model is attractive as it provides access to the banks' existing distribution network and customer base and the opportunity to bundle their services with bank services to create more compelling offerings.

In contrast, the Banking as a Service model positions the bank as a distributor of core financial services through TPP or partner-owned distribution channels. Following this model, banks establish themselves as developers of APIs and services to promote core financial services (e.g., payments, loans or investments). From an organisational standpoint, this business model is most suitable for banks with strong technological and development capabilities and the processual competencies to facilitate the necessary back-end interactions and flows. This model is attractive because it enables banks to expand their distribution channels and market reach by leveraging the customer base of external partners, effectively reducing associated costs. For TPPs, this model is attractive as it enables these actors to increase revenue based on service offerings they may otherwise not be able or interested in providing.

In reality, both models must be understood as two points on a spectrum. Banks will likely situate themselves somewhere in between or have several business models depending on individual market circumstances and strategies (see Figure 15.2). Alternatively, it may even be possible for banks to consider starting entirely new organisations independent of their headquarters' legacy and influence.

Independent of the business model configuration, all models show that banks will need to rethink their approach to value creation differently from traditional banking, emphasising customer needs, portfolios of initiatives, new interpretations of customers and orchestration of the system resources (Bracket et al., 2018).

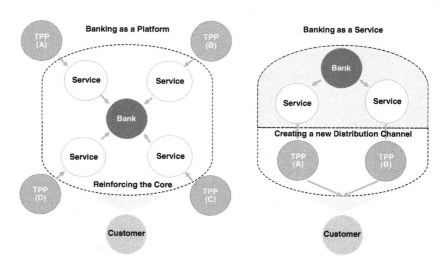

Figure 15.2 Business model configurations for open banking.
Source: The author.

To create value within open banking, it becomes essential to be better at identifying customer pain points. Banks must develop an intimate understanding of crucial segment customer journeys and realise what aspects of their journey represent unmet needs. Gaining this clarity will position banks to determine business model configurations and associated offerings and avoid resource waste.

Moreover, banks will need to break free from traditional approaches to service design that focus on few one size fits all offerings and start to nurture portfolios of different service initiatives. The portfolio approach enables banks to capitalise from more innovative concepts that may otherwise not be considered feasible or seen as unrealistic at least initially. This approach will require constant experimentation and evaluation of the most suitable offerings. Hence, successful agile development practices become essential, emphasising speedy trial and error iteration cycles of continuous learning and modification. Moreover, it implies a more flexible and fluent organisation willing to embrace change, which requires significant investments into employee development and structural change.

Open banking also challenges the definition of who is a customer or a resource for value creation. As the presented business models suggest a limited view, focusing on individual or corporate account holders is not timely anymore. For example, TPPs are increasingly sought-after candidates. However, to attract these actors' banks must understand what characterises value for TPPs. Two elements stand out: access to a significant customer base and the ability to support seamless integration of TPPs APIs and services into the existing bank system. Therefore, banks must also develop sufficient capabilities such as partner marketing or onboarding practices and resources like software development kits, design templates or developer environments and communities.

Success in open banking also requires banks to balance the forces of their development initiatives and TPPs resources. What is particularly complex in this situation is that some of these elements may compete with one another, highlighting the challenge of coopetition. Depending on the bank's strategic choice, this will require more or less alignment of governance and technology across the open banking service system. Particularly from a technological standpoint, banks should open up to the idea of engaging with standard practices of developer environments native to digital-first TPPs. That includes transparent communication of service initiatives and underlying technologies in developer communities. Moreover, this transparency can contribute to enhanced collaborative opportunities and potentially avoid competitive challenges.

Risk of Negative Implications in Open Banking

The previous discussion on the implications of value creation in open banking (e.g., source of value and business model configurations) shows that open banking differs significantly from closed banking. At its core is the notion that APIs facilitate data exchange, promoting value creation opportunities. However, this new paradigm also entails risks, affecting actors' value creation.

From a customer perspective, many concerns around security and accountability arise. For example, customers of financial services now begin to deal with new and perhaps unestablished TPPs, demanding a credit of trust that these actors are as trustworthy as well-known banks. This question relates to the concern of whether TPPs such as FinTech start-ups will have the ability to provide the same degree of protection of finance and data as established banks. In addition, considerations of appropriate data use are valid. Financial customer data holds valuable information such as consumer behaviour and patterns, financial position or timetables, which unregulated TPPs may exploit. Technological developments may also pose a threat. APIs are at risk of inefficient code practices that do not adhere to best-practice coding standards. Similarly, the authentication of identity and secure data transactions must be ensured at all stages of the service process. These concerns are complicated for customers to evaluate, for instance, in terms of actor credibility or reliability. Hence governments and/or lead institutions must develop strict governance and quality mechanisms to avoid adverse customer outcomes.

From a bank perspective, perhaps most imminent is the threat of being disintermediated from customers and becoming an underlying infrastructure provider (e.g., data storage and provision) with limited potential for value capture. Arguably, disintermediation is inevitable, and there is no getting around it. Why is it inevitable? On the one hand, other open banking actors will utilise technological workarounds such as SS to access customer data independent of the bank's approval, creating an expensive arms race to prevent these actions. On the other hand, it is unlikely that one bank will have sufficient resources and capabilities to offer an attractive portfolio of open banking services continuously. Hence, other actors such as TPPs will always be involved and potentially in between the bank and their customers (see Figure 15.3). However, the degree to which this happens and what implications this may have for the banks' ability to create and capture value is dependent on how banks will position themselves, which relates to the careful design of new business models in line with market directions.

Furthermore, from a system perspective, open banking seems to suggest that open systems will be more resilient because of enhanced resource diversity and opportunities for resource integration across system actors. This notion relates to the concept of agency in that open banking should enable actors to freely choose which resources to integrate depending on their current needs.

However, each integration process has implications for actor agency because they involve costs (e.g., asset specificities). Therefore, actors will need to carefully evaluate associated costs, which suggests that actors will naturally strive for the most cost-effective outcomes. Likely, achieving the

The Emergence of Open Banking and its Implications 289

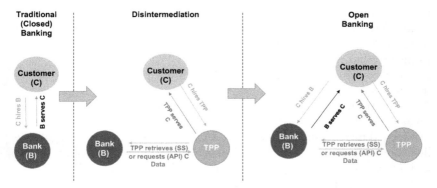

Figure 15.3 Transformation of the value chain – traditional vs open banking.
Source: The author.

most cost-effective results will be possible by partnering and integrating resources from actors with solid network effects such as API aggregators or banks with a significant customer basis. That raises the question of whether open banking is genuinely open and if the construct may not rather be temporary until resource consolidation has established dominant actors. Such a scenario favours those who understand how to build attractive platforms like Big Tech (e.g., Apple, Alphabet or Microsoft), which points towards a potential risk of banking or finance becoming monopolised in the hands of a few technology leaders. Most apparent may become the risk of dominant platform owners dictating specific attributes of actor value propositions (e.g., design standards or scope of functionality), limiting the system actor's individual ability to create value.

Therefore, the danger of market concentration open banking points towards the importance of understanding differences in interpreting what creates value across actors. For instance, incumbent banks may consider tight control and limited access for TPPs as essential for value creation. In contrast, TPPs may believe data access and barriers prevent value creation. Dealing with this disagreement across actors will be inevitable as open banking limits the degree of choice whether actors want to interact or not. For example, banks within the EU are forced to provide APIs that provide access to customer data. Hence TPPs can, with the customer's permission, utilise that data no matter what banks think about that or not. Thus, developing appropriate mechanisms to achieve reciprocally beneficial outcomes and/or to have strong alternative service offerings that offset unintended interaction costs is critical.

Open Banking across the Globe

The state of open banking system maturity across the globe is very diverse, which can be related to various factors. Among them are differences in types of markets and associated regulative forces, customer readiness, technology and competition. Therefore, open banking across the globe will break at different times, giving rise to distinct markets and shaping various forms of value creation.

The two most dominant market forms of open banking are regulator-directed and market-led markets. Regulator-directed markets like in the EU and Australia show are characterised by a strong regulative push for open banking and the definition of regulatory frameworks. In contrast, market-led markets such as the US and Canada have little to no regulative developments but show industry-led developments by incumbent actors and TPPs (Center for Regulatory Strategy, 2022; Mallick et al., 2021).

The development of the open banking system within the EU has been driven mainly by the promotion of the PSD and PSD2, forcing actors to engage and take steps to implement open banking. While these directives were initially met with compliance, today, sophisticated open banking solutions and platform constellations are emerging. Because of these developments, some countries like Brazil consider the EU regulation as a blueprint for successful open banking implementation. However, differences across European countries are significant. The UK and Nordic countries with the Nordea Group and DNB Banks as their frontrunners are leading in developing open banking systems (Brodsky & Oakes, 2017; Harrison, 2020).

Open banking as a concept in the US is not new. Incumbent banks and TPPs have initiated many industry-led initiatives because of recognised commercial opportunities. However, value creation and the actual effectiveness of open banking in this market are limited. Open banking actors in the US experience inconsistent rules and practices due to disconnected industry-led initiatives (e.g., partnerships between Chase with Intuit and Wells Fargo with Xero and Finicity) (Brodsky & Oakes, 2017; Harrison, 2020), leading to various conflicts of interest.

Considering these differences across markets enables a fruitful discussion on value creation. A point of departure in this discussion are questions like whether value creation and capture are simultaneous events, what implications a potential disconnect has on long-term system resilience and for whom value is created.

It seems that regulator-directed markets emphasise long-term value creation for the system or society while market-led markets emphasise immediate value creation for the individual actor. A backdrop to the motivation of open banking regulation in the EU is helpful to understand this assumption more clearly. The EU initiated open banking because they were unsatisfied with its financial system's degree of competition and innovation. This inertia is concerning considering the importance of the financial system for the overall economy, as the financial crisis of 2007–2008 has shown, and the increasingly blurry boundaries between industries, particularly beneficial BigTech firms. Now the regulative push for open banking broke traditional closed systems of value creation and encouraged a systemic perspective of actor-to-actor exchange.

Indeed, open banking actors were forced to make investments that may cannibalise existing businesses and may not create sufficient supplementary returns. However, these pressures also facilitated the development of new business models and mechanisms of value creation more aligned with the demands of digital markets. This development may cause some actors to disappear, and others may momentarily experience a limited ability to create and capture value. Yet this competition and innovation also enhance the chances of the remaining actors to stay competitive within new future market paradigms.

On the other hand, market-led markets like the US without open banking regulation are characterised by conflicts of interest and incumbent actors utilising market or bargaining power to limit the degree of system openness. While this enables these actors to create and capture value for themselves today, it remains questionable if this approach will prepare them for future market paradigms potentially threatening system resilience. For example, successful open banking actors within the EU establish themselves as platform players, learn how to develop a working relationship with diverse system actors and create new services such as premium APIs and embedded finance solutions. In contrast, US actors continue to fight over concerns about whether data should be shared across actors and to what degree this should be possible, limiting learning and innovation.

Now, this discussion cannot point out which system will eventually create more or less value. That is because value comes in various forms (e.g., economic, well-being or viability), and its creation is dependent on multiple diverse factors sometimes unique to a given context. This discussion highlights that innovation can drive system resilience, positively affecting overall value creation, and its initiation may increasingly be dependent on systemic change (e.g., regulative developments).

The Future of Open Banking

It is highly likely that open banking is only the first step in a more profound change process of value creation on a systemic level. For example, as of now, open banking in the EU is limited to AIS and PIS services, or in other words, payment-related services. Other countries have already taken first steps towards a broader scope of services. The UK is preparing for an open finance system that is not limited to AIS or PIS, but includes anything finance related such as insurance, pension or wealth management. Beyond this is what is referred to as open data. Currently, Australia is defining what this may mean. In theory, open data will enable customers to control and manage their data connected to any service such as telecommunication, utility or healthcare. Considering these developments, it becomes clear that the future points towards interconnected data networks that will fundamentally change how value is created and captured (Harrison, 2021a; Mallick & Kapoor, 2021). What remains to be seen is whether this seemingly accessible and inter-connected future will indeed be so open as examples of Chinese ecosystem mega players like Alibaba or Tencent show. Their services increasingly offer everything captured by the open banking, finance and data concepts within one single-walled garden, the so-called mega apps, with the firms being the gatekeepers (FinTech Futures, 2020).

Conclusion

This chapter introduced an account of the emerging open banking eco-system and discussed its implications for value creation. It shows that open banking is characterised by significant complexity, manifesting itself in di-verse market and business model configurations, depending on factors like regulative maturity. At the core of these developments is the connection and integration of previously dispersed resources (i.e., data) through the use of technology (i.e., APIs). This change has established new sources of value such as ecosystem resource orchestration and integration capability.

However, all of this development is relatively new, and much remains un-clear, particularly with the outset of open banking evolving to open finance and eventually open data. Future studies should investigate potential risks involved in the transition, including system resilience and competition and innovation perspectives. Moreover, value creation within the open banking context remains underinvestigated. For example, future research may want to explore how to innovate within complex service systems (e.g., customer co-creation) or what business model configurations may be the most appropriate forms of market and regulative frameworks? In addition, as technology reduces boundaries for re-source exchange and integration, studies should investigate the implications on customer well-being (e.g., service experience and desire for privacy).

References

BBVA (2019). *Everything you need to know about PSD2*. BBVA. https://www.bbva.com/en/everything-need-know-psd2/. Accessed on 10 September 2021.

Bracket, T., Dab, S., Kok, S.A., & Peeters, M. (2018). *Retail banks must embrace open banking or be sidelined*. BCG. https://www.bcg.com/publications/2018/retail-banks-must-embrace-open-banking-sidelined. Accessed on 10 September 2021.

Brodsky, L. & Oakes, L. (2017). *Data sharing and open banking*. McKinsey. https://www.mckinsey.com/industries/financial-services/our-insights/data-sharing-and-open-banking. Accessed on 20 October 2020.

Center for Regulatory Strategy (2022). *Open banking around the world*. Deloitte. https://www2.deloitte.com/global/en/pages/financial-services/articles/open-banking-around-the-world.html. Accessed on 15 April 2022.

FinTech Futures (2020). *Is the future of banking not open but closed?* FinTech Futures. https://www.fintechfutures.com/2020/03/is-the-future-of-banking-not-open-but-closed/. Accessed on 20 October 2020.

The Emergence of Open Banking and its Implications   293

Harrison, H. (2020). *Open banking around the world*. Mastercard. https://www.mastercard.com/news/perspectives/2021/mapping-out-the-world-of-open-banking/. Accessed on 20 October 2020.

Harrison, H. (2021a). *Mapping out the world of open banking*. Mastercard. https://www.mastercard.com/news/perspectives/2021/mapping-out-the-world-of-open-banking/. Accessed on 25 September 2021.

Harrison, H. (2021b). *What is open banking? Your essential guide*. Mastercard. https://www.mastercard.com/news/perspectives/2021/open-banking-101/. Accessed on 25 September 2021.

Mallick, A. (2020). *Two business models for monetising open banking*. Accenture. https://bankingblog.accenture.com/two-business-models-for-monetizing-open-banking. Accessed on 20 October 2020.

Mallick, A. & Kapoor, A. (2021). *Unlock the promise of open banking market infrastructure*. Accenture. https://bankingblog.accenture.com/unlock-the-promise-of-open-banking-market-infrastructure. Accessed on 25 September 2021.

Mallick, A., McIntyre, A., & Scott, E. (2021). *Ready to catch the open banking wave?* Accenture. https://www.accenture.com/dk-en/insights/banking/open-banking-moving-towards-open-data-economy. Accessed on 25 September 2021.

Meichenitsch, E. (2016). *Open Banking is here to stay*. Banking Hub. https://www.bankinghub.eu/innovation-digital/open-banking-stays#:~:text=Anew banking world&text=In a nutshell%2C Open Banking, have access to this data. Accessed on 20 October 2020.

16 Trans-fur-able Resources? Strategic Responses to a Crisis in the Danish Mink-Related Ecosystem

Michael S. Dahl, Louise Brøns Kringelum, Agnieszka Nowinska, and Thomas Roslyng Olesen

Introduction

On the 4th of November 2020, the Danish Prime Minister held a press conference stating the spreading and risk of mutation of COVID-19 at Danish mink farms (Ministry of the State of Denmark, 2020). To act timely and contain the spread of the virus, the Danish state ordered all minks to be destroyed. The total shutdown of Danish mink production created ripple effects for the sub-suppliers and related industries closely linked to this specialised production field, which are now forced to rethink the strategic direction of their companies.

The strategic direction of companies rests on decision-making. However, strategic decision-making during and at times of after-shock events has been consistently overlooked (Bonn & Rundle-Thiele, 2007). Since the COVID-19 pandemic, the theme has gained attention and based on the experiences from the past years, firms' strategic responses to a crisis are now regarded as a critical and growing topic for both research and practice (Kozachenko et al., 2021). When facing a crisis, firms are forced to make strategic responses to ensure survival. Strategic responses and the direction taken by a firm based on strategic decision-making never occur in a vacuum. The decisions regarding the strategic direction can create bull-whip and ripple effects. These effects relate to the influence on other actors in the supply chain and the whole ecosystem. The bullwhip effect pertains to the actors upstream from the focal organisation, and the ripple effect relates to the ones downstream, thus, affecting both organisations in direct transactional interaction with the company through the common value chain and parts of the broader ecosystem affiliation. In that sense, it can represent a process of strategic decoupling from an ecosystem perspective.

This chapter explores the interplay between organisational and inter-organisational resilience of an ecosystem exemplified by the Danish mink-related industry. Following Adner (2017, p. 40), the ecosystem can be defined as *"the alignment structure of the multilateral set of partners that need to*

DOI: 10.4324/9781003326731-16

interact for a focal value proposition to materialize". This definition highlights the **structure** of interdependent activities that are interlinked to create a value proposition across organisational boundaries. While each organisation in an ecosystem has its business model, they are interconnected in producing a joint value proposition.

Through the ecosystem perspective, we focus on the multilateral set of actors that maintain value creation processes which are central to creating the joint value proposition of high-quality mink fur. This allows us to look beyond the linear transactional flow of the supply chain to the interdependencies across the ecosystem. Further, by showcasing the process of ecosystem breakdown as an effect of the total shutdown of Danish mink production, we explore the resilience of the individual mink-related firms when they become decoupled from the joint ecosystem value proposition, they were previously part of. In this case, mink-related industries cover feed kitchens and affiliated sub-suppliers, equipment producers, wholesalers, veterinarians, transportation providers, pelters and auction houses that are directly dependent on the breeding of mink (see Figure 16.1).

The mink-related industries represent a tightly coupled ecosystem with a focus on resource efficiency and cost reduction, which has reduced the resilience of the whole ecosystem. Because of the shutdown of the Danish mink industry, the Danish state has negotiated financial compensation for mink farms and those mink-dependent related industries that cannot be converted to other types of production (Ministry of Finance, 2021). For this reason, the mink-related sub-suppliers now find themselves in a position where they are accessing both resource and competency pools to identify possibilities for survival as their strategic response to the crisis.

Crisis and Resilience in Ecosystems

There is vast literature on crisis and crisis management. A crisis can be defined as a *"disruption that physically affects a system as a whole and threatens its basic assumptions"* (Pedersen et al., 2020). Compared to other disruptive events, the COVID-19 pandemic was unprecedented since it did not fit the linear crisis lifecycle models with a specific pre-crisis period (i.e., the stages of a crisis are pre-crisis, crisis emergence, crisis occurrence, crisis aftermath and post-crisis. In the crisis emergence and occurrence phase, the managerial tasks are preparing, postponing, reacting, responding and recovering.) (Pedersen et al., 2020). Facing such a rare and harsh critical event, scholarly attention has turned to study firms' behaviour (Kozachenko et al., 2021). This inquiry is crucial since the way decision-makers respond to a crisis will largely determine whether they survive and thrive.

Four main strategies were identified as strategic responses to crisis, i.e., retrenchment, persevering, innovation and exit (Wenzel et al., 2020). Retrenchment refers to a strategic narrowing down of the scope of firms' activities including *"reductions of costs, assets, products, product lines, and overhead"*

296 *Michael S. Dahl et al.*

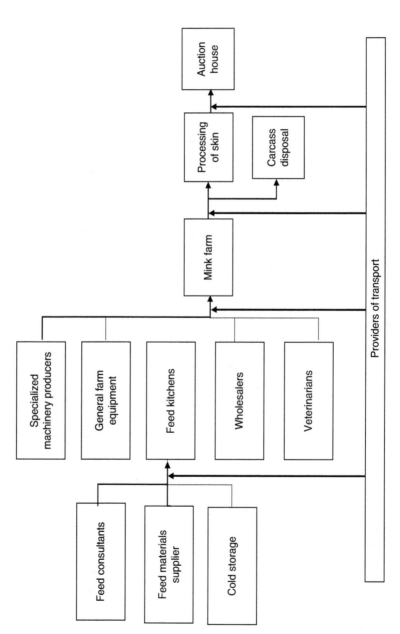

Figure 16.1 Overview of actors in the Danish mink production industry.
Source: The authors.

(Pearce & Robbins, 1993, p. 614). This strategy is effective in the short run, as prolonged crises may lead to severe performance losses for firms. Perseverance relates to sustaining firms' activities and avoiding strategic renewal and re-configurations. The strategy has proven more effective than venturing into strategic renewal too early. The strategy is efficient in the medium run and is conditional on firms having slack resources. Innovating is a long-term strategy that firms may use to substitute persevering. It may require excess capacity and the ability to do "bricolage" and exploit the fungibility of the firm's resources. Finally, the exit strategy means the discontinuation of firms' activities. It may occur once other strategies prove inefficient, but it may also be used strate-gically, paving the way to a strategic renewal of another new venture.

Scholars further elaborate on different types of strategy firms use during a crisis. Implementing such strategies is linked to financial, social and technological capital and is crucial for establishing resilience. Alternatively, Kozachenko et al. (2021) identify alternatives, including stakeholder relationship revival, pricing mechanisms and organisational compliance. Stakeholder relationship revival re-flects the change of interactions with stakeholders during a crisis, which is especially evident when firms tighten their links with stakeholders that are critical for the operational activities of the firm:

Ivanov and Dolgui (2020) suggest that *"the analysis of survivability at the level of ISN (intertwined supplier network) requires a consideration at a large scale as the resilience of individual SCs (supply chain)"* (Ivanov & Dolgui, 2020). ISN encapsulates entireties of interconnected SCs which, in their integrity, se-cure the provision of society and markets with goods and services (p. 2095). Studying individual responses to crisis allows us to understand changes and survivability of larger structures such as networks or ecosystems of firms with the distinction of down and upstream effects of the event studied (respectively ripple and bullwhip effects). A well-functioning ecosystem requires coherency, and the coherency between ecosystem actors affects the degree of system-level resilience (Tsujimoto et al., 2018). Indeed, more nuanced distinction between the bullwhip and ripple effects has been studied by Dolgui et al. (2018), accounting for the magnitude of shock related to the location in the supply- or value chain.

Further, data collection during the initial lockdown of the mink fur production in Denmark is presented. Based on this, we elaborate on the ecosystem structure of the Danish mink industry and explore the immediate strategic responses of the companies engaged in upstream, midstream and downstream activities of the Danish mink ecosystem. This analysis identifies potential drivers of the strategic responses across the ecosystem and the effects on both individual and joint resilience.

Data Collection

To study strategic responses to a significant exogenous shock in the Danish mink-related industry, in-depth qualitative insights are required. We started

298   *Michael S. Dahl et al.*

by identifying suppliers in the industry using secondary data. We reached out to local Chambers of Commerce (Erhverv Norddanmark, Dansk Industri), local consultancies specialised in agriculture (Agrinord) and the government agency in charge of agriculture. In agreement, these institutions advised us that a comprehensive report or single industry identifiers did not exist for the broad and diverse industry of mink suppliers. We, therefore, kept records of all companies mentioned in media outlets reporting on the collapse of the mink industry and its consequences industrywide from the beginning of November 2020. In December 2020, we had a list of more than 40 companies originating from different media outlets, internet searches and "snowballing", i.e., investigations of companies with profiles similar to those already identified through local company databases (proff.dk). At that stage, we also established contact with a newly formed Mink Suppliers' Industry Association (Dansk Minkerhverv), which shared a list of its members, including 45 companies. We crosschecked the overview developed through desk research to identify all relevant suppliers' categories based on this list.

At the beginning of January 2021, we started reaching out to various categories of firms by email explaining the purpose of our study (see Figure 16.1). We used a vouch from the Industry Association or the local chamber of commerce in some cases. Additionally, we supplemented such a direct approach with information from secondary, publicly available sources such as newspaper articles and company web pages. Table 16.1 lists the category of firms we collected data on, the type of data (primary or secondary interviews) and the number of cases within each category.

Our interviewee selection had several goals: first, we attempted to target interviewees from various suppliers, spanning multiple categories to achieve

Table 16.1 Data sources

Category	Sources	Number of cases
Auction house	Newspaper articles + webpage	1
Carcass disposal	Interview with manager + webpage	1
Cold storage	Interview with manager + webpage	1
Feed consultants	Interview with manager	1
Feed kitchens	Newspaper articles + other interviews	1
Feed materials supplier	Interview with manager + webpage	1
General farm equipment	Interview with manager + webpage	1
Mink farm	Interview with owner/manager	1
Processing of skin	Manager/owner + webpage	1
Providers of transport	Newspaper articles + other interviews	1
Specialised machinery producers	Interviews with managers + webpage	4
Veterinarians	Interview with manager + webpage	1
Wholesalers	Interview with manager + webpage	1

Source: The authors.

a balance among them. Second, we tried to vary firms and different indicators, while choosing firms within each category. For instance, among equipment producers, we aimed at covering various types of equipment and diverse firms (small vs. giant, older and younger, etc.).

We contacted around 20 firms by email, and 11 agreed to participate in an online interview. Several firms who responded to our call are simultaneously present in two different supplier categories. In addition, three other companies are part of the same corporate structure. We used a single interviewee per firm.

We conducted most of the interviews virtually in January and February 2021. During each interview, two interviewers were present. We followed a semi-structured protocol with four interview parts: the first one is dedicated to company characteristics (assets, activities, suppliers and customers, following the structure of the business model canvas); the second part focuses on a summary of the firm's situation after the shock in November; in the third part, we covered the strategic response, and finally, all interviews were concluded by discussing the outlooks for the future of each firm. We used the first part of the interviews to analyse firms' value propositions and activities using the Business Model Canvas. The interviews were used to qualify firms' strategic responses. The interviews lasted between 30 and 90 minutes and were all recorded and transcribed. The research team members have worked independently to classify the firms' characteristics and their strategic responses. After that, diverging cases were discussed in the forum until a consensus could be reached. Based on the classifications and both individual and joint value propositions, and the firm- and ecosystem-level activities and resources, the following section will present the ecosystem for the Danish mink-related industry.

The Ecosystem of the Danish Mink-Related Industry

The ecosystem of the mink-related industry is organised around the shared value proposition of producing high-quality mink fur. The mink fur from Danish farmers has traditionally been of high quality, which has been reflected in their ability to obtain a higher price for the skins (Hansen, 2014).

The ability to produce high-quality skins has evolved by developing the ecosystem of mink production in Denmark since the 1930s (Hansen, 2014). This has led to the establishment of ecosystems of mink farmers, especially in the northern and western regions of Jutland. These ecosystems are comparable to regional innovation systems in which concerted strategic actions enable knowledge creation, sharing and learning between companies in close proximity (Lundvall, 1992). Through the close transactional links of the actors, they have been able to produce a value proposition of high-quality mink fur by establishing a solid ecosystem of relational capital, knowledge and innovation.

All firms have their approach and intent when part of an ecosystem (Adner, 2017). Thus, organisations in the ecosystem naturally take on various roles

300 *Michael S. Dahl et al.*

during the establishment of the ecosystem and continuously adapt their activities to the reciprocal relationship with other actors (Jacobides et al., 2018). The ecosystem of mink fur production is centred on the mink breeders (the mink farms), who, to a large extent, both directly and indirectly organise the activities of the other actors due to the dependency on the breeding and production of minks. Following the definition of Adner (2017), the Danish mink industry ecosystem shows a tight alignment structure based on multilateral relations united by joint value creation efforts to create a focal value proposition.

The alignment structure is shown through the positions and activity flows between actors. The Danish mink industry is characterised by many upstream and downstream activities organised around the mink farms. A generic overview of the central business actors in the mink production industry is illustrated in Figure 16.1.

The generic overview reflects the ecosystem centred around the mink farm, with related industries representing both upstream and downstream.

Upstream, the supply chain comprises companies supplying goods and services for the mink farms. These upstream activities can roughly be divided into five categories. The first group of suppliers is the producers of different types of specialised machinery for the mink farms and the pelting firms. These suppliers produce feeding machines and other types of equipment for the farms. They furthermore provide a wide range of machinery to the pelting firms. This includes drums, conveyor belts, machinery for skinning, fleshing and pinning the minks and equipment for drying and cleaning the skins. In this group, you find a combination of large firms and smaller and specialised workshops highly dependent on the mink industry.

The second type of suppliers is the suppliers of equipment for the mink farms and the pelting firms. For the mink farmers, these suppliers provide sheds, watering systems, manure systems, food silos, cages, breeding boxes, traps, etc. The pelting firms provide supplies of sawdust, mink paper, etc. In this category, you will find firms that are also present in the first category and firms engaged in the construction of farms or providing equipment and supplies to the pelting firms. The firms in this category vary in their dependence on the mink industry.

The third type of supplier is the specialised feed kitchens that produce the feed for the mink farms. The feed kitchens have a range of suppliers that may be divided into four groups. The first group provides the ingredients for the feed, which mainly consists of animal by-products from pigs and fish. The firms in this category are intermediaries that will buy the elements from the food production industry, the fishing industry and butcheries. The second group of firms provides cold storage capacity for the suppliers. The third group of suppliers provides the machinery and equipment for making and storing the food (such as cookers, mixers, choppers, grinders, silos, etc.). Finally, the fourth group includes consultants that advise the feed kitchens on optimising the food quality based on the ingredients available. The feed kitchens may have this service in-house or outsourced. The feed kitchens that provide feed for the mink farms are highly specialised and thus, highly dependent on the mink industry.

The fourth type of supplier is the wholesalers of equipment to the agricultural sector. These suppliers provide general supplies of clothing, tools, farm equipment, etc., and to some degree also specialised equipment for mink farmers, including cages, pest control, cleaning equipment, etc. As this group of suppliers services many different parts of the agricultural sector, they are not dependent on the mink industry.

The fifth type of supplier is the veterinarians visiting the mink farms. These companies provide two types of service – vaccines and flea control and prevention. The veterinarians are supplied by 4–5 apothecaries/pharmacies licensed to provide drugs to farm animals. Large multinational pharma firms produce these drugs. Neither the veterinarians, the apothecaries, nor the pharma firms are particularly dependent on the mink industry. They mainly provide medicines and services to other production animals such as cows and pigs.

The downstream supply chain encompasses the companies that handle the disposal of mink carcasses and pelting firms that process the fur. In 2020, there were five large pelting firms in Denmark. These firms are almost 100% dependent on the Danish mink farmers. The mink fur is brought from the pelting firms to an auction house (99% to Kopenhagen Fur), where they are sold to fur manufacturers and fur traders before they are brought to retailers and finally to the end consumers.

The remaining parts of the skinned minks from the pelting firms are disposed of by firms that operate as intermediaries between the pelting firms and the bio-energy companies. Some of these intermediaries are highly specialised (and thus highly dependent) on mink, whereas others deal with the remains of a wide range of different types of production animals. The animal fat is transported to a biodiesel plant and turned into biodiesel. The mink carcasses are transported to a biogas plant, where the corpse is turned into energy or used as fertiliser components.

Throughout the supply chain, the providers of transportation play an essential role. This group will transport the raw materials (meat and fish) to the feed kitchens and the feed from the feed centres to the farms. They are furthermore responsible for bringing the minks from the farms to the pelting facilities, transporting the carcasses and the fat from the pelting to the biomass and biodiesel plants and transportation of the furs from the pelting firms to the auction house and onwards to the retailers and finally to the end consumers. The transportation may be conducted in-house (e.g., by a feed kitchen) or outsourced to third parties. The transportation providers include large and small firms with varying degrees of dependence on the mink industry.

The Danish mink-related industries are characterised by the co-operative movement, with both auction houses and feed kitchens being owned by

302   *Michael S. Dahl et al.*

mink farmers. This reflects the multilateral relations representing the ecosystem that cannot be reduced to several bilateral interactions due to the tight coupling of activities. The efforts toward creating common value in producing a value proposition are naturally challenged when the ecosystem's structure is eliminated. In the following, we explore what drives individual organisation's strategic choices and resilience when an ecosystem characterised by a high degree of coherency and tight coupling is closed down overnight.

Analysis

As mentioned earlier, the Danish mink industry provides a unique context to explore the factors that drive immediate strategic responses and affects both individual and joint resilience when an entire ecosystem is hit by a shock, such as the one caused by the Covid crisis. The recent study by Wenzel et al. (2020) points to four strategic responses to a crisis – retrenchment, persevering, innovation and exit. However, their study does not explore (1) what factors influence the different strategic choices and (2) how the company's position in the value chain will affect the strategic responses to the crisis. In the analysis, we will examine the immediate strategic responses of the companies engaged in upstream, midstream and downstream activities of the Danish mink ecosystem (see Figure 16.2).

Upstream Activities

When exploring the upstream part of the mink ecosystem, we find that companies in the five main areas have pursued three different strategies. The mink farms' feed kitchens and most specialised machinery manufacturers have generally decided to exit when they saw their customers disappear. The wholesalers, veterinarians and the suppliers of general farm equipment are pursuing a retrenchment strategy, while the sub-suppliers (and one machinery producer) are attempting to innovate their way out of the crisis.

When analysing our interview data, we find that the main reason for the machinery producers and the feed kitchens to exit was their almost total dependence on the Danish mink farms. The equipment developed and produced by the machinery manufacturers was tailor-made for mink farms and could not readily be modified to serve other types of farming. Furthermore, it was not considered a viable solution to target mink farmers in other countries. There were two reasons for this: first, the demand for machines in other countries was much lower than in Denmark. All the machinery producers we interviewed had customers abroad. Still, foreign markets only made up a small part of the total turnover, as these markets relied on cheap labour rather than investments in machinery. Consequently, they evaluated that an expansion in these foreign markets could not nearly replace what had been lost when the home market

Trans-fur-able Resources? 303

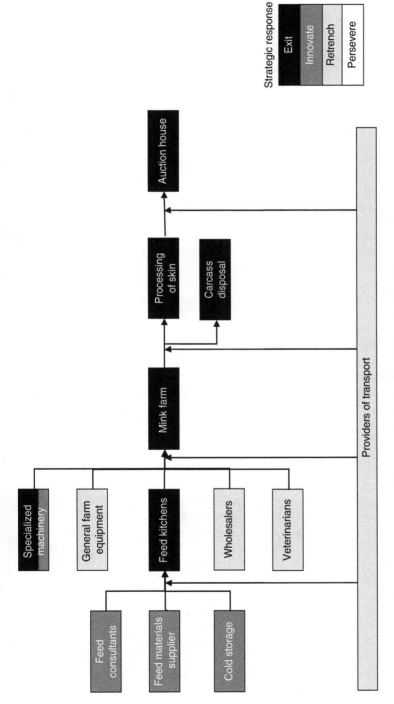

Figure 16.2 Immediate strategic responses of the actors in the Danish mink production industry.
Source: The authors.

collapsed. Second, our interviewees expected that the international market would be flooded with cheap second-hand equipment from the closed Danish mink farms for years to come. Developing other types of business model innovation – for example, applying the know-how and manufacturing facilities to produce different equipment – was also not considered a viable solution.

The managers of the feed kitchens also pursued an exit strategy. These firms were even more dependent on the Danish mink ecosystem than the equipment manufacturers, as they were established to serve the farms in the Danish mink ecosystem. Consequently, they shut them down at a short notice when the mink farms stopped purchasing animal feed.

The groups of wholesalers, veterinarians and suppliers of general farm equipment pursued a different strategy: retrenchment. These firms were characterised by a more diverse customer group than the feed kitchens and the specialised equipment providers. This meant that even if they were an essential part of the mink ecosystem, they were far less dependent on it than the feed kitchens and the machinery producers. A manager of a large veterinarian firm explained that even if they had a 40% market share in the Danish mink farming, this only made up approximately 10% of their total turnover. The remaining turnover came from cows and pigs. The immediate response of the firm was to quit the mink segment and focus their attention on the other areas rather than attempting to engage in something new. The wholesalers and providers of farm equipment found themselves in a similar situation. The more diverse customer portfolio allowed them to focus on their remaining business areas (e.g., other types of farming or other industries) and merely consider the mink industry a lost business opportunity. Even so, this decision was not without consequences, as the manager of a wholesaler of farm equipment explained:

> Mink made up around 33% of our turnover. So it was a pretty big part of our business that we lost.
>
> (Manager of a wholesaler)

Finally, the group of companies consisting of sub-suppliers to the feed kitchens (and one machinery producer) attempted to pursue an innovation strategy to respond to the closure of the mink farms. The group of suppliers to the feed kitchens shared some similarities with the firms seeking the retrenchment strategy – most importantly, they were not relying 100% on the Danish mink ecosystem. Several of these firms attempted to use their competencies and production facilities in new ways. The manager of a freezing factory that produced blocks of frozen raw materials for the (now closed) feed kitchens explained it in this way:

> We have tried to become more independent of the mink industry. We obtained permission to handle consumer fish … [and] … we also had the idea that we would try to produce salmon oil. We developed an installation that could do this.
>
> (Manager of a freezing factory and a cold storage company)

It was, however, not an easy task to pursue this strategy, the manager explained. The intake of consumer fish is fluctuating which created new problems. In order to keep a qualified staff at the site, the factory needed to have other activities when the intake was low. Providing feed for the mink sector was important in that regard (i.e., providing critical mass). The salmon oil installation was also dependent on the mink farms. In order to be profitable, the company needed a buyer who could use the by-products from the oil production. Previously, the Danish feed kitchens could use this by-product, but it was difficult to find new customers. Searching for new markets abroad (i.e., feed kitchens in other countries) was not considered a viable solution in the long run, due to the low value of the product which would not make up for the cost of transportation. In the short run, the only solution was to destroy the by-products or sell them to mink farmers and feed kitchens abroad. Both solutions incurred a loss for the firm. This exemplifies, that even if the firm was able to venture into new areas, it was difficult to pursue a profitable innovation strategy that was completely disconnected from the mink industry.

The manager of another company that imported meat and fish to produce mink feed and pet food explained that they would attempt to develop their products into pig feed.

Only one producer of specialised machinery for mink farms decided to pursue an innovation strategy. Based on their know-how on farm equipment, they were developing electrical machinery for use in gardening, farming and light construction works. The manager expects it to be a tough turnaround as the company was relying 90% on the mink industry.

The aforementioned examples demonstrate some "bullwhip" effect on upstream suppliers in the mink industry as several categories of suppliers decided to exit and retrench. The bullwhip effect, however, did not prevent other suppliers from innovating.

Midstream Activities

The midstream activities of the mink ecosystem are made up of the mink farms, the firms that do the pelting and the firms that process the mink carcasses. Contrary to the firms engaged in upstream activities, the firms in the midstream have almost exclusively pursued an exit strategy.

The government forced the mink farmers to put down all their minks in November 2020. Once the breeding animals had been killed, it was difficult to start over again. According to the farmers we interviewed, it was impossible to use the production facilities (cages, buildings, machines, etc.) for other types of farming. Consequently, most farmers decided to exit the business. By April 2022, only 13 out of 1259 Danish mink farmers had applied for permission to restart their farming activities (Berlingske, 2022).

The closure of mink farms had immediate consequences for the firms that pelted the animals. These firms were utterly dependent on minks from

306   *Michael S. Dahl et al.*

Danish farms, as the current regulation prevented the firms from importing minks from mink farms in other countries, as explained by the managers:

> *We have this thing called viral plasmacytosis, a disease you have abroad. So the Danish Veterinary and Food Authorities will not allow ... imports of mink from Poland or Lithuania, Latvia or the Netherlands.*
>
> (Manager of a pelting company)

Without the supply of minks from the Danish farms, the managers of the five major pelting firms decided to exit the business.

The closure of the five pelting companies had immediate consequences for the firms that were specialised in handling the waste products from the pelting process. This activity mainly consisted of buying mink carcasses and mink fat and selling them to bio-plants. The manager of one company explained that they were 100% dependent on Danish minks. He furthermore explained that they had considered an innovation strategy – namely to enter into the market for handling waste products from pigs and chickens. However, he explained that this market is consolidated with high entry barriers, which were deemed impossible to face. Consequently, the firms have been without activities after the closure, and an exit strategy was most likely.

In sum, the effects of COVID-19-induced closure of mink producers were severe on the midstream suppliers and all of them adopted the exit strategy.

Downstream Activities

The single most crucial downstream activity in the Danish mink ecosystem is the auctioning of mink fur. Almost all fur from the Danish farms was sold through the Copenhagen-based auction house Kopenhagen Fur. Shortly after the decision to shut down the mink farms, the CEO of Kopenhagen Fur announced that the company would pursue an exit strategy and shut down within the next 2–3 years (Fagbladet3F, 2021). In sum, the downstream activities have greatly suffered from the ripple effects as they adopted an exit strategy.

Providers of Transportation

The transportation providers consist mainly of trucking companies present along the entire supply chain. The upstream activities transport meat leftovers from the slaughterhouses to the feed kitchens, and the processed mink feed to the farms. In the midstream activities, they transport the minks from the farms to the skinners and the carcasses from the skinners to the bio-plants. And finally, in the downstream activities, the fur is transported to the auction houses and to buyers. The providers of transportation mainly pursue a retrenchment strategy. The manager of a trucking company explained that his company had specialised in servicing the mink business over the past 25 years and that the industry accounted for around 60% of his turnover. The cooled bulk trailers for handling the mink feed are very specialised and cannot be used for anything else. However, he expected to be able to find new customers for around 50% of his 10–12 trucks that are specialised in this transportation:

> *I need to look for alternative cargo in a market under pressure, so I will have to adjust the company activities accordingly.*

(Manager of a trucking company)

Discussion

The analysis earlier suggests that the companies engaged in upstream, midstream and downstream activities of the mink ecosystem have responded very differently to the COVID crisis and shut down the mink production industry. Firms engaged in mid- and downstream activities (farmers, pelting firms, companies that handle the waste products from the pelting and the auction house) were all characterised by total dependence on the Danish mink ecosystem. Furthermore, these firms contained resources that were not very fungible. This includes exceptionally specialised resources for servicing this particular ecosystem and could not easily be applied or converted to something else. On the other hand, the upstream activities were characterised by different degrees of dependence on the ecosystem and more generic (fungible) resources that could be applied for other purposes. This could be activities in other industries in Denmark or abroad. Based on these initial findings, we propose that: (1) the dependence on the ecosystem and (2) resource fungibility are essential factors when determining the strategic decisions in response to a crisis such as the one that followed the COVID.

Figure 16.3 presents an overview of the actors' responses in the Danish mink-related industry based on their dependence on the ecosystem and the fungibility of their resources. The figure suggests that firms with high dependency on the ecosystem have pursued an exit strategy – regardless of whether their resources were fungible or not. Firms seek the innovation strategy with medium dependence and highly fungible resources. Two factors may explain these findings: First, a firm needs time and money to respond by innovating, regardless of whether the innovation takes form by developing new products, growing new markets or changing the organisational setup.

A company that loses its total turnover overnight has little time to redirect its resources. The feed kitchens are a good example. They could potentially have used their competencies and production facilities to produce pet food or feed for other types of farm animals. However, their entire customer base disappeared without warning, leaving them without any

308 Michael S. Dahl et al.

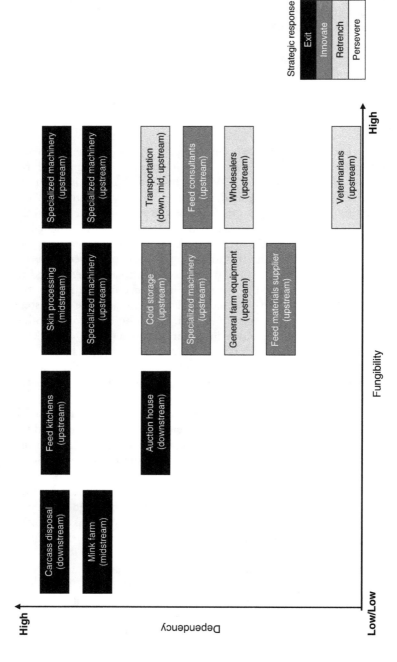

Figure 16.3 Ecosystem dependency and resource fungibility in the Danish mink-related industry.

Source: The authors.

chance of recalibrating their business. A company with a significant equity pool could potentially pursue an innovation strategy. However, the Danish mink ecosystem firms had suffered from poor market conditions for several years and were in no position to make such a move.

On the other hand, a diverse customer portfolio can offer companies sufficient time to redirect their resources. A study of industrial transformation by Olesen (2016) suggests that it takes firms several years (from the crisis) to unleash their innovative potential and venture into new markets or develop new technologies. This also corresponds with the paper by Wenzel et al. (2020), who categorise the innovation strategy as a long-term response to the crisis. Therefore, those firms that had other sources of revenue – but for whom the mink ecosystem was still important – had the opportunity to pursue an innovation strategy.

A second explanatory factor may be that managers of firms utterly dependent on the Danish mink ecosystem may be unwilling to venture into a new market or industry. Several of the firms in this study had been part of the Danish mink ecosystem for decades. They had had the same customers and suppliers for years, creating strong relations with no need to look outside their existing network. Consequently, the barriers to making such a radical shift could be considered too high. The manager of a company that developed specialised equipment for Danish mink farms explained it in this way:

Could we target other areas? Maybe we could, but then you could just as well start a new business?
(Manager of a manufacturer of specialized equipment for mink farms)

The manager of another manufacturer of specialised equipment voiced a similar concern. However, his management team decided to try their luck and pursue an innovation strategy by venturing into new areas:

We have been looking into developing some other machines[for a different industry]. But ... I mean ... this is something completely different. I mean ... we are working with mink. This is what we are good at ...
(Manager of a manufacturer of specialised equipment for mink farms)

Other firms are less dependent on the ecosystem. These firms have experience with other business activities or other markets. This also suggests that these firms have the necessary resources to pursue an innovation strategy.

The third strategy identified by Wenzel et al. (2020) – the retrenchment strategy – was mainly pursued by firms with low or medium dependence on the ecosystem. Most of these firms simply decided to write off the mink-related activities and continue with their remaining activities. Wenzel et al. (2020) suggest that the retrenchment strategy is a short-term strategy

310   *Michael S. Dahl et al.*

pursued while you wait for the market (or, in this case, the ecosystem) to recover. However, the ecosystem ceased to exist in our case, as only 13 of the 1,259 farmers decided to apply for permission to resume production. We argue that the retrenchment strategy is not necessarily a short-term strategy but maybe a mid-term or even long-term strategy under certain circumstances, i.e., when a whole ecosystem collapses. Finally, we did not find any cases where the companies pursued a perseverance strategy. Again the particular circumstances, i.e., the ecosystem ceased to exist from one day to the other across Denmark, i.e., the national ecosystem collapsed, made it virtually impossible for the affected firms to sustain their current level of business activities.

However, our analysis suggests that dependence and fungibility are not sufficient to explain the strategic choice of a manager who is faced with a crisis. Looking closer at the strategic response of actors in the Danish mink ecosystem, we find that several firms with highly fungible resources and high dependence on the ecosystem still decided to pursue an exit strategy. This is surprising, as these firms are among those heavily influenced by the crisis and have the potential to innovate their way out of it. The manager of a provider of machinery for the mink farms recognised that their competencies could be applied for other purposes:

> *We could do service on other types of machinery. We have milling cutters and lathes, which we could use as suppliers for other firms. You could also move to Ukraine [where there is a large mink industry] and continue there [with service activities].*
>
> (Manager of a machinery provider)

Even so, he had decided to pursue an exit strategy:

> *We have talked about doing other things … but you can say that we are a bit discouraged. It [the entire process] has been too hard on us. So we have decided to shut down.*
>
> (Manager of a machinery provider)

The manager of a pelting firm had the same concerns. Even if there were opportunities to use the firm's resources in new ways, he was not willing to pursue these opportunities:

> *We have been very good at developing machines [for pelting]. I am a smith, and we have a development unit where we develoedp many of our machines. We could [move the business abroad and continue what we are doing], but it would require that I take my family and move to Poland. I have small kids here. So, of course, we could do it, but it comes with a price, right? So we have decided to shut down.*
>
> (Manager of a pelting firm)

The two aforementioned examples and several others suggest that high dependency and high fungibility are not enough to drive innovation to respond to a crisis. A third factor is equally important and even conditional for adopting strategies other than exit: *Willingness to act*, which is at the level of the entrepreneur as a key decision-maker.

Our study empirically tests firms' strategic responses proposed by Wenzel et al. (2020). The bullwhip and ripple effects are present but not of equal magnitude. Moreover, we found that suppliers with the same location in the supply chain displayed heterogeneous responses to the crisis based on various drivers.

Our findings are summarised in Table 16.2. First, based on Wenzel et al. (2021), we expected that firms with high dependence and high fungibility would either innovate or exit. The increased reliance on the ecosystem would prevent them from pursuing the retrenchment or perseverance strategies. However, it would also force them to react. We expected that the fungibility of their resources would allow them to innovate or exit. However, we found that these firms decided to exit in our empirical setting, as explained earlier. This may be because the actors in the ecosystem had experienced poor market conditions for several years, which was also combined with a promise from the Danish government to be compensated if they decided to exit.

Second, we expected firms with high dependence on the ecosystem and low fungibility to exit. This was confirmed in the empirical study. Third, we expected the firms with inadequate support and high fungibility to retrench, persevere or innovate. The low dependence on the ecosystem suggested that these firms would not be severely hit and therefore. an exit strategy seemed unlikely. Furthermore, the high level of fungibility indicated that these firms had the potential to pursue an innovation strategy. Our empirical study confirmed that these companies pursued retrenchment or nnovation strategy, but not the perseverance strategy. This may be due to the particular practical context where the ecosystem ceased to exist. Finally, we expected firms with low dependency and low fungibility to

Table 16.2 Summary of main findings regarding firm characteristics and strategic response

Firm characteristics		Strategic response	
Dependence	Fungibility	Expected findings based on Wenzel et al. (2020)	Empirical findings in current study
High	High	Innovate/exit	Exit
High	Low	Exit	Exit
Low	High	Retrench/persevere/innovate	Retrench/innovate
Low	Low	Retrench/persevere	Retrench

Source: The authors.

312   *Michael S. Dahl et al.*

pursue a retrenchment or perseverance strategy. In this case, an innovation response was unlikely due to the low fungibility of the resources, and exit was unlikely due to the expected dependence on the ecosystem. In the empirical study, we found these firms to pursue a retrenchment strategy, but not a perseverance strategy – for the same reasons that were mentioned earlier.

Conclusion

In this chapter, we have explored the immediate strategic responses by different types of actors along with factors that drive the strategic responses in line with Wenzel et al. (2020): retrenchment, persevering, innovation and exit. Specifically, we studied the crisis that hit the Danish mink-related industry ecosystem when the government decided to close all activities in November 2020. Exploring the response of the individual actors in the ecosystem, we find that firms engaged in midstream and downstream activities pursued an exit strategy. In contrast, firms involved in upstream activities pursued retrenchment or innovation strategies. This suggests that the extent of the ripple effect has been more severe than the one of the bullwhip effect in this empirical case. We found three factors that influenced the choice of a strategic response to the crisis: (1) dependency on the ecosystem, (2) fungibility of the resources in the company and (3) the willingness of the owners (who are often also the managers) to pursue new opportunities.

We find that firms highly dependent on the ecosystem prefer to pursue an exit strategy. It takes time to innovate, and this is something you do not have if your current market disappears overnight. Low dependency on the ecosystem allows firms to retrench and continue their activities outside the ecosystem. If a firm's resources are fungible, they may even pursue an innovation strategy to repurpose these resources in other areas. Exit is usually not a preferred strategy for firms with low dependence on the ecosystem, as the business will often be able to continue its activities. However, for a firm to pursue an innovation strategy, the owner needs to be willing to do so. We find several cases where the owner can see a way out of the crisis (through innovation) but is unwilling to pursue it.

Regarding the time perspective of the various strategic responses, we propose that retrenchment strategy may, in some cases, be a long-term response to the crisis (and not a short term as presented by Wenzel et al. (2020, see also Figure 3/Table 2). Finally, we propose that the perseverance strategy is only relevant when an ecosystem is temporarily hit by a crisis and not (as in this case) a more or less permanent closure of the industry. With this empirical study of a crisis in a (geographically limited) ecosystem, we thus shed more light on the drivers and time-horizons of the strategic responses to crisis proposed by Wenzel et al. (2020). However, a business ecosystem can hardly be expected to be resilient enough to mitigate a politically driven decision to shut down an entire industry. However, the strategic responses of the different actors reflect the interplay between firm-level and ecosystem-level resilience that is affected by the degree of decoupling across the ecosystems, as exemplified throughout this chapter.

There are two boundary conditions to our study. Our interviewees indicated the existence of strong and informal ties governing the formal transactions within the ecosystem, recently also formalised in a network organisation. We speculate that the importance of social capital may be, through a "lock-in" effect, affecting firms' subsequent strategic responses. The "lock-in" effect occurs when firms keep doing business with partners, they already have experience with and knowledge of, regardless of transactional outcomes. Such influence may prevent firms and decision-makers from innovating, effectively restricting the range of available strategic responses. Second, similar effects may materialise because of the political context. Our empirical study unfolded following an unprecedented political decision to stop all mink farming activities in Denmark. All actors in the ecosystem were offered a compensation if they declared an exiting strategy. Based on the nature of this political decision, the firms we sampled may have been more inclined to express their willingness to exit or, conversely, less likely to mention the use of any other strategic response for fear of affecting the compensation negotiations with the government.

We are aware that the nature of the unique, extreme case of the Danish mink-related industry means that the generalisability of our study is limited to a significant, exogenous shock targeting a whole sector in a context with a strong institutional field. In addition, the political context and the role of relationships are non-trivial here. We, therefore, suggest that future research studies exogenous shocks of various intensity and strategic responses in cases free of political pressure or implications. Also, scholars could study firms' strategic responses in a non-networked industry. We also suggest exploring the dynamics of strategic responses in a longitudinal research design. Possible changes and evolution or even the configurations of strategic responses used over time may show novel insights into the strategy-making process.

References

Adner, R. (2017). "Ecosystem as structure: An actionable construct for strategy", *Journal of Management*, vol. 43(1), pp. 39–58. 10.1177/0149206316678451

Berlingske (2022). 13 Minkavlere søger om penge til at genoptage erhverv", 2 April 2021, https://www.berlingske.dk/danmark/13-minkavlere-soeger-om-penge-til-at-genoptage-erhverv (Accessed on 10 May 2022).

Bonn, I. & Rundle-Thiele, S. (2007). "Do or die – Strategic decision-making following a shock event", *Tourism Management*, vol. 28(2), pp. 615–620.

Dolgui, A., Ivanov, D. & Sokolov, B. (2018). "Ripple effect in the supply chain: An analysis and recent literature", *International Journal of Production Research*, vol. 56(1–2), pp. 414–430.

314 *Michael S. Dahl et al.*

Fagbladet3F (2021). "Kopenhagen Fur lukker ned: Frustrerede ansatte føler sig ladt i stikken", 21 May 2021. https://fagbladet3f.dk/artikel/frustrerede-ansatte-foeler-sig-ladt-i-stikken

Hansen, H.O. (2014). *Den danske pelssektor – struktur, konkurrenceevne og international placering.* København: Jurist- og Økonomiforbundets Forlag.

Ivanov, D. & Dolgui, A. (2020). "Viability of intertwined supply networks: Extending the supply chain resilience angles towards survivability. A position paper motivated by COVID-19 outbreak", *International Journal of Production Research*, vol. 58(10), pp. 2904–2915.

Jacobides, M.G., Cennamo, C. & Gawer, A. (2018). "Towards a theory of ecosystems", *Strategic Management Journal*, vol. 39(8), pp. 2255–2276. 10.1002/smj.2904

Kozachenko, E., Amitabh A. & Shirokova, G. (2021). "Strategic responses to crisis: a review and synthesis of promising research directions", *Review of International Business and Strategy* (forthcoming).

Lundvall, B.-Å. (Ed.). (1992). *National Systems of Innovation: Towards a Theory of Innovation and Interactive Learning.* Pinter Publishers.

Ministry of Finance (2021). Bred aftale sikrer fuldstændig erstatning til minkavlere og følgeerhverv. Available at: https://fm.dk/nyheder/nyhedsarkiv/2021/januar/bred-aftale-sikrer-fuldstaendig-erstatning-til-minkavlere-og-foelgeerhverv/ (Accessed on 10 May 2022).

Ministry of the State of Denmark. (2020). Pressemøde d. 4. November 2020. Available at: https://www.stm.dk/presse/pressemoedearkiv/pressemoede-den-4-november-2020/ (Accessed on 12 May 2022).

Nordjyske (2020). Bump på vejen: Mink-krise rammer vognmand. 26 October 2020. https://nordjyske.dk/nyheder/thisted/bump-paa-vejen-mink-krise-rammer-vognmand/978ef042-a062-418b-ad92-79e6854431fe (Access on 10 April 2022).

Olesen, T.R. (2016). *Da Værfterne Lukkede: Transformationen af Den Danske Værftsindustri 1975-2015.* Odense: Syddansk Universitetsforlag.

Pearce, J.A. & Robbins, K. (1993). "Toward improved theory and research on business turnaround", *Journal of Management*, vol. 19(3), pp. 613–636.

Pedersen, C.L., Ritter, T., & Di Benedetto, C.A. (2020). "Managing through a crisis: Managerial implications for business-to-business firms", *Industrial Marketing Management*, vol. 88, pp. 314–322. 10.1016/j.indmarman.2020.05.034

Tsujimoto, M., Kajikawa, Y., Tomita, J., & Matsumoto, Y. (2018). "A review of the ecosystem concept – Towards coherent ecosystem design", *Technological Forecasting and Social Change*, vol. 136, pp. 49–58.

Wenzel, M., Stanske, S. & Lieberman, M.B. (2020). "Strategic responses to crisis", *Strategic Management Journal*, vol. 41(7/18), pp. V7–V18.

Wenzel, M., Stanske, S., & Lieberman, M. (2021). "Strategic responses to crises". *Strategic Management Journal, Virtual Special Issue*, vol. 42(2), pp. O16–O27. 10.1002/smj.3161

Index

5V framework 1, 11, 123, 127

abductive research 164, 168
Account Information Services (AIS)
    281–282, 285, 291
action 21–23, 120–123
adaptability 4, 84, 92
advantage exploration 142, 151, 154
after-shock events 294
agency 120–123, 288, 185, 288, 298
Agrinord 298
Alexander von Humboldt 118
Alphabet 289
ambiguity 6, 165
American workforce 265
Apple 86, 89–90, 197, 289
architecture 1, 67, 110, 123, 155, 222
Armenia 244, 246–247, 250
Arthur Tansley 118
artificial intelligence (AI) 10, 13, 44–45,
    104, 107, 111, 138, 143, 204, 206–207,
    216–219, 222, 225, 281, 285
Australia 73, 290–291
authority 103, 118, 135, 146, 217

biology 118
Bionomics 118
Black Swan 22, 120–121, 124
blueprint 1, 28, 290
boundary theory 264–265
Brazil 189, 290
breakthrough markets 34–35
Britain 33
bullwhip effect 294, 297, 305
business model adaptation 4, 7, 242
Business Model Canvas (BMC) 1, 15,
    27–28, 44, 86–87, 299

business model change 4, 11, 21–23,
    66–68, 76–77, 86–88, 92, 102,
    242–243, 246, 251–253, 282–284
business model compatibility 42
business model elements 2, 4, 7, 67–69,
    76–78
business model erosion 4
business model evolution 4, 67–70
business model innovation 4, 9–11, 44,
    67, 82–95, 99–104, 114–115, 128, 185,
    242, 304
Business Model Navigator 28
business model pathways 28
business model reconfiguration 4–13, 48,
    66, 77–78, 91, 100
Business Model Zoo framework 28
business opportunities 1, 4, 83, 128
business-to-business 10, 98–115

Canada 290
capability 4, 9, 61, 74, 122, 216, 222, 292
capital markets 20
Casandra call 18
case study 8–10, 14, 31, 67, 69, 82, 84–85,
    103, 132, 136, 167, 186, 243, 253, 268
cash 22, 123, 128, 248–249, 252
central banks 19–20, 124–126
change 4–7, 13–14, 18–23, 30, 47–48,
    118–123, 127–129, 173–176, 180,
    185–187, 204–207, 216–217, 224–225,
    237–239, 251–253, 259–260,
    265–266, 297
China 6, 20, 21, 124, 125, 189, 190, 238
choice 120–123
clinical practice 216
Club-Med 21
cognitive dissonance 19–20, 204–205

316 *Index*

collaboration 8, 26–27, 31, 33–44, 89, 109, 134, 142–149, 157, 166–167, 176–180, 189–191, 194, 207, 217, 219, 224–227
collaborative advantage 28–29
collaborative ecosystem 26–27, 33–45
collaborative leadership approach 28
collaborative organisation 29
collective action 29, 42, 206
collective mindset 29
collective system of action 27
competition 4, 8, 11, 45, 85, 93, 98, 101, 112–114, 131–136, 139–157, 166–167, 171, 173–179, 241, 282–285, 290–292
competitive advantage 8, 51, 59, 100, 119, 123, 134, 146, 165, 170–179, 242
complementors 10, 12, 98, 131–136, 153–158, 163
complex system 10–11, 23, 119
complexity 1–2, 5–6, 8, 23, 90–94, 121, 135, 153, 166, 192, 209, 217, 220, 225, 283–284, 292
confluence 18
construction industry 10, 88–89
consumer price inflation 20, 125
content analysis 31
context 1–5, 12–14, 156–158, 168, 224–225
continuity 5, 19, 94, 123, 240
continuous development 118
coopetition 11, 131–158
core product 1
corporate governance 18–21
cost and revenue models 1–2
cost structure 27–28
country-level drivers 8, 47–50, 53, 55–61
Covid-19 5–6, 47, 61–62, 85–86, 121–125, 185–187, 193–197, 216–220, 236, 242–243, 294–295
credit 21–23, 125, 152
crisis 14–15, 19–23, 59, 120–121, 124, 195, 236–253, 294–297, 302, 307–313
critical event 121
critical internal and external assets 1–2
critical jolts 5–7, 10–11, 128–129
critical juncture 119–121
cultural distance 71
culture 9, 12, 42, 66, 164–166, 170–173, 179–180, 185–196
customer 10–12, 163–180
customer intimacy 164, 170–171, 176–180

customer needs 36, 92–94, 111, 164–165, 171–178, 282–286
customer orientation 11–12, 163–180
customer portfolio 304, 309
customer value 12, 87–88, 98, 163–180
customer–bank relationship 281
customer-oriented culture 170–172
Cyprus 244, 251

Danish mink ecosystem 129, 297, 302–313
Danish mink farms 294, 302–304, 309
Danish mink-related industry 15, 297–299, 307–308, 312–313
Dansk Industri 298
data analytics 9, 82, 108, 113, 115
data-driven innovation 83–95
data-driven services 82, 90, 93
data-driven solution 88, 91, 205, 217, 220
debtors 21
decision paths 23
decision-making 29, 48, 62, 103, 105–107, 112–113, 137–139, 146, 165, 176, 194, 205, 207, 216, 219, 258, 294
decoupling 1–15, 82–95, 98–115, 204–238
decoupling of production and markets 6, 124
deflation 19
Denmark 189, 297, 299, 301–302, 307, 310, 313
digital care 11, 135–140, 147, 157
digital economy 131
digital learning 110–111, 194
digital platform 69, 73, 76–77, 104–115
digital services 9, 66, 71, 285
digitalisation 9, 13, 82–83, 93, 98, 101, 106, 108, 122, 127, 204–228, 239
disintermediation 99–100, 288–289
disrupted supply-demand relationships 124
disruption 7–8, 14, 20, 82, 101, 118, 222, 236–238, 240, 251, 295
distributor 72–77, 286
diversification 6, 62, 85, 247–248, 252–253
diversifying suppliers 123
DNB Banks 290
downstream supply chain 301
drilling contractors 35
Dubai 244, 245, 251
dynamic capabilities 4, 82

Index   317

earnings logic 87, 91
economic growth 26, 53
economic sanctions 20
ecosystem 1–15, 18–23, 26–45, 48,
    59–60, 62, 68–69, 83, 103, 112–113,
    118–129, 131–141, 144–158, 163–171,
    178–180, 204–206, 216–227, 238, 240,
    281, 292, 294–313
ecosystem breakdown 15, 295
ecosystem-based business model 29
efficiency gains 6–7, 126
emergency planning 22
emerging markets 126–127
energy sector 31, 125
entrepreneurial opportunities 236
entrepreneurship 14, 95, 220, 224,
    236–241, 258–276
entry barriers 13, 113–115, 118, 204, 306
environment 1–11, 18–23, 26, 30, 42,
    48–49, 51, 61, 68, 82–84, 110, 115,
    118–121, 124–129, 149–150, 166–167,
    185–189, 194–196, 206, 224, 236–243,
    245–247, 266–267
environmental dynamics 19
equipment suppliers 35
Erhverv Norddanmark 298
Ethics 216–219, 222–227
Europe 6, 19, 26, 52, 54–57, 76–77,
    124–125, 196, 238, 245, 282, 290
European Central Bank 21
European Union (EU) 54–55, 103, 282
Euro-zone 21
exit strategy 15, 297, 304–307, 310–312
expansion 21, 62, 73, 118, 156, 302–304
exploitation 4, 49, 83, 101–103, 113–114,
    151–154
exploration 101–103, 113–114, 121,
    151–154, 215–216
exporting 122

fair treatment 22
feedback 76, 176, 194
feminine entrepreneurship 267
financial crisis 19, 55–59, 120–121, 124,
    240, 290
Finland 66, 70–77, 136
firm-level drivers 8, 47–49, 51–63
flexibility 41, 50–51, 82–84, 105, 135,
    148, 152, 168–170, 197, 222, 242–243,
    252, 260, 264–266, 275, 287
flexible production ability 22
food industry 169, 272–273, 300

foreign market entry 66–78
foresight 7, 19, 23
fragmentation 12, 21, 190
fragmented world 18
France 189
freemium solution 35
full-service provider 35, 39
fungibility 297, 307–313
further offshoring 8–9, 47–63
future 6, 15, 19–20, 23, 45, 62, 82, 84,
    87–95, 108, 124–128, 195, 238, 241,
    251, 291–292, 299

gatekeeping 42, 132, 141–144, 152–158
gender segregation 260–276
General Electric 190
geographic proximity 42
geographical dimension 2–4
geographical distance 71
geopolitical turbulence 13, 236–253
Georgia 246–247, 250
German economic policy 21
Germany 189–190, 245, 259
global classroom 192–193
global decoupling 5–7, 123
global financial crisis 120–121
global reach 11, 26, 150
global virtual teams 12, 185–197
global virtual university 191–197
Goldman Sachs 18
Governance 1–2, 18–19, 39–42, 131–135,
    142–143, 148–157, 196, 287–288
Government 11, 15, 19–21, 45, 47,
    53–54, 59, 62, 125–126, 186, 196, 227,
    237, 288, 298, 305, 311–313
great resignation 22
great retention 22
greenflation 21

healthcare implementation 13, 206–219
healthcare industry 222
healthcare landscape 205–228
healthcare professionals 140, 144–145,
    204–205, 222
higher education institutions 12, 186,
    191–197, 263
household income 20, 126, 261
hyper-globalisation 6, 126

IBM 190, 238
importing 122, 306
incumbent platforms 11, 132, 141–157

318   *Index*

India 189–190
industry 13, 28, 48–51, 76, 85, 102, 104, 118, 153, 169, 193
Industry 4.0 50–51, 219, 224
inflation 7, 11, 18–21, 23, 124–127, 248
innovation 4, 8, 11, 13, 15, 26–28, 31, 36, 39–45, 53, 68, 72, 76–77, 83–87, 91–94, 98–102, 107, 112, 115, 118–122, 135–136, 150, 155–157, 185, 188, 190–192, 197, 204, 206–208, 217, 219–225, 239, 242, 266, 282, 290–292, 295, 299, 302, 304–312
insurance firms 35
Integration 11, 30, 76, 82, 87, 131–158, 224, 259–260, 270, 287–288, 292
integrative logic of the firm 2
integrator 34–35
interdependability 121
interdependency 2
interdependent activities 15, 295
interdisciplinary research 13, 228
interest rate 7, 11, 20–23, 124–127
interlocked communities 118
internal resilience 119
internal resources 1
internationalisation 4, 47–51, 59, 66–68, 70, 77, 185, 241, 252–253
internet of things (IoT) 10, 13, 108, 204, 219
interorganisational resilience 294
inter-platform complementarity 133, 136, 157
intertwined supplier network 297
Israel 14, 190, 215, 217, 258–276
Israeli labour market 258–260
Israeli society 258–267
IT entrepreneur 13, 236–253
IT services 89, 281
Italy 194

Jacking Solutions International 32, 38–41
Japan 9, 66–78, 245
Jerusalem 269
Johannes Eugenius Bülow Warming 118
Jutland 299

Kazakhstan 246, 248, 251
Ken Fisher 23
Kfar Sirkin 269
knowledge 2, 5, 8, 11, 23, 28–29, 35, 43–44, 49, 53, 61, 69, 73, 76–77,
121–122, 127, 176, 190, 193, 216, 222, 241–242, 269, 299
knowledge-sharing 132–135, 143–156, 225–226
Kopenhagen Fur 301, 306

labour intensive sectors 20
labour model 14, 258–276
Latvia 306
leadership challenges 118
legally binding contracts 22
liability of newness 239
liability of smallness 250
liquidity 22, 125
Lithuania 306
localisation 4–5, 67–68, 76
localising production 122
location decision 47–48, 52–62
logistics suppliers 35
long bear market 19
loose coupling 42

management consulting 12
management innovation 197
manager interviews 12, 69–76, 139–150, 163–164, 167–180, 298, 304–310
managerial perspective 165–180
market dominance 11, 119, 145–146, 149, 152–155
market size 71, 245
market superiority 141–143, 145–148, 153, 156–157
masculine entrepreneurship 267
matched-pair case 9–10, 82–85
means of value delivery 1–2
medical data engineering 205–209, 213
medical tech industry 137
mental model 21, 121, 164, 170–171, 175–176, 179–180
metal and engineering 85
Mevasereth Zion 268–269
Microsoft 194, 238, 244, 289
midstream activities 305–306
Mink Suppliers' Industry Association 298
modularity 28–29, 135
Moscow 237, 244
motivation matrix methodology 31, 41
multinational companies 26
multiplatform ecosystems (MPEs) 11, 131–158
multisided platforms 136, 139

narrative test 27
Netherlands 259, 306
Network 5, 8–14, 28, 31–42, 67–68, 72–78, 87, 109, 111, 122, 127, 134, 153, 164, 166–170, 186–191, 194, 197, 241–243, 250–253, 313
network relationships 77–78, 105–106, 109, 112–114, 122
network theory 77
network-based business model 8, 27, 31
new entrant platforms 144, 146, 149–154, 157
Nordea Group 290
Nordic countries 290
NorSea Denmark A/S 32, 37
North Sea region 33
Norway 33, 52, 150, 259
numbers test 27

Odum 118
offshoring 8–9, 47–63, 190
oil prices 19
One-network 39
online work 187–191
open banking 14–15, 281–292
opportunity exploration 142, 151–153
orchestrator 42, 122
organisation 2–5, 15, 27–30, 42, 45, 51, 100, 122, 128, 163–166, 170–180, 185, 294–295
organisational boundaries 15, 217, 295

Paris Agreement on climate change 19
partner 33–45, 68–69, 74–76, 87–93, 109, 113–114, 176–180, 246–250, 270, 285–287, 294–295
partner network 87–88, 91
part-time employment 260
part-time jobs 259–260
Payment Initiation Services (PIS) 281–282, 285, 291
Payment Service Directive (PSD) 282, 284, 290
Penta-Helix mindset 45
perseverance 297, 310–312
personal networks 73
platform 10–11, 27, 34–41, 69, 73–78, 89–93, 98–115, 194–195, 244, 247, 285–286, 289–291
platform business model 98–101, 103, 110, 285
(inter-)platform competition 132, 134

platform ecosystem 8, 27–28, 31, 35–42, 103, 131–135, 156
platform governance 134, 156
platform leader 131–136, 153–156
platform-based ecosystem 27
platform-to-platform openness 135, 139, 141–143, 145, 149, 151, 154–155, 157
Poland 306, 310
Port of Esbjerg 31–33, 37–41
power 29–30, 217, 240
producer prices 20
product inventory 123
protective measures 18, 119
psychological behaviour 20
public debt 19
public health 215
purchasing power of customers 20

qualitative research 11, 136, 227
qualitative study 31
quality 13, 31, 53, 61, 107, 134, 165–167, 172, 204, 217–225

real asset holders 21
real interest rates 20
redundancies 22
regionalisation 62, 123
Rehovot 269
relational capacities 42
relationships 6, 9, 11, 29–31, 41, 72, 77–78, 88–91, 105–109, 112–114, 122–124, 165, 191
relocation decision 48, 51, 60
renewal 4, 85, 93, 118–119, 297
reporting process 27
resilience 1–15, 26–27, 42–43, 82–85, 89–95, 128, 222, 236–237, 240, 243, 250–253, 290–292, 294–297
resources 1, 7–8, 45, 49–51, 59, 61, 83–84, 87–94, 100–103, 113–114, 166–168, 222–225, 240–243, 250, 263–264, 285–289, 297, 307–312
retrenchment strategy 302–312
revenue 32, 54, 56–57, 83, 99, 169, 285–286
revenue stream 27–28, 67, 89–91, 101–102
Rig Quip Drilling Services Ltd. 32, 38–41
ripple effect 294, 297, 306, 311–312
risk 6–7, 20–23, 31, 49, 124, 127–128, 148, 238, 244–245, 266–267, 287–289
robustness 49, 84, 240

320 *Index*

Rothschild 118
Rotterdam 33
Russia 18–20, 237–238, 243–253
Russian start-up market 14, 237, 243–253

sales 49, 71–72, 89, 123
scalable business models 26
scenario thinking 22, 128
segregation 21, 260–262, 275–276
Semco Maritime S/A 32, 37
service companies 35
service hub 31–36, 39–44
severity 121, 125
slack resources 297
small and medium-sized enterprise
(SMEs) 6, 9–10, 26, 82–86, 93, 99,
103–104, 112, 114, 186, 236, 239, 242
small open economies 122
social capital 313
social inequality 21
social unrest 21
Society 5.0 44–45
software companies 35
software industry 10, 35, 66, 104, 169
spare part shortages 19
speed of changes 18
Sri Lanka 126
stability 6, 30, 37, 120, 265
stages 10, 29, 44, 118, 132, 141, 153,
157–158, 288, 295
stagflation 7, 11, 20, 124
stakeholder 10–11, 23, 27–29, 35, 41–45,
68, 99, 111, 114, 131, 135, 139–155,
163, 166, 168, 192, 195–196, 224, 297
standardisation 5, 225
start-ups 14, 113–115, 237–253
stimulus packages 19
strategic and operational logic 1
strategic decoupling 294
strategic direction 128, 294
strategic partnerships 26–28, 123, 285
strategic renewal 297
strategic response 15, 236–239, 294–299,
302–303, 308, 310–313
strategy 1, 4, 8–9, 15, 27–30, 47–48, 51,
59, 82, 113–114, 119, 135, 152,
155–156, 164, 170–180, 185, 226,
238–239, 297, 302, 304–313
Strengths, Weaknesses, Opportunity, and
Threats analysis (SWOT) 225–227
Stroke-Data 136–152, 158
structure 1, 14, 294–297, 300–302

structured systems of action 27
sub-suppliers 15, 294–295, 302–304
supplier dependency 123
supply 11, 18, 20, 100, 121–122, 124–128
supply chain 7, 19, 22, 29, 61–62, 109,
124, 219, 222, 224, 295, 297,
300–301, 311
survival 5, 85, 101, 127, 134, 167,
237–238, 251, 294–295
switching costs 118
Switzerland 125
system 2, 5, 10–11, 23, 27–32, 41–43,
118–121, 166, 196, 204–205, 220–228,
282–292, 295

target audience 1–2
team performance 188–189, 193
technology 13, 42, 44, 49–57, 86, 89–95,
99, 136–139, 144–145, 158, 191–196,
205–209, 219–222, 225–228, 289–292
Tel-Aviv University 269
tensions 11, 21–22, 62, 76, 131–135,
141–143, 147–148, 150–158, 205
theories of cultural feminism 261
transformation 5, 13–14, 29, 50, 114, 187,
1921, 197, 204–205, 224–226,
239–244, 247–248, 251–253, 261, 272,
275, 289, 309
triangulation 10, 105, 246
trigger 55–58, 87, 120–121, 124, 141,
185–186
trust 22, 42–43, 123, 144, 186, 188–191,
281, 288
typology 28

Ukraine 5–6, 18, 47, 121, 125, 238, 310
uncertainty 6, 8, 11, 21, 26, 29, 33, 42,
50, 124–128, 135, 236, 238, 240, 253
Unilever 186–187
United Kingdom (UK) 32, 259, 290–291
United States (US) 21, 120, 124,
189–190, 193, 195, 238, 244–246, 249,
259, 265, 284, 290–291
upfront payment 34–35
upstream activities 15, 300, 302,
305–307, 312
US exporters 6

value capture 1–2, 6, 11, 67, 98–99,
121–123, 127–128, 242, 247–248,
252–253, 288
value chain service provider 34–35

Index   321

,-creation 167

v configuration 1, 11, 127, 142, 151, 153

value creation 5, 10, 12–13, 15, 26–27, 30–44, 67–68, 83–84, 88–90, 98–105, 112–115, 131–134, 155–157, 163–164, 166–171, 175, 179, 242, 247–249, 251–253, 282–292, 295, 300

value delivery 1–2, 68–69, 74, 77, 91, 98, 122

value network 1, 6, 9, 11, 67–69, 72–77, 82, 122–123, 127–128

value proposition 1–2, 8, 11, 15, 26–27, 31–33, 36, 39, 42, 44, 83, 87, 101, 119, 122–123, 127, 153, 155, 174, 176, 206, 242, 248, 251, 253, 282, 284, 289, 295, 299–302

value segment 1, 6, 11, 122–123, 127

value-creating decoupling 98–106, 108, 112–113

value-eroding decoupling 10, 98–105, 109–115

velocity 8, 20, 121, 126, 236

virtual teams 12, 185–197

virtual work 187–189, 196

volatility 6, 18, 50, 236–238, 248, 252

wall of worry 23

Walldorf 190

Warren Buffet 23

West Diesel Engineering A/S 32, 38–41

white label products 11

women entrepreneurs 243, 258, 266–276

work-life balance 14, 263, 266–270, 274–275

Printed in the USA
CPSIA information can be obtained
at www.ICGtesting.com
LVHW012000160324
774517LV00004B/491